CHINA'S UNRESOLVED ISSUES

CHINA'S UNRESOLVED ISSUES

Politics, Development, and Culture

Suzanne Ogden

Northeastern University

Prentice Hall, *Englewood Cliffs, New Jersey 07632*

LIBRARY OF CONGRESS
Library of Congress Cataloging-in-Publication Data

Ogden, Suzanne.
   China's unresolved issues : politics, development, and culture /
Suzanne Ogden.
      p.   cm.
   Bibliography.
   Includes index.
   ISBN 0-13-132739-9
   1. China--Politics and government--1949-   2. China--Economic
policy--1949-   3. China--Social policy.   4. Socialism--China.
I. Title.
DS777.75.O35 1988
320.951--dc19   88-5864
                                                            CIP

Editorial/production supervision and
   interior design: *Mary A. Araneo*
Cover design: *Ben Santora*
Manufacturing buyer: *Peter Havens*

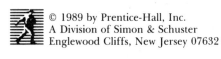© 1989 by Prentice-Hall, Inc.
A Division of Simon & Schuster
Englewood Cliffs, New Jersey 07632

Printed in the United States of America

10 9 8 7 6 5 4 3 2 1

ISBN   0-13-132739-9

Prentice-Hall International (UK) Limited, *London*
Prentice-Hall of Australia Pty. Limited, *Sydney*
Prentice-Hall Canada Inc., *Toronto*
Prentice-Hall Hispanoamericana, S.A., *Mexico*
Prentice-Hall of India Private Limited, *New Delhi*
Prentice-Hall of Japan, Inc., *Tokyo*
Simon & Schuster Asia Pte. Ltd., *Singapore*
Editora Prentice-Hall do Brasil, Ltda., *Rio de Janeiro*

To the memory of my parents,
Victor Algernon Peckham
and Vernie Holmes Peckham

CONTENTS

Chapter Five
SOCIALIST DEMOCRACY   144

Chapter Six
SOCIALIST LEGALITY AND SOCIAL CONTROL   187

Chapter Seven
CLASS AND CLASS STRUGGLE: IS CHINA UNITED
OR DIVIDED?   235

Chapter Eight
ECONOMIC DEVELOPMENT: THE CONFLICT BETWEEN SOCIALIST AND DEVELOPMENTAL OBJECTIVES   258

PREFACE

This book addresses China's key unresolved issues, those issues that plague the Chinese system now as they have since the Communist takeover in 1949. In so doing, the book offers both a conceptual and thematic perspective on China's accomplishments and failures. With this perspective, readers will be able to sort out what are at best quite complicated pictures of rapid and repeated turnarounds in China's policies, objectives, and leadership. The overarching theme presented herein—that it is the interaction of three variables, political, developmental, and cultural, which created the conditions for problems being resolved or left unresolved—will serve to pull together the complex and diverse elements of Chinese politics.

The book is, therefore, a thematic and issue-oriented study. Although the major policies adopted after 1949 to address China's problems will be examined, the text does not pretend to explain every change in China's objectives, policy, ideology, leadership, and institutions. These are important matters for specialists, but they are confusing for those being introduced to Chinese politics. The book begins by offering a theoretical framework for understanding Chinese politics after 1949. This is followed by an overview of China's history and culture and a summary of the major policies followed by the Chinese Communists after 1949. The book then examines seven major unresolved issues in the People's Republic of China:

the leadership and bureaucracy, socialist democracy, socialist legality and control, class struggle, economic development, education and political culture, and finally, the meaning of socialism in China today. This approach will, I believe, offer readers a solid basis for understanding the nature of the Chinese political system and how it has functioned since 1949.

CHINESE SYSTEM OF SPELLING USED FOR THIS TEXT

This text will use the Chinese phonetic alphabet (*pinyin*) system of spelling for Chinese names, terms, and places. The only exceptions are the established and internationally accepted spellings of the Kuomintang, Chiang Kai-shek, and Sun Yat-sen. For Chinese names, the surname is the first name given: Mao is the surname of Mao Zedong.

The only letters that are pronounced in a significantly different manner from what an English speaker would expect are: "C," which has a "ts" sound as in *its*; "Q," which has a "ch" sound as in *China*; "X," which has an 'sh' sound as in *shop*; "Zh," which has a "j" sound as in *jar*. "Z" by itself has an ordinary "z" sound as in *zero*. "Q" is not necessarily followed by "u". In some cases, alternative spellings using the Wade-Giles system, the system commonly used before the adoption of *pinyin*, have been put in brackets beside the new *pinyin* system.

ACKNOWLEDGMENTS

I am deeply indebted to my colleagues who read part or all of my book in manuscript form, and who provided invaluable comments and criticisms of my work: Gordon Bennett, Timothy Cheek, Donald Clarke, James Feinerman, B. Michael Frolic, Robert Hunt, Donald Klein, Barrett McCormick, John Moon, Andrew Nathan, Louis Putterman, Lucian Pye, Stanley Rosen, Vivienne Shue, Ralph Thaxton, Robin D. S. Yates, and David Zweig; to Philip Kuhn and Roderick MacFarquhar, the former and present directors, respectively, of the Fairbank Center for East Asian Research, who have provided me with an office at the Center and access to Harvard's libraries; to my colleagues at the Fairbank Center for endless inspiration during lunchtime conversations and in weekly colloqia; to my colleagues in the Department of Political Science at Northeastern University; to the Chinese scholars and graduate students for their insights about Chinese culture and politics; to Kau Yingmao, for the training that made such a work as this possible; to Karen Horton, the political science editor at Prentice Hall who unstintingly supported my project; to Ann Holmes and the editors at Prentice Hall who helped this book come to fruition; to Henry and Lydia who were mystified but patient with my endless excitement about China; and to my friends and students for asking the kinds of questions that stimulated me to write this book. I alone, of course, bear responsibility for the errors and shortcomings of this study.

China

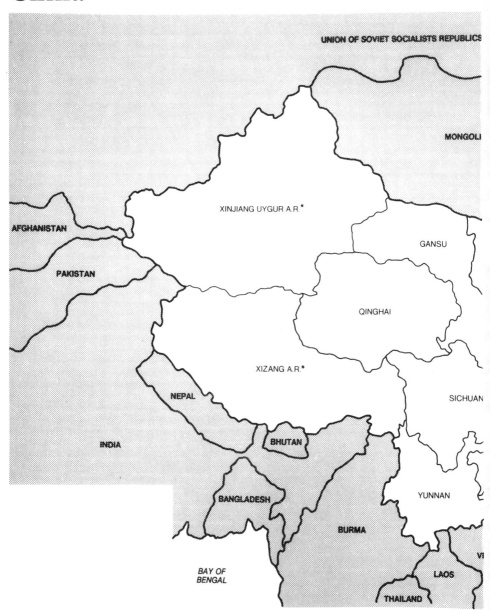

UNION OF SOVIET SOCIALISTS REPUBLICS

MONGOLI

AFGHANISTAN

PAKISTAN

XINJIANG UYGUR A.R.*

GANSU

QINGHAI

XIZANG A.R.*

NEPAL

SICHUAN

INDIA

BHUTAN

BANGLADESH

YUNNAN

BURMA

BAY OF
BENGAL

VI

LAOS

THAILAND

*A.R.: Autonomous (Self-Governing) Republic

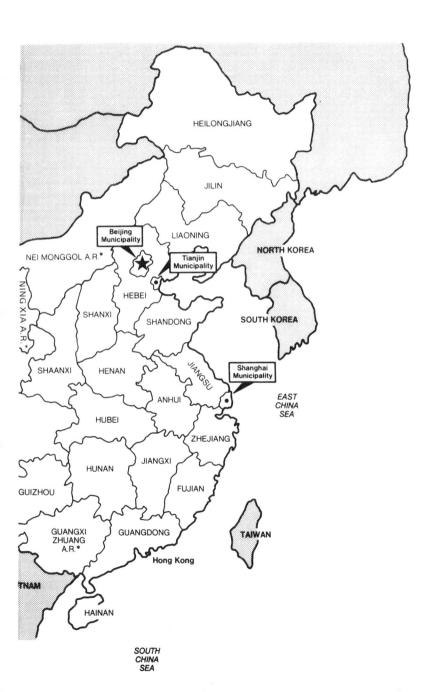

CHINA'S UNRESOLVED ISSUES

Chapter One
A FRAMEWORK FOR UNDERSTANDING CHINESE POLITICS SINCE 1949

Though of less value than communist moral standards, traditional moral values can be used as a moral foundation. Unlike material production, moral codes can transcend history. Furthermore, communist moral values cannot be developed independent of tradition; their development should grow out of the traditions of the country. Only when the traditional moral values are distilled and sublimated, can true communist ethics be established.[1]

Communist rule in China has been marked by stunning successes and resounding failures. But underlying these successes and failures have been unresolved issues, issues that have seemingly eluded solutions and have continued to absorb the energy and attention of both the Chinese leadership and the people since 1949. Without an understanding of these unresolved issues, the present problems of the People's Republic of China will remain unfathomable, and the future prospects of this great country will remain obscure.

DEFINING THE ISSUES

In the period immediately following the Communist victory in 1949, the new leaders of China did much to change basic structures and values. Attitudes changed with these structural reforms, and new policies evolved. One could safely hypothesize that the initial series of policies implemented after 1949 were successful in large part because they were relevant to China's needs of that time and because they could become firmly rooted in the structures and values that the Chinese Communists were simul-

1

taneously cultivating. As time went on, however, policies either became increasingly ineffectual or they created new problems. Sometimes the solutions were worse than the problems.

Western Versus Chinese Communist Definitions

The problem of defining China's major unresolved issues pits Western values and perspectives against Chinese and socialist values. Many of the values American Sinologists have used to assess China's achievements and failures reflect either their own society's dilemmas or the nature of the U.S. bilateral relationship with the People's Republic of China (PRC) at the moment. These assessments, and reassessments, of the nature of Chinese achievements and problems are, therefore, colored by America's own internal politics, the excitement and disappointment about its relationships with the Chinese, and the emotional and intellectual perceptions of the "way-things-ought-to-be" at home and abroad.[2]

More broadly, Western scholars have frequently been accused of "intellectual imperialism" in their use of Western values and standards for judging and analyzing issues that are both Chinese and communist. Which values are used is a subjective determination in any event and profoundly affects the conclusions reached. Subjective perceptions emanating (perhaps unconsciously) from a discrete set of values and standards necessarily affect any analysis. The real question is, do students of China really understand the Chinese situation better when Western liberal democratic values, concepts, and models with which they are familiar form the analytical framework?[3] Or does their use simply distort understanding, since different values, ideals, concepts, and objectives motivate the Chinese Communists? How far can one push the argument that Chinese and communist values are not as concerned with Western concepts of individual liberty, human rights, and democracy, and that these are not, therefore, fair or accurate standards by which to judge the situation in the PRC? Could one argue further that they are not even "issues," either for the leadership or the masses? Could it at least be argued that the introduction of a market economy and economic freedoms into China has had many consequences they would not have had in a non-Chinese or a noncommunist state?

The alternative to adopting Western evaluative standards—and the one scholars sympathetic to the goals of the Chinese Communist revolution and those pleased with the U.S. relationship with the PRC most frequently appropriate—is to accept the Chinese leadership's definition of the situation. According to this viewpoint, what really matters are Chinese and communist values, ideals, models, and objectives and whether or not they have been realized. Even if one rejects Chinese values and goals as not worthy, or not worth the sacrifices involved, the ability of the Chinese to attain them is still relevant.

If we accept the findings of modern psychology, which indicate that matters treated as problems often become problems, then we must certainly treat the Chinese leadership's definition of problems seriously. The Chinese leaders have utilized all the media, in addition to a unified leadership structure, to ensure that the entire country has received the same message about what the issues are. Subsequent policies are usually addressed to rectifying whatever the leadership has said those problems are. In China more than in most countries, then, saying it makes it so—or at least policies respond *as if* it is so. If the leadership states that "bourgeois attitudes" are an issue that must be dealt with, policies will be formulated to eradicate these attitudes, the bulk of the people will start searching for bourgeois attitudes in others, conceal their own, and generally become concerned, if not distressed, over the issue of being "bourgeois." If they are told the issue is "right-wing deviation," the collective angst of the Chinese people will similarly become focused on this issue. This seemingly happens regardless of whether most Chinese people accept the regime's definition of the situation or not.

The value of an exegesis of Chinese statements that define the issues is greatly enhanced by the additional use of "rational" (although not necessarily Western) criteria for defining the issues. An example would be the determination of whether China's present problems take the form of recycled old problems or evolve forward because solutions have created new and more advanced stages of problems that are themselves the result of an improved situation. Of course, going back to old values or institutions may be the best means to move forward.[4] This is, in fact, one of the few possibilities for a system with rigidly orthodox pretensions: Such a system does not permit going out and beyond it for alternatives. So it must resurrect and amend the limited number of alternatives that *are* permitted. Yet, going back to old methods and ideas may simply indicate the leadership lacks imagination: It can not see beyond its ideological and cultural boundaries.

China's unresolved problems must, therefore, be viewed in the context of what has already been achieved. The Chinese government has, in fact, made considerable progress in addressing many of its major issues, particularly when compared to most developing countries. Thus, the question is one of defining and measuring "progress" and "success."

First, have the Chinese, according to their own criteria, achieved successes? For example, "development" according to communist values is frequently at variance with a Western liberal conceptualization of it. Western liberals, unlike the Chinese Communists, have not seen the destruction of the capitalist class as an element of development. The Chinese Communists defined "development" as the movement to ever-higher forms of economic structures, from primitive communism, to slavery, feudalism, capitalism, socialism, and then to communism. And in the past, they tended to equate bigger units of production with better, more efficient units of production. The problem is that even these standards of development and achievement are not consistent over time. This makes it unwise to adopt them as the criteria for our own judgments.

Second, accepting Chinese statements about their achievements in resolving their problems is risky because China's leaders insist on an upbeat presentation, even when unprecedented disasters strike. Only later, when the regime is intent on reversing a particular policy, do the leaders inform the people that it was an unmitigated disaster,[5] and a newly formulated policy, which represents the current embodiment of "truth," is to be followed without questioning. As Lu Xün [Lu Hsun], China's preeminent critic of the 1930s and 1940s, so aptly put it, the Chinese take the statement as the fact, as if stating that something is true really makes it true, and itself creates a new reality.[6]

Thus, several problems arise in accepting Chinese Communist evaluative standards. First, some policies do not lead to "development" at all, according to what Western liberals believe are unbiased, objective standards. Second, it is difficult to accept some of the values explicit in certain Chinese assessments of success, to wit: "The world is in great disorder and this is a good thing." Third, China's leaders seem uncertain of what they really want. This makes it virtually impossible for them to create consistent standards for evaluating the success of their policies. In any event, when it comes time to assess what went wrong with a policy, the leaders have usually resorted to blaming cadres at one level or another for improper implementation, rather than blaming the policy itself.

Because the Chinese tell us little about why some of their most important problems have not been successfully addressed, we must dig out all the relevant data to make our own assessments. Inferences thus have come to constitute a large part of the diet of students of China: If what the Chinese termed *successful* policies are subsequently undone, we may infer that they produced unacceptable results. To illustrate, the rapid succession of rural economic policies after 1949 brought the Chinese full circle from individual landholdings through ever-higher levels of collectivization and back to individual landholdings some thirty years later. Yet at each step, China's leaders announced that their latest policy confirmed the Communist Party's wisdom and embodied an unquestionable "truth."

Thus, the methodological problem posed by the need to discover what elements China's successful policies encapsulate requires students of Chinese politics to use additional evaluative criteria. In each issue area addressed in this study, the criteria for assessing whether the Chinese succeeded in achieving their goal and why will be stated. The value clusters that surround three key variables—traditional, developmental, and political—and that interact to provide the conditions and catalysts for policy change will also be considered: *China's achievements must be judged by criteria appropriate to a developing country with socialist and traditional Chinese cultural values.*

Misidentifying or Misrepresenting Real Issues

If we accept the Chinese leaders' statement of the issues, we must consider two other possibilities. The first is that the leaders, intentionally or not, misidentify the issues. For example, China's fundamental problem may not be the inapplicability of Marxist theories, but rather the leadership's distortion of China's reality: framing problems of corruption in terms of Marxist class analysis, when the real problem may be scarcity of goods in the context of traditional Chinese bureaucratic practices; or attributing "bureaucratism" to "feudal remnants," when the real issue may be the socialist structure. If the leadership purposefully defines the problem incorrectly, what is its motivation? Are the political implications of confronting reality potentially explosive? Or do such factors as insufficient information, inadequate inputs by experts, and ideological blinders lead unintentionally to an incorrect definition of the problem, which results in a misdiagnosis? Whatever the reason for incorrectly defining the issue, problems arise when policies are made *as if* the leaders were infallible.

The second possibility is that the leaders correctly identify the issues for themselves, use policies to resolve the issues, but publicly misrepresent them.[7] For example, is "Mao Zedong Thought" not really "Mao's thought," as the reform leadership suggested? And why does the leadership want to make this point? Were Mao's mistakes those of "a great revolutionary and Marxist"? Was the "gang of four" really a "gang"? Is the cause of the overconcentration of power in Mao's hands attributable to the remnant influence of "feudalism," or to the power that any victorious wartime leader would acquire?

Part of the problem of assessing how issues become issues, and whether they are being misidentified or misrepresented, is that it is difficult to learn anything reliable about the process of policy formulation in a polity where all discussions and decisions are made behind closed doors. Students of Chinese politics are thus thrown back to inference from data and policy outcomes.

THE TRADITIONAL, DEVELOPMENTAL, AND SOCIALIST VARIABLES

The underlying theme of this book is that tensions among the three clusters of values represented by the traditional Chinese cultural, developmental, and socialist variables are responsible for the turbulent nature of Chinese policies, and therefore, for the unresolved issues to which these policies have been addressed. The Chinese dilemma is this: Until the 1980s, China's leaders wanted development, but they wanted development that was both Chinese and socialist. Development that was not socialist, or development that challenged their Chinese identity, was unacceptable. This had the effect of making Chinese policies appear cyclical rather than linear: The leaders busily rushed from one spot to the other and back again inside a small room from which they could not escape. The set of values which was of greatest importance varied depending on the issue, but by and large the ideological/political values and institutions emanating from socialism provided the major stumbling block to a broader range of policies to address China's problems. Cultural values and practices, on the other hand, doomed many socialist policies to failure.

Although it is certainly true that in many instances one set of values has been supportive of another, rather than in tension with it, this is usually *not* the case with China's unresolved issues. In determining policy, China's leaders have tried to reconcile the conflicts among these three sets of values. Precisely because of their need to satisfy simultaneously all three sets of values, they have been confined to a narrow range of alternative solutions.

By way of illustration, the problems and tradeoffs which leaders face in formulating policy in less developed countries (LDCs) like China are substantially different from those of a developed state. Considerable evidence indicates that most LDCs have, in fact, far more in common with other LDCs of *any* ideology than with developed countries of the same ideology. The relevant "objective" criteria to judge China's success in resolving issues in the post-1949 period should, therefore, be those used to evaluate development in any LDC. But one of the problems for the Chinese is that, because they are also using *socialist* criteria for assessing progress, criteria which are sometimes in direct conflict with developmental criteria, they cannot agree on whether or not a policy has achieved acceptable results. Thus, the PRC has achieved certain socialist objectives; but having done so, it discovers that they were detrimental to achieving certain developmental objectives, such as higher productivity, more efficiency, and less wastage of material and human talent. The institutionalization of a Leninist-style bureaucratic system, which has become so concerned with its own existence and problems that it hardly has time to address issues of economic development, need only be cited to illustrate a case in which socialist institutional objectives have severely hampered economic development.

In the 1980s, however, it appears that the Chinese have to some degree reconciled these three clusters of values at the expense of socialism. In fact, the leadership seems far more willing to sacrifice socialist values than Chinese cultural values in the pursuit of development. If we pose the question of what is the most crucial element in a Chinese person's identity, what is a Chinese person most afraid of losing, it would be his or her Chineseness. "I am a Marxist" has a hollow ring. "I am a modern person" defies reality. But "I am a Chinese" speaks to a fundamental identity.

As the following chapters illustrate, the Chinese leadership has seemingly developed a far greater tolerance for market forces of supply and demand, which challenge socialism, than for Western values which might pollute Chinese culture. Outside the economic realm, the appeal of Western models and values is limited by the central leadership's concern for protecting China's Chineseness. This is not to assert that among groups outside the central leadership, and especially among the younger generation, a similar concern exists with maintaining a pure Chinese identity. Indeed, their curiosity about—and their craving for—the vast intellectual and material wealth of the West seem to surpass by far their fear of losing their Chinese identity.[8] Although the Chinese are not yet blindly imitating, much less worshiping, the West, clearly they would like to *enrich* their lives with Western culture and tradition: modern and classical Western music, architecture, artistic concepts, fashions, intellectual values, democratic forms, science, technology—the list is endless. In part, this reflects the response of a tiny privileged segment of China's highly educated people to their first exposure to the outside world. They have a deep, perhaps unconscious, need to fill in the cultural and intellectual void in China today: to reach out for new values which will give life more meaning in the absence of the leadership's ability to supply a meaningful set of values in a time of ferment and change.

The leadership's failed efforts to supply these values were evident, for example, in the uninspiring campaign launched in 1981: the "four beauties and five stresses" campaign.[9] This campaign illustrates a common strategy of the leadership: cloaking values which call for the restoration of Chinese values, which are in this case really humanistic values calling for simple decency in the relationship of one person to another, in the garb of socialism. In other words, this campaign castigated the Chinese people for their poor behavior as socialists and called on them to raise the level of "socialist culture," when in fact the objective was the restoration of Chinese traditional values that undergird decency in human relationships.

Paradoxically, although the Chinese government now fights to shield the Chinese from outside forces that would undermine their cultural heritage, prior to the 1980s it purposefully attempted to eradicate much of that heritage, all in the name of eliminating "feudalism." Yet Chinese culture endured in spite of these policies, and even the Chinese leadership under Mao Zedong clung tightly to a Chinese identity. In reality, the efforts to make China secure from foreign invasion have appealed to nationalist, culturally based sentiments, not to a concern for protecting a socialist state disembodied of Chinese values.

In today's China, the desire to become socialist pales in comparison with the desire to become modern. The concern with conforming to socialist values has been replaced by a concern for developmental and Chinese values, even while maintaining socialist values cosmetically. In fact, as the following chapters suggest, the only socialist value the leadership has consistently insisted on keeping is that of the Party's "infallibility." This, however, may well reflect less of a concern for supporting socialism than for maintaining political power, and—as the Chinese so euphemistically put it—not "hurting the feelings" of China's 40 million Communist Party members.

The perceived need to satisfy all three clusters of values simultaneously has repeatedly frustrated efforts to formulate successful policies. Few policies are able to embody simultaneously all three sets of values, precisely because they are usually in conflict with each other. Today, China's leaders are redefining socialism in a manner that will permit them to develop China by the best means possible. Although these means may be permitted to undermine their previous interpretation of the values of socialism, they must not threaten a sense of identity as Chinese. Indeed, in spite of the Chinese leadership's devastating blunders, the people continue to cooperate with their government's policies precisely because they want China to be wealthy, powerful, and secure, not because they want it to be socialist.

On the other hand, if students of China choose culture as the key variable in explaining China's unresolved issues, they must consider the limits to its explanatory power. Foremost among these is that if socialism failed in China because of culture, then why did it also fail in almost all other countries that tried to implement it as state policy?[10] Further, if culture explains the failures of socialism after 1949, then what variable explains the failure of democracy and capitalism in China *before* 1949? Each of the three variables, then, has limited explanatory power, but taken together they go far in pinpointing the key elements in China's major unresolved issues.

SUBSIDIARY VARIABLES

Many of the conflicts within the leadership are over which of the three sets of value clusters should dominate in policy formulation on a given issue at a particular time; but there are also subsidiary determinants of policies. These can hardly be ignored when considering why China has so frequently changed course in its efforts to resolve its problems. The following sections briefly highlight some of the other principal factors in policy formulation that supplement the concern for asserting cultural, ideological, and developmental values.

Unsatisfactory Results

Often in China, the leaders simply reverse policies that have not succeeded, whereas governments functioning under more flexible ideologies and in more stable political environments are more prone to tinker with policies in order to correct the mistakes or excesses of existing policies,[11] fine-tuning them through a dynamic process of trial and error. The narrow range of responses to policy failures until 1978 seems to reflect the rigid ideological constraints that only permitted the Chinese leadership to define issues within strict Marxist-Leninist-Maoist parameters. In the 1980s, the Chinese moved beyond these ideological parameters only by redefining the ideology itself as one primarily concerned with developmental issues.

External Pressures

External pressures for policy change occurred repeatedly after 1949: in the early 1950s, the Soviets' insistence that if the Chinese wanted aid, they must do things the Soviet way; by the late 1950s, a greater need to emphasize "self-reliance" because of the withdrawal of Soviet aid—a posture accentuated by China's complete rejection of, and by, almost all countries in 1965 and thereafter; by the mid- to late 1960s, the fear of the consequences of its own destabilizing policy when it found itself surrounded with hostile forces, including the United States in Vietnam and a threatening Soviet Union to the north; and, more positively, changes in policy in the 1970s and 1980s as a by-product of improved relations with the West.

Internal Pressures

Promises once made must be fulfilled, or the polity's leaders may find that their right to rule is questioned. For example, in the 1980s, China's leaders themselves fueled the "revolution of rising expectations," a process that possessed its own internal dynamic and required the leaders to make still further changes to accommodate its gathering momentum. Lifting the lid of a tightly controlled, impoverished society led in a short time to the rapid accretion of demands for both institutional and policy change.

Other unresolved problems reflect pressures from the political opposition, often composed of those who are the "losers" because of a particular policy. For example, those bureaucrats and others who achieved their job status simply by seniority, revolutionary war credentials, activism, or being "good and honest" oppose the present "modernizing" policies, which require expertise, skills, and/or education. The unintentional victims of new policies, such as unemployed youth, constitute another source of opposition to policies that do not guarantee employment. The new policy in the early 1980s to permit and even fund small collective enterprises was a response to the growing alienation of unemployed Chinese youth and to popular discontent over the paucity of services and the limited variety and quantity of goods.

Changes in the Context for Policy

Some new contexts in which problems must be resolved are the result of unanticipated events or events beyond anyone's control. The events of the "Cultural Revolution" provided a framework out of which emerged the issues and themes of the late 1970s. Mao's death in September 1976 provided an entirely new context for policy-making. Western and Japanese involvement in China's economic modernization, although the result of a conscious policy decision, has simultaneously generated both new economic opportunities and new political and cultural tensions. The force of biological determinism is itself providing a new context as an entire generation of leaders who have ruled China since 1949 passes from the scene. And changes in the political power equation will inevitably lead to changes in policies.

Further, China's leaders have repeatedly manipulated the *psychological* context, often without ever changing any other actual conditions. When will China achieve communism? Tomorrow, if everyone rushes into communes and helps China "leap forward." And when the country "trips" instead of leaps? Lowering expectations, again a manipulation of the psychological context, is one way to make lesser achievements appear greater. Basically what China's leaders do, in a style perhaps not unique to China, is to increase the expectations if they want the people to work harder, and decrease the expectations when they realize that no amount of hard work will attain their goals according to the original timetable. Alternatively, they find scapegoats for these policy failures.

Thus, new contexts are created by the playing out of the results of policies. Changes in the social and economic structure, the political culture, political participation, the leadership, or demographic changes alter the policy context so profoundly that "even if there is a tendency to follow an oscillating pattern of mobilization and consolidation, long-term evolutionary change alters the issues and context so that earlier patterns cannot be repeated."[12] The result is that problems are addressed step by step, and "success" occurs along a continuum. One measurement of success is a leadership with sufficient control to *choose* which problems it will address, in contrast to a leadership which is forced to address problems thrust on it. Each issue this book addresses must be put on a continuum. None has a final solution.

There are problems, of course, whose solutions appear worse than the problem themselves and problems that elude solutions. In particular, the tenacious hold of Chinese culture has inhibited satisfactory solutions. Political efforts to eradicate what are in fact culturally supported attitudes and habits have been the least successful of all efforts. But issues evolving out of social institutions and the political power structure have also resisted reform. The real problem is that the Chinese Communist Party's claim to ideological truth has created the narrow and often stifling context within which all issues must be addressed. And the nature of this "truth" has been interpreted in a rigid, yet inconsistent, manner.

• • •

Let us begin, then, with an examination of the historical framework, which provides both the context for China's present issues and the traditional cultural values that affect how those issues are resolved.

NOTES

[1] "Traditional Mores of Modern Value," *Gongren Ribao (Workers' Daily)*, in *Beijing Review* *(BR)*, No. 21 (May 26, 1986), p. 26.

[2] For a discussion of these general issues, see Harry Harding, "From China, with Disdain: New Trends in the Study of China," *Asian Survey*, No. 10 (October 1982), pp. 934–958.

[3] For a discussion of Western models, see Steven I. Hofman, "Development in Post-Revolutionary China: An Analysis of Western Models as Descriptive Tools," *Asian Forum*, Vol. X, No. 2 (Winter/Spring 1980), pp. 1–7; and Harry Harding, "Competing Models of the Chinese Policy Process: Toward a Sorting and Evaluation," in Chang King-yuh (ed), *Perspectives on Development in Mainland China* (Boulder, Colo: Westview Press, 1985), pp. 61–84.

[4] For details as to what they might recycle, see Gordon Bennett, "Traditional, Modern, and Revolutionary Values of New Social Groups in China," in Richard Wilson, Amy Wilson, and Sidney Greenblatt (eds), *Value Change in Chinese Society* (New York: Praeger Special Studies, 1979), pp. 94–99. As Bennett notes, the recycling of revolutionary values and patterns (which have usually been superimposed on *traditional* patterns) may themselves become obstacles to modernization. And in the PRC, it is far more difficult to get rid of something bearing the shibbolith of "revolutionary" than to eliminate something designated as "traditional."

[5] As an example, in 1984, after blaming the leftist policies of the "ten bad years" from 1966–1976 for all of China's problems in the following seven years, the Chinese leadership suddenly admitted that, actually, the "ten bad years" registered a respectable average annual growth rate in the GNP of 6.8%. But since the "Lin Biao and Jiang Qing counterrevolutionary cliques" could not be given credit for such growth rates, the author of the article (Director of the State Statistical Bureau) characterized the "ten bad years" as a "tortuous course of 'two ups and three downs,' " with the leftists held responsible for all the dips, and the Deng Xiaoping–Zhou Enlai leadership accorded all the credit for each year of progress. See Li Chengrui, "Are the 1967–76 Statistics on China's Economy Reliable?" *BR*, No. 12 (March 19, 1984), pp. 21–26.

[6] Harriet Mills, seminar on Lu Xun, at Fairbank Center Seminar, Harvard University (May 20, 1983). The problem as Lucian Pye sees it, however, is that the rhetoric becomes increasingly divorced from practice, that is, from reality. Thus, codewords and "ritual rhetoric" diverge from practice (such as bureaucratic obstructionism) and even from the policies of the leaders engaged in the rhetoric. See Lucian Pye, *The Dynamics of Chinese Politics* (Cambridge, Mass.: Oelgeschlager, Gunn & Hain Publishers, 1981), p. 60.

[7] For a general discussion of this problem, see Chalmers Johnson, "What's Wrong With Chinese Political Studies?" *Asian Survey*, No. 10 (October 1982), pp. 919–933.

[8] In 1985, student protest marches occurred in several cities, allegedly to protest China's "Open Door" policies toward foreign investment. (See John F. Burns, "China Fights Student

Protest Against Open Door," *The New York Times* (November 27, 1985), p. A7.) But these apparently nationalistic protests were actually cover-ups for the real cause of discontent among the young: Deng's economic policies, which brought high levels of inflation to the cities and the many workers there on fixed state salaries; and Deng's policies of implanting a young "third echelon" of leadership in place, thereby preempting positions for this generation of youth.

[9]The inability of this campaign to inspire the ordinary Chinese is, I think, evidenced by my own totally random sample of Chinese, both in the United States and in China in 1981 (and thereafter) in which *none* of them were able to list even half of what the "five stresses" and "four points of beauty" were. ("Stress on decorum, manners, hygiene, discipline, and morals; beautification of the mind, which means cultivating a fine ideology, moral character, and integrity, and upholding the Party's leadership and socialist system; beautification of language; beautification of behavior, which means doing useful things for people, working hard, being concerned for others' welfare, observing discipline, and safeguarding collective interests; beautification of environment . . . paying attention to personal hygiene and to sanitation in houses and public houses." See "Notes," *Beijing Review*, No. 36 (September 7, 1981), p. 3.

[10]Socialism has failed in the sense that it requires coersion to be sustained, and in the sense that a socialist economic system has generally encountered difficulties of greater magnitude than in states implementing a liberal capitalist system.

[11]See Dorothy J. Solinger, "The Fifth National People's Congress and the Process of Policy-Making: Reform, Readjustment, and the Opposition," *Asian Survey*, Vol. XXII, No. 12 (December 1982), p. 124.

[12]James R. Townsend, *Politics in China*, 2nd edition (Boston: Little, Brown, 1980), pp. 148–149.

Chapter Two
THE HISTORICAL AND CULTURAL CONTEXT

Our national history goes back several thousand years and has its own characteristics and innumerable treasures. . . . Contemporary China has grown out of the China of the past; we are Marxist in our historical approach and must not lop off our history. We should sum up our history from Confucius to Sun Yat-sen and take over this valuable legacy.[1]

This book focuses on China's unresolved issues in the 1980s. But, because one of the key variables involved with the Chinese Communists' success in addressing their problems is a several-thousand-year-old culture, and because the leadership since 1949 has so frequently referred to this culture as the source of many of its most serious problems, an understanding of China's historical and cultural development is indispensable.

China's history supplies strong evidence of the importance of Chinese culture and "ideology," whether Confucian, republican, nationalist, or communist. It also suggests how powerful individuals have manipulated culture and ideology to gain power over China and its people, and how they have shaped China's political development. China's history further reveals the roots of China's attitudes toward foreign countries, and how these attitudes have influenced the direction of China's foreign relations. The following brief history of pre-1949 China will focus on those aspects of China's historical and cultural development most relevant to its present-day issues.

IMPERIAL CHINA

Isolated from its neighbors by the vast wind-swept deserts of central Asia and the mighty Tibetan plateau to the west, by tropical forests to the south, and by the Pacific Ocean to the east, China developed a civilization and cultural tradition independent from the rest of the world, even though it accepted many inventions and ideas created elsewhere.[2] For its first 6000 years, China's civilization evolved with minimal contact with the other great centers of archaic civilization in the Asian continent. It is only in the last two centuries that China has joined the global community. The problems China has been trying to resolve ever since the Communists' victory over the Nationalists in 1949 derive in part from this geographical isolation and its resulting independent cultural tradition. Perhaps we should say that it is only in the last two centuries that other countries have become part of China's world, for the Chinese called their land *Zhongguo*, the "Central Kingdom," where a civilization superior to all others flourished.

Recent discoveries by Chinese archaeologists have shown that, contrary to previous opinion, Chinese civilization did not grow out of a single source, the Yellow River valley, but rather, developed out of a mixture of different ethnic and cultural traditions. Beginning with the Neolithic period (roughly 5500 B.C. to 2000 B.C.), Chinese tradition was formed out of a multitude of ethnically and linguistically distinct cultures located in different regions of the vast East Asian subcontinent. Even today, China is a multiethnic nation with over fifty major groups. The largest single group is the Han, who speak Chinese as their native tongue and who have dominated their neighbors in historical as well as present times. It is indeed remarkable that the Chinese people have been able to maintain their unity over so many hundreds of years, given the variety of their country's geography and the diversity of the ethnic groups inhabiting the region. The major reason for this unity is the strength of Chinese culture, which has often extended far beyond the boundaries controlled politically by the central government.

China entered history with the Shang Dynasty, which was located in the lower Yellow River valley and which ruled in the second half of the second millennium B.C.[3] Our knowledge of the Shang is drawn to a very great extent from records of divinations, which were scratched upon the shoulder blades of cattle and the shells of tortoises to preserve the answers of the gods to the questions put to them by the Shang kings. These date from circa 1350 B.C. to circa 1050 B.C. and are the famous "oracle bones" or "dragon bones" as the peasants, who first found them at Anyang, Henan province, at the turn of this century, called them. From these inscriptions we can see that the Shang had developed to a stage which is recognizably "Chinese." First of all, they possessed an elaborate writing system that was obviously the result of a long process of evolution, for it had developed far beyond the mere "ideographic" and was no longer "picture-writing." Writing was the means of communication between the world of humans and that of the gods, and it preserved the knowledge of the past, which, derived from the ancestors, could be used to predict the outcome of events in the present. As such, writing was sacred, and it continues to this day to be treated as sacred, though for reasons of politics rather than religion.

The Shang king took a personal and active part in all activities relating to the running of the government and stood at the apex of a religious and political hierarchy. In political terms, he was the head of a conical patrilineal clan, and the kingship passed through the male line, often through brothers and then from uncle to nephew, rather than directly from father to son.

The Shang elite spent their time in religious activities, predominantly sacrifices, and warfare with neighbors. Success in warfare provided captured warriors, who were ceremoniously butchered at the altars together with cattle, sheep, and pigs, to keep the Shang ancestors fed and favorably disposed toward the living. The ancestors could influence every aspect of daily life, from success in warfare to the weather to harvesting grain, and were even capable of inflicting toothache upon the king. They therefore had to be continually supplicated and worshipped.

In the mid-eleventh century B.C., the Shang were conquered by one of their neighbors and former subordinates in the west, the Zhou [Chou] people. Zhou propaganda claimed that the Shang had become morally corrupt and, as a result, the Supreme Deity or Power of the Zhou, Heaven, transferred the right to rule from the Shang to the Zhou. This right the Zhou called the "Mandate of Heaven," and the concept became an essential component of later Chinese political theory, particularly that associated with Confucianism.

Because the size of the territory that fell to the Zhou after their victory was enormous, they decided to give fiefs to members of the Zhou royal lineage and the leaders of the other lineages who had helped their cause, at strategic locations throughout the land so that they could maintain control over the conquered people. Because of this new system, the Zhou Dynasty has been interpreted by Western scholars as China's "feudal" age, but many Chinese Marxist scholars believe that the "Three Dynasties"—Xia [Hsia], Shang, and Zhou—actually represent the slave stage of society in China. Later Chinese writers and philosophers, particularly Confucius (551–479 B.C.) and his followers, looked back to the Western Zhou as a golden age, when all was good and all people behaved in a morally proper fashion, and there was peace and prosperity in the land. The founding fathers of the Zhou, such as King Wen, King Wu, and the Duke of Zhou, were hailed as paragons of virtue and wisdom. Whether this was actually the case is hard to tell because of a lack of reliable sources; but this image and these noble names are still considered reference points for morality in China today.

The Zhou were defeated by an alliance of some of their vassals and

raiding nomads and were forced to move their capital east to Loyang in 770
B.C. The period from this move to the final destruction of the dynasty in
256 B.C. is known as the Eastern Zhou and is divided by historians into the
Spring and Autumn (722–464 B.C.) and the Warring States (464–222 B.C.).
During these 500 years, the Chinese tradition became definitely established, and the Chinese first came to be conscious of themselves as distinct
from all other people. A sense of moral and philosophical crisis. This in
turn led thinking people to reevaluate their fundamental worldviews and
resulted in the flowering of the "Hundred Schools" philosophy. Of these,
the most important was Confucianism, which over the years coexisted with
or absorbed some of the values of Daoism and Legalism. Confucius and his
followers Mencius and Xunzi (Hsun-tzu) elaborated Confucianism; Daoism
(Taoism) grew out of the texts attributed to Laozi (Lao-tzu) and Zhuangzi
(Chuang-tzu); and Legalism was advocated by a number of leading statesmen and philosophers as essential for the smooth running of government.

When the Zhou transferred their capital to the east, they lost almost
all power over their nominal vassal states, retaining only religious authority
over them. These vassals fought among themselves, asserting their political
independence from the throne. Gradually, political power came to be centered on only one or two lineages. Thus, a centralized bureaucratic administration developed and, for the first time, individuals were appointed to
official positions based on their own personal capabilities and not only
because of their family ties. Consequently, a need arose for educating
people. Confucius was the first independent teacher, and his students came
from all backgrounds. They went on to become administrators and officials
in various states. This change inaugurated an institution that eventually
came to be central to the Chinese tradition: Social status was achieved by
receiving an education and then serving in the government bureaucracy.
For most periods of Chinese history, it was, therefore, much more important to be a scholar than to be either wealthy, born into an aristocratic
family, or to possess exceptional military prowess. And the tradition of the
scholar's loyalty to the state remains a central feature of the issues still
facing China's intellectuals today.[4]

Confucianism

Secular worldview

Confucius believed that both the world and its people were essentially
moral and that it was the duty of superior minds to train themselves in
benevolence or humanity (*ren*) and then extend this out to all people.
Benevolence began in filial piety and fraternal submission and ended in
helping everyone. The duty of the government was to nurture the people
both physically and spiritually, particularly by teaching them virtue and

ceremonial rites. Only if the people failed to respond were the instruments of punishment and government rules and regulations to be applied to them.

Certain consequences of Confucius' attitudes were fundamental to Confucianism as it developed in the hands of his later followers. First of all, Confucius' philosophy was not a formal system as Platonism and Aristotelianism were in the West. His thought was practical and ethical and oriented toward the here and now of everyday life; it was not theoretical or metaphysical or concerned with the hereafter or with first questions about the origins and meaning of life. Confucius refused to discuss death and the spirits. He was not irreligious, but rather he viewed the world of the sacred as continuous with that of the secular: The universe was one organic whole. People, he believed, should therefore act morally not to save their souls, as in the Christian tradition, or because they would receive some reward in this life, but because it was their nature to be ethical.

Further, people could be educated to learn morality. (This idealistic faith in the educability of people contributed to the development of a strong Chinese idealistic strand that is a central part of Chinese Communism.) The fundamental moralistic orientation affected the outlook of educated Chinese throughout the imperial period and partially explains why later Western missionaries failed to convert Chinese in large numbers. The Chinese simply did not believe that there was one God who had created the universe at a particular moment, or that humanity had fallen away from God through sin and needed to be saved and returned to God. Further, the underlying religious and philosophical beliefs of Calvinism, that people serve God by being productive and making money—attributes of Protestantism that contributed to the rise of capitalism in the West—simply were not present in China. Thus, the merchant retained a low status.

Hierarchical organization

A second consequence of Confucius' attitudes was the family-based hierarchically organized nature of society. The fundamental loyalty of an individual was to one's family and closest kin, not to the state or the public good as a whole. A person certainly *could* be public-spirited, but not at the expense of one's family. Confucius encouraged submission of younger generations to their elders, of women to their menfolk, and of all to the ruler of the state, who was the "father and mother" to all the people. Gradually, Confucianism evolved the "five relationships": ruler–subject, father–son, husband–wife, older brother–younger brother, and friend–friend. Except for the last, all of these relationships were based on difference of status and expressed differences of power in the society. In cases of conflict between the two partners in the relationship, the person in the superior position was favored both by society and the law. Nevertheless, the superior person was expected to take care of the inferior person—provided, of course, that the latter fulfilled his or her own duties. But, Confucianism encouraged obedience, submission, and loyalty among inferiors. Independence of the individual was actively discouraged during the process of socialization in childhood.

The emphasis that the Confucians placed upon correct ritual behavior and proper social relationships tended to dampen the spirit of innovation and imagination of the individual. This is not to deny that the Chinese were remarkably capable in inventing new techniques and new machines. Rather, the Confucian emphasis on harmony and order, on the values of the group at the expense of the individual, and on the acceptance of social hierarchy, prevented the Chinese from ever fundamentally challenging their basic worldview. These values, reinforced through rituals, have remained an integral part of rulership under Chinese Communism.

The Emperor's right to rule

A third consequence of Confucius' attitudes was that later Confucians accepted the early Zhou concept of the "Mandate of Heaven." The king's, and later the emperor's, right to rule was premised on his ability to maintain harmony between heaven and earth, between himself and his officials, and between the officials and the people. He was conceived to be personally responsible for the welfare of the world. By being morally upright, ruling righteously, maintaining proper relationships, and performing the correct rituals in their seasonal order, he could, as the Son of Heaven, guarantee peace and abundance for the world. If there was famine or floods, if comets or solar eclipses appeared, if women gave birth to cows, or if the peasants rose up in rebellion, it was the ruler's fault and evidence of his immorality. It was then permissible to criticize his conduct. Should disorders continue, however, Mencius argued that the people had a right to remove the ruler and install a more moral leader. It was not that revolution was justified, but rather than an immoral ruler was not a ruler at all: He was merely a commoner. The "mandate of heaven" had been withdrawn and was offered to someone else who was worthy of it. Thus, this mandate offered the option of legitimate rebellion in Chinese life, but not revolution. It permitted a new ruler, but not a new system. Some commentators even suggest that Mao Zedong's supreme power during the Cultural Revolution stemmed at least in part from this perhaps unconscious but deeply ingrained cultural acceptance of a single supreme leader.[5]

An educated elite

In the second century B.C., Confucianism was adopted as the state ideology. As a result, those who were appointed to positions in the imperial bureaucracy came to be chosen not just for their family connections or for their technical expertise, but also for their moral qualities. Bureaucrats were deemed to require an education in those texts thought to have been either written or edited by the hand of the master Confucius himself, for true understanding of morality was believed to rest in a thorough absorption of the hidden meanings and value judgments expressed by Confucius in the wording of the classics.

Although Confucianism suffered an eclipse after the Han Dynasty fell in A.D. 220, some three centuries later, the Sui emperor realized the value of Confucianism as an ideology that helped legitimize central autocratic rule. Therefore, he reintroduced the examination system, in which candidates for official appointment were tested primarily on their knowledge of the Confucian classics. From this time, China was administered by members of a ruling class who were educated as scholars of the classics and were experts in morality, rather than in any particular technical field, such as agriculture, law, commerce, or later, industry and science. These scholar-officials invested their income in land, thus forming a scholar-gentry class. Because of their superior knowledge of morality, they formed the basis of a system of rule by men rather than rule by law. This provided the basis for one of the issues which China confronts today.

The scholar-gentry class dominated Chinese society, both at the local and at the central level. It was only the Mongols who, as rulers of China from 1279 to 1368 (the Yuan Dynasty), felt that they could dispense with their services. But even they found it expedient to reinstitute the examination system which they had previously ignored. And the Manchus, who later invaded China from the northeast, overthrew the Ming Dynasty (1368–1644), and founded the last imperial dynasty, discovered it was necessary to come to an accommodation with the scholar-gentry and accept their bureaucratic expertise. To legitimize their seizure of power, they accepted Confucian social and intellectual values and turned themselves into the defenders of Confucian moral and ritual orthodoxy.

The very existence of an institutionalized system of recruitment based on educational achievement sets China apart from most other civilizations and countries. Of course, nepotism and ascribed characteristics sometimes were crucial, but the examination system was the dominant form of recruitment until it was abolished in 1905. Thus, another one of the central issues confronting China today—namely, how to select leaders and administrators, and what kind of training to give them—was first raised in 1905. In the nineteenth century, ethical education proved to be an insufficient preparation for bureaucrats addressing the innumerable problems posed by the advance of the Western nations into China, as well as by internal economic and social collapse. The besieged Manchu rulers chose to emphasize Western-style learning over Confucian ethics in a last-ditch effort to strengthen China through modernization; but the problems China confronted as a consequence, and particularly the fear that Chinese culture would be weakened if not destroyed by the modernization process, caused each of China's future leaders to face painful dilemmas in reforming the educational system. The belief that China was and should be ruled by a morally superior elite remained central in China's efforts to meet the challenge. A correct ethical and ideological orientation continued to be considered superior to technical expertise, an attitude which is just as strong in the post-1949 period as it was in imperial China.

China as the 'Central Kingdom'

The tributary system and confinement of foreigners

The logical implication of the Chinese emperor possessing the "mandate of heaven" to rule was that China was the "central kingdom." Since this was the case, all other civilizations and groups of people were necessarily inferior and "barbarian." Traditionally, this value was expressed in practice through the "tributary system," a practice under which non-Chinese peoples expressed their acceptance of the superiority of the Chinese emperor by giving tribute. This symbolic system of honoring the Chinese emperor's superior moral authority not only was a method by which the barbarians could maintain peaceful relations with a powerful China. It also disguised what was actually a very important and complex system of informal trade, wherein the Chinese, upon receipt of tribute, would send back "gifts" of nearly equivalent value. Sometimes it was a system of bribing the tribes not to attack or pillage China.

The assumptions underlying the tributary system are important in explaining China's refusal to countenance trade and diplomatic relations on the basis of equality with Western countries when these countries pushed for relations in the nineteenth century. China was willing to export Chinese goods such as porcelain and tea to the West, but only in exchange for gold and silver bullion. China had little interest in acquiring the manufactured products of what it considered a morally inferior civilization. The British, who watched their treasury disappear through a one-way trade with China, countered with selling the Chinese the one product they seemed to have acquired a taste for: opium. In the end, China's refusal to permit the West to establish reciprocal trade on a basis of equality resulted in the West forcing entry into China, and bringing with it not only its industrial technology, but also its own social and political values. Although the Chinese lost the Opium War (1839–1842) to the British, they felt that they had struck a good bargain in the Nanking Treaty (1842), which was drawn up at the war's end. According to the treaty, the British would be permitted to establish themselves in "treaty ports" for the purpose of trade with China. But from the Chinese perspective, this treaty, as with subsequent treaties forced upon the Chinese with each defeat in battle against the Western imperial powers, *confined* these foreign barbarians to the treaty ports.[6] Barbarian values would, it was hoped, be contained in isolated areas of China, leaving China to be as it had always been.

Basic to China's xenophobic attitudes was both the belief in the superiority of Chinese values and the belief that it was better to forego the alleged benefits of foreign advances in technology and industry if they threatened the integrity of China's own values. In any event, in the nineteenth century, the Chinese rulers seemingly did not believe that Western industrialization mattered very much: Industrial power would be no match against the superior Chinese civilization. Even after the Chinese realized the virulence of these industrialized countries, and the potential implications for military conquest of China, they persisted in an attempt to isolate Western technology from Western values. To the extent they succeeded in doing this, one could either argue that they also succeeded in obstructing China's own more rapid modernization, or, on the other hand, that they thereby maintained the last strands of values that kept China from losing its identity in the face of crisis.

By the end of the nineteenth century, China had suffered from repeated foreign incursions and defeats at the hands of both the Western powers and the Japanese. Reeling from the combined effect of imperialist invasions, internal dissent and rebellion, inept and corrupt rule, and an inability to rally the people to unite in an effort to modernize in either the reforms of the 1860s or 1898, the ruling Manchus, who were themselves foreigners, eventually succumbed to defeat. China's nineteenth-century history of internal rebellions, and successive defeats by the imperial powers from the Opium War on, is a bitter story of a slowly decaying empire whose ethical axioms had for almost 2000 years played a key role in the ordering of the Chinese empire; but these conservative axioms came to obstruct the Chinese from acquiring a broader vision of how to rule effectively in a world that had, in terms of absolute economic, political, and military power, outstripped the Chinese. China, wallowing in an ethics-based educational and political system, which was not only unable to modernize but was itself disintegrating, was no match for the military and industrial power and aggressive nationalism of both the Western powers and Japan.

Stunning parallels exist between China's traditional attitudes toward the outside world and its post-1949 orientation under Communist rule. The theme of trying to keep foreigners out of China and, in the face of failure, isolating those who would come to China in small enclaves—largely out of fear of the potentially disruptive social and political effects of foreign values—is a theme that appears relentlessly in Chinese history and one that has profoundly affected China's relationships with the outside world since 1949. Similarly, as the issues analyzed in this text illustrate, it was precisely China's undying belief in the superiority of its ethico-political system, based in post-1949 China on a belief in the superiority of both

Chinese and socialist values, which inhibited China's modernization. The same concern for maintaining Chinese identity and protecting Chinese values that characterized imperial China carried through into the Communist period and goes far in explaining the dilemma the Communist leaders have faced in their efforts to modernize with Western technology and investments.

One hypothesis that might partially explain the continuing reliance on a claim of ethical superiority is Chinese insecurity about their own identity in a world which is no longer at their command. This seemingly compels them to rigidly insist on defining proper values as if they can thereby claim the higher moral ground.

The collapse of barbarian rule and the imperial system of governance

In the nineteenth-century, the Chinese could blame China's weakness and vulnerability to challenges from both outside and within on barbarian rule. The Manchus, who assumed the dynastic title of Qing (Ch'ing), and who adopted most Chinese social and ethical values, ruled China from 1644 until the 1911 Revolution. But the restoration of Chinese rule did little to reestablish China's central place in the world. China under Chinese rule proved no more able to rid itself of foreign control and the infiltration of foreign values than it was under the Manchus. In part, the centrifugal forces set in motion during the last decades of Manchu rule led to a regionalism that was not easily eliminated with the establishment of the Republic of China in 1912. "Warlordism" ultimately undermined the power of any central Chinese government to govern effectively.

But there was more to the story than this. Oddly enough, the 1911 Revolution was inspired by a man educated outside of China, a man who looked to Western political ideas for inspiring a new vision of China's future. Sun Yat-sen, taking the ideas of "democracy," "nationalism," and "the people's livelihood" from an eclectic group of Western statesmen and writers to form the "three people's principles," hoped to reshape China's image of its future and its identity. Sun's ideas failed to take root, however, not just because of his superficial understanding of them or because they were, in most respects, alien to China, but also because of the hold of Chinese culture and tradition on the perception of authority, power, and the role of the people in government. Bound by the Confucian heritage to believe that the common people had no role to play in governing unless the Emperor lost his Heavenly Mandate, and that officials were to be obeyed and feared, not voted in and out of office, the Chinese did not easily grasp the Western democratic notion of the power of the people.

This is not to deny the importance of China's low level of development, which offered little in the way of political, economic, and social institutions to provide a basis for democracy. Even literacy, the bare minimum for an effectively functioning democracy, was limited to a small percentage of the population. But, at some point, a traditional system must decide whether it will modernize and cast aside its traditional heritage. Having overthrown an imperial system that had existed for some 2000 years, the Chinese were in a critical position to eliminate those traditions and values which inhibited modernization while building on those which supported modernization. Yet they were, for one reason or another, unable to grasp this opportunity.

Let us examine, then, China's history from 1911 to the Communist victory in 1949 in the context of this effort to modernize, to democratize, and, ironically, to discover a new identity for China by looking to the West for value structures. It is this tension between a belief that the vibrant West holds the answers to China's problems and a countervailing fear that those same Western values can undermine China's identity and its ethical value structure that we still see today as China's leaders continue to wrestle with foreign values while striving to modernize China.

THE REPUBLICAN PERIOD

China's millennium-old heritage of nondemocratic procedures and institutions provides a backdrop for a cultural and historical understanding of the limits of democracy in China. What democracy could mean in the Chinese context has been an issue ever since the first attempts to turn China into a democratic republic with the overthrow of imperial China in 1911. The Kuomintang (KMT), the "Nationalist Party," failed to find a relevant form of democracy for China that could be implemented with the amount of political power available to it. The meaning of "democracy" for China, as opposed to its meanings for Western states, was left to the Chinese Communists to determine.

The debate over democracy from 1895 to 1911 focussed on the *form* democracy should take: constitutional monarchy or republic. When after 1912 the Chinese failed to establish democracy within the context of a republic, the debate turned to the issue of the best *means* for establishing an operative form of democracy in China. Finally, with the Communists in the 1920s and thereafter, the question turned to the *meaning* of democracy in the Chinese context. The concept of democracy is particularly valuable as a perspective from which to view China's history from 1911 to 1949, because it indicates which types of values and institutions concerning the economy, education, the leadership, and the political system could find fertile ground in China.

The Form of Democracy

Chinese reformers and revolutionaries at the turn of the twentieth century had some notion of there being certain preconditions necessary for the establishment of democracy in China which differed from those in the West, but their concept of democracy was largely only theoretical. It was a rational conception,[7] based on the idea of democracy rather than on experience, for the Chinese lacked any significant experiments in democracy, and none at the national level. After the 1911 Revolution, their conception changed.

China's revolutionaries and reformers did not really care whether their democracy was just like that in the West. From the late nineteenth-century on, the underlying reason for wanting democracy in China was not for its Western-based ethical rationale: namely, that all people should be free to develop without impediment from those more powerful than themselves, and that people would voluntarily exercise their individual freedom by participating in the political process. Chinese intellectuals were not really committed to individualism, freedom, or equality per se, nor did they believe it was unethical for some people to exploit others. There was no Jeffersonian idea that those who exercise power cannot be trusted to keep in mind the public interest. Instead, they saw democracy as contributing to economic progress in the West, and they hoped it would bring wealth and power to China as well. "Democracy" was offered as a prescription for establishing a nationally unified and strong modern state.[8] The values and the political institutions of democracy were adopted without much advance preparation and without sufficient consideration of the social, cultural, and economic changes required to allow the political institutions of democracy to function in China. The Chinese were unaware that these institutions could not be introduced into a completely different social system and be expected to function.

The desire of many Chinese to overthrow the Qing imperial monarchy in favor of a republic seemed less a protest against the privilege of one group over another (although the Chinese did, for racist reasons, want to rid themselves of the alien Manchus), or a desire for something called "freedom" and "equality," than a protest against the inability of the Manchus to make China into a strong modern state and to defend it from the new European barbarians. Neither Liang Qichao (Liang Ch'i-ch'ao), the reformer, nor Hu Hanmin and Sun Yat-sen, the revolutionaries, appear to have thought or written much about the more abstract philosophical concepts connected with the establishment of representative government.[9] Instead, they concerned themselves with its mechanics, with the problems it might face in China, and its most appropriate form for Chinese conditions. "Democracy," the term they used when referring to various forms of representative government, was considered desirable because it would unify and strengthen China, thus enabling China to resist foreign aggression. Their vision was strictly utilitarian.

Liang did, however, have serious doubts about implementing democratic practices in China. Having traveled to the United States in 1903 and having observed the practices of the Chinese living there, he concluded that Chinese people, even if they lived in a free and democratic society, were not prepared to practice democracy. So how could they possibly practice democracy in China, where there was a lack of social order or sense of national identity, and where the public ethos was corrupt? For the Chinese masses, said Liang,

> Freedom, constitutionalism, republicanism—this would be like wearing summer garb in winter, or furs in summer: beautiful, to be sure, but unsuitable. . . . [T]he Chinese people must for now accept authoritarian rule; they cannot enjoy freedom. . . .[10]

Sun Yat-sen's conception of democracy as he presented it in 1906 is one of the key documents for the Chinese in the twentieth century. Entitled *The Three People's Principles,* it characterizes democratic government as government responsive to the will of the people. This popular will, however, could not be allowed to weaken effective centralized authority. Given the pressing demands China faced, it could not permit the people to interfere with the administration of the state, as they did in Western liberal democracies. Such an interpretation of democratic government fit well with China's existing conception of the role of the government. Whether imperial, republican, or communist, the Chinese seemed bound by their history and culture to favor a powerful and elitist government at the expense of popular democratic rule. The chaos of periods when China was under less than authoritarian rule has, to this day, confirmed in the Chinese view the correctness of their perspective.

Sun Yat-sen further believed that the idea of democracy would give rise to the adoption of democracy. Monarchy merely had to vanish, a "republic" declared, and the Chinese would start practicing democracy. The adoption of democracy would, in turn, inspire social and economic changes that would dispel traditional Chinese authoritarianism. Sun therefore saw no need to prepare for a democratic republic by establishing conditions conducive to the successful practice of democracy. With the benefit of nearly eighty years of hindsight, it seems odd to observers today that China's reformers or revolutionaries would have assumed that democracy was China's for the taking. Equality, whether social, economic, or political, was totally foreign to China. For 2000 years China had accepted a system that emphasized the strict ordering of interpersonal relationships according to Confucian hierarchical standards. It was a system adminis tered by an educated elite, and its unity depended upon the maintenance of a relationship of power dominance by superiors over inferiors.

Sun's "Three Principles" were democracy, nationalism, and "people's livelihood," or what the Chinese Communists later called *socialism*. "People's livelihood" indicated Sun's concern for economic equality. Then referred to as "land nationalization" or "equalization of land rights," it would allow all landowners to keep whatever they had, but the state would appropriate all future increases in the land value. Sun's target was urban property holders, whose land values were increasing rapidly, especially in the coastal ports. "Equalization of land rights" was not, therefore, aimed at equalizing land distribution, nor at eliminating economic classes. Rather, it was meant to prevent landlords from becoming inordinately wealthy.[11]

The Means to Achieve Democracy

Once the monarchy had been destroyed and a republic established, the historical context within which democracy was addressed was obviously quite different. The Republic formed the new political structure, but it failed to function successfully. By 1915 the national parliament had become a tool manipulated by the warlords, not a representative body for the Chinese people. It was devoid of political power. The government made and unmade constitutions and ignored the "people's rights." No attempt was made to propagate the ideas of democracy among the vast Chinese population. The people remained unaware that they were supposed to consent to their government. Democratic political institutions, standing isolated amidst a culture and society not predisposed by its tradition to democratic forms, could not succeed. The power of the *idea* of representative government had not sufficed to cause the peasants to abandon their culture-bound, hierarchical patterns of thinking about power nor to exercise their rights as individuals.

The "New Culture Movement" was a response to the perceived need to find the means for giving content to democratic forms. Its major proponents, notably Ba Jin [Pa Chin], Hu Shih, and Chen Duxiu [Ch'en Tu-hsiu] argued that a cultural transformation was needed to inject vitality into the institutions of democracy. Members of the movement denounced China's Confucian heritage as feudalistic and incompatible with individual freedom and a constitutional regime. As Chen Duxiu noted, "All our traditional ethics, laws, scholarship, rites, and customs are survivals of feudalism."[12] Chen focused on the family as the basis of the absolutism of Confucianism. Traditional family and societal concepts needed to be destroyed before China could have a true democracy, a society in which individuals would be free to pursue their "enlightened self-interest."[13] But the masses also needed to attain a political consciousness if representative government were to survive, and this required educating them. Lu Xun,

China's literary giant of the first half of the twentieth century, also advocated the liberation of the individual from the ties of tradition and from the ignorance and submissiveness that tradition had bred. In his famous story of "Ah Q," Lu Xun's point is that the Chinese Republic "would never become anything more than a republic in name" until the Chinese peasantry was liberated from ignorance and submissiveness to tradition and authority.[14] Hu Shih led the attack with his advocacy of *baihua,* or "plain language," the vernacular which in its written form came to replace the classical form of Chinese writing in the 1920s.

The Chinese Communists adopted as their own the New Culture Movement's theme of the need to educate the masses. Likewise, they continued to attack the traditions of Confucian China, which had bred submissiveness to authority and ignorance. In addition, the nascent Communist movement added an explicit concern with economics and democracy. Li Dazhao [Li Ta-chao], a co-founder with Chen Duxiu of the Chinese Communist Party [CCP] in 1921, insisted on the important role the intellectuals had in arousing the peasants out of their passivity and making them aware of their economic oppression. He believed fully in the Marxist theory that economic inequalities had to be addressed. In his view, "The solution of the economic problem is the fundamental solution."[15]

New Meaning of Democracy

Perhaps the Chinese Communist conception of democracy appeared more relevant in the Chinese context than did prior Chinese conceptions because it appeared to offer a more comprehensive solution to China's problems. The leaders of the pre-Republican period sought a total solution in political (representative) democracy, and those in the Republican period from 1916 to the mid-1920s sought a solution in social-cultural democracy. It was only the Chinese Communists who, after laying down an *economic* conception of democracy as fundamental, proceeded to outline a comprehensive organization and ideology for a form of democracy relevant to China's needs and culture. Perhaps unknowingly, the Communists responded to China's need for orthodoxy, a common need of systems in crisis.

The Communists considered representative political institutions to be capable of producing only political factionalism and provincial warlordism; but they still held "democracy" as the highest value. Moreover, they believed that economic equality was critical to true democracy and defined democracy in terms of political activism and the economic relationships between the people and the means of production. Democracy would require the participation of the people in the political system, so that they could attain a political and class consciousness, which would give them the reasons for overthrowing the old system. The traditional hierarchical social structure and authoritarian attitudes had their roots in economic in-equalities. In Marxist terms, until this economic "substructure" was changed, the cultural and political "superstructure" could not become democratic.

Finally, the Chinese Communists encapsulated its new definition of democracy in two main organizational precepts: "democratic centralism" and "the mass line." These and other aspects of "socialist democracy" will be discussed in Chapter Five. Let us now examine the political environment of the Republican period, in which the CCP rose from its position as a small Marxist study group to become the ruling party of the world's most popu-lated nation.

The Environment of the Republican Period

China's pre-1949 political history may be viewed as an explosive com-bination of the Chinese search for answers to China's problems in Western political thought, a hatred of foreigners, and the reality of civil war and continued foreign incursions into China. While intellectuals and political leaders talked in lofty terms about democratic aspirations, the power hun-gry went about their daily business of seeking power and exploiting both the people and the government. China was a country at war against itself since the death in 1916 of the dominant warlord, Yuan Shikai, who had imposed at least a measure of order for the first few years of the Republic. Thereafter the Chinese battled each other, first as warlords, then as oppos-ing political parties.

In the meantime, Japan took advantage of China's weakness. First, in 1914, the Japanese declared war on Germany and immediately laid claim to the German concession in Shandong Province—as if China had no sov-ereign right to reclaim its own territory. At the end of World War I, the Japanese shrewdly negotiated with the Western powers at the Versailles Peace Conference of 1919 to have continued control over Shandong. This left the Chinese with the distinct impression that the West had sold out China's interests to Japan. (Only in 1922 did Japan at last return the for-mer German concession in Shandong to Chinese control.) The Japanese aggressively reaffirmed their challenge to Chinese sovereignty by issuing the "21 Demands," which, if accepted, would have turned much of China into a mere appendage of Japan. While the response of intellectuals and students to this Japanese threat was the vibrant May Fourth Movement (which included the New Culture Movement), and while protest strikes and boycotts of Japanese goods ensued, China's warlords and politicians con-tinued to battle for primacy. The Western powers who had treaty port concessions in China, although of a mind to return them to the govern-ment of China, could not determine from the rival claims just which group truly represented and ruled China.

The Northern Expedition, an effort to reunite China, was led by the new leader of the KMT, Chiang Kai-shek. He had succeeded Sun Yat-sen as the KMT leader upon Sun's death in 1925 and had become commander-in-chief of the army. With the support of the CCP, Chiang Kai-shek's army defeated the contending warlords. In 1927, however, the unity forged by the Nothern Expedition came to an abrupt halt with the KMT slaughter of the Communists, who were growing ever stronger within the KMT-CCP "united front." Thus ended the dominant theme of warlordism and began another theme of civil war, this time between two political parties.

Founding of the Chinese Communist Party

The founding of the CCP in 1921, with the support of the Comintern (the Soviet-run "Communist International") in the form of advisers to the CCP, represented the political institutionalization of what had hitherto been no more than a small Marxist study group of intellectuals concerned about China's problems. Like so many other intellectuals during the May Fourth Movement, they hoped to find a panacea to all of China's problems. Marxism seemed to provide that panacea. The Soviets, however, had a different set of priorities. Concerned about the power of Japan on their eastern flank, the Soviets wanted a united China that was strong enough to resist Japan's power and that was friendly toward the Soviet Union. Believing that the CCP was too weak to control China in the near future, the Soviets insisted that the CCP gain strength by merging in a united front with the KMT. Soviet aid flowed, therefore, to the KMT, in hopes of creating a loyal ally.

The fledgling CCP was not the primary beneficiary of Soviet interests in China, whether at its inception or later in the civil war against the KMT. Indeed, with the Soviets actually training and funneling aid to the KMT-led military, it was really the Soviets who made it possible for the KMT to so effectively decimate the ranks of the CCP. The Soviet Union further contributed to the CCP's overall weakness after the 1927 collapse of the united front by demanding that the CCP pursue an urban strategy. Locked into a mind-set that insisted upon strict ideological adherence to the Marxist model of an urban revolution, wherein the workers would rebel against the industrial capitalists who exploited them, the Soviets prevailed upon the CCP to organize in the cities. But because the KMT exercised nearly complete control over the cities, and because there were minuscule numbers of Chinese industrial capitalists and, hence, urban workers, the urban strategy proved devastating to the CCP. Three times in succession, the Soviet-appointed leadership of the CCP (Qu Qiubai, followed by Li Lisan, and then the "28 Bolsheviks" or "returned students") led the Party to incur heavy losses in the cities.

Intraparty conflict

Within the CCP itself serious conflict existed over the wisdom of continuing to follow an unsuccessful urban strategy. Proponents of an alternative strategy, namely, a rural-based strategy emphasizing the development of guerrilla-base areas, were able to demonstrate its advantages against Chiang Kai-shek's encirclement and annihilation campaigns, but were unable to gain leadership over the CCP. In 1934, the final straw for Comintern influence over the Chinese Communists strategy occurred: the KMT's encirclement of Communist forces in the Jiangxi Soviet. The Red Army, breaking through the circle, fled from the KMT army by a circuitous and arduous route, which came to be known as the Long March.[16] At last they found refuge and a place to rebuild their decimated ranks in a desolate place called Yen'an, in Shaanxi Province.

It was in January 1935, during the Long March and after bitter intraparty struggle at the now famous Zunyi conference, that Mao Zedong emerged as the leader of the CCP. Under Mao's guidance, the Party emphasized the importance of winning the support of the rural peasantry (some 85 percent of the total population), guerrilla tactics in warfare, the importance of correct thought for defeating the enemy, and the importance of Communist ethics for recruitment into the Party. Ethical leadership, this time based on Marxist-Leninist, not Confucian, ethics, once again provided the rationale for leadership, albeit a revolutionary leadership which did not yet have control over China.

Japanese aggression and the second united front

While the Chinese warred against each other, the Japanese seized the opportunity offered by China's weakness. In September 1931, Japan invaded China's three northeastern provinces. Manchuria, the industrial heartland of China, was suddenly in Japan's hands. The League of Nations, unable to take action against this military aggression, stood by on the sidelines. The United States, not a League member, wistfully issued the Stimson "nonrecognition" doctrine: The United States would not recognize Japan's control of China.

This served to confirm to the Japanese that they had a free hand in China and that the West would not intervene. No one was able to thwart Japan's aggression. Chiang Kai-shek himself, bent on fighting the Communists, paid little heed to the strengthening of Japanese power, now within the confines of China itself. The CCP agreed, perhaps under pressure from the Comintern, to enter a second united front with the KMT to fight the Japanese. But Chiang would have no part of it. Finally, on December 12, 1936, Marshall Zhang Xueliang (Chang Hsueh-liang), who was in charge of Chinese troops attempting to push back the Japanese in Manchuria—but who had received no support from Chiang Kai-shek (who wanted Zhang to fight the Red Army, not the Japanese)—took the extraordinary action of placing Chiang Kai-shek under house arrest. Only when Chiang agreed to temporarily suspend the civil war with the Communists and join with them in a united front was he released. This event, known as the Xian (Sian) Incident, resulted in Chiang's reluctant acquiescence to a second united front. In the Marco Polo Bridge incident of July 7, 1937, Japan attacked the Nationalist troops just outide of Beijing (Peking) thereby launching what became World War II in the Asian theatre. The Communist leadership announced that its troops would fight under the leadership of the KMT Army against the Japanese.

This second united front was a case of too little too late. Within a short time the Japanese controlled the entire eastern seaboard of China. It was, in fact, only the endless sacrifices and hard work of the Chinese people, combined with effective Communist-led guerrilla activities, which prevented the Japanese from expanding their control farther westward. Although the Japanese repeatedly bombed the wartime capital of Chongqing (Chungking), they were unable to destroy the city or to take the territory that lay between it and the occupied eastern seaboard.

But the story of China's war effort against Japan is not entirely one of valor and bravery. In fact, the evidence is fairly persuasive that once the United States formally entered World War II at the end of 1941 by declaring war on Japan, the KMT wartime government grew increasingly corrupt and effete. Apparently convinced that the United States would now win the war for them, the Nationalists' elite corps, safely ensconced in Zhongqing, engaged in the easy life, and bade their time until the war was over to once again fight the Communists. America's wartime supplies, intended to supply the KMT's rank and file, instead were siphoned off and held in storage for the elite corps to use later against the Red Army. Thus the KMT's forces went into battle against the Japanese in freezing temperatures with cloth boots and inadequate clothing, ammunition, and food.

The Communists were not, of course, innocent in all of this. Although they had no access to American supplies, they too had their own agenda for the postwar period. But their approach was different: to strengthen their troops through battle experience and to build popular support in their base areas. In 1944, the United States, sensing the upcoming civil war, sent Ambassador Patrick Hurley to initiate negotiations between the CCP and the KMT, a mission that was doomed to fail.

Thus, when World War II ended in Asia in August 1945, with the dropping of two American atomic bombs on Japan, the Red Army was battle-hardened and able to rely on minimal weaponry, whereas the KMT elite corps was, by comparison, soft and dependent on superior weaponry supplied by the United States. Although the United States tried repeatedly through the Hurley mission, and then the Marshall mission (1946–1947), to halt the civil war between the Nationalist and Red Armies that began almost the day Japan surrendered, these efforts failed. The Nationalists fought as they had always fought, holding the cities and ignoring the need to gain control over the vast countryside.

By contrast, the Red Army had been steadily building support among the peasantry, even during the war against the Japanese. They were thus well-prepared, through a combined strategy of people's war, guerrilla tactics, and confrontational battles when they held the advantage, to wear down KMT forces, isolate them in cities, and cut off their supplies. For this reason, the cities eventually fell to the Red Army. But who would claim the final victory was not at all evident until the spring of 1949, just months before the Communists routed the KMT and declared the founding of the People's Republic of China.

Sinologists continue to debate whether the Communists "won" or the Nationalists "lost." Put differently, there is as much evidence to suggest that the Nationalists defeated themselves as there is that the Communists defeated them. It is certainly true that Chiang Kai-shek was unwilling to make the kinds of reforms that would have strengthened China's economy and addressed social grievances, such as the massive exploitation of the Chinese peasantry. But from Chiang's perspective, these reforms were politically unfeasible. His major political and financial supporters controlled the very financial and commercial institutions that he should have reformed. Further, landlord support in the countryside made rural land reform unattractive to Chiang. By not addressing China's major social and economic tensions, Chiang lost an opportunity to further integrate the Chinese economy and unify the society. China was, therefore, in a weaker position than it might have been to face the Japanese.

Further, after World War II ended and the Japanese were repatriated, China's social and economic tensions continued. They were, of course, exacerbated by the strains on the economy caused by the war. Because the civil war with the Communists immediately resumed, even more money was poured into the Nationalist war effort rather than into the country's economic production. The resulting inflation undermined the economic position of many of Chiang Kai-shek's supporters, and it reduced those already in the lower classes to utter destitution. The productivity of the Nationalist-run economy suffered, leaving the KMT government little with which to appeal to the people. In the context of a deteriorating economy, the KMT's political platform of the "three people's principles" had a hollow ring. Its demagogic, corrupt governance offered neither democracy, national unity, nor economic livelihood. It could, of course, be argued that the circumstances of eight years of war with the Japanese, combined with the Japanese occupation of the entire eastern seaboard and China's industrial heartland, would have undermined the economic strength and political power of any Chinese government, regardless of its political persuasion. For this reason, it could be argued that there were certain circumstances beyond Chiang Kai-shek's control that doomed the KMT to lose permanent control over the mainland.

The Communists held the advantage of the party out of power, which could claim that it would offer the "three people's principles" to the people if they gained power: democracy (albeit socialist-style democracy); nationalism (unification and the ousting of foreign imperialists); and "the people's livelihood" (a socialist economy and guaranteed state support to provide adequate food, clothing, and shelter for everyone). Further, the Communists could claim to be China's true nationalists, because they had put China's interest as a sovereign state above their own political interests by actively fighting the Japanese, whereas the KMT had only reluctantly stopped fighting the Communists and joined in a united front with the CCP.

In the end, it was in the vast hinterland that the war was won. To what extent the ability of the Chinese Communists to establish successful models of CCP-run villages influenced the loyalties of the peasantry is not known; but it must have been a positive factor. Having learned from their past experience not to simply abandon a village once land reform had been carried out—because the former landlords who had been dispossessed would simply reassert their power—enough Communists remained behind in the villages to assure that their reforms were not reversed. Moreover, as one area of China after another fell under Communist control, the "bandwagon effect" eventually took over: Peasants joined in supporting the Communists precisely because it appeared that they were going to be the winners. And KMT troops, with their morale steadily eroding as they lost ground, and feeling that the leadership of the KMT army cared little for their welfare, often surrendered en masse to the Red Army.

Eventually, the Red Army routed the Nationalist Army, and several million of Chiang Kai-shek's elite military, commercial, and industrial supporters fled to Taiwan, with help from the United States. The Soviet Union, always concerned about being on the winning side of the Chinese war, had immediately after World War II permitted the arms from the demobilized Japanese troops to fall into the hands of the Communists. Yet, when it looked as if the KMT would win the civil war, Soviet support had again flowed to the KMT. Only when it became evident that the Communists would be victorious did the Soviets switch to supporting the Red Army.

This history of Soviet duplicity, the selling out of the CCP's interests for their own objectives, no doubt played a role in the CCP leadership's cautious dealings with the Soviets after 1949. In fact, it is remarkable that, in the context of this history, they would have anything to do with the Soviets at all. But faced with the U.S. refusal to aid the newly founded People's Republic of China, Stalin's offer of aid and "advice" was the only option the Chinese Communists really had. What is extraordinary is that even in the 1980s in China, virtually none of the Chinese people seem to be aware of the Soviets' duplicitous dealings with the CCP before 1949. After 1949, the Communist leadership, desperate for Soviet aid, and facing a hostile anticommunist world, skirted over past issues and emphasized the positive aspects of the Sino-Soviet relationship. Even after the open break with the Soviets in 1963, China's leaders did not reveal to the Chinese people the true nature of their pre-1949 relationship with the Soviets.

With this history in mind, then, let us examine the events of the post-1949 period, the period of the People's Republic of China. Although international events and China's foreign relations are important in gaining a thorough understanding of China's politics, space limitations require that they be discussed within the context of China's unresolved issues rather than as a separate chapter.

NOTES

[1]Mao Zedong, "The Role of the Chinese Communist Party in the National War" (1938), in *Selected Works*, Vol. II (Peking: Foreign Languages Press, 1967), p. 209.

[2]Chang K. C., *The Archaeology of China*, 4th ed. (New Haven, Conn.: Yale University Press, 1986), p. 1.

[3]Robin D. S. Yates (Harvard University), correspondence, October 1986. I am indebted to Professor Yates for much of the detail on the Shang and Zhou Dynasties.

[4]Timothy Cheek, correspondence, June 1987.

[5]Timothy Cheek, correspondence.

[6]The system of treaty ports for Europeans was actually quite similar to the arrangements the Chinese set up in central Asia some years before. Until the treaty ports were established, European merchants could only trade through Macao and Canton, which functioned as official government monopolies. The Chinese treated the Europeans as they treated all tribute-bearing barbarians. See John K. Fairbank (ed.), *The Chinese World Order: Traditional China's Foreign Relations* (Cambridge, Mass.: Harvard University Press, 1968).

[7]Giovanni Sartori, *Democratic Theory* (Detroit: Wayne State University Press, 1962).

[8]For a study of Yen Fu, who wrote about these ideas for the Chinese in the late nineteenth-century, see Benjamin I. Schwartz, *In Search of Wealth and Power: Yen Fu and the West* (New York: Harper & Row, 1968).

[9]For a biography of Sun Yat-sen, see Lyon Sharman, *Sun Yat-sen: His Life and Its Meaning* (Stanford, Calif.: Stanford University Press, 1968); for a biography of Liang Ch'i-ch'ao, see Joseph R. Levenson, *Liang Ch'i-ch'ao and the Mind of Modern China* (Berkeley: University of California Press, Berkeley 1967).

[10]Andrew J. Nathan, *Chinese Democracy*, (New York: Alfred A. Knopf, 1985), pp. 60–61.

[11]Hu Hanmin, "The Six Principles of the People's Report," in Wm. Theodore deBary (ed), *Sources of Chinese Tradition*, (New York: Columbia University Press, 1964), Vol. II, pp. 104–105.

[12]Chen Duxiu, "Appeal to Youth," *New Youth* Vol. I, No. 1 (Sept., 1915), p. 2, in Olga Lang, *Pa Chin and His Writings* (Cambridge, Mass.: Harvard University Press, 1967), p. 35. On Hu Shih, see Jerome B. Grieder, *Hu Shih and the Chinese Renaissance* (Cambridge, Mass.: Harvard University Press, 1970).

[13]Benjamin I. Schwartz, *Chinese Communism and the Rise of Mao* (Cambridge, Mass.: Harvard University Press, 1964), p. 9.

[14]Huang Sung-k'ang, *Lu Hsun and the New Culture Movement of Modern China* (Amsterdam: Djambatan, 1957), p. 59.

[15]Li Ta-chao, "Again on Problems and Isms," (August 17, 1919), referenced in Maurice Meisner, *Li Ta-chao and the Origins of Chinese Marxism* (Cambridge, Mass.: Harvard University Press, 1968), p. 111.

[16]Of some 300,000 individuals who joined the Long March along its route, only about 30,000 made it to Yen'an.

Chapter Three
THE PEOPLE'S REPUBLIC OF CHINA IN SEARCH OF ITS GOALS, 1949–1988

From the metaphysical point of view, a mistake is a mistake. . . . But from a dialectical viewpoint, a mistake is not merely a mistake. It is often the precursor of what is correct.[1]

THE PRC'S INITIAL PERIOD OF CONSOLIDATION AND GROWTH: 1949–1955

Conditions Affecting the Formulation of Policies

There are six important factors to consider in how the initial period of consolidation and reconstruction took shape within the People's Republic of China (PRC):

1. The sudden victory of Communist forces;
2. The Korean War, and China's subsequent inability to secure economic and military aid and advice from anyone but the Soviets;
3. The rural nature of the Communist movement;
4. A united political leadership;
5. The need to rebuild and unify China, which required control;
6. The need for the Communists to repay the peasants for their support.

The outcome of the civil war between the Communists and Nationalists was not evident until the spring of 1949, just months before the Communists would claim final victory in October. The Chinese Communist Party (CCP) leadership, fighting the final battles against the Nationalist Army, had little time to contemplate blueprints for the future. It was ill-prepared to move from war to reconstructing China. Suddenly, the CCP leadership was sitting in the citadels of power. During its initial period of consolidating power, it continued policies that it had started as early as 1947 in the rural areas; but it had few specific policies to address the problems of an industrial economy and commerce, and few ideas about how to integrate and unify the country politically and socially.

In addition, in the context of the cold war, the Communist leadership won little sympathy from the major protagonist of hostile anticommunism, the United States. Because the CCP had routed the Kuomintang [KMT] forces and seemed bent in at least some degree on a postrevolutionary bloodbath, the West approached the new revolutionary regime with caution. Any amount of sympathy that the Communists might have gained was destroyed with the onset of the Korean War in June 1950. Regardless of the facts of that conflict as revealed long after the event, in 1950 the United States viewed China as the aggressor in a Moscow-orchestrated attempt to spread communism in Asia. In the cold war hysteria generated in the United States by Senator Joseph McCarthy, which focused on America's "loss" of China to the Communists, U.S. responsibility for China's invasion of North Korea, in response to the steady march of U.S.-led United Nations troops all the way to the Chinese border, was conveniently overlooked. From the American perspective, China's participation in that war, regardless of China's legitimate concern for its own security against imperialist aggression, was dispositive evidence that it was an aggressor, to be contained by surrounding it with military bases.

The West's vitriolic reaction to the new government of China was only rational in the context of a firmly held belief that Peking had fallen under the control of an aggressive monolithic communism, directed by Moscow. The People's Republic of China was quickly written off as a Communist lackey, totally at the disposal of the Soviet Union. Worse, the fact that the KMT government set up its headquarters in exile in Taiwan permitted the United States and its allies to go one step beyond containment: Because no one could deny that "China" existed, and, indeed, had been recognized as one of the five great powers which were given the veto on the United Nations Security Council, the United States pressed the point of view that the *government* which had the right to *represent* China was the KMT government in Taiwan. It had retained the name of the "Republic of China," the name adopted by the newly established republican government in 1912. Claiming that this was the legitimate government of all of China, the United States went beyond containment in an effort to *isolate* Communist-controlled China (about 600 million Chinese) from participation in the international community outside of the Communist bloc. With the support of the United States and its allies, the Nationalist government was able to claim that it, not the Communist government, was the true representative of the Chinese people. The government of the PRC was, therefore, excluded from participation in any international forum, from most diplomatic circles, from trade with almost any country outside the Communist bloc, and from participation in international scientific and technological circles.

Under these circumstances, and in spite of the bitter pre-1949 experience the Chinese Communists had had with the Soviets, they had no choice but to turn to the Soviets for both aid and advice on how to consolidate power and rebuild their country. In addition, given the rural background of most of the Communist leaders and of the revolutionary movement they led, they needed advice on the formulation of urban policies and the governance of a country which encompassed a wide variety of resources, industries, and peoples. Thus, with the Soviet Union the only successful model of a Communist state, and with nowhere else to turn, China "leaned to one side," the Soviet side, in this initial period of consolidation and reconstruction.

The Chinese reliance on the Soviet model was so complete that the Chinese copied the Soviets in almost every major area: the Soviet style of industrialization, economic policy, commercial and banking policies, the legal system, and the Party and government structure. In spite of the deterioration of Sino-Soviet relations in the late 1950s, these models remained in place, if only because the people who had formulated policies and built institutions according to the Soviet model, as well as many of those trained in the Soviet Union, also remained at the top of China's power hierarchy. In fact, Deng Xiaoping's reforms initiated in late 1978 may in some respects be seen as an attempt to replace the Maoist model with the Soviet model.

It is here, in the initial period of Communist rule, that we can see the roots of the institutional and ideological trap in which the Chinese found themselves: Once having adopted centralized planning and administration, capital-intensive industrialization, and other aspects of the Soviet model, these policies and institutions became built into the fabric of Chinese rule and were increasingly difficult to eradicate or reverse. Mao's efforts to do so may be viewed as the source of many problems. Yet, in the *initial* stages of consolidation and reconstruction, the Soviet model may have been the most effective one that the Chinese could have adopted. In the context of more than a hundred years of war, starvation, misery, and disunity, a model of centralized "totalitarian" governance, which could unify the country and abort regionalism, civil war, and violence, as well as provide a successful model of economic modernization—this was perhaps the most appropriate model for China in its first years under Communist rule.

The following analysis focuses on the rural and urban components of the new leadership's policies after 1949. Economic policies, and sociopolitical policies related to the redistribution of property, class, and class struggle, are the focal points of discussion.

Rural Policies, 1949-1955

Class struggle and land reform, 1949-1952

Even before the Chinese Communists achieved final victory in October 1949, they carried out land reform in the rural areas that they had "liberated" by redistributing the landord's property to the peasants. In so doing, the new Communist government fulfilled its revolutionary promise of "land to the tillers," one of the major components of its pre-victory platform. Local Party cadres could not confiscate and redistribute land equitably, however, until they had determined from whom to take it, and to whom to give it. The designation of each individual's class was, then, a necessary prerequisite for land reform,[2] and for determining the targets of class struggle.

"Work teams" entered the villages and meticulously calculated each individual's social role and "class background" on the basis of each individual's source of economic support for the three years preceeding 1949. The appropriate class designation was further refined by calculating the amount of the "means of production"—land, tools, machinery, and human labor—each person owned or had at his disposal.

The percentage of income derived from "exploitation" of other people's labor might be used to distinguish "rich" peasants from merely "well-to-do middle" peasants. The work teams calculated the number of years of exploitation to determine who fell into the landlord category. They created detailed formulae to determine the family status in ambiguous cases, such as when a landlord had married a poor peasant.[3] Then they assigned to each person one of several class labels: "feudal," "enlightened," "bankrupt," "tyrranical," "reactionary," or "hidden" landlord; "rich" peasant; "poor" peasant; "landless laborer," or one of several graduated categories of "middle" peasant.[4] Class labels were inheritable in the male line. If the father had not been self-supporting in the three years preceding liberation, then both the father and his children would bear the class label attached to the grandfather. In borderline cases, readjustment of class status occurred whenever new information came to light.[5]

After determining which class labels applied to whom, the work team confiscated all the property that belonged to landlords and redistributed it to the peasants at the lower end of the spectrum of peasantry. Once this was done, the process was repeated. The work teams confiscated the "surplus" part of the means of production owned by "rich" peasants,[6] then "upper-middle" peasants, and so on. They then refined the lower classifications, such as by drawing distinctions between "middle" and "lower-middle" peasants, and between "lower-middle" and "poor" peasants. However, because there was so little to redistribute in many parts of China, petty calculations entered into the formulae, with mere ownership of more cooking pots or shovels serving as evidence that a peasant belonged in a higher class category.[7] For many of the poorest areas, the increment in wealth was virtually nil. Poverty was simply redistributed. As of 1952, land reform had been completed throughout the countryside, and all peasants within a given geographical area were, theoretically, equal in their ownership of the means of production.

Land reform was not, however, just a process of redistributing the means of production. It also involved "struggle," a psychological and political process by which all became involved in "speaking bitterness" against those who had used their possession of property to exploit others. Mao Zedong was convinced that one of the key aspects of Chinese culture that permitted the people to be exploited was their submissiveness to authority and their willingness to endure suffering, to "eat bitterness." Rather than stand up against the landlords, the peasants would, out of both fear and respect for authority, say nothing. Thus the work teams in charge of land reform in the villages, instead of merely redistributing the land and other means of production, insisted that the peasantry "speak bitterness": that they stand up and denounce those who had exploited them. The purpose was to mobilize class hatred as a tool for politically uniting "the people" against the "enemy classes." A large number of landlords were executed. As a percentage of the total population, however, those executed probably did not exceed one-tenth of 1 percent.

The assignment of class labels to individuals and their families as a part of land reform played a dual role. First, it determined from whom property would be taken away, and to whom it would be given. Second, it determined, for the next thirty years as it turned out, who fell into the catch-all categories of "friends" and "enemies" of socialism, or the "people" and "nonpeople." These distinctions were fundamental to the future distribution of opportunities and, consequently, of limited resources, for if one's class designation was bad, it could mean that certain career paths, such as in the military or the Communist Party, were blocked indefinitely; that one's chances of getting into the best schools and universities were limited; and that a person could repeatedly become the victim of class struggles long after this original class struggle to end all class struggle occurred.

In this initial period, however, once land redistribution and class struggle were carried out in the countryside, and the key enemies of socialism were eliminated, the individual peasant was rewarded with property of his own. By breaking up the large landlord holdings, the Communists established a nearly universal pattern of individually owned, small land holdings. This policy fulfilled promises to the peasants in return for their support of the Communists during the civil war. Whether because of the enthusiasm that individual property ownership inspired, or because of the low base upon which future gains were projected, agricultural production shot up. Free markets flourished, formerly "rich" peasants often grew rich again, and the life of the peasantry as a whole improved.

The move toward collectivization, 1953–1955

Nevertheless, the Communist leadership was concerned that permitting the peasants to remain "individual producers" over any extended period might create the same problem for China that the Soviet Union faced in the 1920s after Lenin implemented the New Economic Plan: that is, the establishment of an economically and politically powerful "kulak" class composed of the more clever or hardworking peasants, who would quickly prosper and who might even use their greater wealth to exploit less capable peasants (or peasant families with less disposable labor power). There is fairly substantial evidence, in fact, that the former class of "rich" peasants reemerged and flourished during this period. Moreover, individual ownership of scattered plots in China postponed the supposed economies of scale that would arise from large economic units, notably large-scale mechanization of agriculture, sharing of expensive machinery unaffordable to individual peasants, and organized cooperative peasant labor.

Thus the leadership first encouraged the peasantry to join "mutual aid teams," groups composed of a few neighbors, who pooled their production resources (land, labor, and tools), but maintained individual ownership of their land. By 1953, the leadership had initiated the First Five-Year Plan. In agriculture, this plan introduced the first stage of collectivization, "Lower Level Agricultural Producers' Cooperatives" (APCs), equivalent in size to what were later called "teams," in which thirty to fifty households pooled their land, labor, tools, and animals but still retained ownership of these pooled assets.

But within a month of having officially announced (in July 1955) the First Five-Year Plan, China's leaders decided to accelerate collectivization. Mao Zedong declared that the objectives of the First Five-Year Plan were fulfilled, and that the peasants would now move into a higher stage of collectivization. The key accounting unit for the peasants became the "Higher Level Agricultural Producers' Cooperatives" (the equivalent in size of what were later called "brigades"), in which the assets of some 200 to 300 households were pooled and owned by the cooperative. Peasants were paid according to the number of "work points" they earned. The value of each work point was determined by dividing the total number of work points earned by the APC into the total value of the output of the brigade. An individual's actual number of work points was calculated on the basis of the type of labor done and number of hours worked. Peasants still maintained private ownership of 5 percent of the land, and they were also allowed to engage in household sideline production and to raise farm animals. Whatever was produced privately could be sold in the still flourishing rural free markets; and as is so often the case in socialist economies, the peasants produced a disproportionately large amount (25 percent) of China's total agricultural products from their small private plots and privately owned farm animals.

Urban Social and Economic Policies

A gradualist approach: 1949–1955

The urban areas only fell under the Communists' control after their victory in 1949. The Communists were less concerned with determining class status in the cities, however, because the issues of exploitation, redistribution of the means of production, and mobilization of class hatred were neither as compelling nor, as we shall see, as desirable for attaining their objectives as they were in the countryside. Because there was little in the way of native Chinese capitalism, there were few workers who had been exploited by the capitalist class. For this reason, an orthodox Marxist worker-led revolution against urban capitalists made no more sense after the Communist victory than it made in the 1920s or 1930s. Urban residents were apparently asked to designate their own class backgrounds, which the Party in their work unit or neighborhood then examined and verified.[8] The Communists did seize the property of, and summarily execute or send to "reform through labor," members of the urban "reactionary capitalist class," who had collaborated with the KMT and were firmly anticommunist. However, how to deal with the few remaining "capitalists" posed a dilemma for the Communist leadership. On the one hand, it wished to confiscate their property and equitably redistribute it in perfect adherence to Marxist theory. On the other hand, given the CCP's rural roots and its limited urban support, the Party needed all the support it could muster in the cities from the capitalists, the educated technicians, managers, and the intellectuals.

To consolidate their control over the cities after 1949, the Communists tried to co-opt the urban industrial capitalists and educated elite. Only their expertise could keep the cities running, and their political cooperation was essential to establish CCP control of the cities. Mao justified recruiting some former capitalists to the Communist cause by arguing that people's *chengfen* (class background) could improve if they accepted Party discipline and upheld socialist values.[9] That is, they could overcome their bad class backgrounds by obedience to the Party. The CCP's "soft on capitalism" policies were further justified by the argument that China's national capitalist class had dual characteristics: It had exploited the proletariat but it had also opposed feudalism and "reactionary capitalism." Moreover, after the CCP's 1949 victory, the "national capitalist" class had supported China's laws and had willingly accepted socialist transformation. Thus, this type of capitalist could be considered one element of "the people" and could form a part of China's "united front" to struggle against the enemy or "nonpeople." The policy toward the national capitalists who controlled a mere 20 percent of the entire urban capitalist economy was, therefore, one of "redemption": The state paid them a certain amount of money when it nationalized their property.

In the first few years after 1949, then, the Communists pursued an urban strategy that emphasized cooperation, not class struggle, and that took a gradualist approach to collectivizing urban businesses. They assured members of the urban bourgeoisie that socialism was a distant objective, and that for the immediate future they would not dispossess them of their property. Some capitalists, however, soon exhibited behavior unacceptable to the Party. In 1952, they were criticized in the "Three Antis" Campaign (against the "three evils" of corruption, waste, and bureaucracy), and the "Five Antis" Campaign (against the "five evils" of bribery, tax evasion, stealing state property, cheating on government contracts, and stealing economic information). This resulted in the execution of many former capitalists who had originally escaped punitive measures.[10]

Nevertheless, in urban handicrafts, small-scale industry, transport and trade, private ownership remained dominant until 1955. When in mid-1955 the leadership launched its collectivization and nationalization campaign, many of these small enterprises were merged into cooperatives. Cooperatives remained the primary form of property relations thereafter, although some peddlers and handicrafts people were left on their own.[11]

In large-scale industry, modern transport, trade, services, and banking, the Communists established a different pattern. China already had a significant public-enterprise sector in these areas since many industrial enterprises were Japanese assets that were turned over to the Chinese Nationalist government at the end of World War II. These enterprises alone accounted for one-third of industrial output. Railroads and several of China's largest banks had also been government enterprises under the Nationalists. Because these enterprises were already state-controlled, much economic power fell into the central government's hands without incurring the hostility and tensions normally generated by nationalization. The Communist leadership was then able to use its state-controlled base for competing with the remaining private enterprises in those same sectors. By 1952, government control was widespread in modern transport and banking; but in large-scale industry and modern trade, private enterprise was still significant. Many entrepreneurs were bought out only after significant economic pressures had brought their enterprises to a virtual halt. Some, for example, discovered that they could no longer acquire the necessary raw materials or energy supplies to keep their factories going. The state-controlled enterprises, which sold their products below market prices, forced other enterprises into bankruptcy. Further, the state imposed high taxes on the private enterprises, and when they failed to pay them, fined them heavily.[12] By 1955, therefore, the government had chipped away at the private sector by a combination of economic pressures and inducements. It did not simply decree nationalization.[13]

Accelerated cooperativization, 1955–1956

Thus, when the state accelerated nationalization in 1955–1956, it was able to buy out private enterprises at prices well below their true value, but still at considerable sums. Dispossessed Shanghai industrialists, while no longer "owners" of their enterprises, were often retained as the leading managers. And as the Chinese people were to discover in the course of their "beating, smashing, and looting" campaigns in the late 1960s, these former capitalists lived far above the standards of all but the very highest Party elite. They had retained their private houses, enormous yards (walled in from public view), servants, and bank accounts. The real problem, in fact, was that they had no way to spend such large amounts of money in an economy where there were so few consumer goods. Stories abound of their bizarre exploits, such as hiring a taxi to drive them from Shanghai to Beijing (about 650 miles), as an alternative to the dull fare otherwise available to them.

As a result of the government's socialization of urban private enterprise, by the end of 1956 there were two major forms of ownership patterns in the cities: joint state-private ownership, and exclusive state ownership, with the latter by far the dominant pattern.[14] "Socialist transformation" was, in the eyes of the Chinese leadership, virtually complete. The Party had redistributed the property of the exploiting classes in both the countryside and the cities, thus eliminating the economic bases of these classes. Although the acceleration of collectivization in the countryside was meeting considerable resistance, close to 90 percent of all peasant households were in advanced producers cooperatives by the end of 1956; and the "enemies of the people" had been eliminated. For this reason, the leadership could now turn its attention elsewhere.

THE 'ONE HUNDRED FLOWERS' CAMPAIGN AND THE 'ANTI-RIGHTIST MOVEMENT,' 1956–1957

The Chinese Party leadership seems to have made a generally positive evaluation of the economic and political situation by late 1956. But there were problems in the international Communist movement. The Polish and

Hungarian uprisings of late 1956 sensitized the Chinese leadership to the dangers of a Communist Party that suppressed the views of the people. In the context of China's own positive situation, and wanting to avoid the mistakes of the Eastern European Communist parties, the Chinese leadership invited the people, and especially the intellectuals and experts, to speak out and criticize the Party so it could improve itself. In imitation of the May Fourth Movement of 1919, the Party launched the "One Hundred Flowers" campaign in 1956 with the slogan "Let a hundred flowers blossom, let a hundred schools of thought contend." In Mao Zedong's view, democracy would be a means to serve the Party's end of resolving remaining "contradictions" in Chinese society. The only way to discover correct ideas, and to assure their victory over incorrect ideas, was to use discussion and criticism. In this way, the leadership could promote correct ideas and expose wrong ideas.[15] After much prodding and reassurance from the Communist Party that to criticize Marxism or the Party would not be considered antisocialist, many did so.

The Party's response was swift and brutal. Expecting only mild criticisms that would help the Party fine-tune its policies and operations, the leadership was not prepared for the harsh criticisms which the campaign elicited. The more educated, whom the Party labeled as "intellectuals," were particularly critical of the Communist Party, its policies, and socialism itself. In Mao's view, they had stepped beyond the bounds of acceptable criticism and into the territory occupied by those whose hearts, if not their ownership of the means of production, were antisocialist. This led Mao to conclude that, although socialist transformation had eliminated an unequal distribution of the means of production, it had not eliminated the exploitative bourgeois *attitudes* of those who had once belonged to the capitalist class (as most intellectuals had). This apparently convinced Mao that class struggle was a long-term issue. The deeply ingrained class attitudes of former members of the capitalist class meant that class struggle must continue within the context of what was, in economic terms, a socialist society; but the struggle would now be between class ideologies, not between actual economic classes.

Thus, in early June 1957, the Communist Party launched its "Anti-Rightist" Movement, which lasted in its various phases until 1959.[16] Work units were assigned quotas of rightists to ferret out. Like production quotas, work unit leaders had to fulfill quotas of rightists. Intellectuals were the primary targets. Many accused of being "rightists" lost their jobs in their primary fields of expertise and were reassigned to jobs in which they could exercise no influence. Some were exiled to distant provinces, to return to their homes and original jobs some twenty years later with a "reversal of verdicts" against rightists. Some rightists were imprisoned. All were socially and politically ostracized. The Anti-Rightist Movement was soon supplemented with a party rectification to cleanse the Communist Party of unreliable elements who had sneaked into it when it was massively recruiting members to control and organize China in the early 1950s. The result now was a deafening silence: Dissenters both inside and outside the Party dared say nothing critical of socialism or the Party.

The Anti-Rightist Movement marked the beginning of what was later to be called the "twenty bad years" in China: a period characterized by repeated class struggles, rectifications, and sharp reversals of Party policies; a period in which the administration of all sectors gradually fell into Party hands and became increasingly politicized; and a period in which the legal system was steadily undermined. Although the Chinese who look back and remember the pre-1957 period as the "golden years" of Communist rule may have distorted the past somewhat, what did exist at that time was a strong faith in the correctness and virtue of the Party leadership, a belief that socialist policies were improving the livelihood of the Chinese people, the appearance of a united Party leadership, and a strong sense of law and order. During these first years of Communist Party rule, the country was unified and prosperous in a way its citizens had not experienced in their lifetimes. Then suddenly, euphoria turned to fear, and the Chinese people were to experience both personal and national tragedy.

THE GREAT LEAP FORWARD AND THE THREE BAD YEARS, 1958–1961

The Maoist Model

Although the overall gains were impressive, productivity was at a much lower level toward the end of the First Five-Year Plan (1953–1957) than in its first years. The bulk of the available investment capital, largely coming in loans from the Soviet Union and the profits squeezed out of the agricultural sector, went into purchasing capital goods for heavy industry, which benefitted at the expense of both the light industrial and agricultural sectors. This was in full accord with the Soviet model of development. The costs of following this model were, in Mao Zedong's view, excessive: China simply lacked sufficient funds to continue to finance heavy industrialization with purchases from the Soviets. China had huge numbers of workers but little money. Further, Mao believed that the Soviets wanted to hold back rapid Chinese development for fear that China might surpass Soviet production levels.

Thus, Mao proposed an alternative model for economic development, one which became known as the "Maoist" model. Its emphasis was on higher levels of collectivization in order to achieve greater economies of scale; organizing China's large population to take the place of expensive capital equipment; decentralization of decision making down to the level of the commune; the importance of political thought for greater productivity;

"redness" and "politics in command"; egalitarianism; and "spiritual" rather than material rewards.

In the meantime, the Party rectification to supplement the Anti-, Rightist movement of 1957 had cleared out unreliable cadres from the Party, thus paving the way for the grandiose visions of the Second Five-Year Plan. The decline in productivity gains toward the end of the First Five-Year Plan was, in Mao's view, the result of either unreliable cadres or lazy ones who "lagged behind the masses" in enthusiasm for attaining socialism. In the rapid buildup of the Party and state organizations after 1949, recruitment criteria had been minimal. Tens of thousands of ambitious individuals who wanted only to advance their personal careers had slipped into the Communist Party. With Party ranks consolidated through rectification, Mao felt confident of a reliable and enthusiastic Party leadership to promote the Second Five-Year Plan.

The Great Leap Forward in the countryside

Under this plan, which became known as the "Great Leap Forward," the key economic unit in the countryside would be the commune. One of the major economic purposes of this high level of collectivization was to merge the governmental (administrative) unit of the township (*xiang*) with the economic production unit that it controlled. Communes varied greatly in size, but could include as many as 10,000 households (about 40,000 to 50,000 people), or as few as 1,200 to 1,500 households in more desolate areas.

The commune was intended to achieve economies of scale. Its large size would permit it to become the basis for agricultural mechanization and for an expanded educational, medical, cultural, and scientific network in the countryside. Thus, a commune could support a high school, a hospital, a "cultural palace" or sports complex, a militia unit, an agricultural research station, power plant, radio station, stores, a bank, irrigation and road-building projects, and similar large-scale efforts that smaller collective units could not. Most importantly for Mao Zedong, the commune was to become the basis for the "backyard furnace" program, by which peasants would become industrialists: They would industrialize the rural countryside by building heavy industries, especially steel. In this way, China could surpass the Western industrialized countries in steel production in just three years.

Thus, communes were to be locally self-contained, self-reliant units that could provide for all their members' needs. They would be responsible for both political and economic decision making from the commune level down. From the perspective of the production units below the commune level, the commune represented a centralization of authority. From the perspective of the central government, however, communes represented a decentralization of political and economic control and production. But general policy guidelines were still set at the national level, and communes were responsible for implementing them correctly.

In the communes, peasants were no longer permitted to own private plots, engage in sideline industries, or raise their own farm animals. Everyone was to receive the same wage, regardless of work effort or talent, in fulfillment of the Communist axiom, "From each according to his ability, to each according to his need." Through a continuation of "politics in command," and new planting techniques, the Great Leap Forward was supposed to lead to such excess grain production that the existing granaries would be inadequate to handle the surplus. No one need worry about having their "needs" satisfied.

As success stories of doubling, tripling, and even quadrupling agricultural production filtered into the press, cadres who were desperate both to escape criticism and to advance their careers filed fraudulent record growth reports. What resulted could be viewed as the workings of "the big lie": The leadership started out with wildly unrealistic statements about what the new economic policies could produce. Rural cadres, under pressure to fulfill and then exceed these already unrealistic production quotas, reported back success in achieving them, when in fact they had failed. The central leadership, believing the production figures, pressured the cadres to fulfill even higher production quotas. The cadres, in turn, pushed the peasants until they refused to comply, or collapsed.

As it turned out, the suppositions underlying the communes were invalid. Because the peasants were informed the harvests would be abundant, they did not stint on eating grain. And when the leadership ordered them to relinquish their farm animals to the communes, they slaughtered and ate the animals themselves rather than share them with commune members. The agricultural techniques that the cadres commanded the peasants to use, on orders from distant bureaucrats in Beijing's smoke-filled offices, included such untested practices as double-cropping in single-crop areas, triple-cropping in double-crop areas, close planting of seedlings, and deep ploughing. All this required more labor and more fertilizer than was available. As the Chinese put it, "Three times three is not as good as two times five." In the end, the crops wilted in the fields, and many peasants, too weak from hunger to move, died in their houses.

As for the "backyard furnaces," the peasants, who were forced by their leaders to build steel furnaces about which they knew nothing, hastily contrived structures that often blew up or did not function at all. Working without safety equipment, many peasants were seriously injured. Further, the leadership did not set quality standards, so it made little difference to the peasants what kind of product they turned out. Most of it was unusable. In addition, the leadership had never investigated the question of the sources of raw materials for making steel in the countryside. Not only was coal or coke already in short supply for firing existing furnaces even in the cities, where large steel plants were located, but also there was little ore or metal *of any kind* to smelt. Thus, under the supervision of cadres anxious to overfulfill production quotas that the central government said *other* communes had fulfilled, the peasants ripped out the metal heating units in their buildings, tore down their metal fences, and threw excess pots, pans, and shovels into the furnaces. Even more pathetic distortions occurred as peasants carted metal antiquities, including irreplaceable ancient Buddhist sculptures, out to be smelted in their backyard furnaces. At the minimum, these were one-shot affairs. No continuing source of supplies existed.

Some believe that the Chinese peasants would have nevertheless endured all the sacrifices the communization program entailed had it not been for one final administrative flourish: communal messhalls. Most peasants had already grown accustomed to a centralized cooking system at the brigade level. This system was intended to free housewives for productive labor. Now, at the commune level, the leadership told the peasants that they could no longer take the collectively cooked food back to their own houses to eat. Instead, families were ordered to eat in communal dining halls. This was the final straw, and the peasant resistance that erupted sent the commune program reeling in reverse. The number of communes plummeted from roughly 70,000 to about 50,000. Cadres were helpless in the face of incensed peasants to maintain many of the features of the commune system.

In the following years, the commune nevertheless remained the local governmental and administrative unit. It also retained certain economic functions such as tax collection, agricultural experimentation centers, management of communal industries, supervision of compulsory farm procurement quotas, as well as functioning as the primary market for those villages within the area covered by the commune. Further, it expanded its role in providing health care and administered rural hospitals. And in education, the commune became the level at which secondary schools were located.[17]

But many of the communes' features were eliminated, notably the communal messhalls and the backyard furnaces. By 1962, private plots, household production, and private farm animal production had been restored. The level of accounting in most cases devolved by 1959–1960 down to at least the brigade level, and by 1962 to the team level. Peasants were once again paid on the basis of their work points, rather than "all eating out of the same pot."

The Great Leap Forward in the cities

Although Chinese cities were not immune to Great Leap Forward policies, they had already reached a high level of socialization of property. By 1956, most urban enterprises had become cooperatives or state-owned, and the "eight grade wage scale" was already on the books. Thus the cities did not face the same crises of communization and new wage rates that the villages confronted. In fact, the enthusiasm in the cities for the "Great Leap" initially was immense. The idea of China catching up with the industrialized countries in a few years excited the imagination of many urban Chinese. Children now went to school only half days (which began earlier), and spent the other half of the day (which ended later) either working in a school industry or trying to find raw materials to put into their own backyard furnaces. These were often constructed in the school's own grounds, such as on the basketball court or the playing fields, and they were supervised by older students or teachers whose only qualification to run industries was their higher level of political activism.

In the end, the Great Leap Forward slogan of "more, better, faster" had a devastating impact on urban industry. Under pressure from Party authorities, plant managers were prodded to speed up production. When they responded by saying that even if the workers could increase output, their engines, boilers, furnaces, or other equipment could not, the Party cadres accused them of holding back the tide of socialism and insisted that the plant machinery be speeded up. The result was predictable: Under intolerably high pressure, boilers exploded and equipment broke down. Exhausted from longer hours, workers caused damage to their machinery, injuries to themselves, and produced shoddy goods. On the basis of factor input, that is, the ratio of what (materials and labor) was put into production compared to what was produced, production actually declined in urban enterprises even though production figures rose. Then it declined in absolute terms.

The Lushan Party Plenum, 1959

Finally, at the Lushan Party Plenum in July 1959,[18] the Party leadership tried to end the Great Leap Forward policies inspired by Mao, but they were too late to prevent irreparable damage. The Soviets, enraged by Mao's "adventurism" in the Taiwan Straits Crisis of 1958, in which he seemingly tried to drag them into a war with the Americans, and by Mao's refusal to listen to their warning not to skip the socialist stage of production, summarily withdrew their economic advisers and technical personnel in 1959. The Soviets left with blueprints in hand. Unfinished factories that could not be completed without Soviet assistance and direction had to be scrapped. The Soviets even refused to provide spare parts to replace defective industrial or military equipment that they had supplied. To compound the injury, the Soviets withdrew military assistance and ripped up their nuclear-sharing agreement with the Chinese.

The Soviet withdrawal of aid is said to have set China's economic and technological development back many years. The Chinese were left on their own, isolated now from almost any source of outside aid or assistance.

The combination of the Soviet withdrawal and the Greap Leap Forward policies set the stage for the "three bad years," in which an estimated 20 million to 30 million Chinese died from starvation and diseases arising from malnutrition. The lesson of this period is clear: "Mistakes by one single political leader in a centrally planned economy can lead to *national* economic disaster."[19] But this was a lesson the Chinese leadership was slow to act on.

The Great Leap Forward shook the foundations of faith in the stability of the Communist Party, and for the first time it exposed to the Chinese people a divided leadership. As a result of the harsh criticism which Mao's policies received from some veteran Party leaders at the Lushan Plenum in 1959, Mao again reassessed the issue of class struggle. Such leaders as Minister of Defense Peng Dehuai not only had impeccable class backgrounds but they had also fought together with Mao to achieve a victory for the Communist Party before 1949. Some had even joined the Party in the 1920s. But, according to Mao's new assessment, these socialist victors had become the enemy of the people. They were bureaucrats who, within the context of *socialist* institutions, especially the People's Liberation Army, the Party, and state organizations, had advanced their own self-interest at the expense of socialism. The socialist system, which spawned a hierarchy of power and privilege, was not, in Mao's view, responsible for the appearance of this antisocialist behavior. Rather, it resulted from the influence of remnant bourgeois elements and, as Mao was to conclude later, from the influence of Soviet revisionism. By reassessing the criteria for determining class in 1957 to make criteria behavioral and not property or bloodlines based, Mao had paved the way for later purging veteran Party cadres who criticized his policies.

The Lushan Plenum culminated in the removal of Peng Dehuai from his position as Minister of Defense. After Mao lurched back into Great Leap Forward policies once more, those policies were finally abandoned in 1960. Mao himself retained his position of Party Chairman but relinquished his position as Chairman of the State to Liu Shaoqi. This, however, had been planned before the failure of the Great Leap Forward and need not be seen as a power shift resulting from it. Nevertheless, with Liu Shaoqi in charge of the administrative apparatus, and Premier Zhou Enlai at the head of the State Council, the country quickly abandoned the Maoist model and returned to the Soviet model of development. Efforts to restore the strength of the economy were, however, impeded by bad weather, the withdrawal of Soviet economic assistance, the damage done by the policies of the Great Leap Forward, an intellectual class silenced by the Anti-Rightist Campaign of 1957, and by yet another anti-rightist campaign, this time against "die-hard" rightists. Further, the now disheartened and fearful middle and lower level cadres who were at this point criticized by the Party for "commandism" (ordering the masses to act without any previous discussion) and "communism" (forcing the masses to accept communist values and institutions before they were ready to do so), were of no state of mind to work hard.

RECOVERY AND THE SOCIALIST EDUCATION CAMPAIGN, 1962–1965

As the Chinese struggled to get back on course after the "three bad years" of economic chaos and massive starvation, the leadership tolerated virtually anything that worked. The Chinese people, whose only real concern was their livelihood, gave little thought to class struggle or revolutionary causes. But in Mao Zedong's view, a "spontaneous capitalist tendency," reasserted itself among the former landlords and rich peasants. They took advantage of the difficulties that surfaced in the "three bad years" to undermine the collective economy. These "bad elements" preferred to act as individuals rather than as members of collectives. They left agriculture for urban jobs whenever possible. Rich peasants who remained in the countryside relied for income on their private plots and sideline industries, not on the wages they earned in the collectives. Other "unhealthy tendencies" emerged, such as the corruption of rural cadres, who used public funds for their own purposes. In 1962, therefore, the government reasserted guidelines and structures to move a now-recovered economy along a socialist path and to rid China of "unhealthy tendencies," which, according to that part of the now divided central leadership represented by Mao Zedong, paved the way for counterrevolution in the countryside.[20]

Politics once again, then, interfered with pure economic considerations, this time in the form of the Socialist Education Campaign (1962–1965). This movement involved intense class struggle in the countryside and resulted in the purge of some 2 million rural Party officials and administrative cadres.[21] It had the additional objectives of attacking the elitist attitudes of urban youth while at the same time closing the rural-urban gaps in the standard of living and educational level. This would be done by shortening the school year down to six months, and for the other six months sending students out to the countryside to educate the peasantry.

Thus, even though Mao had lost his control over economic policies, he was able to retain dominance in the sphere of ideology. Maoist or "leftist" values pervaded propaganda, culture, and education. Mao also advanced his values through the People's Liberation Army (PLA). Having replaced Peng Dehuai as Minister of Defense with Lin Biao, a man whose ideas were far more in tune with Mao's own concept of a revolutionary model than were Peng's, and who adhered to the Soviet model of military professionalism, Mao was able to recast the PLA in the image of the preliberation Red Army. Rank and insignia were abolished in an effort to rid the officer corps of elitism. Guerrilla tactics, hand-to-hand combat, and low-level weaponry were relied upon in an overall strategy of "people's war." Without Soviet military assistance, the slogans of "man over weapons" and "politics in command" provided the perfect rationale for a resource-poor military. Ideological indoctrination replaced battlefield training: Correct political thought would provide the weapon to conquer a materially superior enemy.

Because expertise was of limited value in such a military, the role of the military became more diffuse. Not only was it responsible for defense but also for growing its own food, making its own clothes, and reclaiming vast areas of wasteland. In 1963, the PLA initiated the "Learn from Lei Feng" campaign. Lei Feng was a bizarre choice of revolutionary heroes; for although he had allegedly been a tireless worker for the revolution and was able to overcome all adversity by reliance on correct political thought, he had died an ignominious death when a telephone pole fell on his head. Nevertheless, Lei Feng served as the *national* model of selfless service. In 1964, the Party supplemented this campaign with the "Learn from the PLA" campaign, a movement that emphasized the PLA's attention to the thought of Mao Zedong.

It was also during this prelude to even greater radicalization of Party policies that Mao's wife, Jiang Qing, emerged as a political actress (as was befitting of her former role in life). Together with two other figures, Zhang Chunqiao and Yao Wenyuan, later to become co-conspirators with her in the "Gang of Four," they moved to the forefront of the sphere of propaganda and culture and promoted their objective of creating a new proletarian culture to replace China's traditional "feudal" culture.

This more radical "Maoist" group in the central leadership was not pleased with the Socialist Education Campaign. Mao apparently believed that a "two-line struggle" was emerging within the Party, and that the mildness of the methods used to promote class struggle and socialist education in the countryside exposed the existence of a faction within the Party reluctant to underwrite "continuous revolution." The Maoist faction sensed that the more conservative wing of the Party, represented most notably by Liu Shaoqi and Deng Xiaoping, was obstructing continuous revolution because they had formed "power kingdoms" within the communist hierarchy. They perferred to reap personal gains through policies which promoted stability, not class struggle. For these reasons, the Maoist faction aborted the Socialist Education Campaign and replaced it with a far more revolutionary movement, the Great Proletarian Cultural Revolution. Its methods were really an extension and intensification of those already initiated in the Socialist Education Campaign. But the effect was to turn the Party itself into a victim, and ultimately to destroy it.

THE 'TEN BAD YEARS,' 1966–1976

What Mao Zedong declared the "Great Proletarian Cultural Revolution" lasted only from 1966 until 1969, when he officially declared it was over and ordered the Red Guards home; but the Chinese now generally refer to the entire decade from 1966 to 1976 as the Cultural Revolution. To avoid chronological confusion, this text adopts the terminology of the "ten bad years" to describe events of this decade if they occur generally throughout, and Cultural Revolution to describe those events limited to the years 1966 to 1969.

The following analysis highlights those events most important for understanding China's present unresolved issues. The motives of China's various key leaders during this period can only be intimated. The debate among Sinologists and Chinese alike as to the major causes of the "ten bad years" has focused on such factors as the deteriorating conditions for successful revolution internationally; Mao's own quest for revolutionary immortality, and hence for an institutionalization of Maoist values; Mao's concern for continuing the revolution; a power struggle between two major factions, or perhaps among a number of various factions over the course of ten years. Most analyses tend to connect any differences in policies among China's key leaders during this period to factional alignments and power struggles.

Whatever perspective one adopts, many Chinese today believe that Mao Zedong was basically correct in his analysis of China's problems in the mid-1960s. Party members had grown elitist and self-aggrandizing. Party leaders had built up independent power bases, and only reluctantly implemented programs that furthered socialist goals. They used their political power against those who crossed them, for acquiring personal privilege, and for patronage. They opened the narrow doors to success only to those who were loyal or willing to do favors for them. Throughout organizations, those empowered treated their subordinates with disdain. A highly centralized system of leadership, which permitted those at the top to make critical professional decisions affecting the opportunities and resources allocated to those below, aggravated the situation. Even though it was the workers and peasants who were supposed to have been the primary beneficiaries of the communist revolution, they, as well as those in the lower ranks of bureaucracies, were exploited. Political exploitation had simply replaced economic exploitation. The new "bureaucratic class" which emerged under socialism *acted* as if it were a capitalist class, using its power (instead of capital) to exploit the workers.[22]

Thus, although the Chinese condemn the *methods* of class struggle and "politics in command," which Mao utilized to remedy this situation, they at least believe that Mao's analysis of the problem was accurate. For this reason, it is hardly surprising that when the first salvos of the "Cultural Revolution" were fired, there were countless individuals eager to embrace the opportunity to attack those in the leadership of their work units. Little did they realize that they too would soon become the victims of the class struggle that seethed throughout a decade.

The Chinese Leadership and the Struggle for Power

Because the decade from 1966 to 1976 embodies an internal leadership struggle, a knowledge of the major protagonists is essential to understanding both policies and the issue of the succession to Mao Zedong. Mao himself was, of course, the central figure. This is not to suggest that he was at all times the power behind the scene, the instigator and manipulator of policy and people, since so much of what happened can be explained by the interaction of developmental, ideological, and cultural factors. Nevertheless, in an overall assessment of this period, Mao's stance was central to events. And, it was Mao's personal power, policies, and theories that were crucial in the leadership's debate. Mao, and those other leaders who were caught up in the succession issue will also be discussed. These include: Liu Shaoqi, Deng Xiaoping, Lin Biao, and the Shanghai radicals or "Gang of Four." Other leaders of exceptional importance must, regrettably, be omitted from the following discussion.

Mao Zedong

Mao Zedong was a member of the CCP from its founding in 1921, but only after years of bitter leadership struggles was he confirmed as its leader in 1935. He remained Chairman of the Party until his death in September 1976. While the Party leadership after 1949 was a collective leadership, Mao became the symbol of a unified China. Thus, when dissent arose within the collective Party leadership in the late 1950s, and Mao allegedly no longer listened to his colleagues, the Party refrained from publicly criticizing Mao. This was in spite of the disastrous Great Leap Forward and its aftermath, the "three bad years." Apparently, the leadership feared that to criticize Mao might raise questions concerning the legitimacy of Party rule. Thus Mao remained a popular leader, precisely because the leadership kept the people ignorant of Mao's culpability for the Great Leap Forward. Nevertheless, behind closed doors he lost much of his power.[23] Mao resented this. His concern about China's revolutionary vitality diminishing as it became petrified into a new class society provided the justification for his efforts to reassert power. Those who opposed "continuous revolution" became in Mao's eyes both "counter-revolutionaries" and his own personal enemies. They, the bureaucrats, the "revisionist capitalist clique," led by Liu Shaoqi, President of the State, had become entrenched powerholders who had to be evicted. Mao used a two-pronged approach to progress toward modernization and communism: rectification and class struggle. Mao's methods were highly destabilizing and were part and parcel of the "leftist line." After the smoke had cleared and the victims were removed from the bloody battleground, Mao averred he had launched the Cultural Revolution to renovate the Party, not to destroy it.

Those who had most ardently endorsed extreme leftism, whether with Mao's doddering consent or not, survived Mao politically by only a month. The following Chinese leaders were all, in turn, victims of Mao's changing viewpoint and quest for power during the "ten bad years."

Liu Shaoqi

Liu Shaoqi, a member of the Chinese Communist Party from the early 1920s on, held impeccable Party credentials—or so it seemed until his precipitous demise. He was one of Mao Zedong's closest "comrades in arms" throughout the preliberation period and had popularized the idea of "Mao Zedong Thought" as early as 1943. He may have been considered the number two man in the CCP leadership by 1945, when he became the General Secretary of the Party's Secretariat. He held this position until 1955. In the post-1949 period, Liu was the capable administrator, the leader firmly aligned with Mao, who attempted to take Mao's somewhat inchoate ideas and unformed visions and turn them into workable policies. But the principles behind the "Great Leap" of 1958 bothered Liu; and ultimately Mao's assumptions about principles of economic and social organization came to divide the two men.

When Mao relinquished his position as Chairman of the State (the equivalent of President) in late 1958, the National People's Congress elected Liu to succeed him. In 1961, Mao confirmed that Liu Shaoqi would be his successor.[24] As the archetype of the good administrator in the postrevolutionary phase of China's development, Liu was attuned to concepts of stability and "rational" organizational development. He was in charge of the state bureaucracy, and with the help of Deng Xiaoping, he launched policies in the early 1960s that were to be condemned as revisionist by 1966. For the most part, these policies were rooted in the need to reorganize China after the failures of the Great Leap Forward. Actually, Liu's policies were similar to those the Chinese leadership had followed in the 1950s. It was Mao who had changed. Caught up in his revolutionary vision, Mao now parted ways with those who did not share that vision and labeled them "revisionists" and "renegade scabs." But Mao could not really attack Liu's policies as such since they were also Mao's policies of the earlier 1950s. Thus, Mao attacked Liu on personal grounds, denouncing his "bourgeois character."[25]

The struggle between Mao and Liu perhaps encapsulates one of the greatest sources of intraparty conflict: the clash between the "revolutionary" and the "bureaucratic" political cultures.[26] For Mao, Liu Shaoqi went too far in shaping the Communist Party in a way which made it the "vanguard," but not the "representative," of the proletariat. Liu insisted that criticism of the Party be permitted only *within* the Party. Those outside the Party owed unquestioning obedience and loyalty to it.[27]

Liu became Mao's primary target after he tried to intervene in the Cultural Revolution by sending in "work teams" to curtail the attacks of the self-avowed revolutionaries on leading Party officials. In the chaos of 1966, Mao succeeded in having the Central Committee demote Liu from second to eighth place in the Politburo. Mao's supporters concocted a case against Liu that dated all the way back to his student days in the 1920s. By the fall of 1968, the Central Committee had stripped Liu of all his offices, arrested him, and cast him upon "the garbage heap of history." In late 1969 he died in disgrace.[28]

Lin Biao

Lin Biao, as the commander of the Fourth Field Army, was one of the greatest of the Communist military leaders during the anti-Japanese war (1937 to 1945) and civil war (1945 to 1949). His impeccable revolutionary credentials were matched only by his contribution to the defeat of the KMT. During the 1950s, he disappeared from view, convalescing from tuberculosis. But when Mao Zedong dismissed the Minister of Defense in 1959, he chose Lin Biao as his successor. The appointment highlighted the tension between Mao's revolutionary line, which in military policy meant "men over weapons" and "politics in command," and the bureaucratic-consolidation line, which favored stabilizing society, and operating through a bureaucratic-hierarchical framework led by experts.

Mao had the firm support of Lin Biao, if not all the army leaders. When the Cultural Revolution began in earnest, and Mao's youthful Red Guards encountered resistance from the bureaucrats and Party leaders whom they had targeted for "re-education," Mao turned for support to the People's Liberation Army. While it is beyond the scope of this book to recount the chaotic situation which the PLA suddenly confronted, it is important to note that the PLA made its debut in civilian politics reluctantly. The already significant divisions within the PLA between the professionally and politically oriented groups, and between the central and regional commanders, were further exacerbated by the PLA's forced involvement in the complexities of local politics. By the time the Cultural Revolution was officially declared at an end at the Ninth Party Congress in April 1969, however, a highly fragmented PLA had asserted control over civilian politics through its dominant membership in the "revolutionary committees" that had replaced the Party in the governing structure, and in the Party's Central Committee and Politburo. The new Party Constitution named Lin Biao as the man who would succeed Mao Zedong as Party Chairman.

But history was cruel to Lin Biao. The Ninth Party Congress turned out to be the pinnacle of his career, the prelude to his denouement. As both Chairman Mao and Premier Zhou Enlai tried to restore the Party as the dominant political institution, many of those Party bureaucrats who had fallen into disfavor and had been maligned and mistreated during the Cultural Revolution returned to their positions. They had little love for Lin Biao. The growing tensions within the PLA over Lin Biao's leadership, combined with Mao's discomfort over the military's dominant role in civilian politics, sealed Lin Biao's fate. No doubt Mao's concerns went beyond the PLA's tenacious hold and its refusal to relinquish power when told to do so, to a personal anxiety that Lin Biao was moving into the citadels of his own power before Mao had even gone "to see Marx."[29] The critical juncture seems to have come during the rewriting of the State Constitution in 1970, with Mao allegedly arguing that there was no need to replace the deceased Liu Shaoqi as President of the PRC.[30] Lin Biao was apparently anxious that this position be revived in the hopes that he would eventually hold both it and the position of Party Chairman when Mao died. Were Premier Zhou Enlai to remain the key figure in the state apparatus, Lin Biao's leading position in the Party would be counterbalanced.

Lin Biao seems to have pushed his point until he antagonized, even infuriated, Mao.[31] It appears that at the minimum, Mao did not want any *more* power to fall into Lin Biao's hands. Mao's refusal to let Lin Biao have his way, Mao's campaign to rid the army of "arrogance and complacency," efforts to rotate the positions of military commanders out of the regions where their power was rooted, and attempts to get the military out of politics and positions of power were all maneuvers directed at curbing the PLA's, and specifically Lin Biao's, power. Knowing full well how cruel Mao could be, and having himself participated in the efforts to humiliate and mistreat Liu Shaoqi, Lin Biao could anticipate his own fate if Mao drew his forces together faster than he did.

The result was the alleged "Lin Biao plot" of 1971. Few accounts agree on the details, but all accuse Lin Biao and his closest supporters of plotting to assassinate Mao Zedong. When their plan was foiled, they fled in haste to the airport, boarded a plane with insufficient fuel and crew, and headed for the Soviet Union. The plane crashed in Outer Mongolia, killing all aboard. The Soviets were the first to arrive at the scene of the crash.[32] However, no real evidence is at our disposal for assessing the story's validity. We really only know what the Chinese government, which has its own skeletons to hide, wants us to know. Thus, the Lin Biao plot remains a matter shrouded in mystery.

A campaign was launched after Lin Biao's death to rid the military of all those associated with him. In this "Criticize Lin, Criticize Confucius" campaign, Lin Biao was decried as a "closet Confucianist," an "ultra-rightist" in disguise, a man of unlimited personal ambition. How could the man who had irrefutably been an ultra-leftist, who pushed Mao's theories of continuous revolution and class struggle, who had contributed more than almost any other commander to the defeat of the KMT in the civil war, and who was one of Mao's closest "comrade in arms" since at least 1959, now suddenly be an "ultra-rightist"? In the acrobatic logic of Chinese ideology, it was argued that by purposefully pushing the Chinese masses too far to the left, he hoped to alienate them from socialism. Thus he was really an "ultra-rightist," and could be associated with the likes of Liu Shaoqi. At the Tenth Party Congress, Premier Zhou Enlai denounced Lin Biao in a statement that was almost a caricature of the way in which Lin Biao had denounced Liu Shaoqi four years earlier at the 1969 Ninth Party Congress. As usual, the denunciation took a one-sidely negative perspective and alluded to Lin Biao's allegedly political, moral, and personal failings, not to his policies, theories, or to the facts:

> Lin Biao, this bourgeois careerist, conspirator and double dealer, engaged in machinations within our Party not just for one decade but for several decades. . . . At important junctures of the revolution he invariably committed Right opportunist errors and invariably played double faced tricks, putting up a false front to deceive the party and the people. . . . Lin Biao and his like, who were capitalist-roaders in power working only for the interests of the minority and whose ambitions grew with the rise of their positions, overestimating their own strength. . . .[33]

Later, Lin's name was linked to the ultra-leftist "Gang of Four;" but they in fact had little in common, bar the desire of each to attain supreme power, with Mao as a stepping stone. And, although Mao's wife had collaborated with Lin Biao when his star was on the rise, she quickly abandoned him when it began to fall. It seems that Lin Biao did not make the sort of friends in high places who would "reverse verdicts" on him after his death.

Lin Biao was the second case of Mao's ill-fated designated successors. His ignominious fall from power raised serious questions about the infallibility of both the Party and its leader, Mao Zedong. Reports from China indicate that, for many people, their real doubts about the infallibility of the Party only began with the ludicrous reasoning in the "Criticize Lin, Criticize Confucius" campaign.

The "Gang of Four"

The Shanghai radicals or so-called "Gang of Four" were Jiang Qing,[34] Wang Hongwen,[35] Zhang Chunqiao,[36] and Yao Wenyuan.[37] The term "Gang of Four" derived from Mao's admonition to his wife and the other three at a Politburo meeting in July 1974 not to form a "gang of four," although our knowledge of this is strictly confined to publications by the Gang's political opponents. Presumably in response to Mao's criticisms, Jiang Qing, in a "self-criticism" in June 1975, submitted that she now had a new awareness that a "gang of four" existed, and that it may have contributed to sectarian splits in the Party's Central Committee.[38] She apparently never said she had any intention of dissolving the Gang, however. The term was never used publicly until after the arrest of the four on October 6, 1976. Since then, it has been universally used in China as a derogatory epitaph to refer to the four individuals involved.

Whether they ever formed a gang, that is, a group of conspirators united in common purpose, is, moreover, a matter for conjecture. Although the post Gang leadership has encouraged the acceptance of a united conspiracy theory, there is, in fact, substantial evidence to indicate serious disagreements existed among the four; and that had they ever assumed complete power on their own after Mao's death, a falling out among them would quickly have occurred.

Regardless of the accuracy of the Chinese epitaph, the Gang was arrested, and beginning in late 1980 tried in a court of law. Whether or not the accusation of counterrevolutionary crimes was valid, the key point is that the four members of the Gang and their associates came to symbolize leftist extremism, the distortion of Marxism, and unbridled political ambition and power. The Gang of Four used power in the cultural and ideological sphere to introduce sweeping changes throughout every aspect of Chinese life, including the economy, the military, the educational and legal systems, the government, and the Party. Members of the Gang are also held responsible for the deaths of tens of thousands of Chinese, who died victims of political persecution and the human despair generated by the leftist line.

The Gang left a legacy from which China has not yet completely recovered. Most notably, at least half of the Party and governmental cadres who remained in their positions after 1976 were appointed during the turbulent decade from 1966 to 1976 on the basis of their leftist credentials. Although their numbers have gradually been reduced, enough have remained to slow down reform. Nevertheless, the Gang of Four served a useful function as the primary scapegoat for almost all of China's problems and failings until the mid-1980s.

Deng Xiaoping

Deng Xiaoping's revolutionary credentials are flawless. His ties with Mao Zedong and the rest of the central Party leadership go back to the very beginnings of the Communist movement. Joining the CCP in 1924, he participated in the Long March, the anti-Japanese war, and the civil war. In the post-1949 era, Deng quickly became a member of the Party elite. By 1956, he had risen to the position of the Party's General Secretary, in which capacity he worked closely with both Mao Zedong and Liu Shaoqi. He deserves no small amount of credit for helping to formulate some of the key policies between 1956 and his first downfall in 1967. Yet somehow he escaped being publicly identified with Mao's mistakes. In 1980 he even admitted his own culpability in formulating the Great Leap Forward, just enough to lend the appearance of honesty without really taking blame or setting himself up for others to criticize.[39] However, Deng's identification with Liu Shaoqi's revisionist policies after the failure of the Great Leap Forward and his refusal to endorse Mao's and Lin Biao's policies in the 1960s brought about Deng's downfall during the Cultural Revolution. Most notably, Deng adamantly opposed the idea of continuous revolution, preferring instead to consolidate the gains of China's revolution, to stabilize the political environment, and to spur on economic growth with "whatever works."

The societal, administrative, and economic breakdown, and the destruction of the Party during the Cultural Revolution, combined with the PLA's refusal to graciously relinquish its recently acquired dominant political position even after Lin Biao's death in 1971, seemed to have brought about a change of heart for Mao. Believing the left had gone too far, Mao apparently requested, or at least acceded to, a return of the preeminent administrator and arch pragmatist, Deng Xiaoping, to restore order and get the country moving.

As a man who did not care "whether the cat is black or white, as long as it catches mice," Deng was fated to offend those who pretended to ideological purism, notably the Gang of Four. His emphasis on the importance of research, science, technology, education, material incentives, stability, and contact with the Western capitalist countries, and his pursuit of a "reversal of verdicts" for victims of the Cultural Revolution set him at odds with the objectives and policies of leftist leaders. Until 1976, the struggle between the left and right was complex and did not yield any winners. However, Zhou Enlai's death in January 1976, after which Mao named Hua Guofeng, not Deng Xiaoping, as acting premier, and Mao's own frailty contributed to the strength of the leftists. In the immediate aftermath of the April 5, 1976 Tiananmen Incident,[40] Hua Guofeng was named both Premier and First Vice-Chairman of the Party's Central Committee. Deng Xiaoping, held responsible for this "counterrevolutionary" incident, and for the leadership of the "Right Deviationist Wind," was dismissed from all his leadership posts.

The Ideological Variable: The Leftist Line's Impact on Class Issues

At the outset of the Cultural Revolution, Mao's analysis of class refocused on class labels as symbols of political behavior and ideological orientation. A capitalist class had arisen *within* the Party. Intraparty conflicts over ideology and policy were really conflicts between social classes.

Loyal Maoists represented the proletariat, whereas those opposed to continuous revolution and the Maoist model of development (followers of Liu Shaoqi) represented the capitalist class.[41] The necessary product of this class struggle within the Party was that it could no longer claim infallibility. A detailed analysis of the issues surrounding class struggle will be taken up in Chapter Seven. The point to be made here is that Mao's power was sufficient for him to carry out policies based on his own analysis. Thus, the "Maoist," or leftist, line prevailed during the "ten bad years" from 1966 to 1976, and even, many would argue, from the Anti-rightist Campaign of 1957 to 1976, making it "twenty bad years." This line was characterized by its emphasis on "redness" (political commitment); mass class struggle; political attitudes and behavior as the basis for advancement; ideological stance and ideological status;[42] and the socioeconomic category assigned to individuals before 1956.

The Developmental Variable: The Leftist Line's Impact on the Economy

The leftist line caused considerable setbacks to economic development. Although production figures for the "ten bad years" are not all bad, the lost opportunity costs incurred under the guidance of the leftist line were substantial. Under a more appropriate economic strategy, growth rates could have been significantly higher with the same amount of raw materials and labor.

The main features of the leftist line in economic policy fluctuated, but may generally be summarized as follows. First, Dazhai Production Brigade, introduced in 1964 as a model of "self-reliance," became the national model for agriculture. As a result, by 1968–1969, work teams were eclipsed by brigades as the basic production and accounting units for agriculture. Peasants again found themselves merged into the larger units, where their contributions were more anonymous and less visible than at the team level. More importantly, with the leftist line of "learn from Dazhai" enthroned as policy, the work point value of the individual peasant's labor was affected by the local leader's interpretation of his or her political attitudes and activism. Presumably, a peasant with the proper ideological viewpoint would contribute more to production, whether through increased production or through the peasant's positive effect on the production of others. Thus, a politically articulate but lazy peasant could earn as many work points as a hardworking but reserved peasant. From the leftist perspective, adequate fertilizers, appropriate weather conditions, and sufficient water resources were insignificant in comparison with a peasant's political thought. Politics took command, and experts were ignored or even struggled against. This policy in agriculture was complemented by the "learn from Daqing" policy in industry, a policy motivated by the same theory and values.

Second, as during the Great Leap Forward, the leftist line required that all "eat out of the same pot," and that goods be distributed according to "need," not according to "work." Egalitarianism thus became a cornerstone of leftist economic policy in both industry and agriculture.

Third, some radical agricultural techniques that had failed during the Great Leap Forward, such as triple-cropping (growing three crops per year) in double-crop areas, were reintroduced. And as before, planners did not take into account the additional costs of production of multiple crops, including extra seeds, the increase of insects and crop diseases, and additional labor costs.[43]

Perhaps most catastrophic for agriculture was the leftist leadership's introduction of a new target for China in the early 1970s: self-sufficiency in grain. The damage of this one policy to China's economic growth was immeasurable. Ordered to grow grain, regardless of climatic and soil conditions, and regardless of the comparative advantage for some localities to grow other crops, peasants cut down fruit orchards and rubber trees, which took some twenty years to mature, and planted rice paddies in their place. Cotton fields and grasslands were ploughed under in order to grow more grain. China did attain self-sufficiency in grain, but at colossal expense: Growing grain in unsuitable weather and soil conditions cost more, and China then had to import the very products, such as cotton, which it had replaced with grain.

In addition, the leftist leadership revived the Great Leap policy of *autarky*, and extended it down to the level of counties and even prefectures. Like regions, these areas were supposed to establish independent industrial systems and function as virtually independent economic units. By the mid-1970s, exponents of autarkic policies were advocating near self-sufficiency for each major economic region. Further, leftist policy required each province and antonomous region to become self-sufficient in general consumer goods. The result was "a maze of local smaller industries and clear waste of resources as exemplified by the existence of motor vehicle plants in every province."[44] The same policy applied to the manufacture of farm implements and a host of other products. Without national standardization of parts, and with production targets emphasizing the production of completed products, not spare parts, once any part of a machine malfunctioned, the entire machine was rendered useless. Cannibalization of other machines in disrepair was the only solution.

Although not every year during the tumultous decade from 1966 to 1976 witnessed economic decline, 1976 was one of the worst. In some sectors and regions, economic production literally ground to a halt. The combination of the deaths of three of China's top leaders (Zhou Enlai, Zhu De, and Mao Zedong), years of political upheaval, loss of faith in the Party leadership, and a society fabric ruptured by politically engendered hatred combined with the people's dissatisfaction with the meager rewards for years of sacrifice and hard work to create an environment amenable to a major change in leadership. The Chinese people had no say in choosing Mao's successor, but their enthusiasm for the arrest of the "Gang of Four" signalled a need to reconsider the policies of the preceding decade.

The Cultural Variable: The Leftist Line's Impact on Cultural Life

There can be little question that the leftists were committed to eradicating the entrenched elitism of traditional Chinese culture. Their efforts to present the peasant as the model of Chineseness, to glorify the simple, hardworking, self-sacrificing values of peasant life, were evident in their endorsement of a handful of "revolutionary operas," peasant papercuts, short stories and novels written by groups of workers, and pictures collectively painted by peasant brigades. These efforts to promote a "proletarian cultural revolution" with populist, mass values often resulted in propagandistic hack writing that reduced Chinese culture to a banal statement about pseudo-egalitarianism. But amidst the hack writing and crude paintings and operas were jewels, works of arts that did indeed glorify the workers and peasants, works that brought a new consciousness to all Chinese of the centrality of the peasantry in China's history and the revolution, and the contribution both the peasants and workers continued to make to China's development. In this sense, then, leftism really went beyond socialist realism in art forms by confirming an important strand of Chinese culture that China's museums, films, operas, and paintings ignored even after 1949. In so doing, it reinforced the value of traditional culture for fulfilling political objectives.[45]

THE TRANSITION FROM THE LEFTISTS TO THE REFORMERS, 1976–1978: HUA GUOFENG

The story of the transition in both policy and leadership during 1976 is in large part the story of the rise of Hua Guofeng to power. Born and educated in Shanxi Province, Hua Guofeng joined the Anti-Japanese Resistance in 1937 and became a member of the Chinese Communist Party. With the Communist victory in 1949, he was transferred to Hunan Province. There he remained until 1971, rising rapidly through the ranks of the Party and performing many tasks. By the time he was called to Peking, he was First Secretary of the Hunan Party Committee. He apparently suffered little, if any, during the "ten bad years," no mean feat for someone in his position. Perhaps this reflected Mao's personal protection, for Hua had loyally served Mao in Mao's home province of Hunan. In any event, in 1973, Hua was elected to the Politburo. In 1975, he became a Vice-premier and Minister of Public Security.[46]

Upon Zhou Enlai's death in January 1976, Hua became premier.

Although this may well have represented a compromise between forces on the left and right, Hua's credentials for the position were considerable. Perhaps he lacked Deng Xiaoping's remarkable intelligence; but he apparently compensated for this with a superb talent for organization. He was "a consummate politician," and when he entered national politics, he managed to convince each side that he was not identified with the opposing side.[47]

Clearly Hua Guofeng benefitted from Mao's support, or at least Mao's presumed support, as expressed on a little piece of paper allegedly written by Mao in April 1976, but apparently without either an addressee, signature, or date. It stated, "With you in charge, I am at ease," and "Take it easy. Do things according to established principles." Regardless of the validity of this little piece of paper, it provided the basis of Hua's claim to the position of Party Chairman after Mao's death on September 9, 1976. At that point, Hua held the highest position in both the state and the Party, much to the distress of the Gang of Four. With Mao's death, the Gang intensified its efforts to undermine Hua's power. Hua arrested the members of the gang in October, at least partly because they posed a considerable threat to his own position. Nonetheless, the Chinese people appeared to view it not as a power play but rather as an act done on their behalf, to end the despair, chaos, and terrorism that had accompanied the Gang's policies. The people willingly endorsed efforts to lionize "wise Chairman Hua." And Hua, in an attempt to further consolidate his power, and perhaps to enhance his visibility among the people, built up his own personality cult.

In the meantime, Hua oversaw the restoration of Deng Xiaoping to his former posts in 1977, even if he did so only in response to Politburo pressures for Deng's return. Circumstantial evidence indicates that Hua, who lacked a strong factional basis comparable to Deng's, was too weak politically to resist these pressures. Still, there were advantages for Hua in restoring Deng: Deng's revolutionary credentials and his close link to the deceased Zhou Enlai and even to Mao Zedong would lend a legitimacy to the Party's rule, which it sorely needed.

Hua's path was a difficult one: not to identify with the leftist policies of the Gang of Four, and yet to identify completely with Mao's leftist policies, including his "correct" policy of the Cultural Revolution. Because the policies of Mao and the Gang were often indistinguishable, indeed, one and the same, this was a nearly impossible task. The fact that Hua's power was eclipsed by 1981 confirms the impossibility of his position in the face of powerful opposition from the right. Little did Hua imagine that one day the rightist "reform" faction would criticize him for affirming rather than correcting "the erroneous theories, policies and slogans of the "Cultural Revolution," or for aggravating "the seriously disproportionate development of the national economy" when he endorsed 120 large construction projects, thereby seriously jeopardizing the state's financial situation.[48] His slowness to "reverse verdicts" on the Party leaders victimized during the "Cultural Revolution" and the Tiananmen incident of 1976, and his assumption of the premiership without prior ratification by the National People's Congress, and subsequently of the Party chairmanship without prior ratification by the National Party Congress, were no doubt the lesser of his errors. His real mistake was that, regardless of his own capability, Hua's career had blossomed at Deng Xiaoping's expense.

In spite of Hua's attempts to distance himself from the leftist policies of the Gang of Four, his effort to maintain the mantle of leadership by espousal of the "two whatevers" policy (praising whatever policies Mao made, and carrying out whatever instructions Mao issued), persuaded many that he too wore leftist clothing. Hua's lopsided expansion of investment in heavy industry meant the continued neglect of the agricultural and light industrial sectors and serious financial crisis; for expansion was heavily premised on a miscalculation of petroleum production.

In the end, Hua's power proved no match for Deng's. Hua lacked sufficient political allies and successful economic policies to solidify his delicate claim to power. Within a short time after Deng was restored to all his former posts in 1977, he acquired all of Hua's power, and subsequently removed Hua from his positions of both Premier (1980) and Party Chairman (1981). The Third Plenum of the Party's Central Committee in December 1978 set the stage for the final confrontation. Hua and his "whatever" faction unsuccessfully opposed the Plenum's announced policies, which reflected the dominant influence of Deng and the "reform" faction. Except for Hua himself, all members of the "whatever" factions were forced to resign from the Party's Central Committee in February 1979.[49] Later, Deng skillfully used the trial of the Gang of Four to implicate Hua. The reform leadership's criticisms of Mao's post-1957 policies further undermined Hua's basis for a claim to power. Although Hua never suffered from the same level of personal vilification as other senior leaders, even being allowed to retain a symbolic position on the Politburo, his fall from the citadels of power was complete. Rumor has it that he attempted to commit suicide.[50] Hua's case illustrates once again the fluidity of the power that accompanies various positions within the Chinese leadership hierarchy.

THE REFORMERS TAKE COMMAND: 1978 TO THE PRESENT

A New Direction for the Economy

Although the "ten bad years" ended in 1976, it took several years to sort out the leadership issue. By late 1978, the reformers had sufficiently consolidated their power within the leadership to embark on a major shift in policy. At the December 1978 Third Party Plenum, they repudiated both the leftist and the Soviet model of development, as well as Hua's plans for rapid expansion of the economy. According to the reformers' assessments, the Soviet model was too advanced for China: The model *assumed* a high level of development, but was in fact having to perform within the context of China's underdeveloped economy. One of their key criticisms of the Soviet model, an indictment of the very foundations of a centrally planned socialist economy, was that it rejected the role of the market in determining prices, production, and distribution. Instead, the Soviet model relied on administrative control: The entire national economy was managed "as a single 'big enterprise.' "[51]

After December 1978, China moved gradually, if not steadily, away from a centrally administered economy to a more decentralized system in which all types of enterprises, including farms, gained more autonomy. Markets became the major pricing mechanism for virtually all agricultural and many industrial products. The state continued to set the price of most industrial raw materials and certain commodities. Contracts rather than centrally determined production targets became the major instrument for determining production. Some have labeled the resulting system a form of nascent market socialism. The Chinese prefer to call it "socialism with Chinese characteristics." They contend that ideological commitments to collective production do not preclude production activities of a private character; and that markets do not necessarily create "capitalist" social relations. Whatever it is called, post-1978 economic policies emphasize profits and efficiency more than any other policy since 1949. Chapter Eight will examine economic policy since 1978 more fully.

Scapegoats for China's Failures: The Gang of Four and the "Whatever" Faction

The reform faction could not make progress in its reforms, however, before it had removed a sufficient number of opponents to such reforms. For this purpose, the Gang of Four provided a convenient hook on which to hang most of the problems and leftist errors that China had faced since 1966. But they had not simply made "errors." They had committed "counterrevolutionary crimes"; for unlike Mao Zedong, a committed Marxist who had made "mistakes," the members of the Gang had formulated a counterrevolutionary plot to seize the power of the state and Party.

On November 20, 1980, four years after their arrest, and with witnesses, victims, and piles of evidence at hand, the trial of the Gang of Four and their alleged accomplices began. The prosecution listed almost fifty charges against the accused, not the least of which were connivance with the various leftist schemes of Lin Biao and taking advantage of a weak and doddering Mao. In the most sweeping terms, they were accused of every crime of "leftism" imaginable, including an overemphasis on class struggle, politics, and egalitarianism, and the destruction of both the educational and legal systems. On January 23, 1981, after a carefully orchestrated show-and-tell performance for the benefit of the Chinese public, the international press, and the political fortunes of those then in power, the members of the Gang were sentenced.[52] The Gang had been imprisoned since 1976, their various crimes detailed endlessly before the trial. The process of a public trial for the Gang was, therefore, anticlimatic, and was done largely for political effect. Nevertheless, the trial marked the turning of a major corner: The leadership turned its attention away from the Gang's crimes to focus on Hua Guofeng and his "whatever faction." Like the "Gang of Four," the "whatever faction" relied on the validity of Mao's ideas. The subsequent purge of the "whatever faction," therefore, necessarily raised serious questions about the role of Mao's "thought" in China's past—and in its future.

Mao and Mao's Thought Reassessed

In an effort to put a new perspective on Mao Zedong and his "thought" that would permit the reform faction to attack all those who derived their legitimacy from Mao, while at the same time retaining enough of Mao and his ideas to support the validity of the concept of Party infallibility, the reformers officially reassessed Mao. In 1979, Deng suggested that Mao was 70 percent right, 30 percent wrong. By 1980, the figures were, unofficially, reversed, and talk of "de-Maoification" ensued. But the reformers vigorously denied they were engaged in de-Maoification. Their denunciation of the personality cult and the rectification of leftist mistakes in the Party's work were not, they argued, synonymous with de-Maoification.[53] Perhaps the reform faction had learned from the de-Stalinization campaign in the Soviet Union, for which Nikita Khrushchev suffered serious setbacks. No doubt the reformers had to attack some of Mao's policies in order to clear the path for reforms. Yet the attack on Mao could, and did, open the door to attacks on socialism.

The reformers had to tread delicately over Mao's body. While they tried to draw a theoretical distinction between Mao the committed revolutionary and good Marxist, and Mao a man who made "mistakes,"[54] and between Mao's "mistakes" and the Gang of Four's "crimes," they were hardly kind in their analysis of those mistakes. But, not all leftist mistakes were Mao's. According to the Party, left-wing extremists had twisted Mao's ideas to serve their own purpose. Further, Mao, a "proletarian revolutionary," should be forgiven for his own leftist errors, which had resulted from a lack of practical experience, a reliance on Marxist-Leninist theory that was divorced from reality, and hence from his "subjective" thinking. Lin Biao, the "Gang of Four," and all their associates were, on the other hand, "counterrevolutionary saboteurs." But obviously Mao had set the pace for leftist mistakes. They were many: broadening class struggle, despising mental work, the communes, overemphasizing heavy industry, ignoring the CCP's collective leadership, and extreme egalitarianism, to mention the most serious.

Still, "Mao Zedong Thought" remains valid; for it is the summation of the *Party's* collective wisdom since 1935. *"Mao's thoughts,"* which were a single man's thought, uninformed by this collective wisdom, simply were not "Mao Thought." Thus, if the Party criticizes Mao, it does not thereby question the Party's ideological basis. Anyone indoctrinated in the Byzantine thought patterns of post-1949 China could grasp this concatenated logic.

"De-Maoification" in China was, at best, an incomplete process. By 1980, the problems created by the "democracy movement" and general dissidence caused the reformers to shift away from criticizing Mao to restoring faith in socialism and the Party's leadership. Had the Party been stronger, it could have continued without Mao or his "thought." But precisely because the Party was weak, the reformers could not permit cynicism to spread.[55]

Thus, Mao remains half-buried. His collected works and little red book of quotations are no longer required reading; his portrait is rarely hung in official places; his name is virtually never invoked to justify policies; and his badly deteriorated body is only sometimes available for public viewing. But the leadership is well aware that there might not have been a successful socialist revolution without Mao; that without "Mao Thought" and without *Mao's thoughts,* the Chinese Communist Party might not be governing China today. This point lies at the heart of almost every unresolved issue in China today: At what point can reforms disregard Mao's thoughts?

Former Rightists and Their Allies Gain Power

A necessary corollary of the indictment of leftists was that their victims, the "rightists," must have been unfairly accused. It was absolutely necessary, therefore, to rehabilitate the political status of unjustly accused rightists, even if they had already died. Deng Xiaoping was himself a beneficiary of such a reversal of verdicts. But thousands of others had been left with the stigma of a rightist label.

Most notable among those who had been denounced as rightists was Deng's colleague and the primary target of the leftists during the Cultural Revolution, Liu Shaoqi. Liu's supporters, themselves victimized during the Cultural Revolution because of their association with Liu, have treated their former superior with a certain degree of circumspection. Their rehabilitation of Liu Shaoqi in 1980 was a tepid rehabilitation by Chinese standards and omitted the key element of a true rehabilitation, an intensive study of Liu's works. Denouncing the investigatory material submitted to the Eighth Party Central Committee during the Cultural Revolution as a "frame-up," the Party did clear Liu of his alleged traitorous activities in the 1920s. At the same time, it admitted that after 1949 Liu made "some mistakes and had some shortcomings."[56] Still, in the eyes of the reformers, these mistakes were the usual type Party leaders made, and could have been corrected through criticism and self-criticism. Liu did not represent a "counterrevolutionary revisionist line," nor did he lead "bourgeois head-quarters" of a group of "inner-Party capitalist roaders in power."[57] Beyond this, none of the concrete charges against Liu were mentioned.

The vague and tardy aspects of Liu's official rehabilitation are explainable partly by the existence of significant political opposition, and partly by the dilemma facing the reformers: How could they restore Liu and yet not attack Mao? If Mao sought "truth from facts," how had he mistakely purged Liu? The answer: Mao found it difficult to sort out the truth from the facts in the context of complicated and tortuous political struggles. Thus, to rehabilitate Comrade Liu Shaoqi demonstrated "the Party's determination to restore the true qualities of Mao Zedong Thought," to seek truth from facts and correct mistakes.[58] Probably Chinese children in the 1980s and beyond will learn little more about Liu than a few bare facts. He may never be able to remove himself from where Mao threw him, on the "garbage heap of history."

Deng Xiaoping's return to power

The reversal of the verdict on Deng and his return to power in 1977 made possible the reversal of verdicts for tens of thousands of individuals, many of whom had been languishing in distant provinces since 1957. Deng turned away from class struggle and gradually returned to his old themes. His policies became known as "reforms." These emphasized the importance of education, science and technology, expertise, material incentives, stability and modernization, and most of all, pragmatism. Deng combined Mao's slogan of "seek truth from facts" with Mao's theory of the unity of theory and practice to form the basis for his own slogan: "Practice is the sole criterion of truth."

Deng gradually placed his own loyal followers into leadership positions. Although Deng's power sufficed to strip Hua of power, it was not adequate to remove strong political opposition. At the middle and lower levels of the cadre system, Deng was not easily able to overcome one basic fact: Almost half of those cadres owed their positions to the "left." Many stood to lose what power they had acquired from their leftist political credentials were Deng's policies to be implemented successfully. Thus, while at the national level Deng was able to set policy and to choose his own followers for the higher levels of policy *formation*, resistance to his program at lower levels continued to thwart its *implementation*.

Deng was not, however, able to vilify the leftists completely. He successfully ended Hua's cult of personality, insisted on collective decision making by the central leadership, and imposed limits on any future leader's ability to develop such a cult—though some might suggest that Deng was unable, not unwilling, to pursue his own personality cult. He could insist on material incentives; the end of absolute egalitarianism and everyone eating out of the same pot; the end of the "iron rice bowl"; the ferreting out of inefficient producers and enterprises through market control mechanisms; the acceptance of individual responsibility for poor decisions; and the introduction of markets and profit motives. He was able to establish greater autonomy for certain economic enterprises, but the Party retained the overall right to determine whether enterprises had implemented policy correctly. Deng was able to readjust the "disproportionate development" of the economy by shifting resources out of heavy industry and into light industry and agriculture.

Deng was also able to introduce degrees of political liberalization and to strengthen the legal system. But the 1978–1979 "democracy movement," "spiritual pollution," "bourgeois liberalization," and the student demonstrations of 1986–1987—each in turn caused Deng to retreat from political liberalization until a more auspicious moment. Like the reformers and revolutionaries of the early twentieth century, Deng approached democracy instrumentally: namely, as a tool to gain popular support for his policies and to disgrace the Gang of Four further. Dissidents, however, also used democracy instrumentally, notably as a means to attack the socialist system and the incumbent leadership. Finally, Deng was able to start a "de-Maoification" campaign, aimed largely at removing middle-level cadres recruited during the "ten bad years;" but he had to discontinue it because de-Maoification also became an instrument to attack the socialist system.

Not everyone has benefitted equally from Deng's policies. Some cadres and peasants, as well as certain agricultural regions, have profited from the breaking up of the communes; yet others have fared poorly. Both in the cities and in the countryside, some have grown rich by providing collective or even individual services; but others have lost out completely. In urban work units, those who either already were educated, or had the opportunity to become further educated, have had a far better chance of succeeding under the reformers' policies. Those with little more than revolutionary "red" credentials have found promotions, and even careers, closed to them.

Regardless of what ensues upon Deng Xiaoping's death, one can credit him with extraordinary achievements one decade after his return to power. He grappled successfully with the social, economic, and political malaise that gripped China's industry and agriculture; and commerce truly took "great leaps" under his leadership. The people seemed to be injected with new energy and greater optimism. Rapid strides were made in education and law. China's participation in international trade and its relations with the international diplomatic community increased dramatically; virtually the entire seaboard was opened to foreign investment by a sleight of hand called "free enterprise zones." Although the final assessment of Deng has yet to be written, it seems unlikely that history will treat him cruelly.

Hu Yaobang

Hu Yaobang, the secretary of the Party's General Secretariat and a protege of Deng Xiaoping, was a participant in the Long March. By 1941, Hu was already a subordinate of Deng's. His career has been tied to Deng's ever since. Specializing in youth work early on, Hu became the head of the Communist Youth League in 1952. This provided the power base from which he eventually moved up through the ranks of the Party. He was attacked during the Cultural Revolution because of his ties with Deng and Liu Shaoqi. When Deng returned to power, so did Hu Yaobang. He steadily rose to the top after Deng's rehabilitation in 1977, and at the Fifth Party Plenum in February 1980, Hu was appointed to the Politburo's Standing Committee and to the position of General Secretary of the newly restructured Party Secretariat.[59] Hua Guofeng's demise as Party Chairman made Hu Yaobang the single most important person in the Party, organizationally speaking.

It is hard to envision Hu as anything other than a committed Marxist. He steadfastly supported and carried out Deng's policies to clean up the Party, to permit greater freedom of speech by the intelligentsia, to recruit more competent people for the Party, and to get the Party out of administration and management. With hindsight, however, it appears that Hu went too far: In the summer of 1985, he made an important speech, printed in the *People's Daily*, in which he said, "Marxism cannot solve any of our problems" (later corrected by the editor to say, "Marxism cannot solve all of our problems"). At the time, he seems to have received rave reviews from the public, and he continued to have Deng's strong support.

This outward display of being in control continued until January 1987, when Hu was summarily removed from his position as General Secretary of the Party, although he remained in the Politburo. The formal charges were that he had not insisted upon a rigorous ideological education of students, and that he had permitted the student demonstrations for democracy and against socialism in late 1986 and early 1987 to get out of hand. Further, Hu was accused of permitting China's leading intellectuals to spread "bourgeois liberalism," a code word for Western values that challenged both Chinese and socialist values.[60]

Whether Deng himself chose to remove Hu, or whether it was Deng's hard-line "conservative" colleagues who forced him to sacrifice Hu if he wished to save his economic reforms, is still not known. Yet surprisingly, at the Thirteenth Party Congress in October 1987, Hu retained his position within the Politburo of the Party. In fact, Hu received more votes from delegates to the National Party Congress to become a member of the Central Committee (from whose members the Politburo is chosen) than almost anyone else. In addition, almost all the newly elected members of the Politburo were Hu's supporters.[61] They replaced the very hard-line ideologues who had been so opposed to his endorsement of liberalization.

Zhao Ziyang

Although Zhao Ziyang had a fine career in the Party before he was attacked during the Cultural Revolution as a "revisionist," his leadership rank was never higher than first Party secretary at the provincial level (first in Guangdong, and then in Sichuan in 1975) until Deng Xiaoping's rehabilitation. After that, Zhao rose rapidly. Sichuan Province, then under Zhao's leadership, was singled out by Deng as outstanding in several policy areas, especially economic management and population control. Like Deng, Zhao was a pragmatist who put "economics in command." At the Fifth Party Plenum in February 1980, Zhao was elevated to the Politburo's Standing Committee. By April, he was Vice-Premier of the State Council, and quickly took over its day-to-day work, which had been Deng Xiaoping's responsibility. By September 1980, Zhao had replaced Hua Guofeng as Premier, and was named to a high Party position, Party vice-chairman, in June 1981.[62] With Hu Yaobang's removal, he became Acting General Secretary of the Party. At the Thirteenth Party Congress in October 1987, he was named General Secretary, and in November, relinquished his position as Premier to Li Peng, his protege. (Li Peng then became Acting Premier until his confirmation as Premier at the National People's Congress in the spring, 1988.) The success of economic liberalization and of China's relationship with the outside world, policies to which Zhao is strongly tied, and for whose implementation Zhao has been responsible, will influence his future power.

• • •

With this background in mind, the following chapters will investigate some of China's major unresolved issues and how the three variables of development, culture, and ideology have interacted to shape China's remarkable successes and its failures since 1949.

NOTES

[1] Li Honglin, "The Chinese Communist Party Is Capable of Correcting Its Mistakes," *BR*, No. 25 (June 22, 1981), p. 18.

[2] Richard C. Kraus, *Class Conflict in Chinese Socialism* (New York: Columbia University Press, 1981), p. 23.

[3]Ibid., p. 23.

[4]James L. Watson, "Introduction: Class and Class Formation in Chinese Society," in James L. Watson (ed), *Class and Social Stratification in Post-Revolution China* (Cambridge, England: Cambridge University Press, 1984), pp. 4, 5; and Kraus, *Class Conflict*, pp. 22, 23.

[5]Jonathan Unger, *Education under Mao: Class and Competition in Canton Schools, 1960–1980* (New York: Columbia University Press, 1982), p. 13.

[6]As Vivienne Shue has illustrated, however, Mao believed that rich peasants were more clever than the other peasants, and he did not want them to be treated badly during land reform. See Vivienne Shue, *Peasant China in Transition* (Berkeley: University of California Press, 1980).

[7]For a detailed presentation of this process of land redistribution, and how class struggle and land reform went together, see William Hinton, *Fanshen, A Documentary of Revolution in a Chinese Village,* (New York: Vintage Books, 1966); and Isabel and David Crook, *Revolution in a Chinese Village: Ten Mile Inn* (London: Routledge, 1959), for a commentary on North China.

[8]Kraus, *Class Conflict*, p. 24.

[9]Watson, "Introduction," *Class and Social Stratification,*" p. 7.

[10]For a critical study of these campaigns, see Robert Loh (as told to Humphrey Evans), *Escape From Red China* (New York: Coward, McCann, 1962).

[11]Alexander Eckstein, *China's Economic Revolution* (Cambridge, U.K.: Cambridge University Press, 1977), pp. 74, 75.

[12]Ibid., p. 76.

[13]Ibid., pp. 75, 76.

[14]Ibid.

[15]Mao Zedong, "On the Correct Handling of Contradictions Among the People," speech made on February 27, 1957 at the Eleventh Session of the Supreme State Conference, in Anne Fremantle (ed), *Mao Tse-tung: An Anthology of His Writings,* (New York: Mentor Books, 1962), pp. 264–297.

[16]For a moving account of this campaign, see Yu Daiyun and Carolyn Wakeman, *To the Storm* (Berkeley: University of California Press, 1986).

[17]Eckstein, *China's Economic Revolution,* p. 83.

[18]For rich detail on the Lushan Plenum, see Roderick MacFarquhar, *The Origins of the Cultural Revolution,* Vol. 1 (New York: Columbia University Press, 1974).

[19]Gregory C. Chow, *The Chinese Economy* (New York: Harper & Row, 1985), p. 73. Emphasis added.

[20]Richard Baum, *Prelude to Revolution: Mao, the Party and the Peasant Question 1962–1966* (New York: Columbia University Press, 1975), pp. 12–15.

[21]Ibid., p. 4.

[22]Ahn Byung-joon, *Chinese Politics and the Cultural Revolution* (Seattle: University of Washington Press, 1976), provides a good account of these social problems, particularly the exploitation of factory workers in the early 1960s.

[23]An alternative interpretation is that Mao truly retained his authority until his final years. Proof of this would be that during the Cultural Revolution, China's most powerful leaders were unable to resist Mao's attacks or form a coalition against him. Even those leaders who were repulsed by Mao's Cultural Revolution policies nevertheless supported him as the "leader," because he still exercised authority. Those who could not support his policies withdrew, rather than disobey or oppose him. Only in Mao's final years, when he was sick and failing, and either unable or unwilling to choose between contending factions, did policy drift away from Mao's control. Frederick Tiewes, *Leadership, Legitimacy and Conflict in China* (Armonk, N.Y.: M.E.Sharpe, 1984), especially chapter 2.

[24]John Gardner, *Chinese Politics and the Succession to Mao* (New York: Holmes & Meier, 1982), pp. 10, 11. For biography of Liu, see Lowell Dittmer, *Liu Shao-ch'i and the Chinese Cultural Revolution* (Berkeley: University of California Press), 1974.

[25]*Renmin Ribao* Editorial, "Restore True Qualities of Mao Zedong Thought: On the Rehabilitation of Comrade Liu Shaoqi," *BR,* No. 21 (May 26, 1980), p. 13.

[26]James Townsend, *Politics in China,* 2nd edition (Boston: Little, Brown, 1980), pp. 170, 171.

[27]Carol Hamrin and Timothy Cheek (eds), *China's Establishment Intellectuals* (Armonk, N.Y.: M.E.Sharpe, 1986), provides a vivid picture of the breadth of the bureaucratic approach, especially in Peng Zhen's Beijing Committee, with which Mao had to contend.

[28]Gardner, *Chinese Politics*, pp. 12, 13, 30, 31.

[29]Mao's euphemism for dying.

[30]Position last held by Liu Shaoqi, until his death in 1967.

[31]For the above account, see Gardner, *Chinese Politics*, pp. 44, 45, who bases most of his analysis on Michael Yingmao Kau's edited collection of Chinese documents, *The Lin Biao Affair: Power, Politics and Military Coup* (White Plains, New York: International Arts and Sciences Press, 1975).

[32]For documents concerning this alleged plot, see Kau Ying mao (ed), "The Case Against Lin Biao," *Chinese Law and Government* (Fall/Winter 1972–73), Vol. V, Nos. 3–4.

[33]Gardner, *Chinese Politics*, pp. 59, 60, citing the *Report* in Kau, *The Lin Biao Affair*, pp. 208–209. For the meaning behind the terms of ultra-leftism and ultra-rightism, see William Joseph, *The Critique of Ultra–Leftism in China, 1958–1981* (Stanford: Stanford University Press, 1984), Chapter VII; and for its relevance to Lin Biao here, pp. 228–231, 174–179.

[34]The fourth wife of Mao Zedong, and the person who took charge of proletarianizing China's culture, specifically Peking opera, a year before the "Great Proletarian Cultural Revolution" began. For a biography of Jiang Qing, based on both personal interviews and historical research, see Roxane Witke, *Comrade Chiang Ch'ing*, (Boston: Little, Brown, 1977).

[35]A security guard at Shanghai Textile Mill Number 17 until his "helicopter rise" during the Cultural Revolution to the position of Vice-Chairman of the Party's Central Committee at the Tenth Party Congress in 1973.

[36]Shanghai's Party leader and one of those responsible for establishing in 1966 the short-lived "Shanghai commune," modeled on the Paris Commune of 1871.

[37]A follower of Jiang Qing who, as a Shanghai Party propagandist, cast one of the first sparks to ignite the Cultural Revolution by publishing an editorial in the leftist-controlled *Wenhui Bao*. In it, he attacked Wu Han, a deputy mayor of Peking and an historian, for his stage play, "The Dismissal of Hai Rui." In the play, the Chinese Emperor dismisses a loyal and honest minister. According to Yao, this was a thinly disguised attack on Mao, through the use of historical analogy, for his dismissal of his "loyal and honest" Minister of Defense, Peng Dehuai.

[38]*Ming Bao* (Hong Kong) (October 27, 29, 1976), as referenced in Gardner, *Chinese Politics*, pp. 104, 106, 107.

[39]In 1980, Deng Xiaoping wrote, "Comrade Mao Zedong was overly enthusiastic at the time of the 'Great Leap Forward,' but the rest of us were overly enthusiastic as well. Comrades Liu Shaoqi and Zhou Enlai and I, too, did not object to it, and Comrade Chen Yun kept silent in the matter." Later in 1981, Deng argued that criticism of Mao Zedong's mistakes had become "excessive." Without specifying which mistakes, Deng said, "Responsibility for some past mistakes should be borne collectively, though chief responsibility . . . lies with Comrade Mao Zedong. . . . Of course, what really happened then was that we found it difficult to express objections." Deng Xiaoping, "Talk With Some Leading Comrades of the Party Central Committee on April 1, 1980," and "Talk at a Preparatory Meeting for the Sixth Plenary Session of the 11th Party Central Committee on June 22, 1981," from *Selected Works of Deng Xiaoping*, reprinted in "Suggestions on the Drafting of the Resolution on Certain Questions in the History of Our Party Since the Founding of the People's Republic of China" (March 1980–June 1981), in *BR*, No. 31 (August 1, 1983), p. 23.

[40]The Chinese people, feeling that they had not been permitted to express their grief over the death of Premier Zhou Enlai in January, laid wreaths in Tiananmen Square, Beijing, around the monument to the revolutionary heroes in remembrance of Zhou. But many people also left poems and statements which were distinctly critical of the Gang of Four's leadership. Believing this could lead to political turmoil, and angry at the hostility expressed against them, the Gang ordered the wreaths removed and the crowds dispersed. Violence and bloodshed is rumored to have occurred.

[41]Maurice Meisner, "The Maoist Vision of the Future," in Maurice Meisner (ed), *Marxism, Maoism, and Utopianism* (Madison: University of Wisconsin Press, 1982), pp. 103, 104.

[42]Stuart R. Schram, "Classes, Old and New, in Mao Zedong Thought, 1949–1976," in Watson, *Class and Social Stratification*, pp. 50–54.

[43]Benjamin Stavis and Maurice Meisner (guest editors) "China's Cropping System Debate," *Chinese Economic Studies* (Winter, 1981–1982), pp. 7–24. The real problem with multiple crops may not, in fact, have been the increased costs, but the increased labor, labor that was, as a result, unavailable for making greater profits in sideline work.

[44]Maruyama Nobuo, "The Mechanism of China's Industrial Development—Background to the Shift in Development Strategy," *The Development Economies,* Vol. XX, No. 4 (Tokyo: December 1982), p. 463.

[45]For excellent detail on the arts and literature after 1979, see Bonnie S. McDougall (ed), *Popular Chinese Literature and Performing Arts in the People's Republic of China, 1949–1979* (Berkeley: University of California Press, 1984); and Bonnie S. McDougall, "Preface," *Mao Zedong's "Talks at the Yen'an Conference on Literature and Art"* (Ann Arbor: Center for Chinese Studies, University of Michigan Press, 1980).

[46]Gardner, *Chinese Politics,* pp. 115–119.

[47]Ibid., p. 119.

[48]"A Chronology of Major Events of the Party and State: August 1977–August 1982," *BR,* No. 35 (August 30, 1982), p. 18, 19.

[49]Alan P. L. Liu, *How China Is Ruled* (Englewood Cliffs, N.J.: Prentice-Hall, 1986), p. 54.

[50]For more details on Hua's demise, see Dorothy Fontana, "Background to the Fall of Hua Guogeng," *Asian Survey* (March 1982), Vol. XXII, No. 3, pp. 237–260.

[51]Liao Jili, "On the Question of the Restructuring of China's Economic System," in Xue Muqiao, *Almanac of China's Economy, 1981* (Hong Kong: Modern Cultural Company, Ltd., 1982), p. 332; and Jiang Yiwei, "The Theory of an Enterprise-Based Economy," *Social Sciences in China,* (Beijing), No. 1 (March 1980), p. 64.

[52]It is rumored that Jiang Qing, assigned by "reform through labor" to assemble dolls in prison, continued her defiance by embroidering her initials on each doll, thus making them unsalable. In spite of her conspicuously unrepentant behavior, at the end of two years the authorities commended her "good behavior" and commuted her death sentence to life imprisonment. Reports out of Hong Kong in late 1987 indicated that Jiang Qing, quite ill from cancer, had been released from prison and was living in a villa in the suburbs of Beijing. AP report, "Mao's Widow Free, Magazine Reports," *New York Times* (December 27, 1987), p. 17.

[53]"Notes from the Editors," *BR,* No. 30 (July 27, 1981), p. 3.

[54]See, for example, Deng Xiaoping, "Speech at the Enlarged Political Bureau Meeting of the Party Central Committee on May 19, 1981," from *Selected Works of Deng Xiaoping,* and reprinted in "Suggestions on the Drafting of the Resolution," *BR* No. 31 (August 1, 1983), p. 21.

[55]Stephen Goldstein (Smith College), New England China Seminar, Harvard University (December 2, 1981).

[56]Deng Xiaoping, "On the Reform of the System of Party and State Leadership" (August 18, 1980), in *BR,* No. 40 (October 3, 1983), p. 13.

[57]Editorial, *Renmin Ribao,* "Restore True Qualities of Mao Zedong Thought: On the Rehabilitation of Comrade Liu Shaoqi," *BR,* No. 21 (May 26, 1980), pp. 13–15.

[58]Ibid.

[59]James R. Townsend and Richard C. Bush (compilers) *The People's Republic of China: A Basic Handbook,* 2nd edition (New York: Council on International and Public Affairs, 1981), pp. 40, 41.

[60]According to Chinese sources, Hu loves reading the works of Enlightenment writers, such as Voltaire and Montesquieu, and the writings of Eastern European dissidents. Hu also said in a speech that most Chinese intellectuals would prefer capitalism. He did not then go on to condemn them for it.

[61]*Ta Kung Pao,* Hong Kong (November 5, 1987), p. 3.

[62]Townsend and Bush, *A Basic Handbook,* p. 42.

Chapter Four
LEADERSHIP AND REFORM: DOWN WITH FEUDALISM (AND WITH SOCIALISM)!

Indeed it no longer made sense to ask if Mao was . . . a Maoist. One day he was; the next day he wasn't.[1]

[T]he basic question is, "Who shall rule?" The search is not for ways of limiting the ruler's exercise of power, but rather for ways of making sure that the right person holds it so that it will be used well.[2]

Liberalization in a non-liberal system will generally be a power play. It will be undertaken when it promises gains for those who cause it to be undertaken—one assumes by those with sufficient power to be fully satisfied with it. Once set in motion, liberalization may exceed the purposes of those leaders who fostered it. They may then attempt to reverse the process, but this will nourish doubts about the regime's legitimacy. Elites will have promised more than they can deliver and will find themselves asserting as virtues features of the regime they had a few months earlier condemned as defects.[3]

INTRODUCTION

If it is obvious that traditional Chinese cultural values and political structures have affected how the present-day leadership system has developed, the depth of their influence is nonetheless surprising. No doubt because the ideological system of Marxism-Leninism is itself highly moralistic and utopian, it has built on the Chinese tradition of emphasizing morality in leadership. In repeated purges of Communist Party leaders, it is their personal immorality, as demonstrated in their behavior as ordinary people, not their actual policies as leaders, that is impugned. China today is run as if it were a *moral* polity. And just as the Emperor and mandarinate of imperial China embodied morality, the Communist Party leadership of the People's Republic of China claims it is the repository of moral authority, and is therefore "infallible."

In the 1980s, however, that very repository of moral authority reluctantly admitted that the socialist system had contributed to moral decay, and that the system itself was in need not just of moral rectification, but also of structural reform. The Party leadership has, in fact, admitted that it was the socialist system as structured in China that had permitted its own abuse by leftists and by Mao in particular. In some respects, the Party has, in the 1980s for the first time, moved away from the centrality of its role as moral arbiter to accommodate an additional role of structural reformer. But the general conceptualization still holds: China's unresolved leadership issues are rooted in a complex interweaving of strands of China's traditional values and structural predispositions, with an ideology that itself empha- sizes similar values and structures. The result has been that socialist ide- ology has often built on, rather than eradicated traditional Chinese political culture. If in fact China's leadership dares to claim that socialist ideology destroyed China's traditional feudal leadership structure, it should also confess to supporting (even if unintentionally) what might best be termed a "socialist" form of "feudalism."

Certain traditional cultural variables have been dominant in the in- teraction between culture and ideology: the emphasis on normative con- trols (education and reeducation); the importance of the moral rather than the practical education of leaders; the polarized conceptualization of soci- ety and ideas into moral absolutes of "good" and "bad"; the concentration of power in the hands of a few people; and secrecy, elitism, and fac- tionalism within the leadership. Although such traditional cultural vari- ables may appear in other societies that have adopted a Marxist-Leninist ideology, their manifestation in Chinese society is pronounced. China's emphasis in the 1980s on developing a socialism "with Chinese charac- teristics" is, therefore, ironic: Socialism in China has *always* been very Chinese.

Ideological and cultural variables seem preeminent as sources of un- resolved leadership issues and the key, for this reason, to their resolution; but the developmental variable cannot be ignored. As for so many develop- ing countries, unity, integration, stability, development, and security have been the Chinese leaders' key objectives. Reform within the leadership often appears to be at cross purposes with such objectives. For example, the leadership of a not yet fully integrated polity such as China may well fear that if it is less centralized or permits pluralism within its own body, this may lead to instability and perhaps chaos. Perhaps China's leadership re- forms of the 1980s are, in fact, evidence that its leaders are more secure and less concerned with issues of control.

DEFINITION OF LEADERSHIP

In China, the term *leadership* encompasses a broad range of cadres, but in both political and functional terms, it refers primarily to the Chinese Com- munist Party (CCP). The Party's principal role is political, ideological, and organizational leadership, and it includes propaganda and educational work. The Party is "the vanguard of the Chinese working class" and shoulders responsibility for leading China toward socialism. The Party exercises "overall leadership" for all sectors: industry, agriculture, commerce, culture and education, the army, and the government. Except when "revolutionary committees" replaced the Party as the leadership organ during the Cultural Revolution, the terms *centralized leadership* and *unified leadership* have referred exclusively to the *Party's* leadership.[4]

Until the mid-1980s, the Chinese Communist Party was the repository of all political power. This power monopoly permitted it, and it alone, to determine China's social, political, and economic goals and values. It controlled the selection of all other leadership elites: military, economic, educational, social, and political. In fact, almost all members of these other elites were themselves Party members. Thus the Party's power extended from the political hierarchy into all functional areas, from the central leadership of both the Party and the government, down through the provinces and counties, to the Party branches or cells in factories, shops, communes, schools, army company units, neighborhoods, and enterprises.

The Party as the key leadership organ, then, refers to Party leaders at *all* levels, not just at the center. Although the Party structure in the early 1950s ran parallel to the governmental structure, it later became increasingly interlocked with the governmental leadership structure. This situation has continued in spite of the reforms of the 1980s, which have thus far met with only limited success in separating Party from governmental personnel and functions.

CHARACTERISTICS OF CHINESE LEADERSHIP

Leadership Not Monolithic

In spite of the pervasiveness of the Party, it is not, and never has been, monolithic. Throughout the period of Party control since 1949, the Party leadership experienced fissures, most of which were caused by debates over means, not ends. But, in the 1980s, the Party leadership became publicly divided over objectives as well. The nature of power politics and political culture in China is such that these personal differences become manifest in the formation of factions. Factions ordinarily form around individual leaders, who personify policies. Their major purpose has been, minimally, to keep the power they have in order to protect and support faction members, and then, if possible to gain more power. Secondarily, they line up allies for new distinct directions in policy divorced from power considerations.

Leadership Lacks Totalitarian Control

The Party leadership has also never exercised true totalitarian control over the Chinese people. Our growing awareness of the limited capability of Party authorities to fully control policies at the lowest levels, where the Party elite meets face to face with the masses, chips away at the image of the Party's totalitarian control. The challenges to Party control since the Cultural Revolution suggest that the Party will find it increasingly difficult to assert its leadership, much less its control, over the people.

Not All Leaders Belong to the Party

Not all Party members are "cadres" (*ganbu*), that is, leaders. Of the approximate 42 million members of the Chinese Communist Party, many do not hold leadership positions. On the other hand, not all leaders are Party members, although as cadres move up the governmental, military, economic, and educational hierarchies, it is increasingly probable that they will be. There are notable exceptions to this pattern, especially among intellectuals and "experts," whom the Party persistently blocked from Party membership until the 1980s. Moreover, there is an appalling imprecision in the Chinese usage of the term *cadre*, and especially of the term *local cadre*, which "is itself the result of the imprecise delimitation of official powers,"[5] and adds to the confusion in determining who occupies leadership positions.

Policymakers and Bureaucrats

Finally, China's leadership may be defined in functional terms. As in almost any other political system, China's leadership is divided into policymakers on the one hand, and bureaucrats or managers on the other. The policymakers are the innovators, those leaders who determine goals and values. They form the elite corps of the Party at the center. The bureaucrats or managers, on the other hand, are leaders only in the sense that they are responsible for implementing the decisions made by others. These are the middle- and lower-level cadres, from the provinces down through the counties, communes, brigades, and teams in the countryside, and down through the factories, schools, neighborhoods, state enterprises, and collectives in the cities. Yet it is important to realize that it is these implementors who usually determine the success or failure of a policy; for the vastness of China inhibits complete control over them. To a large extent, the implementors implement, modify, or do not implement a policy as they choose. Of course, to obstruct policy implementation without being caught requires subtlety on their part. Yet it is evident that obstructing or diverting correct implementation of central policies in China is actually quite easy and has become a highly developed art form practiced by many.

The reasons for which middle- and lower-level cadres might not want to carry out the central leadership's policies are diverse. To mention only a few, new policies might conflict with the competing demands of the cadres' local lineage ties; with the exigencies of the local situation; or with the ambitions, careers, or life style, of the implementors themselves. Not surprisingly, then, since 1949, the central leadership has time and again blamed those at lower levels of the leadership hierarchy for policy failures.

This may strike the ordinary observer of politics as commonplace, for in almost all polities this division of responsibility between policy innovators at the top and the implementing bureaucrats at middle and lower levels permits the central leadership to escape accountability for policy failures. There is, however, a major difference between the People's Republic of China and other political systems, especially liberal democratic ones, that are not highly centralized: In the unified, centralized, one-party system in the PRC, the Communist Party central leadership can take disciplinary actions against cadres, including their removal.

Whether or not the lower-level policy implementors rather than the policy itself are the key to its success, the central leadership *acts* as if it believes its own claims. Thus personnel changes usually either precede or are an integral part of policy changes; for those leaders already in power will often be adversely affected by the implementation of a new policy. Alternatively, if the policy innovators at the center choose to implement policy without personnel changes, and the policy fails, a "rectification," "Party consolidation," or "political education" campaign is likely to follow. We might call it a "purge" or "indoctrination" campaign. The assumption is that it is the deficient qualities of individual implementors, not the policies of an infallible central Party leadership, that are to blame. This explains why Party leaders under attack tend to be criticized on *personal* grounds, rather than on the basis of their policies.

STRUCTURE AND FUNCTIONS OF LEADERSHIP

Objectives and the 'General Line'

In addition to the specific functions performed by the various units of the Party central leadership, the leadership has certain broad purposes and objectives. Its basic purpose is, of course, to lead, to make policies that ensure the unity, stability, integration, development, and national security of the Chinese state. The pursuit of these objectives must be in accord with socialist values as interpreted by the Party. To this end, the Party provides a framework to guide the state's programs. China's goals at any particular time are encased in what is called the "general line" (*luxian*). Once the Party announces the general line, the specific ideological and organizational lines for economic, cultural, social, and military realms flow from it. The state leadership is, in turn, responsible for creating policies and methods compatible with the framework envisioned in the general line. Only if state policies deviate from it should the Party intervene in the government's execution of policy. Because the Party leadership is responsible for overseeing the implementation of policies, a vast centralized Party network has come into existence. Because the Party's line cannot be implemented in only one way throughout such a vast and diverse country, the local Party cadres' role is to ensure that policy implementation in their particular locality conforms to current Party policy, while taking into account local conditions.

In its role as the overseer of the correct implementation of policy, the Party leadership attempts to unify China through various control, integrative, and normative measures. Originally the Party's functions were intended to be limited to ideological policeman and organizer, to ensure that the governmental *administrators* of policies adopted measures that conformed to the Party's values and goals. But, beginning in the mid-1950s, the Party increasingly interfered with administrative, nonpolitical functions.

Unity, integration, stability, national security, Communism, and development have remained the broad overall goals of the Party leadership. The question becomes: Precisely who within the central leadership will determine the exact content of these various goals and the methods by which they will be attained? Moreover, how much diversity will be tolerated? How much control over the Chinese people is necessary for unity? How fast will development take place, and at the expense of what other objectives, such as "equality"? And exactly what are Communist values and objectives? An examination of the institutional structure and functions of the Party central leadership will show where the power to make such decisions might lie.

Formal Organization of the State

At the top of the state's organizational chart is the State Council. The premier is the State Council's chairman. The State Council's membership is comprised of China's premier, who acts as its head; vice-premiers; state councilors (who are mostly former vice-premiers or elder leaders on their way out); and ministers. All ministries, commissions, special agencies, and centrally administered banks report to the State Council. In theory, the State Council is responsible to the National People's Congress (whose delegates are elected by lower-level people's congresses) and its Standing Committee. The Standing Committee is supposed to enact the constitutions and the laws. In actual practice, however, until the National People's Congress came under the control of Peng Zhen in the early 1980s, it acted as a rubber stamp for decisions reached in the State Council. Further, because the premier and all the vice-premiers and state councilors of the State Council are concurrently members of the Party's Central Committee, and because all policies adopted by the State Council must be approved by the Party, the Party leadership is instrumental in formulating the very governmental policies that it must oversee.

The 1982 State Constitution (Article 63) delineates the electoral process and limits the term of office for top state leaders (usually to five years and no more than two consecutive terms); and it formally gives the National People's Congress the power to recall or remove from office the president, vice-president, the premier, vice-premiers, and other top state leaders; but at the moment it is unimaginable that it would do so.

The new limitations on the leadership's power have yet to be tested. By the time the 1982 State Constitution was written, the Deng-led reformers had themselves gained control of the central Party and State leadership, through committing the form of travesty typical in leadership successions in China: excoriating the preceding leader, Hua Guofeng, for political and personal errors. They submitted none of their decisions to the National Party or National People's Congresses, much less the Chinese public, for scrutiny and debate. Once they themselves were ensconced in power, it became convenient to talk of "democratic procedures" for the *next* round of the leadership struggle. They did not really permit their own leadership positions to be challenged by further democratization. In the 1980s, in fact, democracy has only been insisted upon when the reform leadership has had the votes.

Provincial-level governments, county-level governments, and basic-level governments provide a hierarchy of governments down to the lowest administrative level (now called the *township*) in order to carry out policies formulated by the central government and approved and supervised by the Party. More will be said later about the governmental leadership below the elite policy-formulating level. (See Figure 4–1.)

Formal Organization of the Party

Organizational principle

The Chinese Communist Party is organized in accordance with Leninist, hierarchical, elitist principles. (See Figure 4–2.) At lower levels of the hierarchy, Party congresses and the Party committees they elect are the leading bodies of local Party organizations. Higher Party organizations are supposed to listen to the views of lower organizations and solve the problems they raise. Lower-level Party organizations are supposed to report their work to, and ask instructions from, higher Party organizations. Regional Party organizations, state organizations, work units, and mass orga-

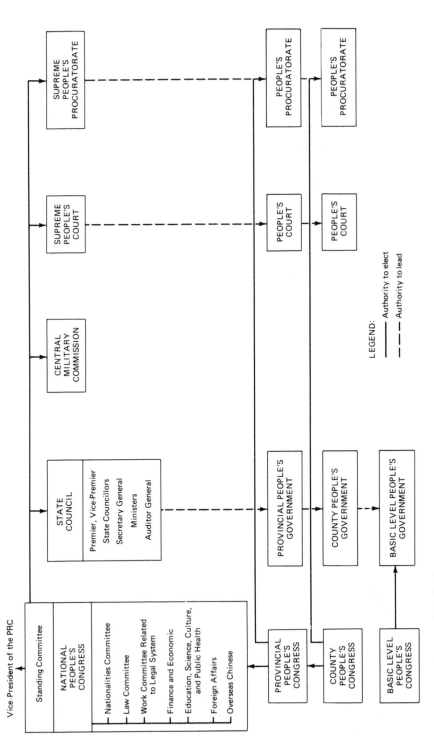

FIGURE 4-1 Structure of the State[6]

President of the PRC

Vice-President of the PRC

Standing Committee

NATIONAL PEOPLE'S CONGRESS

— Nationalities Committee
— Law Committee
— Work Committee Related to Legal System
— Finance and Economic
— Education, Science, Culture, and Public Health
— Foreign Affairs
— Overseas Chinese

STATE COUNCIL

Premier, Vice-Premier
State Councillors
Secretary General
Ministers
Auditor General

CENTRAL MILITARY COMMISSION

SUPREME PEOPLE'S COURT

SUPREME PEOPLE'S PROCURATORATE

PROVINCIAL PEOPLE'S GOVERNMENT

COUNTY PEOPLE'S GOVERNMENT

BASIC LEVEL PEOPLE'S GOVERNMENT

PROVINCIAL PEOPLE'S CONGRESS

COUNTY PEOPLE'S CONGRESS

BASIC LEVEL PEOPLE'S CONGRESS

PEOPLE'S COURT

PEOPLE'S COURT

PEOPLE'S PROCURATORATE

PEOPLE'S PROCURATORATE

LEGEND:
——— Authority to elect
– – – Authority to lead

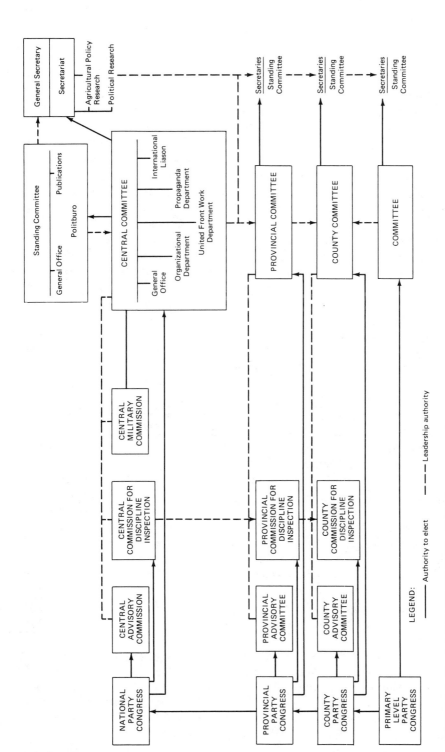

FIGURE 4-2 Structure of the Chinese Communist Party[7]

nizations each elect delegates from among their own Party members to the meeting of the National Party Congress (NPC). These delegates then elect members of the new Central Committee from a slate of candidates given to them by Party leaders at the top. The slate must be drawn from among the delegates to the NPC, but how they are chosen is quite arbitrary and based on power plays at the top. The Thirteenth Party Congress in October 1987 was the first in which the NPC delegates were elected by secret ballot, and the first in which the slate of candidates for the Central Committee was actually larger than the number of seats in the Central Committee. (The Thirteenth NPC had 175 full and 110 alternate members.)

The Central Committee of the Party then elects members from its own body to the Politburo and its Standing Committee. But the slate of candidates, given to it by the top leaders, has only as many candidates as there are seats in the Politburo. The Party General Secretary must be a member of the Standing Committee of the Politburo. Because the Central Committee is usually not in session, and because it is really too large to be an effective decision-making body, in practice it is the Politburo and its Standing Committee which exercise the functions and power of the Central Committee. The Party Secretariat carries out the Party's daily work under the direction of the Politburo and its Standing Committee. The General Secretary convenes the meetings of the Politburo and its Standing Committee and presides over the Secretariat's work.

Biographies of China's leaders suggest what factors have at different times been the key to retaining or seizing power. These include class background and political credentials; wartime experience; loyalty; experience and expertise; and success in implementing policies. Some have argued that from 1935 until a year before his death in 1976, Mao Zedong as Party Chairman selected the members of the Central Committee who were to sit on the Politburo and its Standing Committee. Mao allegedly based his decisions largely on Party seniority and those loyal to himself.[8] Even if Mao did not personally select some Politburo members, they were certainly chosen by Central Committee members loyal to him, which amounts to the same thing. In reality, then, since the members of the Central Committee are chosen by the most powerful Party leaders in the first place, it reflects the power configuration existing at that time. The Central Committee, in short, elects whoever was powerful enough to have chosen the majority of *its* members.

After the Party's central leadership makes a policy, it must submit it to the National Party Congress for approval. In practice, the reports of the Central Committee have rarely received more than a perfunctory examination. On all but a few occasions, the Party Congress has provided a rubber stamp for the decisions of the Central Committee. And it, in turn, has simply ratified whatever the Politburo submitted to it.

The organizational process of "democratic centralism," however, dictates that the Party only make decisions after it has consulted the people. Thus, the people are supposed to participate in the formulation of policy inputs at the lowest level. Their ideas are then passed on to the next level, where the most appropriate ideas are passed on to the next higher level. Finally, at the center, the Party leadership decides policy, theoretically on the basis of the ideas that have "bubbled up" from the masses. The decision to implement the household responsibility system in the countryside in the 1980s is a good example of a policy that was both theoretically and actually the result of pressures from below.[9]

Once the central Party leadership makes a decision, however, the lower levels of the Party hierarchy may only explain the meaning of the policy and discuss how to implement it. It is deemed inappropriate to discuss the merits of a policy at this time. Indeed, the 1982 Party Constitution (Article 15) specifically prohibits lower-level Party organizations from publicly voicing their differences of opinion. This procedure presumes that those who are in the policy-formulating elite have both superior knowledge and wisdom. Yet precisely how the local Party committees choose to interpret and implement central Party policy in light of local conditions may vary considerably from one place to another. Devious lower-level Party secretaries may interpret and implement policy in a direction that favors either their individual needs or those of their locality at the expense of the central Party's policy. On the other hand, those Party secretaries who have implemented central policy without considering local conditions have also been severely criticized and sometimes removed from their positions.

Relying solely on an organizational chart of the Chinese Communist Party is misleading because it does not necessarily pinpoint the locus of power at any given time. One reason for this is that ever since imperial times, power in China has resided in individuals, not institutions.

> Leaders in elite systems tend to capture institutions and then transform them for their own purposes. Institutional change is easy; the numbers of ministries in China, for example, can be increased or decreased with little or no reaction, even from their "clients," to say nothing of the public.[10]

Institutions have only as much power as their leaders; similarly, an individual's power may be totally independent of the presumed power of his or her institutional affiliation. Thus, in the history of the People's Republic of China, individuals with insignificant institutional affiliations have frequently wielded enormous power; conversely, some individuals with powerful institutional affiliations have lacked commensurate power. One need only briefly cite the case as it existed from 1977 to 1980, in which Hua Guofeng simultaneously held the two most powerful institutional positions in the PRC (Chairman of the Party, and Premier of the State) whereas

Deng Xiaoping was a mere Vice-Premier. Yet Deng wielded far greater power. In fact, he was even able to shift the center of power in the Party away from the nominal Party head, the Chairman, into the hands of the Party's General Secretary, a position held by his own supporter, Hu Yaobang.

Of course, powerful individual leaders prefer to gain control over insitutions that already have a certain amount of inherent power. Nonetheless, institutions in the PRC have been created, transformed, and destroyed by individuals, either for the purpose of undermining the power bases of other leaders or for building their own.

The Politiburo, Central Committee, General Secretary, and Central Advisory Committee

The Politburo is another example of the limitations of an organizational chart in pinpointing the actual locus of power. It is supposed to be the highest policy-making body in the Party. The Standing Committee of the Politburo is in charge of its daily work. No Party constitution, however, has ever delineated the Politburo's actual functions, or the limitations on its power, except to say that it carries out the work of the Central Committee when it is not in session; and the Central Committee's work is to direct *all* of the work of the Party.

The Politburo, then, which even appoints all key personnel in the military, Party, and government elites, would seem to have unlimited power. Yet in 1982, Premier Zhao Ziyang stated that the Politburo's Standing Committee only met for a few hours one afternoon a week because most of its members were too old (their average age was over eighty) and too weak to participate effectively in policy formulation. Almost by default, the Party's General Secretariat had to manage the day-to-day work of the Central Committee. This situation was later improved upon as elderly Politburo members "voluntarily" retired. By the end of the Thirteenth Party Congress, all of the elderly were either retired to the Central Advisory Committee, or completely retired. This situation provides additional evidence as to how institutions may lose power officially delegated to them.

The General Secretariat not only formally exerts power over ideology, propaganda, and Party organization and discipline, but also formulates Party policy. By the mid-1980s, an extraordinary amount of power had become concentrated in the hands of the Party General Secretary. Even though Hu Yaobang was removed as General Secretary in 1987, the subsequent appointment of Zhao Ziyang to succeed him further strengthened the power of this position.

As part of the decentralization in the 1980s, some of the power to make day-to-day decisions gravitated downward to the "second and third lines of command," composed of provincial and county-level Party leaders.

Yet the determination of overall Party policy and values remained in the hands of Deng Xiaoping, Chairman of the Military Affairs Commission and the Central Advisory Committee.[11] The latter, a "council of elders" formed in 1982, may advise or be consulted on matters of policy. In actual fact, little is known about this body, or whether any individual on it except Deng Xiaoping has actually affected policy.

The Central Discipline Inspection Commission

The Central Discipline Inspection Commission of the Party reports to the Central Committee. It is responsible for three broad tasks: maintaining Party morality and discipline by correcting "Party style" and disciplining errant Party members; ensuring that Party organizations correctly implement the Party's policies; and investigating claims that Party discipline has been violated (1982 Party Constitution, Article 44). Before 1978, however, it and the Discipline Inspection Commission below it, actually only played a limited role in the control of the Party. Other parts of the Party organization usurped many of their control tasks, no doubt because of "turf" issues within the Party and because the ability to distinguish "between organizational indiscipline and political or ideological dissension" became increasingly difficult and politically sensitive.[12] Then, at the Ninth Party Congress in 1969, when the Party itself was in shambles, the commissions were eliminated. In their place, the "revolutionary masses" were to supervise Party discipline and the correct interpretation and implementation of Party policy through their participation on the new governing "revolutionary committees."

In 1978, the Party Central Discipline Inspection Commission was restored to oversee the work of the Disciplinary Inspection Commissions established at and above the county level in 1977. This was one facet of an attempt to return power to the Party by enforcing Party rules that addressed deviation from Party style and, most importantly, curbing abuses of power in the name of the Party. From 1966 to 1976, slander, frameups, trumped-up charges, and incorrect punishment of Party members had been rife. Some of the first tasks of the new Discipline Inspection Commission system were to investigate the literally millions of cases involving complaints of unfair and unjust charges and punishments; to "reverse the verdicts" on those unfairly accused and punished; and to conduct investigations in order to purge the Party ranks of those members who unquestioningly implemented the leftist leadership's orders or were guilty of "beating, smashing, and looting." "Inner Party discipline" became the shibboleth under which the Central Discipline Inspection Commission sought to rectify Party work style and discipline by ridding the Party of all those who became members through their leftist, activist credentials during the "ten bad years."

In 1980, the Central Discipline Inspection Commission, together with the Party's Central Committee, produced a set of principles for correct Party style. These "Guiding Principles for Inner Party Political Life" amounted to "a catalog of indictments against Mao's personal arbitrary rule and the ills of the Party." Foremost among these principles were collective, not individual, leadership of the Party; "collective discussion by the rank and file of the Party"; decision making by Party committees rather than Party secretaries; prohibition of the practices which fostered a "personality cult"; "tolerance for dissenting views at the discussion stage of policy making"; prohibition of punishment for incorrect statements by Party members "so long as these dissenting opinions do not advocate factional activities or divulge Party and state secrets"; prohibition against waging "ruthless struggle against . . . erring Party members"; the regular convening of Party meetings and elections; the equality of all Party members under Party rules and regulations; the outlawing of graft, corruption, and nepotism; promotion according to ability; and so on. The violent procedures of class struggle and Party rectifications were to be abandoned in favor of a calmer and more reasoned approach. Finally, the Discipline Inspection Commissions were assigned primary responsibility for the fight against economic crimes. Because it is believed that Party members have been central to the growth of criminal economic practices, the commissions have a major role in supporting the reforms of the 1980s.[13]

To ensure adherence to the "Guiding Principles," the Discipline Inspection Commissions serve as the "Party court." They determine when Party discipline or the rules of inner Party political life have been violated and how to address these violations. In doing so, they must distinguish "among work mistakes, political mistakes, line mistakes, and counterrevolutionary actions." Because Party cadres assigned to Disciplinary Inspection Commissions have the power to take punitive actions against other Party members, they are highly vulnerable to intimidation and retaliatory measures.[14] But, as is noted in Chapter Six, permitting the Party to function as a court that sits in judgment of its own members, determines innocence or guilt without legal defense, and sanctions punitive measures gravely interferes both with the principle of an independent judiciary and legal system, and with the principle of equality before the law.

The Organization Department

The Organization Department is central to the management of cadres, and it is the only department specifically assigned to personnel. Organizational work is so crucial to the socialist system in China that "Even the most rudimentary Party branch committee with only three members always assigns one member to organizational work."[15] But it does not appear that the Central Organization Department directly controls the organization departments of all the lower-level Party committees. Rather, each organization department reports to the Party committee at its own level and is under its leadership. Nevertheless, the importance of the Central Organization Department cannot be dismissed, as it is the department that issues the guidelines for collecting, selecting, and retaining of information for Party personnel decisions. Further, the organization departments are responsible for cadre evaluation and for maintaining personnel dossiers on cadres,[16] a sore point for the many who would like to see these dossiers destroyed; for whoever controls what does or does not go into a dossier has inordinate power over cadres.

The Military Affairs Commission (MAC)

Like the Central Discipline Inspection Commission, the Military Affairs Commission (MAC) is institutionally responsible to and reports to the Party's Central Committee. But unlike the Inspection Commission, the MAC basically functions on its own and exercises independent power. Originally, it was structurally tied to the Party's Central Committee, since the Party Chairman automatically served as the chairman of the MAC. With the abolition of the position of Party Chairman, however, it is only required that the MAC chairman also be a member of the Standing Committee of the Politburo. Deng Xiaoping claimed this position for himself in 1978. The very fact that this was the only organizational position that Deng wanted indicates how important Deng considered control over the MAC to be for his own power. Yet in this position, Deng has, in fact, switched power away from the MAC, sent the military back to the barracks, and reasserted Party control over the military. At the Thirteenth Party Congress, Deng allegedly tried to resign as chairman of the MAC, but was forced to stay on since there was no one acceptable to the military to take his place. He did, however, succeed in getting the Party General Secretary Zhao Ziyang chosen as the MAC's Permanent Secretary. This will help Zhao build the relationships with the People's Liberation Army (PLA) that are necessary if he is ever to become an effective head of the MAC.

Overall Party control of the military (except during the Cultural Revolution when the PLA "seized command") has brought a level of stability to China not enjoyed by most developing countries. In China, the Maoist dictum that "Political power grows out of the barrel of a gun; but the Party shall always control the gun" has governed policy. Thus, it is the MAC, a Party-controlled body, that supervises the selection and dismissal of military personnel. More broadly, it determines the criteria for selection and promotion within the ranks of the PLA. For example, in 1984, the MAC mandated that anyone hoping to become an officer or to be promoted within officer ranks must attend a military academy. This, of course, dealt a fatal blow to the ambitions of the many PLA officers who had been chosen on the basis of political activism, class background, and affiliation with leftist policies, and who had thought their careers would advance without obstacles.

Within this context of overall civilian Party control over the military, the MAC may even determine the military's strategy and tactics, alter its command structure, and decide on its daily activities in peacetime. Thus, when Mao chaired both the CCP and the MAC, and in the late 1950s decided to put "politics in command," the PLA's strategy, command structure, and daily activities all fell into line with the new policy. In 1959, Mao Zedong replaced Minister of Defense Peng Dehuai with Lin Biao, who implemented Mao's leftist policies. Rank and insignia for officers were abolished. The guiding principle became "Man over weapons": Soldiers equipped with proper political thought could defeat an army equipped with technologically superior weapons. Hence, sophisticated and expensive weaponry supplied by the then-despised Soviets was unnecessary. Members of the PLA participated in major agricultural reclamation projects, grew their own crops, and even made their own clothes. All this was in accord with Mao's personal preferences for an anti-expert, pro-red orientation.

The PLA's development under Lin Biao and Mao's direction demonstrates that the Party leader who truly controls the MAC can well take the PLA along a path that diverges from the preferences of the rest of the central political leadership, as happened in the early 1960s. It also demonstrates the potential importance of the MAC as a power base: Although Mao had lost his grip on the central *political* leadership after the disastrous results of the Great Leap Forward, his control over the military gave him an adequate base to catapult himself back to the power apex during the Cultural Revolution.

Deng's astute coalition-building in the 1980s succeeded in allying the broadest possible base of nonmilitary forces in opposition to the generals. Deng also gained loyalty from various elements in the PLA because of some of the policies he supported in the past. Had it been otherwise, the PLA would almost surely have more adamantly resisted Deng's many policy changes that were unfavorable toward the military. Not the least of these were the "four modernizations" policy that severely curtailed the military budget; and the removal of the military from the bastions of political power that it had assumed during the Cultural Revolution.

In short, knowing the formal place of the MAC in the lines of communication within the Party leadership only hints at what its real power might be. As with other central Party units, who leads the MAC is central to understanding where it really fits in.

UNRESOLVED PROBLEMS

Problems Attributable to Culture

*Feudalism: A code word for distorted behavior arising
from culture*

The Chinese use the general term *feudalism* (*fengjian juyi*) differently from the way Western historians use it. Western notions of feudalism include the concepts of knightly contracts to do military service and a hereditary system of aristocratic titles and ranks that are part of the structure of a rigid hierarchically ordered society. Society is decentralized to the extent to which each overlord is permitted to exercise autonomy within the area under his control. Mobility is limited. Both rank and succession to power in the social hierarchy are determined by birth. Lords give out pieces of land, called *fiefs* (manors), to their retainers or vassals. Within the overlord's manor, power is highly centralized and concentrated in the hands of the lord. Loyalty to one's overlord is absolute and unquestioning and usually precedes loyalty to the "overlord's overlord."[17] Feudalism refers to the type of society that existed in medieval Europe in the ninth through the thirteenth centuries. Its major components include a subject peasantry; widespread use of fief (instead of salary) in exchange for military service; specialized warriors who formed the dominant class; a society bound together through ties of obedience and protection; and fragmented authority.[18] The period of feudalism was preceded by the Dark Ages and was followed by the period of the growth of mercantilism in Early Modern Europe, culturally known as the Renaissance.

China was not feudal in this sense for the 2,000 years before the Communist takeover in 1949. A specialized group of warriors did not form the dominant class. China's social classes during this period, moreover, were relatively open. A person's birth did not immutably determine that person's social class. If a young man were talented, his clan might underwrite the expense for his education so that he could rise above his humble peasant background and enter the scholar-official class. Entry into officialdom was determined by performance on a civil service exam, not through kinship inheritance. In these respects, traditional China's social structure superficially bore many similarities to the social structure of relatively modernized societies.[19]

In spite of their history, Chinese Communists use the term "feudalism" as Marxists do, and describe traditional Chinese society as "feudal." Although Marx was Western, his view of feudalism did not conform in most respects to European feudalism, largely because his intent was different. For Marx, feudalism refers to a period associated with a rural peasant economy. Marxist "historical determinism" is an economic interpretation of history that asserts that a society must move in a linear path through a series of stages based on the development of the economic substructure. It postulates that a society moves from primitive communism, to slavery, then to feudalism, capitalism, socialism, and finally to communism. Certain economic and social characteristics are associated with each period. Most important for Chinese Communists, "feudalism" is associated with rural agricultural societies and the "peasant mentality." To become "capitalist" requires that a society become industrialized. In short, Marxist historians offer a rigidly deterministic viewpoint of societal evolution from which interpretations of societal development cannot deviate.

As committed Marxists, then, Chinese Communists necessarily adopted this deterministic historical interpretation. Because in their view China had not been a "slave society" since the Zhou Dynasty, and because even committed Marxists could not claim that China was in any sense industrial, hence capitalist until the 1920s,[20] Chinese Communist historians had little choice but to claim that China was feudal for over 2000 years (even if there were "sprouts of capitalism") until a brief interlude of capitalism interceded before socialist transformation.

With the Communist victory in 1949, the leadership claimed that feudalism in land-holding patterns would be eliminated, and laws concerning marriage, women, and religion were soon enacted to address other aspects of China's feudal culture. Although the leadership recognized that "feudal remnants" had survived the demise of the feudal *system*, these were dismissed as largely rural phenomena, unaffected by China's alleged movement into capitalism. As a result, China's ideologues, still clinging to a Marxist interpretation of development, asserted that China had wiped out feudalism and could now move from capitalism to socialism. Most policies after 1949 were therefore directed against capitalist features.

Feudalism was not again an all-encompassing issue until late 1978, when the reform leaders reshaped China's problems and reinterpreted history. Until that time, in fact, those who dared to suggest that China was feudal risked political censorship, criticism, and even punishment; for not only did such a suggestion deviate from the Chinese Communist usage of Marxist categories of history, but it also was (accurately) perceived as an implicit attack on China's leaders and the socialist system. Yet this reinterpretation of history still clung to Marxist categories. Thus, according to the interpretation put forth in the late 1970s, China's capitalism had been too weak to carry out adequate industrialization. As a result, China entered the socialist stage prematurely, without a sufficiently high level of industrial development. China therefore needed to focus on modernization, and even to revert to the "mode of production" and "relations of production" of the capitalist era, in order to achieve an adequate level of industrialization.

In short, since China had never experienced adequate capitalism, the Deng leadership could claim China had, in many respects, never left the feudal period. The same problems of feudal practices and institutions that had existed before 1949 still remained: "patriarchal clan" attitudes and behavior, a bureaucratic system, an autocratic work style, elitism, overconcentration of power, and factionalism. The reform leadership even used the term "feudal" to refer to rigidity, dogmatism, cadre competition, and lifetime positions for rulers.[21] Feudalism in the ideological and political realms had become the "key contradiction" that stood in the way of rapid modernization.[22] Hence, it, not capitalism, had to be eliminated. Capitalism in a Marxist framework is, in fact, the antidote to feudalism.

The reform leaders, without ever suggesting that socialism had created its own form of feudalism, and without offering the slightest credit to the leftist leadership of the preceding twenty years for having pinpointed the problems, simply relabeled them. How, after all, could they dare to find themselves in agreement with Mao's analysis, which pointed to these very same issues as the source of problems within the Chinese leadership, and vindicated the attacks on China's Party and state leadership during the Ten Bad Years. Further, if the elimination of many of China's cultural traditions and practices had not eliminated problems which plagued the leadership, then what would? Evidently, feudalism was the perfect scapegoat, but the attack on feudalism amounted to an attack on socialism—and *that* was tantamount to the socialist leaders attacking themselves. Perhaps as a reflection of a far more realistic assessment, this time it was the leadership itself, and the system of socialism that officials had implemented, which stood accused.[23] But to protect themselves, they used the shibboleth of feudalism both to attack those aspects of Chinese culture that had impeded the proper implementation of socialism, and to attack those elements of the socialist system that contributed to a reinforcement of traditional culture (such as patronage, the overcentralization of power, and the unequal position of officials vis-à-vis the ordinary people).

As became evident, however, everything associated with feudalism could actually be associated with Maoism, and even with socialist practice generally. Feudalism became a code word for the distorted practice of socialism in China that resulted, in large part, from socialism being grafted onto Chinese traditions. Given the reformers' interests in attacking Mao on only a few crucial issues so as to avoid the dangers of "de-Maoification," and given their concern that socialism's validity remain intact, it was politically expedient to attack feudalism instead.

Mao can hardly be blamed for all the elements of traditional Chinese political culture that remained in socialist China; but he can certainly be blamed for permitting his own socialist policies to build on and accentuate those very elements of traditional culture that ultimately discredited socialism and thwarted modernization in China. Mao, and all other leaders, whether "leftists" or "pragmatists," did try to address those elements of traditional culture which led to problems in the practice of socialism, but they associated them with capitalism, counterrevolution, or revisionism. As examples, the *sanfan* or "three antis" campaign against corruption, waste, and bureaucratism in 1951–1952; the *xiafang* ("sending down") of bureaucrats to the countryside and to factories to share in labor with peasants and workers in order to rid them of their elitism; the "simplification" campaigns to clean out bureaucracies; the 1958 campaign against "waste" and "conservatism" among officials; the many rectification campaigns against the Party bureaucracy; campaigns to open up recruitment to the bureaucracy; the 1964 "socialist education" campaign; and the efforts to rid officialdom of the "bureaucratic class" and to "seize back power from capitalist roaders in the Party" during the Cultural Revolution—all these were actions allegedly aimed at capitalist and revisionist influence. Most of these campaigns against bureaucratism and corrupt or inefficient leadership assumed that the officials' personal values and political orientation, not the socialist system, caused organizational problems. Thus the solution was indoctrination, study, criticism, and self-criticism.[24]

Mao intended the Cultural Revolution to be the final solution to the problem of bureaucracy. The initial enthusiasm with which so many of China's scientists, intellectuals, "experts," staff, and workers joined the Cultural Revolution was stunning testimony to their frustration with the leadership in their work units. Chinese youth's disaffection with the leadership caused many of them to join Red Guard units. Although they had been brought up in the post-1949 period and taught that communism would mean a better life for the masses, what they observed was "Party cadres cynically preoccupied with personal and bureaucratic aggrandizement."[25]

Of course, Mao had intended the Cultural Revolution as far more than a mere uprooting of the entrenched leadership.[26] One need not debate here the power struggle, the "struggle between two lines" within the central leadership that created the rubric of the event. But it is important to note that, from the "leftist" perspective, bureaucracy was the major obstacle to continuous revolution: The bureaucrats had built up their "independent kingdoms" of power and had become entrenched, rigid resisters of revolution.[27] The conclusion was the same, whether seen from the Maoist perspective of concern for continuous revolution, or from the perspective of the Chinese people who had grown frustrated and angry with the bureaucratic process and their own helplessness as individuals to effect change in the face of that powerful bureaucracy.

The methods adopted to attack feudal practices in the post-1949 period did not, however, fit the ends. Political campaigns, mass movements, political criticism, class struggle, and purges (rectifications) not only failed to eliminate bureaucratism, elitism, patriarchy, and related problems of feudalism, but they also created problems—victimizing innocent people, sowing suspicion and distrust among the Chinese, raising doubts about the ability of China's leaders to govern effectively, denigrating the value of education, science, and technology, dividing Chinese into "factions" for their own protection, and forcing people to use the "back door" to get what they needed.

Other far less political, less subjective methods might have been more effective in eliminating these problems. In fact, these are precisely the measures which the reform faction tried to implement in the 1980s: a broadened legal system; carefully defined laws and punishments; an emphasis on expertise, education, and efficiency; more accurate accounting and auditing procedures and a better and more open collection of statistics and data; ridding the workplace of "irrational and defective procedures"; getting rid of outdated customs; and enhancing democratic procedures. Results thus far suggest that these are more appropriate and effective methods for dealing with problems of so-called feudalism.[28]

Feudalism and capitalism

The reform leadership's focus on feudalism provides a convenient decoy to lure attention away from, and also to justify, the emphasis on capitalist methods in China's "four modernizations" program. By claiming that China's problems have feudal roots, the leadership obviates the need to decry capitalism. If they were to blame capitalism for China's problems, it would be difficult to rationalize the introduction of yet more capitalist methods. Thus, the official line on free markets as a method to determine supply and demand, prices, and to improve quality is that China needs the healthy competition that capitalism engenders. Capitalism provides a therapeutic antidote to an economy and leadership burdened with feudal values and practices. The government insists that it is closely controlling the development of capitalism so that it will not become exploitative. Only when China reaches a high enough level of economic development can it revert to socialist methods.

The Source of Many Leadership Issues: The Interaction of Chinese Culture and Socialist Ideology

Political culture provides a medium, a lens through which people perceive and interpret sociopolitical institutions and their role in them. The same aspects of a political culture may at different times in a country's development be either supportive or detrimental to modernization. Many of the obstacles to, and actual targets of, political reform in China are, however, socialist in nature, even though it may be cultural predispositions that have distorted the implementation of particular socialist policies and institutions. As a result, although the leadership has been attacking Chinese culture as a major obstacle to China's development since the May Fourth Movement of 1919, in the 1980s, the leadership has also made outright attacks on socialist ideology and institutions. In addition to admitting that some problems have arisen from the *practice* of socialism in China, that is, "certain unscientific methods and imperfect systems in our work resulting from lack of experience," the leadership has suggested that the socialist system must be improved both organizationally and in work style.[29]

Most of the unresolved issues of the leadership system attributed below to the socialist system and socialist ideology are problems because *socialism has had to be grafted onto Chinese culture.* Within the context of this Chinese culture, and at China's level of development, another type of leadership system and idology might have been more appropriate. The Chinese leadership itself has articulated many of the points made below, mostly in the context of stating the need to formulate a socialism "with Chinese characteristics."

One caveat: Chinese culture is extraordinarily rich and complex. Within the mainstream culture, one can find subcultures and contrary tendencies (such as egalitarianism and hierarchy) that provide a substantial repertoire of culturally acceptable themes, attitudes, and behaviors. Socialism has attempted to draw on those aspects of Chinese culture which best suit its needs. But China's leaders have found that certain strands of their culture that are inimicable to socialism persevere, regardless of their best efforts to suppress them.

Party infallibility and submissiveness to authority

Since the earliest days of the People's Republic of China, the leaders under Mao Zedong shared the belief that certain aspects of China's traditional political culture, such as the Chinese people's respect for and submission to authority, their desire for an authority that ensures social order, their acceptance of the (Confucian) concept of the hierarchical ordering of society, and of the superiority of officials over the common people contributed to the continuation of practices incompatible with socialism. The Chinese have experienced periods of change, but "within a framework of cultural continuity."[30] The leadership's approach to land reform after 1949 was an extraordinary effort to overthrow these traditional values and attitudes by forcing the Chinese peasants to "speak bitterness" and to denounce their superiors, the landlords. In spite of the Communists' success in getting the peasants to stand up for their rights at the time, culture and tradition continue to weigh heavily on the ordinary person's view of officials.

Most Chinese consciously or unconsciously collaborate in the perpetuation of traditional practices: Believing that the ordinary person is powerless to change the system, they accept the concentration of authority at the top and the power of officials over their lives, even when they are being treated unfairly or inhumanely; and they tolerate the arrogance of officials and their abuse of power, and accept traditional power relationships between the elite and masses. For this reason, even though China embraced socialist egalitarianism and a socialist economic system, most Chinese remained predisposed to submit to official authority.

> China had been an autocratic, feudal country for thousands of years. Autocracy in China has a historical tradition and a social basis. The new democratic revolution led by our Party completely freed China from the feudal economic and political systems. However, because we focused our attention on the decisive role of the transformation of the economic system, we overlooked the role tradition plays in the people's thinking and failed to systematically criticize and repudiate the ideological influences of feudal autocracy that were still prevalent in political and social life. As a result, remnants of such ideology and traditional practices as the personality cult, patriarchism, privilege, and hierarchy found their way into our Party.[31]

Thus, it is the people's willingness to accept the cadres' arrogance and abuse of power that distorts the socialist system. For this reason, China's Leninist bureaucracy and mistaken policies need not shoulder the entire blame for the pathologies of centralized bureaucratic power. Indeed, socialist bureaucracy may be portrayed as the helpless victim of feudal Confucian culture.[32]

The reform leadership faces the dilemma of preceding leaderships, however, in deciding how far to go in modifying the predisposition of the Chinese people to submit to authority, for this has facilitated maintaining political order and carrying out centrally orchestrated policies. The leadership's insistence upon unquestioning obedience in a sense perpetuates that very traditional political culture that it hopes to eradicate. To move beyond the narrow, if necessary, objective of control, it must actively involve the people in changing the old superior-inferior relationships. This requires political consciousness-raising of a nature which neither the leadership nor the people seem prepared for. The official ideology continues to insist on Party infallibility, which requires the *submission* of the masses to Party leadership. This perpetuates both elitism and centralism. Thus socialism actually accentuates China's "feudal" political culture, which, in turn, reinforces the overconcentration of power that comes from socialism's highly centralized socialist policies.

Secrecy and elitism

Secrecy within the Chinese leadership permits its scandalous behavior and policy errors to escape public censure. Here again, Chinese culture has helped shape institutional practices in today's China. Secrecy concerning affairs of state is as old as China: Decisions by China's emperors were always made "behind the curtain." Under socialism, the leadership's tradition of secrecy has continued to the point that only a handful of leaders know precisely how and why decisions are made. Such secretiveness makes it almost impossible for the Chinese people, or even other leaders, to know who said what, how decisions were reached, upon what information decisions were based, and what alternatives were possible. It is widely believed, for example, that the major reason China stopped publishing economic statistics from 1959 to 1978 was the dominant leadership group's desire to prevent other leaders from challenging their position with hard economic data. The result was that even those few leaders in a position to *make* economic policies lacked sufficient information to do so.

Potentially embarrassing situations, or those that could undermine the authoritativeness of the leadership's decisions, are still carefully guarded secrets. Thus the proposed agreement in 1984 between General Electric and the PRC to dump radioactive nuclear waste from Western European countries in western China was never made public within China. The circumstances surrounding the forced return to China in 1984 of a defector who skipped a delegation while in the United States was never revealed.[33] And on broader issues such as the problems accompanying policies of decollectivization and the responsibility system, the Chinese people are only told what the leadership wants them to know. Even in international affairs, the leadership retains exclusive control over the dissemination of information. Until the 1980s, most reports from abroad were classified as internal (*neibu*) and could only be seen by specified levels of officials. The presumption seemed to be that the ordinary Chinese citizen would not know how to interpret foreign news correctly. The Chinese elite thus has been free to obfuscate the issues and is unfettered by a free press and "freedom of information" acts. Most Chinese will continue to know only what the leadership wants them to know about Mao Zedong, Jiang Qing, Peng Dehuai, Lin Biao, Hua Guofeng, and other leaders.

Secrecy makes it difficult to carry out political reforms aimed at eliminating the power of officials over the people, assigning individuals responsibility for their acts, or ending corruption. Shielding the policy-making process from public debate and scrutiny allows the leadership to make decisions on the basis of power, bureaucratic struggles over turf, or factional ties. It need not reveal its information base, nor what alternatives it rejected. The real reasons for official attacks on an individual leader or for policy reversals can be carefully disguised. Arguably, only an informed elite should make policy, and perhaps the catering of liberal democracies to diverse interest groups and public opinion often acts to the detriment of sound policy.[34] But the history of the PRC reveals that time and again, the test of the validity of a policy has come too late: during the implementation stage. The problem that secrecy creates for the Chinese leadership is this:

Policies that the people played no role in formulating receive feedback in a form determinental to the leadership's objective—mass resistance to the policies.

Other cultural factors such as the traditional orientation toward the collective (the family or the clan) contribute to the Chinese penchant for secrecy. Each clan or family is distinct from all other clans and families. They rarely join forces. Thus, Chinese traditionally do not envision the expansion of the boundaries of their primary affiliations. Similarly, today's faction members identify with the faction and distance themselves from outsiders, whom they treat as strangers if not pariahs. Factions contribute to leadership problems by breeding a conspiratorial atmosphere shrouded in secrecy: Factions contend for power, and followers dare not expose their own hand. Factions are, after all, illegal, and exposure of membership in a faction can mean political death. Of course, debate occurs within the central leadership, but factional dissent must be narrowly circumscribed if the political climate is unfavorable. Hence, there is a propensity toward secrecy and little vision of getting somewhere on one's own, without one's group.

Although cultural contrasts are a matter of degree, secrecy is far more pervasive in Chinese political institutions than in the West. Efforts in the 1980s to open up the system to public scrutiny represent a major turnabout in China's policies. The deliberations of the National People's Congress, the Politburo, and the Central Committee have been publicized far more than ever before—but still only to the extent that it serves the dominant faction's purpose. Domestic and foreign newsmen were, for the first time in the history of the PRC, permitted to cover the meetings of the National Party Congress in 1987—but only the opening and closing speeches, not the discussion in between. Newspapers and television, because of new policies that encourage more aggressive reporting (part of the reformers' efforts to eliminate corruption, bureaucratism, and feudalism), have brought into the public domain far more information than the Chinese people have ever had before about their leaders. The greater powers that have devolved to congresses at the provincial, county, and enterprise levels give the people greater control over their leaders; and the research, investigation, and publication of an immense amount of detailed information about China's economy, society, and people in the 1980s has meant that both China's people and its leaders are better prepared to make effective assessments of the best policy alternatives.

As China continues its political reforms in the 1980s, some of the high walls behind which leaders have hidden are crumbling. Although tentative and limited, democratic reforms within organizations and in the broader political system are eroding the leadership's protective blankets of secrecy. Meanwhile, China's leaders continue to fear that contending ideas may lead to political instability, perhaps anarchy, or revolution.

Factions

From the Western perspective, factions are not really a problem. In a stable polity, they are simply a healthy form of elite conflict. In fact, Chinese factions may be viewed as parties within the Party. They serve as a check on what might otherwise be hastily ill-conceived policies, for to the extent that factions within the Chinese leadership represent significant interest groups within the polity, policies that ignore or offend them are doomed to encounter serious difficulties.

The Chinese leadership thinks otherwise. From the perspective of whoever is the dominant leadership, factions are almost by definition treasonous, for their purpose is to undermine the leadership's policies, and even to seize power, not to present a loyal opposition. "Going against the tide" is only acceptable *after* the tide is proven wrong. Correct "Party spirit" requires that Party members achieve uniformity of thought. Although the CCP has almost invariably contained factions, the outside world has rarely known this until the faction was publicly attacked and its members removed, or when the dominant leadership was sending out warning signals to potential followers of factions. Before they openly denounce factionalism, the dominant leadership is reluctant to admit its existence; for unresolved disagreement within the Party elite threatens the Party's claim to infallibility.

The Chinese leadership invariably views factionalism as a potential threat to a delicate national unity, a crass ploy by ambitious individuals to achieve more power. According to an official Chinese commentary,

> Factionalism means cliquishness; in the ranks of revolutionaries it is an abominable deviation that disrupts unity, weakens organization and jeopardizes the revolution. . . . Now that the two large [Cultural Revolution] factions [the Lin Biao and the gang of four factions] have been broken up, organized factionalism has long ceased to exist, but factionalism is still to be found to differing degrees in the thinking of some cadres and members of the masses. . . .[35]

Today's dominant leadership thus continues to treat factions as "the enemy," and many of its political reform measures are clearly aimed at controlling factional opposition: (1) by eliminating from the leadership ranks all those with the wrong political credentials (notably those gained through activism during the Ten Bad Years), and those without expertise or education; and (2) by diminishing the power of officials to make arbitrary decisions based on politics rather than law or economic policy. The reform faction, in fact, makes no attempt to conceal its efforts to control, if not eliminate, those who are political enemies. Officials throughout the country were forewarned, for example, that "factionalists may seize the opportunity of promoting young and middle-aged cadres to upgrade their own followers." These factionalists are dangerous and must be kept out of leadership positions. They "must never be promoted: not a single one. And any of them who have already been promoted must be resolutely removed from the leading bodies."[36]

Factions respond to these threats to their own power by attempting to block unpalatable policies. To be 'honest and aboveboard" would simply provide fodder to the dominant leadership. The result is that factions use code words, historical analogies, obscure references, and reinterpretations of orthodox Marxist-Leninist texts (often in articles and policy speeches that appear in the mass media) to express their opposition to the dominant leadership's policies, and to mobilize support for their own faction's beliefs. They may use a "code-word attack" on a leader, or a literary or historical allusion to the nature of good and evil to indicate their dissent from the dominant faction's policies.[37] The consequence of this strategy has been that, except for the years from 1966 to 1976, disputes between factions rarely broke out into the open. Rather, they occurred through subtle, indirect methods, which provided a forum for policy debate, without endangering a unified stable leadership.[38]

Factionalism remains a serious issue because it removes debate from the realm of legitimacy, sequesters dissent, and fuels intraelite conflict, often to the detriment of policy. In the 1960s and 1970s, factional conflict interfered with China's ability to make progress and gave rise to "the most disruptive convolutions in Chinese politics."[39] Factionalism has simply gone too far too frequently in China for the benign Western view of factions—as healthy checks on the exercise of absolute totalitarian power by the dominant leadership—to be relevant to Chinese politics.

The irony is, of course, that almost every newly dominant leadership group was once an illegal faction lurking in the background waiting to seize power. The new dominant faction's legitimacy derives from its garnering of enough power to seize control of the leadership, at which point it outlaws all other factions.

When the Chinese decry "factionalism," then, they are really admitting the existence of conflicting views and contending power configurations within the ruling elite. Sometimes responsibility for an admitted failed policy is laid at the doorstep of a particular faction, but only *after* its proponents have been removed.[40] Presumably this helps maintain the facade of a unified leadership. At other times a faction is blamed for obstructing the dominant leadership's "correct" policies. In either case, factions serve as excellent scapegoats.

The Chinese frequently comment on the baleful effects of factionalism:

> People with factionalist tendencies . . . proceed in all matters from factional considerations, continuing to draw lines according to faction and to make differentiations according to faction; they consider all those in their own faction as friends and all those in other factions as enemies; they are incapable

of treating cadres and members of the masses who formerly belonged to either of the two factions equally, without discrimination.[41]

Finally, although Chinese factions may have policy preferences, the relationship between policies and factions is not predictable. Chinese factions are *not* analogous to interest groups or bureaucratic politics in developed countries. Factions within the Party "rarely, if ever, represent clearly defined institutional, geographic, or generational interests," although such interests may contribute to their formation. Rather, they tend to be personal, "power constellations of clusters of officials who for some reason or other feel comfortable with each other, who believe that they can share mutual trust and loyalties, and who may recognize common foes. More often than not, the real motivation is that of career security and enhancement." The result is that factions may easily obstruct policy implementation, but they contribute little to initiating policy. Newly empowered factions often denounce the policies of the preceding dominant faction, when in fact there is little if any difference in the policies.[42] Thus, the newly arisen reform faction's rhetoric in the late 1970s did not reveal that its "four modernizations" policy was actually announced and launched by Premier Zhou Enlai as far back as 1964, endorsed in 1975 by the Gang of Four, and later propounded by Hua Guofeng.

Why, then, has the Chinese leadership not resolved the issue of factions? The problem is, perhaps, unresolvable in the context of a socialist political system that reinforces, rather than eliminates, the cultural predisposition of the Chinese to form factions. The diversity of latent interest groups within China, each one benefitting more from certain policies than others, the existence of a one-party system, and the nature of power in China make the eradication of factionalism a formidable task. Lacking alternative legitimate means by which to express their grievances, dissent, ambitions, and interests, the Chinese gather, by default, into factions. They collude to obstruct unfavorable policies precisely because it is the best way to protect their own interests in a system that does not permit pluralistic power bases.

Factionalism reflects Chinese cultural influence on perceptions of authority and trust, as well as a fear of social and political ostracism.[43] But it also reflects the bitter experience cadres suffered from the abrupt changes and contradictory policies in the 1960s and 1970s. Cadres learned "that personal ties and mutual help and not correct ideological stance or institutional loyalty, best protect their careers and enhance political power."[44] Officials with factional leanings favor those who shared their views, supported or protected them, or did favors for them during the Cultural Revolution. They are "family" to be "trusted and given jobs, while all others are considered untrustworthy and potential sources of trouble." In some work units, "this has resulted in a concentration of power in the hands of people of one faction."[45]

Finally, Mao's departure from Stalin's practice of executing those purged from the Party has no doubt exacerbated factional tendencies. Because Mao emphasized "rehabilitation through reeducation," every organization in China today contains victims of past purges who are waiting for an opportunity to settle scores.[46] Stories abound of Chinese who, once purged and removed from their organizations, have been rehabilitated only to find that those who were responsible for their removal are still there, sometimes even wearing the clothes they took from them during the "ten bad years."[47] Although the survival of political opposition may be positively viewed as encouraging debate, from the Chinese leadership's perspective it is negative since it encourages opposing factions to obstruct policy implementation.

Guilt by association

Although in most cultures association with someone of questionable character may raise eyebrows, in China, a direct connection is invariably drawn between association and guilt. Whether or not it becomes the pretext for vilifying a person depends greatly on the political climate. No doubt the worst time was during the "ten bad years," when anyone who was known ever to have had contact with foreigners, who was educated abroad or in a foreign-run college in China, who had relatives outside of China— regardless of whether they had ever even met them—or who was at any time associated with someone later condemned for a political crime—all were assumed to be guilty of wrong viewpoints or even crimes. Guilt by association replaced due process of law, much as in the McCarthy period in the 1950s in the United States. Thus the campaign against China's "number one capitalist-roader" was not just an attack on "the renegade, traitor, and scab" Liu Shaoqi. It was an attack on all those who had been associated with his policies and who were, therefore, tainted with Liu's alleged character flaws. The 1980 Party resolution to posthumously rehabilitate Liu Shaoqi illustrates how such frame-ups of leaders and their associates occur. Those guilty by association with Liu Shaoqi, like the night-soil collector whom Liu met one day, during the Cultural Revolution found themselves condemned and cruelly persecuted for their association with the "scab" Liu.[48]

The possibility of guilt by association has posed another sort of problem for ordinary Chinese citizens who are under pressure during campaigns to report or criticize others: If they know that someone else's attitudes or actions are wrong, but knowing it would require a close relationship with the person, then they may find themselves implicated as well; for even if they would necessarily have a close relationship with the person being criticized (for example, because the latter is a family member), suspicions are still aroused as to the adverse effects of the association. The "ten bad years" are filled with stories about the vilification of people with relatives abroad as "bourgeois rightists" or even as spies, because of the assumption that foreign connections, however tenuous, necessarily tainted them; and about couples who divorced in an attempt by one spouse to end the association with the spouse accused of counterrevolutionary crimes.

In the leadership, the assumption of guilt through association relates to the concern about factions: Those who are denounced as factional members taint all those associated with them. Such an assumption was fatal to Hua Guofeng's career; for the Gang of Four's decision to compromise on Hua as successor to the deceased Premier Zhou Enlai was later interpreted as evidence of Hua's *alliance* with the Gang. As a result, and in spite of Hua's subsequent arrest of the Gang, Hua himself was implicitly on trial with them. After all, how could he have known about the inner machinations and personal character flaws of the members of the Gang of Four without a strong personal connection with them?

The assumption of guilt by association inhibits factional mobility and enhances rigid factional lines. Switching factions may prove damning: The original association will always be part of one's past. The former lover who turns in one's partner as a traitor is, nevertheless, still guilty of once having had a close relationship with the traitor. In a system where the only way to get rid of someone in a leadership position is to find something *personally, morally, or politically wrong* with that person, rather than with the person's actual job performance, guilt by association is a useful tool. The campaigns to vilify Liu Shaoqi, Lin Biao, and later, Mao's wife, Jiang Qing, reached as far back as the 1920s to reveal instances of each being guilty of association with the wrong crowd.

The problem thus far has been that, once a person attained a key leadership position, that person remained there not just for four years, but perhaps for forty years. Such individuals did not need to worry about reelection even if they performed their jobs poorly. Under such circumstances, impugning their character, morality, and political values was the only way to remove them. Until such time as a regularized system of election to and retirement from office is institutionalized, the assumption of guilt by association and the personal vilification of leaders are likely to continue. The 1982 State Constitution, which emphasized regular elections and a limited term in office, has formally addressed this leadership issue. Of equal importance are the managerial and administrative reforms that emphasize education, expertise, and competence over politics and personal morality. These provisions may well gradually eclipse the tendency to emphasize personal ties and to associate failures in policy with the character weakness of various leaders.

Overcentralization of authority and power

In many respects, the malaise in the leadership system that has been attributed to feudalism or traditional Chinese culture is really attributable to socialism, for to eliminate feudalism requires eliminating one of the key components of socialism in the political system, namely, *centralism.* Centralism gives each person on the higher rung power over those lower down. This kind of power structure breeds corruption, because without the approval of the next person up, an application, request, or form will go nowhere.

The Party rectification of 1983–1986 exposed many such problems within China's leadership system and provoked the persistent question of how China's socialist system could have spawned *so many* problems. While the Chinese are now willing to entertain the idea that Marx did not envision the problems and needs of societies moving toward socialism in the twentieth century, and while they are willing to concede "organizational" problems and errors in "work style," the suggestion that it is the very socialist model itself that has given rise to these problems is still considered heretical.

The 'iron rice bowl'. The "iron rice bowl" (*tie fanwan*) system is a major contributing factor to overcentralization of power. It is a system whereby almost all workers and officials in state-run enterprises and in the government bureaucracies and Party leadership are virtually guaranteed lifetime employment regardless of performance.[49] The practice of "Once an official always an official" is inherited from traditional China. Chinese authorities attribute the continued existence of the "iron rice bowl" to the PRC's system of guaranteeing "the right to work," and to "the protracted absence of proper regulations in [the] Party for the retirement and dismissal of cadres."[50] This question did not arise in the 1950s because those who led the Communist revolution were still young. In the case of a work unit, if it fires a bungling bureaucrat or an incompetent, lazy worker, it is still burdened with paying his or her wages (even if at a slightly reduced level after a certain time), until or unless it can find the person another job with another unit. Of course, it is most improbable that another enterprise (most likely itself suffering from overstaffing) would want to accept others' rejects.

Further, both the government and Party continue to practice the policy of transferring officials who harassed individuals in one work unit to another unit; or from one unit where an official reached his or her level of incompetence to a commensurate position in another unit. As one commentator noted, "It is ludicrous to think that merely moving such people from job to job can make them recognize their mistakes. . . . What I resent most are the courteous words from the superior department about the transferred official: 'He has achieved much in his years of work, and the transfer is required by the work. . . .' "[51] When the government or Party decides to *reassign* incompetent officials to other work units, these units have no right to reject them. This perpetuates the practice of "once an official, always an official."

The "iron rice bowl" and the high level of centralization of power in work units contribute to other problems. Ordinary workers in state enterprises are also almost guaranteed lifetime employment. But this lifetime assignment is double-edged. Once assigned to a work unit, the person is basically *owned* by that work unit for the rest of his or her life. Granted the workers know they will receive certain basic-level wages and benefits for the rest of their lives, but they also know that they are not free to leave that work unit. From the perspective of ineffective officials or workers, lifetime employment is a great benefit of socialism. But from the perspective of ambitious and well-educated or trained individuals who would like to move upward in their profession, perhaps by switching work units, the system of lifetime employment is actually a trap. Even if the work unit does not need them, it will rarely release them to another unit. The official press has reported repeated instances of enterprises or governmental organizations that continue to deny their employees the right to accept a job offered by another unit, even when they were not being fully utilized by their own work unit. Thus, something that looks as simple as recruiting computer specialists usually involves a catch-22 situation. For example, most of the students who were sent abroad in the early 1980s to study computer science already "belonged" to units. When they returned to China, even though their work units had no need for additional computer specialists, the work unit leaders refused to let them be transferred elsewhere. Similarly, graduates of American MBA programs have been unable to find jobs where their skills are utilized. Work unit leaders, on the grounds that they paid for the students' airplane tickets to the United States, won't let them leave for more relevant jobs elsewhere. Many, therefore, work as translators. Some don't work at all.[52] Although new regulations have made the job market more open, with employees given more flexibility to transfer, and with the wishes of new university graduates accorded more consideration, change has been slow. That this should be the case in a country in such desperate need for educated people makes it all the more lamentable.

The Chinese themselves have observed that under the reform policies, in which economic control is decentralized, the "iron rice bowl" is a deterrent to "full deployment and rational allocation of the labor force:" The "iron rice bowl" at this point in history "violates fundamentally so-

cialist economic laws and is increasingly obstructing the four modernizations."[53] But the practice continues.

The power of work-unit officials. Patriarchy is the system by which those
at the top rule autocratically and gain privilege from their power and
status. When such culturally derived habits are practiced in socialist institutions, it results in individual officials placing themselves above the organization, which is thus bent to serve as their tool. Hence, when the reform
leaders speak of the overcentralization of authority and power, they are
speaking not only of the central Party and government but also of local
power holders: the first secretaries of the Party committees that have existed in almost every organization at all levels throughout the country,[54] and
the officials at the head of *danwei* (work units) and *jiti* (collective
organizations).

The top leadership in work units basically exercises complete control
over both the working and personal life of its employees. It can, and often
does, use its power either to give or withhold privileges, opportunities,
promotions, and benefits. Work-unit leaders control the workers' housing,
residence permits, child care, requests for leave, sick leave, access to overnight nurseries, educational opportunities, travel, entry into the Party, and
a host of other important aspects of the workers' day-to-day life. Under
these circumstances, it is understandable why workers spend much of their
available savings on giving gifts to or entertaining work-unit officials. Lest
it is imagined that this is only the case in urban work units, it should be
recognized that the "feudal" relationship between peasants and local officials was even more all-encompassing; for until the decollectivization of
agriculture after 1978, local officials controlled both the type of labor to
which peasants would be assigned and the number of "work points" (used
to compute their wages) that they would earn. For these reasons, peasants
were often desperate to cultivate good relations with the brigade's Party
secretary.[55]

It is not surprising that, under these circumstances, the officials who
have so much power and patronage at their disposal should often use it for
their own personal benefit. The special problems of the "ten bad years" led
to an unprecedented abuse of these powers; for at that time, goods, salary,
and food were to be distributed according to *need* rather than *work*. Because
production was too low to support everyone's needs, however, in practice
goods were distributed through the "back door" (*hou men*). Once these
practices became entrenched, they were very difficult to dislodge. Even
today, a directive to give gas stoves to intellectuals of a certain rank, for
example, may result in the stoves going to Party leaders "who suddenly
manage to define themselves as intellectuals."[56]

Corruption among local leaders continues in spite of the reforms.
Notwithstanding a chronic and severe housing shortage in China's cities,

leading Party cadres have repeatedly been found guilty of occupying more rooms than they need or are entitled to occupy. In 1984, the Party's Central Discipline Inspection Commission issued a letter which stated that "21,900 cadres at and above the county and regiment level have occupied extra rooms" and required that they be returned (or extra rent be charged).[57] In the aftermath of the 1976 Tangshan earthquake, which left more than 100,000 persons still in temporary shelters in Tianjin in 1981, it was revealed that 93 percent of the leading cadres in one commercial department had moved into the new homes built for the homeless.[58] Other examples reveal the "unhealthy" practice of leading cadres "feasting" at the expense of the government and "squandering public funds on entertaining guests and presenting them with gifts in order to cultivate 'under the table' relationships."[59]

Although this kind of comprehensive authority gives officials extraordinary power, it also contributes to a bureaucratic nightmare; for many other officials simultaneously exercise parallel, overlapping, or superior authority. If someone in an equal but only parallel position—whether in one's own unit or a different one—requests action, it will probably not be acted on. The lack of horizontal cooperation among units, the refusal to share information, and to take common actions contribute not only to considerable redundancy of effort but also to endless red tape. Even purchasing a teapot for an office, or building a toilet for a factory, requires approval by officials at all levels before it can be done.[60] Marriages between individuals in different work units must have the approval of both work-unit leaders.

Throughout the 1980s, the reform leadership has used campaigns to attack official corruption, exposed it in the mass media, and discussed it openly. Literature and plays have also highlighted official immorality as a theme. For example, *If I Were Real,* first performed in China in 1979, was one of the first plays after the reformers gained control of the leadership to openly critique the improper use of official power. The story is about a youth who, pretending to be the son of an important Party official, is able to acquire things that the ordinary person cannot. The play focuses on the eagerness of lower-level officials to cultivate influence with the youth's allegedly important father and suggests that efforts to manipulate connections were continuing even under the reform leadership. The fact that the play was banned from production indicated the central leadership's vulnerability on this issue.

Yet the leadership seems ill-prepared to cope effectively with the influence of "patriarchal clan" ideas from China's past. This is in no small part because they have become institutionalized in socialist practices. For example, the difficulty of switching jobs causes individuals to do just about anything to avoid poor work assignments. Officials, more than anyone, have it within their power, through corrupt use of their office, to help their relatives and friends escape the state's arbitrary allocation of jobs. Further, when officials get to the top of the power hierarchy, their relatives go with them and get assigned to the best jobs. On the down side, when their stars fall, so do those of their relatives, to which the Cultural Revolution bears ample testimony. Similarly, the bulk of the government-sponsored students and scholars chosen to go abroad in the first years after 1979 were well connected (mostly the children and relatives of high-ranking officials). At several intervals during the 1980s, the government passed regulations to restrict this kind of practice, but seemingly with little effect.

The sources of such problems are twofold. First, salaries are trivial in comparison with the benefits officials can get from using the power of their office to acquire goods, services, and gain access to privileges. Thus, even high officials, making the equivalent of $2,000 a year, would probably never be able to afford to purchase private cars. But they could perhaps retain the right to chauffeur-driven, unit-owned cars (at no charge) as long as they remained officials. And they could retain far better housing as officials. The result of this, which is itself a source of problems for a competent and moral leadership, is: Although firing incompetent officials became a firm tenet of governmental policy by the mid-1980s, resistance has thus far made it an unusable option. As with other reform policies, the would-be implementors of such a policy might well also be its victims.

"Patriarchal clan" practices are further institutionalized in today's socialist China in the widespread practice of a work unit giving, upon a parent's retirement, a position to that parent's child in the same work unit. This practice, which is not illegal, is considered a valuable perquisite of office and is openly advertised by many enterprises as one of the material incentives offered to their employees. A similar practice exists within the state bureaucracy. The real remedy to officials using their power to avoid the arbitrariness of the state allocation of jobs would be an open job market; but China's powerful officialdom continues to resist such a challenge to its privileges.

China's leaders have adopted some half-measures to address such issues. For example, in 1983, the State Council abolished the system of permitting any cadre or state employee (even before what would be considered a normal retirement age) to be replaced by a son or daughter, regardless of the offspring's professional qualifications. Under the new system, children must wait for their parents to reach retirement age and then pass examinations to qualify for a position. But when, for example, Guizhou Province abolished the old system of recruiting the children of former employees, there was a lightning-fast response: On the eve of the new policy's implementation, some 7,000 senior cadres in Guizhou Province retired, and some 6,900 of their children were recruited to fill their vacancies. Over 4,000 senior cadres had retired before they were eligible in order to permit their children to have their jobs, and more than

4,000 of the children recruited were "totally unqualified for the jobs." After a Party investigation discovered this, the cadres had to return to work, and those children who were unqualified were sent back to where they had been. (The rest of the young people stayed.)[61] Nevertheless, if they can pass the examination, children of employees will still have priority over everyone else. Thus the present system attempts to combine achievement with ascription of status (that is, inheritance of a parent's position).

Gerontocracy. Another major problem emanating from lifetime employment and contributing to the overcentralization of authority and power is the creating of a *gerontocracy,* a leadership of old people. In China, septuagenarians and octogenarians continue to hold leadership positions in the Party, the state, and throughout the social and economic sectors, but they lack the vigor to administer well (some of them being close to senility and many of them requiring long naps and full-time nurses). By staying in their positions until their deaths, or at least until they are totally incapacitated, they also prevent younger, more energetic, and more talented people from rising to the top. Seniority has been the major criterion for promotion (provided a person's political credentials were in order). Younger and more talented cadres have usually been passed over because they lacked the "experience" of older cadres, and because it would hardly be "fair" to promote younger cadres over older ones. But with the shift from mass political campaigns to modernization, leaders needed different qualifications: education, creativity, and the vigor of youth. Veteran cadres may well have been acceptable when the stress was on mass campaigns because of their revolutionary experience and political credentials.[62] But, since the Thirteenth National Party Congress in 1987, many of China's elderly leaders have been replaced by younger, better educated individuals who bear responsibility for carrying out the four modernizations policy.

Undifferentiated Roles. The overcentralization of political power has been an obstacle to achieving an effective leadership for another reason: Senior bureaucrats in a system victimized by red tape hold overlapping, undifferentiated roles. Party officials concurrently hold administrative or managerial posts and feel free to interfere with technical decisions on the basis of political exigency (personal or official). They "manage" by political directives rather than expert knowledge. The Chinese officially estimate that 20 percent of the personnel in factories, for example, are "nonproductive personnel." That is, they have no other role than specializing "in bureaucratic wrangling, and they do nothing but create troubles for production."[63] This inhibits fast and effective action. Documents are passed around to countless officials without any action occurring. The Chinese are reluctant to admit that this form of "bureaucratism," even if it has its roots in "feudal" China's overconcentration of power at the top, is exacerbated by a socialist system's own propensity toward the overcentralization of power.

In addition, various agencies, bureaus, and enterprises involved with the same concerns function separately, without knowledge of what the others are doing. They do not share information or responsibility; and if cooperation by another unit is required but not forthcoming, it serves to stop any progress, as only higher authorities may override the negative decisions of organizations of parallel authority at lower levels. These problems become evident in such areas as job assignments. Although colleges (which train personnel), work units (which need trained personnel), and personnel bureaus (which assign college-trained personnel to work units) are all concerned with China's future leadership, they do not cooperate with each other. Work units do not know what kind of people are being trained in colleges, and they have no way (with some recent exceptions) of hiring the best and/or most appropriate graduates. Personnel bureaus assign graduates to work units without prior knowledge of the work units' needs, and without regard to the students' qualifications for the jobs. Further, a disproportionate number of graduates are assigned to state-owned enterprises and departments under the State Council, whereas the collectively owned units go begging for additional personnel. To make matters worse, state-owned units refuse to permit their surplus staff members to be transferred to other posts.[64]

Lack of Accountability. The lack of clearly defined responsibilities, roles, and functions, overlapping Party and administrative roles, and inadequate legal, legislative or administrative limitations on the use of power have aggravated the problem of accountability within the Chinese leadership. Because it is difficult to pinpoint who has given the orders, officials may shift blame to others for failed or incorrect policies. In some cases, management or state officials blame the Party, or the Party blames them.[65] In other cases, the central policy-making leaders may shift blame downwards to the lower level officials who administer the policies. In the state sector, for example, each vice-premier seems to have responsibility for certain ministries, but at the same time they are not accountable for the performance of discrete bureaucratic tasks.

> Furthermore, there is little communication at the lower levels between ministries. . . . Issues are passed up to the top of ministries, where they are then transmitted to the amorphous domains of the various vice-premiers, each of whom has every reason to be more concerned with maintaining harmony with his peers and protecting his own power than with fighting for the parochial policy interests of particular ministries, especially when they may have several ministries reporting to him. The key source of Chinese policies is the "Center" (*Zhongyang*), composed of men who are powerful but institutionally vaguely defined, including the members of the State Council, the Standing

Committee of the Politburo, the Politburo itself, and the Military Affairs Commission of the Central Committee. Yet, when the key figures at the Center make their decisions, the institutional capacity in which they are acting is usually unclear.[66]

Leaders are often blinded by the conceit that if policies fail, the cause is human failure, not the intractability and complexity of social and economic problems, nor the inappropriateness or inadequacies of the policies themselves. This encourages leaders to blame cadres at lower levels and promotes scapegoating, usually on political and personal grounds, since on policy grounds even the lower levels are protected by the collective decision making approach.

Collective decision making, which requires consensus to reach a decision, and the bureaucratic style of moving documents through an enormous hierarchy of officials for approval combine to aggravate the issue of accountability. "Up to 200 copies of documents may be circulated to senior colleagues in an effort to drum up support. In turn, leaders will merely indicate that they have read the documents by circling their names in red on the distribution list, without expressing any opinion."[67] By mystifying the line of responsibility, these methods release individuals from personal accountability. In one case, sugar was loaded into train cars which had previously carried coal. The coal dust had not been cleaned out, and so the sugar was grey by the time it was unloaded. It was then stored in a warehouse, which was known to have leaks; but no cadre would take responsibility for having it fixed. Predictably, it rained, and the sugar turned into a grey gooey mess. In another case, Chinese workers mistakenly mixed two loads of different chemicals shipped from abroad when unloading and transported them to a factory that had bought only one of the two. The result was a production loss of more than one million yuan. Even though the leaders had known about the dangers, not one official had taken individual responsibility to avert disaster.[68] In yet another instance, it was revealed that the Zhejiang foreign trade department had in the course of three years been responsible for losses to the state of some 44 million yuan, thanks to the recruitment of unqualified cadres and the willingness of the province's import-export firm managers to blithely sign their names on contracts, even when they knew nothing about foreign trade and could not read foreign languages.[69]

Cult of Personality and Inadequate Limits on Power.   In China, no "separation of powers" doctrine formally ensures an equitable or appropriate distribution of power among leaders of diverse institutions. As Max Weber once observed, when job content is "fluid" because it is not institutionalized or routinized, the position of both leader and supporters may be undercut and their duties and power removed. Such was the case with Premier and

Party Chairman Hua Guofeng and his supporters when Deng Xiaoping, upon his own restoration to power, gradually undercut their theoretically greater institutional power and increased his own duties and power.[70] The lack of well-defined constitutional limits on major leadership bodies and individuals, combined with the Chinese traditional tendency to vest power in individuals rather than in institutions, has allowed individual leaders unusual lattitude to determine the extent of their own power. The primary concern in China about power has historically been whether the *right people* held power, and not with the subsidiary issue of *limiting* power. The problem was with giving unlimited power to *bad* people, and therefore the focus in the PRC has been, as it always was in China, on choosing the right people to rule. Once power was concentrated in the hands of one official, then, not surprisingly "many people felt they had to put their faith in the man and not the law he was supposed to execute."[71] Thus, when this traditional cultural predisposition is combined with a highly centralized socialist leadership system that does not carefully delineate and differentiate roles and functions, an individual such as Mao Zedong and a small "clique" such as the Gang of Four are each able to seize power, to place themselves above organizations and become unresponsive to their demands.

Recent Chinese analysis suggests that the overconcentration of authority at the center, in one person, contributed to bureaucratism, when it was, ironically, Mao who most viciously attacked that very bureaucratism. But in many respects the reformers have overstated the power of Mao in their effort to make him responsible for all major problems since 1956. For this reason, they have exaggerated his contribution to the problem of bureaucratism. In fact, after the failure of the Great Leap Forward in 1958, Mao was not at the helm. During the Cultural Revolution he was able to project himself again into a position of central control. Ambitious people such as Lin Biao, we are told by his detractors, then used Mao for their own purposes by molding a "personality cult" around him. But this did not happen until the late 1960s, and it was allegedly Mao who eventually halted these efforts to turn himself into a demigod.

This "cult of personality" could never have emerged, however, without the appropriate groundwork. Mao's rise to power was predicated upon his image as a symbol of national unity that the Party was loathe to smash in spite of his "mistakes"; but it was also predicated upon a power structure that emerged during the early years of the Communist movement, which gave the Chairman of the Party almost limitless policy formulation power. What members of the Party's reform faction truly objected to was their own limited ability to shape Party policy during the "ten bad years." Power, which was already vastly overcentralized in the "collective leadership" of the top Party leadership, had become even further centralized in one person.

Mao's death in 1976 did not, therefore, mean an end to the problem of overcentralization of authority. In fact, control by one leader continued after Mao's death with Hua Guofeng's succession to the position of Party Chairman, which he added to his role as premier. With these two offices, Hua actually had more institutional authority available to him than Mao had had. Yet Hua Guofeng, a leader without a real constituency, lacked the power that Mao had held. Once the reform faction acquired enough power to undercut Hua, they openly attacked the personality cult which they felt Hua perpetuated.

Had the leadership structure possessed more inbuilt controls, a cult of personality might not have arisen. Yet the very same structure that permitted one man to rise to the very pinnacle of power still permits a small group of leaders at the center to exercise inordinate power today.

Reforms to Limit the Concentration of Power in a Few Hands

In the 1980s, the concern for efficiency, competence, expertise, and honesty has taken precedence over the concern for collective decision making below the central level, and the concern for modernization has taken precedence over the desire for total political control. Implementing a system of individual responsibility would be no less than a total redefinition of the system of policy-making and execution which the Chinese have experienced under socialism. To the extent that political reforms are successfully carried out, they will have an immense impact not only on efficiency but also on the recruitment and promotion of leaders; for in a system which is evaluating the individual performance record of each official, it is far more likely that those with merit, not political credentials or connections, will be promoted.

Reform leadership defines roles and responsibilities

Separation of Party and Administrative/Managerial Roles. The reformers have not been unaware of the pitfalls produced by the socialist system of leadership. Deng himself denounced the "proliferation of concurrent and deputy posts:" "There is a limit to one's knowledge, experience, and energy." Too many concurrent posts impede coming to grips with problems in one's work "and, more importantly, it will be difficult for other more suitable comrades to take up leading posts." Deng announced that "The Party's central and local committees will no longer issue directives or make decisions on government work," even though the political leadership of the Party would continue to supervise it.[72] The roles of Party personnel are to be differentiated from state and managerial roles. Party secretaries are, for example, prohibited from making decisions relating to factory production. The reform leaders have also emphasized the need for individuals to give their undivided attention to just one job so that it is done well and so that they will assume complete responsibility for it. And authority for implementing policy has been delegated to lower levels. All this is an attempt to change the prevailing system in which everyone, in the name of collective decision making, disavows individual responsibility for the *execution* of policy.

> No shifting of responsibility should be allowed on any account. . . . As head of the collective leadership, the first secretary of a Party committee must shoulder chief responsibility for its day-to-day work, while among its other members, stress should be laid on individual responsibility based on division of labor. We should encourage leading cadres to be bold in shouldering responsibilities, and this is totally different from making arbitrary personal decisions.[73]

The emphasis on collective decision making at the center has thus been combined with an even greater concern for individual responsibility at lower levels for implementing policies. Clarifying the duties and functions of leaders at all levels below the center facilitates the process of ferreting out incompetent individuals. Although the state and Party constitutions remain somewhat vague on the functions of the central leadership, numerous policies and regulations in the 1980s have pinpointed responsibility for each decision and its execution, especially in the economic arena. Moreover, detailed job descriptions, codification of a precise system of checks and balances, and limitations on terms in office will, the leadership hopes, prevent the gradual accretion of power into the hands of individuals.[74] The reform leaders have also undertaken massive investigations of ministries and agencies to expose problems of officials shirking responsibility (and to get their political enemies at the same time, of course). For example, the government employed no fewer than 50,000 officials to investigate the Ministry of Post and Telecommunications to determine whether postal workers were fit for their work. They discovered cadres who neglected their duties, unqualified workers, and corruption: 6,338 postal employees were found guilty of graft or embezzlement; and the leaders in over 700 post offices at the county and city levels were removed.[75] In 1987, the Ministry of Supervision was established for the specific purpose of ferreting out those organizations and individuals responsible for signing contracts with foreigners that resulted in a net loss of China's hard currency. The assumption is that they sold out China's interests for their own gains.

Elimination of "Iron Rice Bowl". In a far more radical move, the leadership has tried since the mid-1980s to eliminate the "iron rice bowl" system of lifetime guaranteed employment that permitted officials to escape responsibility for their actions. Reforms have spread the concept of the contract responsibility system from the countryside to urban service industries, and then to officials and workers at all levels in the form of a "labor contract system." Contracts for specified time periods, which stipulate the responsibility, rights, and interests of the state, the collective, and the individual, have been given to both officials and workers. When the contract time is up, if the individual has not done a good job (measured by efficiency, profits, productivity, and other performance criteria), the contract will simply not be renewed. For ordinary workers, poor performance has (in a very few cases) become a reason for terminating contracts in advance of their specified dates, which reflects the present leadership's rejection of the "dangerous" concept of "egalitarianism," or "all eating out of the communal pot."[76] Although productivity of officials is harder to evaluate, clearly there are strong pressures on officials.

Elimination of Opportunities for Cult of Personality.   Reforms aimed at eliminating the possibility of a "cult of personality" emerging have encompassed efforts to develop law and rule by law, greater democracy, and regulations to restrict the power of officials to stand above organizations. These reforms reflect the reformers' view that the institutionalization of democracy in decision-making procedures and laws will *overwhelm* feudalism, bureaucracy, and the cult of personality. The presumption is that the ability of any one individual or small group of individuals to gain inordinate power will diminish as the balance between democracy and centralism is reasserted.

Even while Hua was still Chairman of the Party, the reform faction removed the symbolic aspects of individual power. In 1980, the Party's Central Committee ordered that publicity about individual leaders be toned down: The suggestion that a few individuals make history detracted from efforts to eliminate feudal and bourgeois influence. As a result, the portrait of the Party Chairman could no longer be hung in Chinese embassies abroad, meeting halls, or public places. The intention was not to negate the role played by individuals, but rather not to overemphasize it at the expense of the Party and people.[77]

These, then, were the policies; and yet subsequently Deng Xiaoping published his own "selected works,"[78] in the fashion of Mao Zedong. To the extent that Deng did not do more to promote his image as China's leader, it appears to be a reflection of his personality (or of the power of others who opposed him). Still, his efforts to institutionalize democratic procedures and laws and to limit the power of officials may block the next ambitious leader of China from developing a cult of personality.

The emphasis on collective decision making today is an attempt to ensure that no Party member, *regardless of position in the leadership structure*, can make decisions on major issues alone, or "place himself above the Party organization."[79] This kind of organizational control is meant to obstruct both leaders at the center and Party leaders in the provinces, the military, and elsewhere from developing "independent power kingdoms." No doubt this emphasis will collide with the stress on individual responsibility and the steady decentralization of the economic system; for economic and administrative structures that function in a fairly independent manner, and their internal Party cells that are tied into a more rigid, centralized, and collective command system, are likely to conflict.

Reform leadership implements decentralization

At the heart of the problems associated with the leadership is the key unresolved issue of the balance between freedom and control. Mao Zedong tried to maintain control by centralizing power, without bureaucratization. But bureaucratism not only developed—it flourished. Subsequent efforts at decentralization seemingly led directly to a reemergence of control as an issue. At the same time, decentralization did little to alleviate bureaucratism.

China's leaders admit to having "repeatedly overemphasized centralism and unification in Party work, and . . . the need to combat decentralism and assertion of independence." But in the 1980s they felt this was inappropriate because the Party's central task had shifted from socialist transformation to rapid modernization. In the state sector, the leadership has dispersed much of the centralized power of organizations, ministries, and sectors (*xitong*), in hopes that grass-roots management will prove more effective. For example, in 1984, the State Council suddenly dismembered the Ministry of Heavy Industry, and all industrial enterprises that had fallen under its control were turned over to the cities in which they were located. Similarly, the State Council eliminated the power of the machine-building bureaus to manage enterprises in all provinces and autonomous regions. The purpose was to separate administrative management from production management. The result is that the Ministry of Heavy Industry no longer has to approve every minuscule production decision in the thousands of enterprises scattered across China. This process was slow and subject to error because the Ministry could not possibly keep abreast of developments everywhere. Now it simply supervises industrial development by formulating industrial policies and overall development plans.[80]

The financial sector saw its centralized power weakened by the conferral of ministerial status on the People's Bank of China (which put it on a par with the Ministry of Finance), the subsequent decentralization of its administration, and then the proliferation of banks in the mid-1980s. These banks now basically handle their own local financial affairs, functioning as independent accounting units, even if within the policy guidelines of the center. With control over their own credit funds, China's banks have gained greater flexibility in loan, interest rate, and investment policies.[81] Elsewhere, the State Council and Party Secretariat ordered the Ministry of Water Resources and Electric Power to end the practices by which it monopolized construction in the electrical and water power industry. Any department, enterprise, or individual may now build and run power projects and seek foreign investment. The Ministry of Communications was told to transfer control over all communications enterprises to municipal governments.[82] Perhaps the most significant overall deconcentration of power has occurred in the commercial and service sectors: The State Council disbanded the various organizations under the Ministry of Commerce to stimulate commercial and service activities. Individual entrepreneurs and collectives are now permitted to take over what used to be the preserve of the state. Many state enterprises have been broken up, and competition with state enterprises is permitted in these activities.

Finally, economic decentralization in the countryside after 1978 has put control over production into the hands of individual households. The effect has been to diminish (to a degree) the power of local officials who had formerly headed collective agricultural units. By so doing, this reform removed the vast patronage powers of local officials, their power to demand special favors from the peasants, and their former power to tell peasants what to produce, the number of work points they would receive for their work, and whom they could marry.

The important aspect of these structural reforms is that decentralization, economic pluralism, and competition make it difficult for a few individuals to use their positions at the top of a ministry, sector, unified system, or agricultural production unit as a tool to increase their personal power. Alternatives to the state as the sole distributor of resources, goods, and services now exist. Ideally, moreover, competition will breed greater efficiency, and weaker, less capable competitors will try something else.

Yet decentralization is not necessarily the solution to bureaucratism; for there may be even *more* petty, autocratic, and bureaucratic cadres at the lower levels than at the higher levels. In fact, if one accepts the Chinese view, the issues of feudalism and associated bureaucratism are far greater at the county level and on down than at the center. The basically "feudal" mentality of officials, at whatever levels, is not necessarily changed by mere structural decentralization. Thus, although "competition and bargaining among multiple bureaucratic units" has grown, this may turn out to be just as costly as centralized "bureaucratism."[83] Travelers to China are all too aware, for example, that the decentralization of the China International Travel Service, which used to control tourism throughout China, is causing a larger bureaucratic nightmare than had already existed. Now competing municipal branches of China Travel have their own programs to sell to tourists; hotels make their own arrangements and offer special packages to tourists; and China Airlines and new provincial airlines offer different programs. These various levels of competing bureaucracies have undercut the former power of the centralized tourist bureaucracy; but the system is no less bureaucratic.

Problems Arising from Socialism

The Party has had to confront many issues that arise from its own ideological and institutional roots and from the authority structure created by socialism.[84] Because the Party is the key leadership institution, it must both control the incumbent leadership and recruit new leaders. Although the political leadership in most countries must confront these same two issues, in China's case, the leadership has yet to institutionalize acceptable procedures for either.

Controlling the Party

Rectification Campaigns as a Managerial Form. The timeless issue for societies throughout history has been, "Who polices the policeman?" And "How?" In the case of the People's Republic of China, because the Communist Party has taken up the role of both leading and controlling the country, the question becomes, "Who controls the Party?" Who makes sure that the Party disciplines itself?

Even before the Communist victory in 1949, the leadership of the Chinese Communist Party (CCP) had chosen to use rectification movements, usually referred to in the West as *purges*, as the major form for managing and disciplining the Party.[85] Until the Cultural Revolution, it was the Party itself, not the masses or some outside institution, that was responsible for its *own* purging.

Rectifications weed out Communist Party members who are "bad" according to the current general line by investigating their activities and thoughts. They also try to reeducate those who are reeducable and instill them with correct values. Although routine investigations and discipline of Party members are carried out continuously, they have apparently proven inadequate, for "rectification" movements, evidence of the failure of routine controls, have occurred every few years since 1949.

The issues around which rectification centers vary from campaign to campaign. Because the general line and policies flowing from it often change, Party members cannot know in advance what type of behavior, attitudes, or thoughts might provide the next targets for a rectification. They might be identifiable crimes, such as corruption, tax evasion, bribery; or they might be less tangible targets—deviations in thought such as "revisionism," "commandism," or a "bourgeois mentality." Rectifications may target lower- and middle-level Party cadres, or focus on the highest level.

Since membership in a political party is, by definition, highly political, it does not seem unnatural that CCP members should be recruited and dismissed on political grounds; but the criteria for judging a Party member's behavior are sufficiently vague and ill-defined that the Party is left with an enormous amount of discretionary power to determine just whose work style, attitudes, or behavior is unacceptable. The 1982 Party Constitution does little to advance a Party member's understanding of the limits of acceptable behavior. "Backing good people and good deeds and fighting against bad people and bad deeds" (Article 3) is all very well if the Party can be sure on any given day just who is "good" and who is "bad"; but the definitions of good and bad change frequently. This is precisely what makes labeling of people so important. Similarly, the requirement to oppose "factionalism" is difficult when it is disguised or appears to be an innocent variation on the Party line. Moreover, what would ordinarily be considered a mere personal questioning of a Party decision or principle may, during a rectification campaign, be interpreted as a sign of "factional" proclivities, or anti-Party attitudes. Acting "correctly" is not insurance against criticism and disciplinary actions, for what is correct may still be redefined without prior notice.

The net result of periodic rectification campaigns and a Party Constitution that does little to protect Communist Party members from the arbitrary whim of higher-level Party officials is to diminish the appeal of Party membership. The vicious purge of Party members during the "ten bad years" was no doubt the final straw for many potential applicants. Better to forego the possible privileges accorded Party members than to invite an opportunity to have one's life and career jeopardized through Party membership.

In addition to diminishing the appeal of Party membership, repeated rectifications have destroyed Party cohesion. Members have been turned against each other during Party rectifications, and this has fragmented the sense of common purpose and unified leadership. Uncertainty has left Party officials reluctant to exercise initiative or to question potentially unworkable policies. Moreover, rectification campaigns are time-consuming and wasteful of human resources. With the benefit of hindsight, Party leaders now admit that the costs of rectification campaigns have outweighed their benefits. But, they add, this does not mean the end of rectifications. Rather, they will carry out the next Party rectification campaign *correctly*.

Some of the Party rectifications since the 1950s are understandable from the perspective of an organization that expanded too rapidly, first to ensure its control over China and, later, to collectivize the economy. "Opportunists" and "careerists," as well as people inadequately educated in Marxism-Leninism, were recruited by mistake. The 1950 and 1957 rectification campaigns addressed these issues in their drive for "Party consolidation." But subsequent campaigns both within the Party and in society at large were lavishly political: They had no purpose other than enabling the dominant Party leadership to rid the Party of political opposition. How had so many "bad" elements arisen within the Communist Party? According to Mao Zedong, it was because the Party was unable or unwilling to police itself, to purge itself voluntarily. Therefore, during the Cultural Revolution, the Red Guards were called in to police the CCP and carry out Party rectification from the bottom up.

Having only partially recovered from the decimation of the Party during the "ten bad years," the Party's leadership in the 1980s has had to address the issue of how to impose self-discipline without further impugning the already weak image of the Party. As part of its initial efforts to reassert self-discipline, it promulgated the "Guilding Principles for Inner-Party Political Life." The main theme was the need to correct "Party work style" (that is, attitudes and behavior) in order to strengthen Party leadership at all levels. The "Guiding Principles" addressed the major weaknesses of the Communist Party at that time, namely, that Party members ignored both the law and the rules of the Party, took advantage of their privileges as Party members for personal gain, became corrupt, and questioned those who tried to correct their behavior. Further, "some comrades" drew the wrong lessons from the past turmoil of inner-Party struggle. They were "confused" about where to draw the line "between correct, critical help on the one hand, and the attacks on individuals by Lin Biao and the gang of four, on the other hand." So they resisted engaging again in criticism, preferring to ignore improper work styles. The "Guiding Principles" embrace the "three nots:" "not fault-finding, not recklessly applying labels, and not beating with sticks." Party members may not improperly present a person's "mistakes" as anti-Party crimes. But they may use correct criticism, which relies on objective facts and appropriately combines "rational and emotional appeals."[86]

Just how far Party discipline had deteriorated by the early 1980s was poignantly illustrated by a circular from a provincial Party committee regarding the appointment, dismissal, and transfer of cadres. This circular warned that those leading cadres who were transferred to new positions within the province *"and did not show up for work for six months* may well find that their pay has been stopped." Those who failed to show up for work in their new jobs for one year would be dealt with "promptly."[87] (That is, after one year of not working!)

The 1983–1987 Party Rectification Campaign. The issue of discipline and control of Communist Party ranks touches on the issue of accountability. If the Party is only accountable to itself, problems are inevitable. The Party rectification that began in 1983 staggered to its conclusion three-and-one-half years later. (An additional six months of rectification were tacked onto the end of what was intended to be a three-year rectification because of the unexpected rise of "bourgeois liberalism" within the right wing of the Party just as the campaign against "leftism" was being wrapped up in 1986.) It was concerned with what Party leaders described as the "life and death" matter of "cadre work style." This rectification had first been announced in 1980, but was postponed several times before it was launched in 1983. Obviously there was much resistance to it, especially from "die-hard leftists," and from the military. The military had become a major channel of mobility for the politically "red" during the "ten bad years" and did not want to see its power diminished through a purge of its ranks. The dominant but not omnipotent reformist leadership had to get its own ranks in order first, however, for it was hard to pursue a relentless campaign against its enemies, "leftists remnants from the ten bad years," when it also faced problems from "rightists" and "bourgeois liberals" who had in-terpreted political and economic reforms as the end of socialism and one-party rule in China. Further, the reformers had to respond to their adver-saries' criticisms that their reforms had actually corrupted Party and gov-ernment cadres, who had taken advantage of the opportunities created by economic reforms to engage in nefarious practices.[88]

This Party rectification targeted the reform faction's "leftist" enemies by stages. First targeted were those in the departments of the Party's Cen-tral Committee, the ministries under the State Council, and Party organiza-tions at the provincial level, which involved about 960,000 CCP members. Next hit were those in Party organizations from the county (rural) and prefecture (urban) levels on down, involving about 13.5 million cadres. And finally, the last to be targeted were those in grassroots organizations, such as are found in China's villages, schools, and enterprises.[89] The pri-mary rectification targets were:

1. Those who entered the Party from 1966 to 1976, most of whom attained Party membership because they followed the "leftist line." They had incor-rectly defined "revisionism" in order to ensnare some of China's best top leaders. Estimates are that from one-fourth to one-half of the Party's 40 million members were admitted during this time. All were carefully scru-tinized during this rectification movement and had to resubmit application for Party membership. But many of the cadres in this group continue in the 1980s leadership despite their past politics.[90]

2. Those who "beat, smashed, and looted" during the Cultural Revolution. In general, members of this group were also members of the first group.

3. "Factionalists." While again these could be "leftists," this group could include anyone who opposed the reform faction's leadership and policies. Thus, those who became "spiritually polluted" from contact with the West and adopted "bourgeois liberal" attitudes (that is, they opposed socialism and CCP rule) could also be targeted; for they were taking advantage of Deng's liberalizing reforms to espouse antisocialist values. The "hard-liners" in the Party had clearly put pressure on Deng Xiaoping to guarantee that his reform policies would not become an excuse for attacking socialism. Party Chairman Hu Yaobang, on the other hand, believed that attacks on "bourgeois liberalism" were really attacks on the reforms. Deng's failure to control a surge of "bour-geois liberalism" resulted in his decision in 1987 (whether forced on him by the hard-liner "conservative" reformers or not) to remove the most visible and influential supporters of "bourgeois liberalism" from the Party.

4. Those who abused their position as Party members for personal gain. These were "corrupt" Party officials who, given the dimensions of patronage and privilege in China, had to be judged relatively. They, too, tarnished the Party's image by their behavior, to such an extent that those who wanted to join the Party after 1976 were taunted and disparaged, and their motives considered suspect. The Party's cadre work style had to be rectified for the Party to reclaim its "infallibility." Nevertheless, there was not and is not a simple division of cadres into (a) those who opposed the reforms because they benefitted from their ability to engage in corrupt activities as officials and (b) those who supported the reforms because they wanted to rid China of corruption. Many basic-level rural cadres have, in fact, successfully shifted their basis of authority and responsibility under the reforms, and are therefore still able to engage in profitable, if not corrupt, activities.[91]

To set this rectification campaign apart from all preceding ones in an effort to restore the confidence of the people in the Party's stability, Party leaders emphasized that it was not to take on the witch hunt proportions that "rectification" had assumed during the Cultural Revolution. Criticism of other Party members would be "reasoned" and would "seek truth from facts." Exaggeration and trumped-up charges were impermissible. Party members would even be permitted to respond and defend themselves against charges, a right given to them in the 1982 Party Constitution (Article 4). And the non-Party "masses" were not permitted to participate in this Party affair, as they had from 1966 to 1976, at great expense to the Party.

This rectification was, however, more than just a purge of political opponents and a weeding out of corrupt elements. It was also a *Party-wide education campaign* to communicate and implement the Party's new ideology and organization. For this reason, it also performed the important role of informing Party members about new Party values and objectives, and the new criteria for Party cadres. These criteria, which emphasized youth, education, and competence (Article 34), opened the Party's doors to intellectuals, scientists, technicians, and professionals in all fields regardless of their class origins. In the sense, then, that a rectification weeds out unacceptable Party members, it also lays the groundwork for recruiting new members. Rectifications are in this respect a form of recruitment.

With half the Party membership in 1983 composed of individuals who had only graduated from primary school or were even functionally literate, and with only 4 percent boasting a college education,[92] China's leadership could hardly hope for rapid modernization. Such criteria as that Party members be "revolutionary," therefore, took on a new interpretation with the reform leadership: A truly revolutionary cadre *enthusiastically* and *effectively* promoted the Party's four modernizations policies and emphasized the importance of education, science, knowledge, and technical expertise. The profile of what was "revolutionary" was, as usual, the profile of those who supported the leadership in power.

The reform leadership was particularly interested in keeping a tight lid on this Party rectification because in many provinces, and in certain institutions such as the PLA, a broad-ranging campaign might easily slip into the hands of leftists. Better to move cautiously, expelling major political opponents from the Party, "reeducating" others, and recruiting a new leadership from among those who enthusiastically carried out the reforms. For the most part, this is precisely what happened.

One final element distinguished this Party rectification from other such campaigns and made it a landmark campaign in Party history books: In the first year of the rectification, the relevance of socialism to China's problems was officially and publicly reassessed. This reassessment of socialism interacted with the rectification campaign in such a way as to produce a startling conclusion: *The socialist system* itself was as much to blame for corruption and bureaucratization as corruption and bureaucratization were for undermining the socialist system. It was therefore necessary to refocus the Party rectification campaign away "from exposing unhealthy tendencies" to reforming the authority structure created by socialism.[93]

The reasoning behind this reassessment was this: Although the Party had had repeated rectification campaigns, the very same problems kept reemerging. Thus, the source of recurrent personnel problems must rest within the socialist system itself. Reforming the structure would lead to personnel changes and changes in cadres' working style. As a result, in 1984, the reform leadership decided to change the rules of the game through a dose of economic liberalism and political democratization. "The political structure [had] been identified as the source of trouble, and the way out of trouble [was] to subject everything to democratic political power."[94]

The reformers implemented economic reforms that permitted people to get what they wanted though market mechanisms rather than the "back door" or "connections," and they required that cadres have adequate technical expertise or education. Rectification became coterminous with political and economic reform. In its new guise it effected desired changes without damaging the Party's image and power, something which the old method could not seem to avoid. It thereby made membership in the Communist Party appear as more of an honor than a potentially dangerous trap. Yet much of this progress in image-building was undone with the subsequent attack on "bourgeois liberalism" and the removal of a number of key Party members from their posts.

The Party announced that its three-and-one-half-year rectification campaign had successfully concluded in June 1987 and that approximately 34,000 "unqualified members" (a bare 0.1% of its forty million members) were expelled. Further, over 90,000 others were prohibited from re-registration in the Party; and some 184,000 members "were placed on probation with the Party or otherwise disciplined." What exactly happened to the 5,449 people guity of "rebellion" during the Cultural Revolution, of factionalism, or of "beating, smashing, and looting," who "were cleaned up," or the 43,074 guilty of "serious mistakes" who "were dealt with" is a matter for conjecture. But obviously their punishment was far more severe than expulsion from the Communist Party.

Party Not Above the Law. To gain greater control over Communist Party members, the reform leadership officially supports the principle that those who break the state's laws will be "equal before the law" with all other ordinary citizens. In the past, the primary characteristic of Party cadre status was "the right to be treated according to Party disciplinary rules rather than under a regime of legal rules of universal applicability."[95] It was common practice for a high-level Party official who committed a crime as defined by the state's legal codes to be protected by the Party. The Party would either claim that, since he or she was a Party member, the Party would itself mete out the punishment; or if the case actually went to a court, Party personnel would intervene to protect the Party official. Legal reforms instituted by the leadership since 1978 are an effort to deal with this prejudicial treatment of Party cadres.

On the other hand, these reforms do not speak to the issue of the lack of legal protection (such as the right to defense counsel and a trial) accorded to a Party member accused of an anti-Party crime. As is discussed in Chapter Six, anti-Party crimes are defined by the Party, not by the state. Therefore it is the Party which determines on an ad hoc basis when a crime has been committed, who is guilty of such crimes, and how the perpetrator is to be punished. The Party thereby retains an immense amount of control over itself, completely apart from the state and its law.

Controlling officials in the government sector

At each level of the state structure, the state has its own personnel departments that run parallel to Party organization departments, and which implicitly accept the leadership of Party committees. In fact, workers in state personnel departments and the respective parallel Party organization departments overlap, although political reforms since the early 1980s have tried to reduce such overlap.[96] The equivalent of Party rectification in the state administration sector is the *xiafang* movement. During such movements, leading bureaucratic cadres are "sent down" to lower levels of the government organization or state enterprise to remold their attitudes and behavior. Retrenchment and "simplification" campaigns have also served as nets in which to catch inefficient or "bureaucratic" bureaucrats.[97] In general, however, "sent down" bureaucrats have gradually worked their way back up; and those victimized by retrenchment were usually reassigned elsewhere to equivalent positions. Until the antibureaucratism campaigns of the Cultural Revolution, attacks on administrative bureaucrats were considerably less political, and less harsh, than Party rectification campaigns.

In 1982, the leadership tried to reduce bureaucratism by drastically reducing the total number of ministries, commissions, and agencies reporting to the State Council, and reducing the total number of high-level officials (largely through "voluntary" retirement of elderly officials). These actions helped weed out political opposition by breaking up entire networks of "political patronage in which junior cadres are protected by cadres higher up in the administrative hierarchy."[98] The difficulty was that often those very officials in charge of implementing them were also its intended targets. Indeed, substantial evidence indicates that officials adamantly resisted change; and, even if they were removed, the professional staffs under them remained virtually unchanged. Finally, in spite of reducing the total number of state bureaucratic units, the "merged" or "discontinued" units remained intact. Only the nameplates changed.[99]

Recruitment of party officials

Recruitment for both Communist Party membership and the state administrative apparatus has been a continuous concern for China's leadership since 1949. The issue is the *quality* of China's future leadership, and the difficulty is agreeing upon what "good" leadership means. A Party leadership divided since the mid-1950s over this issue has resulted in shifting standards for recruitment. Whatever faction controlled the Party central leadership would use rectifications to get rid of those state bureaucrats and Party members recruited by the faction previously in power, or would use "reeducation" to change their values and behavior, their "work style."

The quality of cadres was adversely affected immediately after 1949 by the need to recruit large numbers rapidly. Total Party membership, for example, rose from about 4.5 million members in 1949 to about 14 million a decade later. Worse, much of the recruitment took place under time pressures compounded by the need to fulfill a recruitment quota;[100] to recruit the politically active, as they had demonstrated leadership ability; and to recruit largely from the lower classes, particularly the poor peasantry, whose education was at a low level. Similar pressures affected the recruitment of officials for the state sector.

In other words, a leadership committed to socialist objectives had to address many other issues that interfered with recruiting the better educated; but whether it also interfered with recruiting those "best qualified" for leadership is a matter of both judgment and politics. After all, the tasks of local leadership (for which most cadres were recruited) in the 1950s had a great deal to do with organizing and mobilizing the masses, inspiring them to carry out the various tasks set forth by the central leadership, and implementing policies. In fact, once this was done, there was little time left for political study and Party meetings.[101] Obviously the Chinese needed organization and expertise to run the country. But if Party and state cadres were to be responsible for implementing socialist policies, their first qualification had to be a dedication to socialism. Otherwise, those who were "expert" but not "red" would use their expertise to lead the country in the wrong direction. Thus, an ongoing debate over what to emphasize in recruitment—political reliability or expertise—has perpetually plagued the Chinese central leadership. The combination of "red and expert" has been the preferred goal, but it is a goal that continues to elude the Chinese.

Recruitment has been one of the key issues for the central leadership because it is, in fact, the issue of succession. Who would succeed Mao Zedong? The question transcended the issue of succession within the central leadership to embrace leading personnel in the state and Party leadership organizations down to the local level, the level responsible for implementing policies. Certainly one of Mao's major objectives in the Cultural Revolution was to regain his own personal power. But Mao's alleged quest for "revolutionary immortality" was more than a personal quest: His revolutionary immortality would depend on the training of personnel committed to "continuous revolution" to fill cadre positions at all levels. In 1949, 80 percent of the top Communist Party and state elites had revolutionary experience. But over the years this percentage steadily declined until, on the eve of the Cultural Revolution in 1966, only 20 percent of the leadership had revolutionary experience. In Mao's view, this 20 percent had, regrettably, become effete and apathetic, interested in consolidating the gains of the revolution for their own benefit, even if at the expense of the masses. The well-educated youth had had no revolutionary experience and were developing into young technocrats. Would they provide the kind of leadership qualities China needed? Mao doubted it. He saw a need for them to leave school, to mix with the masses, and "to make revolution" in order to experience revolution—even a synthetic one. Those who could show they were truly "revolutionary" activists might well be rewarded with Party membership and a potential path to a leadership position.

Burdened by a history of repeated purges of the Party's membership, with Party cadres the first to come under suspicion if policies fail, and with the Party consuming an immense amount of the time of Party members in criticism and self-criticism sessions, small study groups, and mass-mobilization campaigns, Party membership has lost much of its appeal. Political reforms since 1978 have stripped Party officials of much of their power. And economic reforms permit a market economy to invade areas previously subject to tight centralized allocation policies, which had given Party cadres a stranglehold over scarce commodities and services. In general, the breaking up of the "big back door" has meant diminished power for Party cadres.

Thus, recruitment of new Communist Party members has not been easy in the 1980s. Just at the time when the reformers are anxious to recruit younger and better-educated members who reflect their values, they are reluctant to join. The Party has even changed the label of the formerly disparaged "stinking ninth category" of intellectuals and experts to "members of the working class" (those who "work with their minds"). Party committees in colleges and technical schools have been ordered to actively recruit undergraduates; but they continue to drag their feet. Youth, cynical and even contemptuous of the Party's ability to lead China, are likewise reluctant to join the Party. According to one magazine, only 2.25 percent of Party members from Shanghai are under age 25.[102] As a writer in *China Youth* asked rhetorically, "Why is it that those in charge now were criticized previously, and those now criticized were in charge previously?"[103] The Communist Youth League (CYL), which used to act as a feeder organization to the Party, is unable even to fill its membership. Struggling to recruit new members, it has tried bizarre recruiting practices for such a pristine organization: giving dance lessons to young workers[104] (but only dances that do not "overstimulate" the body) and providing dating services and other ploys to appeal to the nonpolitical side of youth.[105] In fact, the CYL and its puritanical political doctrine face formidable competition from the newly available temptations of materialism and bourgeois Western culture. Since the mid-1980s, the CYL has been under orders to concentrate on economic work. But whether its involvement in China's modernization, rather than in its politics, will make the CYL better able to recruit and train young people to become Party leaders is not yet known.

Recruitment of state officials

By 1982, the reform leadership had undertaken serious measures to force state organizations and enterprises to recruit educated people who were not over age fifty-five. The policy involved recruiting hundreds of thousands of young and middle-aged cadres as "reserve forces" for both central and local leading administration bodies. Democratic procedures of selection were to be combined with examinations to test their expertise. Once recruited, they would be trained and eventually would take over from veteran cadres.[106]

This was the policy, but the practice did not live up to its billing. Subsequent reports revealed that the leadership in work units often refused to train those in the pool of qualified recruits on the grounds that they had in the past made "mistakes." The officials in positions to carry out the central leadership's policy of recruiting younger, better-educated personnel, in short, tried to sabotage this new policy by demanding perfection. Alternatively, they might obey the specific requirements of the new recruitment policies to the letter, but ignore their intention. Thus, rather than giving the younger recruits real authority, the veteran officials might put them in nominal posts without any independent responsibility. Oftentimes they loaded down the new recruits with endless meetings, leaving them no time to do serious work.[107]

The Chinese have, nevertheless, at least prepared the groundwork for recruitment of a younger, more vigorous leadership by first thinning out the top-heavy governmental sector at all levels. China's central administrative network by the mid-1980s was trimmed down from 600,000 to 200,000 administrators, while the ninety-eight ministries, commissions, and agencies were initially reduced to thirty-nine. (However, by 1986 they totalled seventy-two!) Most importantly, the 117 ministers and vice-ministers were reduced by seventy-five percent. The new system of retirement helped these governmental structures considerably in reducing their enormous concentration of elderly officials. At the provincial level, the average age of leading cadres was by 1986 reduced from sixty-two to fifty-three years, and those with college education increased from 20 percent to 62 percent. In the cities at the prefectural level, their average age declined from fifty-six to forty-nine years, and those with college education increased from 14 percent to 55 percent. In rural county governments that had already been reorganized (and many had not), the average age of the leading cadres was reduced from forty-nine to forty-four years, and 54 percent were college educated.[108]

In addition, the leadership drew up plans to have college educated cadres, preferably around age forty, and definitely not older than age fifty-five, replace the managing directors and Party committee secretaries of the 3,000 key state enterprises, and eventually of all enterprises. They would have a limited term in office of only four years, "subject to reappointment . . . or recall . . . if so recommended by the enterprise's workers' congress." The new policies favor those educationally qualified over those with "long work experience." Moreover, they recommend that democratic processes, such as subordinates' recommendations and opinion polls, should play a role in choosing new leaders. But the new criteria for recruitment do not apply to those who "rose to prominence by rebellion" or who "indulged in violence during the decade-long 'cultural revolution'" or who were "still seriously factionalist in their ideas."[109] In short, those with unacceptable political credentials will be excluded from leadership *regardless* of their youth and expertise.

Conspicuous progress has been made in implementing new leadership recruitment policies, but there has been much resistance by cadres at all levels. Further, institutional structures that foster seniority inhibit recruitment of a new leadership for China's government organs and state-run enterprises. The step-system of promotion, whereby organizational personnel in their entirety are in lockstep (an individual cannot be promoted unless the person above has been promoted to the next higher position), thus far remains an organizational fact of life. The institutionalized system of maintaining personnel dossiers hinders efforts to promote young cadres from several levels down because the Party committee at any given level only has access "to a recruitment pool of leading cadres one or two levels below it."[110]

Problems Attributable to Developmental Level

China is not unique in the problems it faces in its leadership. Most poor and developing countries face similar obstacles. Moreover, many of the problems that China labels as "feudal," products of Chinese culture, are endemic to bureaucracy and leadership everywhere: These include red tape, blind observance of absurd regulations, circulating documents endlessly without resolving problems, emphasizing seniority over ability and political reliability over expertise, low morale, corruption, overstaffing, practicing favoritism, and so on. Nevertheless, bureaucracy seems to plague less-developed countries more than developed ones. Even the Chinese recognize "a connection between the existence of bureaucratism" and "the developmental level of the socialist productive forces."[111] In short, because underdevelopment exacerbates issues related to bureaucratism, the assumption is that development will end some of these problems. The fact is, of course, that development itself is slowed down until political reforms that modernize the leadership and bureaucracy are carried out.

Many of China's unresolved leadership issues are rooted in China's low level of economic development. Thus, for example, one of the political reforms envisioned, namely, recruiting skilled and educated officials, is itself thwarted by the shortage of skilled and educated officials. This, in turn, reflects a system that has been too poor to support a broader and more intensive educational system.[112] Similarly, in a country too underdeveloped to provide enough goods and services for the people, and where prices for goods are set artificially low, those people who control distribution of goods and services are tempted to distribute them to people who will return the favor. This kind of problem emerges from the environmental conditions created by combining underdevelopment with socialism: In a socialist but poor country, where goods and services are centrally allocated, even people who have money cannot purchase them unless they have "connections." The result is bribery, patronage, and the continuation of a system in which officials have inordinate power over ordinary citizens.

The problem of distributing goods in a poor country was greatly exacerbated in the PRC by the special conditions emerging from the Cultural Revolution. The support at that time for the Communist theory of "to each according to his need" to replace the socialist theory of "to each according to his work" meant that anyone could claim a "need" for more goods. But production was inadequate to support everyone's needs. The result was that far more goods and services were distributed through the "back door" than before the Cultural Revolution.

Given what is known about how bureaucracies develop throughout the world, China's "bureaucratism" and associated problems of inefficiency, corruption, elitism, and the abuse of power will no doubt continue for some time to come. The real objective of China's leadership reforms in the 1980s is, of course, to cut down on the immensity of the problem, to the point at which other reforms, notably those in the economic arena, can go forward without being stymied by bureaucratic officials.

Problems Attributable to Inertia

Although the forces of inertia—the continuance of movement in the same direction unless something forces change—is not one of the three major variables considered in this book as basic to China's unresolved issues, it is important enough to mention it in the context of leadership issues. Many of the leadership problems confronting China today are the result of the institutionalization of certain leadership practices immediately after the Communists' victory in 1949. The Party had to respond to the pressing needs of governance, but once it institutionalized leadership practices, it was hard to move down a totally new path.

When the CCP gained power in 1949, it was basically a rural peasant movement. Suddenly it found itself needing to control and administer the whole of China, which included some 600 million people and an immense land mass, both urban and rural. Although the Communist movement had since the 1930s already built up a relatively large bureaucracy for the purpose of mass mobilization and managing those areas that fell under its control, the enormity of the task after 1949 required even more organization. As mentioned above, the speed with which cadres were recruited, the severity of China's problems, and, most importantly, the attempt to control all aspects of the people's daily lives, meant that the bureaucracy took on gargantuan proportions. In some ways it slipped beyond the central leadership's control. The bureaucratic process itself became institutionalized, an integral part of "the system." Efforts at organizational reform, whether "leftist" or "rightist" in inspiration, at best met with only temporary victories, and at worst they were totally disruptive without even minor benefits.

The reform leadership's policies address the continued existence of those very same organizational issues. Although the reformers attribute them to "feudalism" and mistakes the Party made after 1949, habit, the prolonged existence of organizations, and human resistance to change that threatens the power and privilege gained from the existing system have significantly contributed to this inertia and obstructed the regime's best efforts at organizational reform. Thus, it is the many leaders already in the leadership system who find it contrary to their self-interests to cooperate in implementing reform policies that helps perpetuate inertial tendencies.

WHO WILL LEAD CHINA TOMORROW?

Even exceptionally inspired crystal-ball gazers have had a hard time since the mid-1960s predicting who would lead China. Extraordinary and unpredicted events occur, leaders die, the doors close, the battle ensues, the doors open, and out walks a new, perhaps shaky, and shaken leader. Whether or not each will be able successfully to consolidate his (or her) power awaits historical confirmation and further struggle against opponents.

In this respect, China has not seen unanimous consent to the leadership of one group or one person since the 1950s. Liu Shaoqi, Lin Biao, the Gang of Four, and Hua Guofeng all lost out before they could fully consolidate their power. So did Deng Xiaoping, the first time. The second time, he simply chipped away at Hua Guofeng, until it could no longer be denied that Deng was in fact China's leader. The choice of Hua as paramont leader in 1976 had itself been a stunning surprise for both foreign observers and the Chinese people. No one outside the very highest leadership seemed to have an inkling of his possible candidacy for China's major leadership positions.

Both the special National Party Conference of 1985 and the Thirteenth Party Congress of 1987 indicated that a particular type of leadership was being chosen to carry out economic reforms. Younger and better-educated individuals were elected to the Party's Central Committee and Politburo. Most of the leadership over age 72 were forced into retirement or, at best, into the ranks of the Central Advisory Committee. Although many of those cadres forced to resign had a military background, a spokesman for the Party noted the difficulty in finding cadres from the pre–1949 generation who did *not* have some kind of military background.[113] Nevertheless, other policies, such as the low military budget, the requirement of military academy training for officer status, and personnel changes, reinforce the impression that leadership changes are at least partly intended to relegate the military and its political leadership role to the background.

Events since 1985 indicate that caution must be exercised in assuming that there is just one "reform" group in the Politburo and Central Committee. In fact, there may be several different "reform" groups, all wanting reform, but differing on the nature and speed of reforms.[114] The removal in January 1987 of Hu Yaobang as Party chairman, a preeminent "reformer" removed by other "reformers," suggested a new leadership dichotomy:

moderate or conservative reformers, such as Li Peng, who wanted reform but felt Hu Yaobang (and perhaps Deng Xiaoping) had permitted reforms to go too far in challenging Party leadership and the fundamentals of the socialist system; and radical reformers, such as Deng Xiaoping and Zhao Ziyang, who have sought even more extensive changes in China's socialist structures. The most important of these has been, first, to change the relationship of the state to the economy by ending state ownership of major enterprises so that their managers "no longer look to state administrative organs as their ultimate bosses," favoring the role of the market over state planning, enhancing the banking system's role in the economy at the expense of the planning, finance and ministerial systems, and permitting greater disparities of wealth; and second, in the relationship of China to the outside world, supporting broader and more open interaction, and favoring interdependence and an international division of labor over self-reliance.[115] But no one should imagine that Deng Xiaoping, Hu Yaobang, Zhao Ziyang, and the other radical reformers had struggled for more than forty years to perfect socialism only to oversee its demise and replacement by "bourgeois liberalism."

What of the future? Caution is in order. Present opinion seems sharply divided, from the extreme of predicting civil war upon the death of Deng Xiaoping because only Deng commands the requisite loyalty and respect of the military leadership, to a belief that the leadership changes in the decade from 1978 to 1988 are such as to ensure progress toward reform and economic growth. Some Chinese people still remain reluctant to implement the leadership's reforms out of a concern that policy might be reversed again, with a renewed class struggle to victimize all those who had managed to "get rich" under Deng's reforms. Thus, the reformers have taken measures to reassure them of the future continuity of leadership. They initially chose a "second echeleon" of new government cadres, 70 percent of whom were under the age of sixty. When the "readjustment" was completed in mid-1985, the leadership chose a "third echelon" of state officials, aged thirty-five to forty-five, to remain in the wings, in training. Center stage was left to the first and second echelons of leaders until several million "voluntarily" retired in 1987 and 1988.

Leadership recruitment criteria stress youth, administrative capabilities, education, expertise, and commitment to the Party's line on the "four modernizations." Seniority, "redness," activism, and class background are no longer supposed to be considered relevant for recruitment. If these criteria are actually put into practice, it could mean that the next 6 million college graduates will become members of China's political elite, bringing about a dramatic change in the kind of political leadership China experiences. Already, more intellectuals and experts have joined the Communist Party, and technocrats were elected to the highest bodies of Party decision making at the 1987 Party Congress. In the meantime, the corrupt, the irresponsible, the inefficient, and of course the politically hostile are gradually being removed from leadership ranks at all levels, a testimony to the growing strength of the reform faction.

Yet many Chinese, especially China's youth, are angered by the leadership having already recruited a third generation of leaders. In their view, this means that China is not moving toward a democratic selection of leaders, or a choice of leadership on the basis of expertise and performance. Rather, it is continuing China's nepotistic pattern of leadership selection. What is really happening is that China's aging leaders have agreed to retire only if their children or grandchildren are first guaranteed a position in the second or third echelons of leadership. Not only does this undermine the reform leadership's promise that China's future leadership will be qualified in education, expertise, and competence, but it also undermines the chances of anyone presently under the age of thirty-five moving into leadership positions in the next thirty to forty years. In addition, because most of those in the third echelon are also from that generation which produced the radically left Red Guards of the Cultural Revolution, and which, as a whole, received less formal education than either the generation before or after it, the question as to whether this group of leaders will be either politically reliable[116] or professionally competent remains to be answered.

If, however, measures of competence and such economic criteria as profits and losses do, in fact, come to form the basis on which officials, especially in management positions within state enterprises, *remain* in office, the days of incompetent cadres will be numbered. They may have gained their positions because of their connections, but they will not be able to keep their positions unless they perform well. In this respect, China will not be that different from many Western nations, in which the right connections may help individuals get their foot in the door, but provide no guarantee of lifetime employment or even promotion.

Regardless of whom the reformers have chosen to succeed themselves, nothing can be expected to remain as they might want it unless other conditions are favorable. The ability of China's leaders to maintain their official positions will depend on the success of present economic and political reforms in bringing visible improvements and sustained economic growth to China. It will also depend on China's relationships with both the capitalist countries and the Soviet Union. If the industrialized nations of the West along with Japan invest heavily in China, and if China is able to avoid war on any of its borders, but especially with the Soviet Union, it will be in a much better position to focus on its internal political and economic development. A strong and growing economy would provide an excellent foundation for a politically powerful leadership to resist destabilizing forces. In particular, it would make it far more difficult for ideologues to reassert Marxist dogma and to return China to class struggle and less progressive political and economic programs.

CONCLUSIONS

It would be a mistake to see the reform leadership's attempts to reform the entire system of leadership as simply part of a "two-line struggle," in which the rising, dominant faction utilizes political reforms to eliminate its opponents. On the other hand, there can be little doubt that the political reforms implemented since 1979 have a hidden agenda that goes beyond organizational reform and the elimination of "feudalistic" practices and attitudes; for integral to each reform is the need to change not just the political system as such but also to change the leadership at all levels.

The reform leadership's singling out of "feudalism" and associated bureaucratism as the major contradictions to China's current modernization policies is really an attack on the socialist system as it has become institutionalized in China. But because so many cadres have been afraid that they would be adversely affected by implementing the mandated reforms, they have resisted doing so. Further, the Chinese people themselves seem culturally predisposed to tolerate passively the continued existence of a system in which they are impotent against officialdom. In any event, the Communist Party has a tradition of reforming itself, and this is not an open process in which non-Party members, who are 96 percent of the population, have a right to participate. Much of the actual change in leadership has occurred not because of reforms directed toward leadership modernization, but rather because of economic reforms. These have directly undermined much of the power and patronage of both Party and state leaders by substituting economic tools for administrative tools to determine the allocation of scarce funds and services.

Of course, cadres who would be targets of reform policies naturally resist them, but even for the reformers themselves, the reforms are double-edged: They are beneficial only if they go as far as they planned, and no further. When the reforms have spilled out beyond the unstated borders of acceptability and threatened the power of the reformers themselves by undermining the concept of "Party infallibility," they have been curtailed. Such was the case in late 1986, when the actions and ideas of students and intellectuals were labeled "bourgeois liberalism" and liberalizing reforms were given a cold shower. The real problem is halting the reforms at just the right moment, to wit, modernizing the system of leadership, and the relationship between the leaders and the masses, but at the same time making sure that both the new leaders *and* the masses remain obedient to the Party. It is the leaders' awareness of the need to carefully orchestrate reform that makes them cautious. Still, it is Party General Secretary Zhao Ziyang's view that the only way to overcome the problems that have arisen in the course of reform is to move ahead with reforms faster.

The reform leadership's willingness to undertake this delicate task may be seen either as a reflection of their confidence and security, for only a secure leadership would dare to take such radical steps as attacking the foundations of its own power, or as a desperate measure—the only path left if they want to consolidate their control further, modernize rapidly, and, in the process, remove as many of their enemies as possible. The latter interpretation assumes that the reform leadership sees its own power base as tired and rotting away at the foundations, incapable of further creativity and energy. That is why reforms, which would reinvigorate it with youth, creativity, and a higher level of technical competence, are necessary. In any event, the reforms may be viewed as a bold attempt to reexamine the strengths and weaknesses of socialism within a Chinese cultural context and to shed those aspects of socialism itself that simply cannot function properly within the Chinese cultural context.

If China's economic and political reforms do not succeed, a billion Chinese might continue to function in what is really a traditional society, a mom and pop shop where things are done on the basis of personal relationships in a patriarchal order that involves obligation, status, and power rather than equality and laws. But it is the socialist system itself, as the Chinese Communists have developed it, with its remaining irrationalities in state administration, and the insistence on Party infallibility that is at the heart of the continued existence of "feudalism" within the leadership.[117] Overconcentration of power at the center, a situation almost mandated by the axiom of Party infallibility, has been at the heart of unresolved leadership issues. The conclusion seems to be emerging in China that enhanced democratic practices and a strong legal system will *overwhelm* feudal patterns of behavior that distort socialism. Both socialist democracy and socialist legality are, however, in a process of becoming. So the prognosis is clouded.

NOTES

[1]Ross Terill, *Mao: A Biography* (New York: Harper & Row, 1980), p. 393.

[2]Donald C. Clarke, "Political Power and Authority in Recent Chinese Literature," *China Quarterly*, No. 102 (June 1985), p. 238.

[3]Peter R. Moody, Jr., "Political Liberalization in China: A Struggle Between Two Lines," *Pacific Affairs*, Vol. 57, No. 1 (Spring 1984), p. 34.

[4]See Pierre M. Perrolle, "Introduction," in Pierre M. Perrolle (ed), *Fundamentals of the Chinese Communist Party* (White Plains, N.Y.: International Arts and Sciences Press, 1976), pp. xxvi, xxvii.

[5]Clarke, "Political Power and Authority," p. 244.

[6]This chart is from John P. Burns and Stanley Rosen (eds.), *Policy Conflicts in Post-Mao*

China (Armonk, N.Y.: M.E. Sharpe, 1986), pp. 362, 363. (Based on the Constitution of the People's Republic of China, 1982; and *Zhongguo shouce* [Hong Kong: Ta Kung Pao, 1984].)

[7]This chart is from Burns and Rosen, *Policy Conflicts*, pp. 360, 361. (Based on the Constitution of the Chinese Communisty Party, 1982.)

[8]Franklin Houn, *A Short History of Chinese Communism*, pp. 89, 90–92, referenced in James C. F. Wang, *Contemporary Chinese Politics* (Englewood Cliffs, N.J.: Prentice-Hall, 1985), p. 80.

[9]Daniel Kelliher, May 1987 seminar given to Government Department, Harvard University.

[10]Lucian Pye, *The Dynamics of Chinese Politics* (Cambridge, Mass.: Oelgeschlager, Gunn & Hain, Publishers, 1981), p. 73.

[11]The Central Advisory Committee (CAC) is composed largely of septuagenarians and octogenarians, whom Deng pressured to retire from the Politburo, Central Committee, People's Liberation Army, and provinces, in order to make way for younger members of the Party. Some, however, refused to retire to the CAC. See James C. F. Wang, *Contemporary Chinese Politics*, pp. 86, 87; and 1982 Party Constitution, Article 22.

[12]Graham Young, "Control and Style: Discipline Inspection Commissions Since the Eleventh Congress," *China Quarterly*, No. 97 (March 1984), pp. 29, 30.

[13]Wang, *Contemporary Chinese Politics*, pp. 85, 86; and Graham Young, "Control and Style," pp. 32, 33, 36, 44.

[14]Wang, *Contemporary Chinese Politics*, p. 86; and Young, "Control and Style," p. 33.

[15]CCP Central Committee, Central Organization Department *1983 Handbook*, p. 193, referenced in Melanie Manion, "The Cadre Management System, Post-Mao: The Appointment, Promotion, Transfer and Removal of Party and State Leaders," *China Quarterly*, No. 102 (June 1985), p. 209, note 30.

[16]Manion, "Cadre Management System," pp. 210, 211.

[17]Marion Levy, *Modernization and the Structure of Societies* (Princeton, N.J.: Princeton University Press, 1966), p. 105.

[18]Marc L. B. Bloch, *Feudal Society*, Vol. I (translated by L. A. Manyon), (Chicago: University of Chicago Press, 1961), p. xiv.

[19]Marion Levy compares traditional China with Tokugawa Japan, concluding that the latter was far more feudal. Yet it modernized much more rapidly than did China. Levy proposes the fascinating hypothesis that "In this comparison . . . strong feudal structures constitute a better basis for rapid and efficient modernization of late-comers than do non-feudal social structures . . . despite the fact that non-feudal social structures may have much more in common with so-called democratic aspects of some relatively modernized societies." Levy, *Structure of Societies*, p. 106.

[20]Even then, most of China's limited number of industries were run by, or even in collaboration with, foreign capitalists.

[21]Moody, "Political Liberalization," pp. 38, 39, 41.

[22]Deng Xiaoping, "On the Reform of the System of Party and State Leadership" (August 18, 1980), published three years later in *Beijing Review* (*BR*), Nos. 40 and 41 (October 3 and October 10, 1983).

[23]As evidence of this, see Li Honglin, "Chinese Communist Party Is Capable of Correcting Its Mistakes," *BR*, No. 25 (June 22, 1981), p. 19, and "Combating Unhealthy Tendencies," *BR*, No. 43 (October 26, 1981), p. 5.

[24]Harry Harding, *Organizing China: The Problem of Bureaucracy, 1949–1976* (Stanford, Calif.: Stanford University Press, 1981), p. 330.

[25]John Israel, "The Red Guards in Historical Perspective: Continuity and Change in China's Youth Movement," in Lenard J. Cohen and Jane P. Shapiro, *Communist Systems in Comparative Perspective* (New York: Anchor Press, 1974), p. 425.

[26]Many informed Chinese would argue that Mao's only real compulsion to attack "bureaucratism" was his quest for total power: Since all the major contenders for leadership were part of the bureaucracy, he chose to attack "bureaucratism" and "capitalist roaders" in order to undermine their power. For the official view which parallels this, without mention of Mao's own role, see Shi Zhongquan, "The 'Cultural Revolution,' and the Struggle Against Bureaucracy," *BR* (December 7, 1981), pp. 17, 18.

[27]"Centuries of familiarity with bureaucratic hierarchy so colored Chinese cultural

orientations toward social interaction that even popular conceptions of Hell are filled with ranked officials and their red tape. Little wonder that contemporary revolutionaries entertain profound suspicions toward developments within the bureaucracy." Richard C. Kraus, *Class Conflict in Chinese Socialism* (New York: Columbia University Press, 1981), pp. 4, 5.

[28]Shi Zhongquan, "The 'Cultural Revolution,' and the Struggle Against Bureaucracy," pp. 17, 18.

[29]Deng Xiaoping, "On the Reform" (August 18, 1980), in *BR*, No. 41 (October 10, 1983), p. 18, and Ibid., in *BR*, No. 40 (October 3, 1983), p. 21.

[30]Lu Xiaobu, "The Reforms in China: A Political Cultural Analysis," *Newsletter* (Chinese Scholars of Political Science and International Studies, New Haven, Conn.), Vol. 2, No. 1 (May 20, 1987), p. 3.

[31]Zhu Yuanshi, *BR*, No. 37 (September 14, 1981), p. 18.

[32]Deng Xiaoping, "On the Reform" (August 18, 1980), in *BR*, No. 40 (October 3, 1983), p. 19.

[33]Jay Mathews, "Mystery Follows Defector's Trip Back to China," *The Washington Post* (September 2, 1984), pp. A1, A6.

[34]Some scholars argue that people in elitist systems actually *expect* decisions to be made without their consent: "In elitist systems, authority—and indeed the entire political process—is assumed to adhere to informal practices and operate in a latent manner. Everyone accepts the idea that leaders must work out their problems in private and that there should be a minimum of constraints on the 'wisdom' and 'moral virtue' of leaders." (Lucian Pye, *Dynamics of Chinese Politics*, p. 72, referring to J. P. Nettl, *Political Mobilization: A Sociological Analysis of Methods and Concepts* (New York: Basic Books, 1967).

[35]Commentator, "Recognizing the Dangers of Factionalism," *Guangxi Daily* (May 23, 1983). Translated in *Inside China Mainland*, Institute of Current China Studies, Taipei (July 1983), p. 5.

[36]Deng Xiaoping, "On the Reform" (August 18, 1980), *BR*, No. 40 (October 3, 1983), p. 16.

[37]Pye, *Dynamics of Chinese Politics*, p. 9.

[38]Merle Goldman, *China's Intellectuals: Advise and Dissent*, (Cambridge, Mass.: Harvard University Press, 1981), p. 7; and Moody, "Political Liberalization," pp. 38, 39, 41.

[39]Pye, *Dynamics of Chinese Politics*, p. 27.

[40]Ibid., p. 28.

[41]Commentator, "Recognizing the Dangers of Factionalism," pp. 5, 6.

[42]Pye, *Dynamics of Chinese Politics*, pp. 6, 65, 66.

[43]Ibid., pp. 7, 20.

[44]Parris H. Chang, "The Last Stand of Deng's Revolution," *Journal of Northeast Asian Studies*, Vol. I, No. 2 (June 1982), p. 6.

[45]Commentator, "Recognizing the Dangers of Factionalism," p. 6.

[46]Pye, *Dynamics of Chinese Politics*, p. 12. For further elaboration on why the Chinese are psychoculturally predisposed to form factions, see Pye, pp. 58, 59, 65.

[47]See Liu Binyan, "The Fifth Man in the Overcoat," in Perry Link (ed), *People or Monsters? Liu Binyan* (Bloomington: Indiana University Press, 1983), in which the rehabilitated writer returns to find that the very person responsible for his removal still has power over him. Also see Ann F. Thurston, "Victims of China's Cultural Revoltuion: The Invisible Wounds," Part I, *Pacific Affairs*, Vol. 57, No. 4 (Winter 1984–1985), pp. 599–620, and Part II, *Pacific Affairs*, Vol. 58, No. 1 (Spring 1985), pp. 5–27.

[48]"Chairman of the State and Night Soil Collector," *BR*, No. 21 (May 26, 1981), p. 22. Also see *People's Daily* Editorial, "Restore True Qualities of Mao Zedong Thought: On the Rehabilitation of Comrade Liu Shaoqi," in *BR*, No. 21 (May 26, 1980), p. 15.

[49]There is no actual law that guarantees lifetime employment, but a web of regulations and years of practice have made lifetime employment a de facto situation, especially for leading cadres.

[50]"'Iron Rice Bowl' Debate Revolves Round Three Views," *China Daily (CD)* (June 16, 1983), p. 4.

[51]"Transfers Cannot Change Ideas," *CD* (June 9, 1984), p. 4.

[52]Edward A. Gargan, "For Chinese, a Mismatch of Job Skills," *New York Times* (December 27, 1987), pp. 1, 16.

53"'Iron Rice Bowl' Debate", *CD* (June 16, 1983), p. 4.

54Deng Xiaoping, "On the Reform" (August 18, 1980), *BR*, No. 40 (October 3, 1983), p. 19.

55For insightful commentary on the relations between peasants and local officials, see William Hinton, *Shenfan* (New York: Random House, 1983); a novel by Gu Hua, *A Small Town Named Hibiscus* (translated by Gladys Yang; Beijing: Chinese Literature, Panda Books, 1983); and Anita Chan, Richard Madsen, and Jonathan Unger, *Chen Village* (Berkeley: University of California Press, 1984).

56 Liang Heng and Judith Shapiro, *Intellectual Freedom in China: An Update* (New York: A Report of Asia Watch Committee, The Fund for Free Expression, July 1985), p. 10.

57An Zhiguo (Political Editor), "Solving Problems While Consolidating Party Leadership," *BR*, No. 11 (March 12, 1984), p. 4.

58"Combating Unhealthy Tendencies," *BR*, No. 43 (October 26, 1981), p. 5.

59"Discipline Commission Circular Bans Squandering," *Foreign Broadcasts Information Service*—Chi-81-249 (December 29, 1981), p. K2.

60Examples such as these are frequently reported in the Chinese press. For this example, see "Bureacracy," *CD* (July 14, 1984), p. 4.

61"4000 Illegal Recruits Lost Their Jobs," *CD* (February 8, 1984), p. 3.

62Shih Chien, "On Qualification by Seniority," from the People's Central Broadcasting Station (May 22, 1983), translated in *Inside China Mainland* (July 1983).

63"President Li [Xiannian] Hits out at Specialist Bureaucrats," *CD* (August 29, 1984), p. 1.

64"Job Assignment Needs Reform," *CD* (August 2, 1984), p. 4.

65See, for example, "Shop Chiefs Seek Greater Freedom," *CD* (October 26, 1984), p. 3, in which managers of some of Beijing's leading stores blame the lack of a clear "separation of function" between the Party and the managers and too many "bosses" for inaction.

66Pye, *Dynamics of Chinese Politics*, pp. 14, 15.

67"Beijing Exhibition Exposes Red Tape," *CD* (February 6, 1984), p. 1.

68Article excerpted from *Economic Daily*, in *CD* (August 20, 1984), p. 4.

69Article excerpted from *People's Daily* (June 7, 1984), in *CD* (June 8, 1984), p. 1.

70Dorothy Fontana, "Background to the Fall of Hua Guofeng," *Asian Survey*, Vol. XXII, No. 3 (March 1982), p. 245.

71Clarke, "Political Power and Authority," p. 240.

72Deng Xiaoping, "On the Reform," *BR*, No. 40 (October 3, 1983), p. 14.

73Deng Xiaoping, "On the Reform," *BR*, No. 41 (October 10, 1983), p. 21.

74H. Lyman Miller, "China's Administrative Revolution," *Current History* (September 1983), p. 273.

75"Nationwide Check-Up to Improve Postal Work," *CD* (December 23, 1984), p. 1.

76"Iron Rice Bowl Debate," *CD* (June 16, 1983), p. 4.

77Deng Xiaoping (August 18, 1980), in *BR*, No. 40 (October 3, 1983), p. 20.

78For an English translation, see *The Selected Works of Deng Xiaoping, 1975–1982* (San Francisco: China Books and Periodicals Inc., 1984).

79Article 16, 1982 Party Constitution.

80Except from *People's Daily*, in *CD* (August 27, 1984), p. 4; and "Machine-building Industry Set for Major Shake-up," *CD* (August 23, 1984), p. 1.

81For excellent articles on both the 1956 and the post-1979 organizational and functional reforms in the financial sector, see Hiroyuki Imai, "China's New Banking System: Changes in Monetary Management," *Pacific Affairs*, Vol. 58, No. 3 (Fall 1985), pp. 451–472; and Carl E. Walter, "Dual Leadership and the 1956 Credit Reforms of the People's Bank of China," *China Quarterly*, No. 102 (June 1985), pp. 277–290.

82"China Seeks More Foreign Cash and New Technology," *CD* (September 12, 1984), p. 1.

83Michael Ng-Quinn, "Deng Xiaoping's Political Reform and Political Order," *Asian Survey*, Vol. XXII, No. 12 (December 1982), p. 1201.

84Two classics on post-1949 Chinese bureaucracy that analyze the roots of its bureaucratic pathologies in far greater detail than can be done here are: A. Doak Barnett, *Cadres, Bureaucracy and Political Power in Communist China*, with a contribution by Ezra Vogel (New York: Columbia University Press, 1967); and Harding, *Organizing China*.

85The first major Party rectification was in 1942–1943. Held in conjunction with a literary campaign, it targeted "liberalism" and "sectarianism." Rectification campaigns since that time have had a wide variety of targets.

[86]Cadres Advised to Practice Self-Discipline," Hangzhou, *Zheijiang Ribao*, October 31, 1981, p. 1, in *Joint Publications Research Service* No. 79822 (January 8, 1982), *China Report*, No. 256, pp. 45, 46.

[87]"Shanxi Issues Circular on Job Discipline Systems," Taiyuan, Shanxi Provincial Service, December 16, 1981, in *Foreign Broadcasts Information Service*, No. 246 (December 23, 1981), PRC Regional Affairs, pp. R1, 2. Emphasis added.

[88]Hu Qili, referenced in "Quarterly Chronicle and Documentation," *China Quarterly*, No. 102 (June 1985), p. 364.

[89]William A. Joseph, "The Dilemma of Political Reform in China," *Current History* (September 1985), pp. 252–255, 279, 280; and Bo Yibo, referenced in "Quarterly Chronicle and Documentation," *China Quarterly*, No. 102, p. 364.

[90]David S. G. Goodman, "The National CCP Conference of September 1985 and China's Leadership Changes," *China Quarterly*, No. 105 (March 1986), p. 128.

[91]Kenneth Lieberthal, "The Future of Reform in China," *AEI Foreign Policy and Defense Review*, Vol. 6, No. 3 (1986), p. 6.

[92]Joseph, "Dilemma of Political Reform," p. 254.

[93]China Daily Commentator, "Rectification and Reform," *CD* (July 23, 1984), p. 4.

[94]Moody, "Political Liberalization," p. 30.

[95]Clarke, "Political Power and Authority," p. 236. Clarke's research indicates how values concerning China's political power are reflected in literature.

[96]Manion, "Cadre Management System," pp. 211, 212.

[97]Harding, *Organizing China*.

[98]Michel Chossudovsky, *Toward Capitalist Restoration? Chinese Socialism After Mao* (New York: St. Martin's Press, 1986), p. 14.

[99]Lieberthal, "Reform in China," p. 5 and note 16.

[100]Roberta Martin, *Party Recruitment in China: Patterns and Prospects: A Study of the Recruitment Campaign of 1954–1956 and Its Impact on Party Expansion Through 1980.* (Occasional Papers of the East Asia Institute, Columbia University, N.Y., 1981), pp. 13–17. See Martin's book in its entirety for excellent detail on recruitment policies.

[101]Ibid., p. 31.

[102]"Accepting More Students Into Party," *CD*, July 23, 1984, p. 4.

[103]China Youth (Zhongguo qingnian), No. 9 (September 1979), pp. 2, 3, in Stanley Rosen, "Prosperity, Privatization and China's Youth," *Problems of Communism* (March–April 1985), p. 8.

[104]"Getting in Step with Dancing," *CD* (August 9, 1984), p. 4.

[105]For fascinating detail on the Communist Youth League, see Rosen, "Prosperity, Privatization and China's Youth," pp. 1–28.

[106]"Younger Officials Enliven Country," *CD* (September 12, 1984), p. 4.

[107]"Young Cadres Key to China's Future," *CD* (September 26, 1984), p. 4.

[108]China Daily Commentator, "Young and Able Leaders," *CD* (September 4, 1984), p. 4; and "Younger People Put in Leading Posts," *BR* (July 7, 1986), p. 7. Frankly, these Chinese sources are somewhat suspect: It is unbelievable that over half of all cadres down to the county level are college educated, when less than 6% of all high school graduates have ever attended college, and when the vast majority of those who did have degrees in science, engineering, or medicine, and are so employed.

[109]China Daily Commentator, "Young and Able Leaders," *CD* (September 4, 1984), p. 4.

[110]Manion, "Cadre Management System," p. 232.

[111]Shi Zhongquan, "The Cultural Revolution and the Struggle Against Bureaucracy," p. 20.

[112]The problems arising from an underdeveloped educational system are exacerbated by the fact that in China, so much time in the educational system has been spent on political indoctrination. Additionally, the Party has always been suspicious of "bourgeois intellectuals," which has itself prevented the educational system from being of more use. Harding, *Organizing China*, p. 358.

[113]Goodman, "The National CCP Conference of September 1985 and China's Leadership Changes," pp. 124, 125.

[114]Ibid., p. 125.

[115]Lieberthal, "Reform in China," pp. 3, 4.

[116]Goodman, "National CCP Conference," p. 127.

[117]Shi Zhongquan, "The 'Cultural Revolution,' " pp. 19, 20.

Chapter Five
SOCIALIST DEMOCRACY

No definition of democracy can adequately comprise the vast history which the concept connotes. To some it is a form of government, to others a way of social life. Men have found its essence in the character of the electorate, the relation between government and the people, the absence of wide economic differences between citizens, the refusal to recognize privileges built on birth or wealth, race or creed. Inevitably it has changed its substance in terms of time and place. What has seemed democracy to a member of some ruling class has seemed to his poorer fellow citizen a narrow and indefensible oligarchy.[1]

THE MEANING OF "DEMOCRACY"

The term *democracy* has a very different meaning in China from what it means in the West. The Chinese must and do wrestle with the issues of freedom and democracy. But it is China's leaders who decide how much freedom to allow to whom, and when and how to limit it. They often use a vocabulary to discuss these issues similar to that used in the West. But in China, democracy is not only socialist in form; it is also Chinese in form, and the Chinese people's experience of it thus bears little resemblance to ours. Further, the Chinese repeatedly assert that democracy as practiced in Western capitalist countries is hypocritical and manipulated by the capitalist ruling class to serve its own purposes.

For the Chinese Communist Party (CCP), democracy means "socialist democracy," a democracy which represents the interest of the workers and peasants. It does not mean "absolute democracy," or "what the masses say, goes."[2] It certainly does not mean "one person one vote." China's form of government is a "people's democratic dictatorship," represented by the Communist Party. Most importantly, the word democracy is part of the organizational concept of "democratic centralism"—the heart of socialist democracy. There are, however, many institutions, concepts and processes in the People's Republic of China (PRC) that lack the barest hints of even "socialist" democracy.

To the extent that either we or the Chinese claim that the PRC practices a form of democracy, how can that claim be justified? It is, in fact, a one-party state; the people did not have a choice of candidates to elect for their representatives until 1980, and even now, all candidates must first be approved by the Communist Party. China has been ruled by men, not by law, and there has been no true separation of powers or system of checks and balances to guarantee that the government does not abuse its power. Furthermore, although there has been greater diversity within the press and a wide spectrum of publications in the 1980s, China still lacks freedom of the press and of speech.

The development of Western democratic theory indicates that the PRC could still in some respects fit within the framework of democracy. The two major Western democratic traditions were, after all, in conflict from the beginning over the most crucial issues of democracy: liberty and equality. The Anglo-American democratic tradition gave primary stress to liberty, whereas the French tradition emphasized equality. The dilemma of democracy has been this: The more freedom, the less equality; and the more equality, the less freedom.[3] While the ordinary person may assume that democracy means both freedom and equality, the fact is that in most polities there is a conspicuous tradeoff between the two. Most modern democratic political systems are theoretically egalitarian in their political spheres, but they are neither in principle nor in practice egalitarian in their social and economic spheres. They permit freedom at the expense of equality: Freedom to pursue individual ends in income, education, and occupational status seems inevitably to permit some citizens to acquire unequal access to resources with which to influence the political system. Further, recent studies have shown that equality derived from social and economic redistributive policies within a political system has less to do with the degree of democratization than with "the nature of the party system and the kind of party in power."[4]

As a socialist polity, the PRC until the 1980s favored equality over freedom. The Chinese Communists were not alone, however, in their belief that development requires equality, and that economic equality is as necessary as political equality. Western theorists of democracy have also held such beliefs. Harold Laski, for example, believed that without economic equality, "no political mechanisms will of themselves enable the common man to realize his wishes and interests. Economic power is the parent of political power." De Tocqueville was convinced that, because equality was a necessary principle of democracy, the state had an obligation to minimize inequalities among people.[5] De Tocqueville argued, moreover, that if a state could not divide the sources of economic gain equally among its citizenry, it would be unable to maintain a democratic form of government.[6] In practice, of course, Western democracies have also stressed the importance of economic equality. In the case of France, which has been influenced by the Napoleonic codes since the nineteenth century, the system of primogeniture was eliminated in favor of equal distribution of property among *all* the children of deceased parents. The graduated income tax in the United States and the inheritance tax in Great Britain have likewise aimed at a more equal distribution of wealth.

The Chinese Communist leadership has justified its interference in social and economic arrangements (and later in political structures) to rid China of vast inequalities on the grounds that those who possessed greater socioeconomic power used it to exploit those without power. Therefore, China's leaders first eliminated the basis for socioeconomic exploitation by redistributing property. Then, in the 1960s they attacked many who had parlayed their better *political* status into unequal access to power and who used it to exploit the people. In the PRC, concern for equality usually overrode concern for freedom. Thus, the *theory* of China's socialist democratic system is not far outside the mainstream of Western democratic theory after World War II in its major emphasis on equality of economic benefits: "Social income must definitely be used to prevent undue disparity between man and man in all the major activities upon which the good life depends. . . . The good life is unattainable where there are wide economic disparities between classes."[7]

Nevertheless, how the Chinese state interferes, and the degree to which the state and one-party system actually represent the people's interests, raise serious questions about the PRC's position within the democratic tradition. The PRC's "democratic dictatorship,"[8] which is far more dictatorial than democratic, is the crucial factor distancing China from the Western democratic tradition. The history of dictatorships indicates that over the long run they degenerate, to the detriment of everyone but those in the ruling class.[9]

At certain times, the Chinese have defined democracy in ways unfamiliar to the West. During China's "democracy movement" of 1978–1979, for example, the term "democracy" merely became the new slogan to replace "revolution" (the prevailing slogan for the years between 1966 and 1976).

According to one commentator in the unofficial[10] press, it [democracy] implied the immediate 'withering away' of party control in basic-level organizations. Others conceived of it as Liberal Democracy, Capitalism or Christianity, and even, as in one case, all three together. Both the United States and

Yugoslavia were suggested as models for democracy for emulation. Wei Jing-sheng defined it in terms of maximum individual freedom and non-Marxist socialism. . . . However, for the most part, *any future democracy was conceived of as being under the leadership of the CCP*, even though at times this might entail some amazing contradictions.[11]

Understandably, young Chinese, with little exposure to writings of democratic theorists, and no experience with the practice of liberal democracy, would be confused as to the meaning of democracy.[12] But even those who have lived in or studied Western liberal democracies in the 1980s have not necessarily understood the meaning of democracy in practice. The few who did have had no conception of how democracy might become meaningful to China—what aspects of democracy that China could successfully adopt, and how China would institutionalize democracy.[13]

The values of liberty, equality, democracy, and dictatorship are, for the Chinese, values laden with connotations different from those in the West. They are also values in conflict with each other. As sure as China's "socialist transformation" in the early 1950s led to greater equality, but less freedom, so the economic liberalization of the 1980s has led to greater freedom, but has threatened the very foundation of equality. Comparative development studies in the West have noted the incompatibility between an emphasis on social and economic equality and economic development.[14] The Chinese leadership has witnessed this correlation in China's experience, and it has in the 1980s chosen to favor more rapid economic development at the expense of the maintenance of "pure egalitarianism," a concept now in disgrace in the PRC.

THE PRACTICE OF SOCIALIST IDEOLOGY WITHIN CHINESE CULTURAL CONTEXT LIMITS DEMOCRATIC DEVELOPMENT

Given the different conception of what is at stake when "democracy" or "dictatorship" are spoken of in the PRC, what, then, are the issues that have and have not been resolved? Although liberal democracy is at odds with Chinese "socialist democracy," China's leaders have done much to realize certain democratic processes and institutions, if not a democratic *system*, that make sense for China. They have institutionalized procedures that guarantee levels of democracy heretofore not experienced by China's peasants and workers. There is, however, some question whether these practices are actually "democratic" in nature: Is the forced participation of the Chinese people in small groups, struggle sessions, mass campaigns, and a one-party system of election and congresses, "democratic" in a meaningful sense? Is it democratic in either its process or its results? And is "democratic centralism," except in periods of extreme decentralization, more than an ideological cloak for centralized despotic Party control?

Without advocating wholesale cultural relativism, it is only fair to judge China's progress in institutionalizing democracy in the context of how far the Chinese leaders *want* democracy to go and in which direction; in the context of their other objectives (such as stability and order, Party infallibility, and economic development); and against the background of the level of democracy which China experienced under Nationalist rule until 1949. Whatever democratic rights or procedures might have existed on the books, endless war and internal chaos combined with the corruption and elitism of the Nationalist Party (KMT) under Chiang Kai-shek to produce a despotic regime. Few people beyond China's privileged economic, political, and military elites felt that the democratic process was available to them under Nationalist rule.

In the early twentieth century, China was unprepared for a democratic system, at least in the Western mold, and there are clear historical and cultural reasons for this. The Chinese had a patriarchal culture, in which values of superior-inferior and subordination prevailed over those of equality; an historical predisposition toward official secrecy; a fear of officials and official power; a traditional repugnance for courts, lawyers, and formal laws, resulting in a legal system inadequately developed to defend democratic rights; and an historical legacy of authoritarianism. Therefore, of the three sets of factors that have hindered the Chinese Communists' ability to define and implement socialist democracy, it is the cultural factors that have provided the context, the outer parameters within which ideological-political and developmental factors have operated.[15] As noted in Chapter Two, introducing Western democratic values and institutions into China from the nineteenth century on had met with insurmountable obstacles, not the least of which were the institutionalized authoritarian relationships between the people and officials and the lack of any experience in the practice of democracy.

Developmental factors (such as illiteracy) which China has in common with other developing countries curtailed the Chinese people's ability to understand and practice democracy,[16] but compared to political and ideological factors, they have been relatively insignificant. The development of even "socialist" democracy has been hindered by political power struggles and by the leadership's fear that greater participation by the people would be detrimental to its own continued control, and to China's stability, security, and development. Indeed, the acting out of "democratic" practices since 1949, in such instances as the 1956–1957 "Hundred Flowers" Campaign, the Cultural Revolution, and the "democracy movement" of 1978–1979, has reinforced the leadership's concern that when the Communist Party does not strictly control the expression of democratic forces, it leads directly to chaos, instability, even anarchy, and a threat to the very existence of Party rule and leadership in China.

With hindsight, it seems inevitable that the combination of a culture with strongly authoritarian, antidemocratic impulses, together with an insecure and unstable political leadership, would result in a distorted implementation of socialist democracy. Socialist democracy provides for laws to protect the people's rights and for institutions to practice democratic centralism and represent the people's interests. But the political leadership, threatened both from within and without, distorted the intended thrust of socialist democracy by insisting on Party infallibility and hence absolute obedience to the Party, by calling for continued class struggle, and by insisting that there was only one acceptable way to think. Further, the Chinese people themselves, conditioned historically (and most recently by the events of the "ten bad years") to fear chaos more than authoritarian control, have done relatively little since 1949 to press the leadership for more democracy than it chooses to give. Indeed, *the spread of democratic procedures in the 1980s was not a response to popular demands* but the result of the reform leadership's conclusion that greater democratization would serve well its own purposes of political reform and economic modernization.

THE ORGANIZATIONAL AND PROCEDURAL CONCEPTS OF SOCIALIST DEMOCRACY

Democratic Centralism and the Mass Line: The Unresolved Problem

When the CCP redefined democracy in a way that would make it more relevant to China's conditions and more effective as a form of government, it emphasized two main organizational concepts: democratic centralism, and the mass line. All other political maxims derive from these two central principles, which encapsulate the dilemma that the Party leadership has faced since 1949, namely, striking the proper balance between democracy and centralism. Even now, the leadership's search for the proper balance between freedom and discipline reflects its concern with the objectives of maintaining stability, law and order, and rapid development. The leadership has found agreement on the appropriate balance of democracy and centralism to be elusive. Until 1979, every swing in the direction of more democracy seemed to be matched by an almost equally marked swing back toward centralism. The swings toward democracy seem to have been propelled by the dominant leadership's belief that its policies were popular enough to let the people participate more, or that its policies (and its own grip on political power) would actually *benefit* from greater democracy. Increased democracy has, in fact, always been orchestrated by the center. The reversals toward centralism appear to have occurred when democracy got out of control, usually because participants stepped beyond the acceptable boundaries of dissent or used democratic channels to promote their own self-interests, which were antithetical to the leadership's objectives.

In 1978–1979, as the pragmatists or "reform faction" under Deng Xiaoping's leadership consolidated their control and attempted to point China in the direction of more democracy, rationales for greater democracy were developed. Some of these rationales were: A belief that the people's support of the "four modernizations" program was so strong, that if they had more institutionalized access to democratic procedures, such as elections, they would vote out the "leftists" who opposed the reformers' policies, and vote in better leaders; and a belief that if the people had more say in policy, they might engage in production more enthusiastically. More than this, the leadership planned for formalized democratic procedures to replace class struggle as the mainstay of the political process. Finally, the dominant leadership hoped that further democratization would create the appropriate environment for its goals of adopting the world's most advanced managerial techniques and scientific technology by providing access to education and political power to those with talent.[17] But greater democracy did not mean Western democracy; and democratic practices continued to be limited by centrally formulated policies, the practices of middle- and lower-level cadres, and China's traditional culture.

Democratic Centralism and the Mass Line: The Theory

Democratic centralism[18] is the organizational principle of all mass organizations, and it is premised on unity and acceptance of Party policy being achieved by guided discussion in small groups. Democratic centralism, acknowledging that political organizations must have roots among the people, takes the broad masses as its base, but those at the lower levels submit to orders from those at the highest levels; and the individual submits to organizational discipline. The "democracy" in democratic centralism is defined as "the regular convening of congresses at all levels and free discussion before decisions are reached." "Centralism" means the minority submits to the majority; and the lower levels obey the higher levels. In operation, the elements of democracy and centralism are supposed to be kept in balance.[19]

The *mass line* is the principle stating the Party's dependence on the masses and the need for the Party to keep in constant contact with the masses. It is also "the method by which Chinese Communist Party policies are executed through a synthesis of Party leadership and mass action."[20] The major concept of the mass line is "from the masses, to the masses."

> This means summing up . . . the views of the masses . . . then taking the resulting ideas back to the masses, explaining and popularizing them until the

masses embrace the ideas as their own, stand up for them and translate them into action. . . . Then it is necessary once more to sum up the views of the masses . . . [etc.].[21]

In theory all policies originate with the masses, but the Party makes the final decisions because of its superior knowledge and experience. Once a policy is decided on, it must then be taken back to the masses for execution.

The mass line requires extensive and intensive mass participation in the political process. This participation is meant to raise the political consciousness of the people and increase their willingness to accept and execute Party policy, not to encourage popular interference in the formulation of policy. As Mao stated, "Unless they are conscious and willing, any kind of work that requires [the masses'] participation will turn out to be a mere formality and will fail."[22]

Democratic Centralism and the Mass Line: The Practice

Ever since the post-1978 economic reforms, the concepts of democratic centralism and the mass line have been all but defunct, except in the state-controlled industrial workplace. As will be noted below, in the countryside there is little to distribute and little to decide that would benefit from the use of the mass line. In many respects, the market place has made democratic centralism and the mass line irrelevant by removing the key control role of the state. Further, by the early 1980s, direct elections up to the county level and elected village councils replaced local Party and state functionaires as the key element in China's socialist democracy.

Nevertheless, for some thirty years, the implementation of democratic centralism and the mass line illustrated how the Chinese Communists attempted to find a balance between freedom and discipline. In practice, most of the living and working conditions of the people were determined at the lowest level (the production teams or villages in the countryside, factory work teams, and residential small groups in the cities). Some of the issues on which these groups have had a substantial impact include local budget allocations to cover production costs, investment, welfare and services; determination of work assignments, pay scales and "workpoint" systems within each unit; the management of the work unit's welfare and service programs, schools, and health care facilities; the mediation of disputes; and the "resolution or transmission upward of mass grievances and suggestions concerning all of the above."[23] At the lowest levels, leaders were chosen by other members from within the work unit, and they usually pressed for local interests at higher levels. They were not the mere tools of a totalitarian state.

Rural democracy

In traditional societies, such as those that exist in China's rural hinterland, "perhaps ninety percent of the governmental decisions affecting a villager are made at the village level and ten percent at the national level." While modernization may bring the ratio closer to fifty-fifty, villagers' political participation is confined to the village level.[24] In China, where close to 80 percent of the population still lives in villages, it is important to consider this fact when assessing the meaning of the peasants' participation in the democratic process.

According to the mass line, the leadership *sums up* the masses' viewpoints in a single policy. The leadership does not formulate a variety of proposals for the people to consider, debate, and choose from. Nevertheless, the central leadership's proposed policy is not in any sense final until the people have implemented it. The key here is how to turn general and often vague policies formulated at the center into specific actions for the people at the lowest levels. Thus, the policy of "In agriculture, learn from Dazhai" required each locality to consider the various concrete ways in which that policy could be realized: What did Dazhai mean for how the fields were prepared and how much fertilizer was used? Once that was decided, the people had to determine who would perform which task, what funds would be used, what machinery purchased, who would maintain the machinery, and so on. It is at this level, of policy specification and implementation, that the people have had the greatest say over crucial decisions affecting their daily lives. Thus, central policy directives have tended to be "clearer about the goals of the policy than the concrete forms which it would take in particular situations" because of the leadership's awareness that turning "policy into action must involve the masses' discretion, based on their knowledge of objective conditions."[25]

Until the introduction of the household contract responsibility system and the breaking up of collective ownership of the land after 1978, the mass line was most suitable for the countryside. There the cadres and the peasants were in close daily contact, a situation which facilitated continuous feedback. Repeated "summing up," "consolidation," and "rectification" campaigns among the rural peasantry bore witness to the leadership's belief that "the masses must be involved directly in policy evaluation." Such a view implies that suggestions and criticism from local cadres and the people frequently led to changes in policies, and that policy decisions were provisional in nature. Perhaps, in fact, the leadership reversed its policies not just because of power struggles or policy failures, but also because it had indeed listened to the people.[26]

Although the role of the cadre is to sum up the masses' viewpoints and report them to the center, if a consensus is lacking, the local cadre is supposed to exercise vigorous leadership to achieve one. Obviously a thin line runs between bullying the people into the leadership's predetermined policies and guiding them until they agree to those policies. But often, cadres have been pressured to persuade the people of the top leadership's wisdom, even in the face of extreme opposition. For example, the peasants' protests against such Great Leap Forward policies as close planting, double and triple cropping, and deep ploughing were ignored by local cadres because they were afraid they would be accused of "lagging behind the masses." This and other cases indicate that Chinese cadres have not always lived up to the ideals of the mass line.[27]

When a clear consensus already existed, the brigade or team members as a group might make a decision. This was particularly true in straightforward cases, cases with relatively insignificant consequences, and cases where the issue seemed to be fair and egalitarian. For example, in a case involving "classification of people into one of four categories for the purpose of grain distribution," the four categories were "strongest male workers, other men, women, and nonlaborers (such as older people and children)." In another case where a clear consensus existed, a production team decided to remove from office a team leader in charge of sideline production.[28]

Usually, however, consensus did not already exist. Higher-level authorities, local cadres, or team members, therefore, had to place an issue on the agenda for discussion. Although team cadres usually set the agenda for team meetings, peasants could add their own items to the agenda. A proposal to address the issue was then discussed until a consensus was reached. Thus, according to the informant from one rural production team,

> When sewing machine coupons came down to the team, people found out about it very quickly. They would immediately start discussing how to distribute them. They'd discuss this while working. . . . They would tell the team head how they felt, and he would concentrate their opinions. Then when it came time to do the distribution, he'd suggest a method and get everyone's approval.[29]

In another case,

> The brigade cadres were actively pushing the campaign to learn from Dazhai. . . . The team committee decided on the specific measures to be used in learning from Dazhai. In our case, they decided to try for fertilizer accumulation and filling in streams. The team committee decided this and then called a meeting to clear it with the masses. The masses then discussed which streams to fill in. The old peasants also suggested ideas (on how to learn from Dazhai) to the team committee which were adopted. For example, some old peasants suggested draining out the fish pond twice a year instead of just once.[30]

The point that comes across most strongly from interviews with peasant refugees is that the central leadership, although it sets policy, leaves implementation procedures up to the peasants. When the central leadership has forced policy implementation procedures on them, rural policies have often failed, in no small part as a result of their sabotaging policy. The peasants are quite conscious of their greater responsibility since the Communist takeover, and of their making decisions now that used to be made by landlords.[31] Nevertheless, the freedom to make many decisions that affect daily life must be viewed within the context of the center's broad policy decisions. After all, once the central leadership has decided that all agricultural producers' cooperatives must be merged into communes, the only thing left for the villagers to be democratic about is how to implement the policy.

Urban workplace democracy: Decisionmaking and democracy in "units" (danwei)

Three different systems of leadership function within all state-run organizations in China, whether factories, hotels, restaurants, stores, or "units" (such as schools, research institutes, and museums). The three systems are: the Party, the administration, and the mass organization. In theory, each of the three represents the members' interests to the central leadership through a democratic process. In practice, the Party has tended to dominate all three systems of leadership.

Mass Organizations. The "mass organizations" that exist in almost all state-run units are supposed to represent the interests of the workers to the top leadership in the work unit, as against those of the administrative and Party hierarchies. The decisions made at the top will then be explained to lower levels, and, in accordance with "centralism," the minority will submit to the majority, and the lower levels will obey the higher levels. In practice, however, the primary purpose of mass organizations is to provide an important network for integrating Communist Party members with non-Party members so that the former may help "guide" the latter. They are an important element, moreover, in the overall Party propaganda effort. During "mass campaigns," they organize discussion groups, criticism/self-criticism sessions, study groups, and if necessary, mass demonstrations. Mass organizations are almost invariably led by Communist Party members.

Trade unions are a good example of how a mass organization operates. The Western view of a trade union is one of an organization that fights for workers' rights: higher pay, shorter work hours, longer vacations, better working conditions, improved safety, more participation in managerial decisions, and more benefits. But China's official ideologues dismiss this perspective on trade unions because it assumes a condition of Western capitalist societies, which is that workers are in conflict with capitalist managers. From a Communist perspective (as in the case of the Polish Communist Party's view of Solidarity in Poland), the Party is the vanguard of the working class, and trade unions are simply mass organizations of the working class led by the Communist Party. Because the Party controls management, the workers do not need to be represented as a group distinct from either the Party or management. There is obviously no need for them ever to strike.[32] Given this presupposition, the role trade unions can play is constricted. Chinese workers, who are fully aware of the trade union's limited power, rarely participate in the union, even if they become members.

What, then, does a trade union do? Basically, it provides a social club for the members of the collective or unit. The club has a room within the work unit for such recreational activities as chess, TV, cards, and Ping-Pong. Occasionally, the union might organize a sightseeing trip for its members. And, since the modernization program in the early 1980s began to emphasize the importance of education and technical expertise for getting ahead, unions have taken on the responsibility for organizing and running night schools for their members.[33]

Trade unions cannot interfere in political affairs or with policy-making, either inside their units or at the national level. If they do, they will find themselves in serious trouble. The national Party leader of trade unions in the 1950s, who tried to put substance into them by demanding satisfaction of workers' needs, was summarily removed.[34] The only exceptions to the powerlessness of trade unions occurred during the Cultural Revolution, when they "seized power" over factories. When in the early 1980s, a workers' union in Shandong Province attempted to imitate Poland's Solidarity movement by confronting the Party with the workers' demands, it was immediately crushed. Perhaps this was why the 1982 Constitution expressly removed the workers' right to strike.

It must be kept in mind, however, that most Chinese workers do not think of unions in the same way that workers in capitalist countries do. In fact, they probably had little awareness of what trade unions in other countries did until the All-China Federation of Trade Unions resumed its membership in the International Labor Organization in 1971.

Other mass organizations have also learned from bitter experience that they can only function as subsidiary organs of the Party, not as personal power bases. When the leader of the Chinese Youth League in the 1950s tried to strengthen the League and to use it as a power base, he too found his power eclipsed. In fact, of all China's mass organizations, only the Women's Federation has never pushed for policies that would challenge the Party's authority, or tried to become an independent power vis-à-vis the Party, undoubtedly because it is usually the wives of China's top Party leaders who have run it! Yet, in spite of overall compliance with Party policy, the Women's Federation has constantly lobbied, with limited success, for improving the social and economic position of women. Undoubtedly Party approval of the Women's Federation derives in no small part from Party confidence in its leadership, and perhaps also from the pressure on socialists to recognize women as equals.

Workers' congresses, which are the trade unions' representative bodies, were originally experimented with beginning in 1957. The Chinese abandoned them during the Cultural Revolution, but in 1978, Deng Xiaoping reestablished them. By the mid-1980s, they were functioning in about 200,000 of China's state-owned industrial, transportation, and communication enterprises at and above the county level. Their purpose is to participate in democratic management and to embody the Party's mass line. The reform leadership believes that democratizing the leadership system in China's enterprises will increase productivity and improve management. But an assessment in the mid-1980s of the congress system indicated that it had failed to democratize worker-management relations in 75 percent of the enterprises in which it functioned.[35]

The powers of the factory workers' congresses are largely limited to the right to discuss and make recommendations. The congresses discuss methods for implementing their respective enterprise's production plans and programs; they debate proposed wage adjustments; and they decide matters relating to the workers' welfare. In some factories where the workers' congresses have been successful, they have taken over all matters concerning welfare.[36] This considerably diminishes the power of the factory director to use welfare benefits, such as the allocation of apartments, to reward and punish workers, and thereby contributes to the democratization of worker-management relations.

The workers' congresses are supposed to function as follows: Workers, many of whom are members of the grass-roots trade unions that form working bodies of these congresses, cast votes to choose leaders from their respective work groups, sections, and workshops. Before the election, a list of candidates for directors and deputy directors of their enterprises is presented. This list is compiled on the basis of opinion polls. The secretariat of the congress then presents the qualifications of those candidates recommended by the workers' representatives to the congress.[37] As fully documented in the 1981 "Provisional Regulations Concerning Congresses of Workers and Staff Members in State-Owned Industrial Enterprises" (Article 5), however, the next higher organ must approve and appoint all such democratically elected cadres. The center maintains control in another way: Although workers' congresses may offer suggestions that differ with a decision or directive from the higher organ of the enterprise, "If the higher organ decides to uphold the original decision or directive . . . the workers' congress is obliged to carry out the decision or directive."[38] Furthermore, although the director of an enterprise must present work reports regularly to the workers' congress and submit to supervision by the congress (Article 6), it is up to the Party discipline inspection departments and state law-enforcement departments to take action if the director has acted improperly (Article 4).

Thus, the workers' congresses are more than advisory and supervisory institutions, functioning as "organs of power by which the workers and staff members directly run their factories and supervise the cadres"; but their control is relative, not absolute, since Party committees oversee and control the workers' congresses, and since their "democratic" acts are always subject to reversal by the next higher level.[39]

The timing of the promulgation of the June 1981 "Regulations" may cynically be interpreted as a response to the labor unrest in Poland, an attempt to outline workers' rights, and the explicit limitation on those rights. More positively, they may be seen as part of China's ongoing drive to modernize and to improve enterprise leadership by subjecting it to some worker supervision. The key question here is whether this step toward a broadening of democratic rights of workers will be solidified over the next decade.

The Administrative Leadership.   The second system of leadership in an organization, factory, or unit is the administrative group, which is in charge of day-to-day administration. Generally, the administrators meet two times a week; but during major campaigns, they have met more frequently. In consultation with the trade union leadership, it discusses financial matters, assignments of work to various staff members, working conditions and safety, and managerial leadership. As with mass organizations, however, this is done under the leadership of the third tier of leadership, namely, the Party. The administrative system of leadership, like the mass organizations, is part of the mass education efforts of the Party.

Although administrators are important for day-to-day management, in Western terms they approach their task obliquely. That is, at their meetings they study the latest editorial in the *People's Daily*, speeches by important leaders, and the current slogans. Then they try to apply the sense or "spirit" (*jingsheng*) of these articulated ideas to their daily administrative work. Alternatives that would challenge the spirit of the Party, as presented in the *People's Daily*, will not be discussed. As noted in Chapter Four, from the late 1950s until the 1980s the administrative and Party hiera rchies of leadership within organizations were, in any event, virtually indistinguishable. The Party interfered with administration, or more precisely, usurped the administrative leadership's functions as its own. This is still one of the most crucial unresolved issues facing China in the 1980s.

In addition to meeting with the trade union leadership, the administrative leadership meets with representatives from the trade union's representative body, the workers' congress. The workers' congress meets only twice a year, but trade union leaders discuss the resolutions of the congress with the administrative leadership during the year.

Problems arising from workplace leadership system

This system of three parallel hierarchies of leadership in the workplace has led to many problems over the years. The Chinese leadership has come to recognize the ill-effects of ignoring the workers' inputs into the decision-making process, perhaps as much the result of exposure to Japanese and Western worker–management relations (and their problems) as the result of self-realization. By the mid-1980s, the Chinese were for the first time experimenting with true worker participation in the administrative system of leadership, and offering workers profit-sharing contracts and the opportunity to buy stock in their own enterprises. These innovations suggest that the central leadership truly believes that greater worker participation might generate more productivity, and more effective management.

An additional problem of three parallel and overlapping leaderships is that it often causes mix-ups. Although the Party has tended to interfere with and control the other two leadership systems, it need not take blame for problems because any managerial decision is submitted to all three leadership systems. As the *People's Daily* put it, since the factory director lacks the power to manage, a factory may incur losses due to interference by those (that is, the Party) who are ignorant about factory management. For this reason, by the mid-1980s the leadership began to institutionalize a "responsibility system" for factory directors, to give them "managerial autonomy in production." This would not, the Party argued, weaken Party leadership. Rather, the responsibility system would permit the Party secretaries more time to attend to the implementation of Party policy in a factory while simultaneously making managerial administrators responsible when problems occurred.[40] This line of reasoning is an obvious sop to the Party hacks who, because of the leadership reorganization and the responsibility system, are losing a substantial amount of their power.

Demands for Greater Democracy

How much do ordinary Chinese workers and peasants care about participating more broadly in the political process, either in the workplace or in the political system? It would be naive to assume that anyone who could gain more power over his or her own life and the allocation of scarce resources would not want it. But not everyone is equally discontent with whatever system one lives under. And many people, although not particularly happy, would have little to say if permitted more freedom. Nevertheless, we must dismiss our notions of the "politically inactive and apathetic citizen" who inhabits Western democracies and contemplate the nearly total, if involuntary, participation of Chinese citizens in the political process. Under Communism, the people have been compelled to participate in the political system on a weekly, and sometimes a daily and even hourly basis. No one need participate more than the "prescribed minimum" to keep his or her record clean, although that minimum has fluctuated dramatically over time since 1949. Those who have wanted to become members of the Chinese Youth League, and thence members of the Chinese Communist Party, have, however, had to be political activists. As one study of émigrés from China indicates, the "lukewarm middle" of apathetic citizens—those who do the minimum necessary to fend off charges of inadequate political participation—constitute some 80 to 90 percent of the entire population. The rest are either "activist" or "backward" elements.[41]

Still, a relatively limited interest in active participation in the political system by the majority of the population is common to many political systems, especially in those long accustomed to democratic traditions. (Witness the problem Western liberal democracies have in getting out the vote on election day.) In China, the people may have even less interest because they perceive their participation as ineffective in getting what they want for themselves. For that purpose, they have found that under-the-table gift-giving to, and entertainment of, local officials, together with developing a "web of connections," are far more effective. Chinese peasants and workers seem inclined to believe that policies change only when higher-level officials mandate it, not in response to popular pressure.

Thus, above the local level most Chinese probably feel that their participation is meaningless, or that serious involvement may lead to serious trouble. For the foreseeable future, memories of mandatory and often distasteful participation in the numerous campaigns and movements from the 1950s through the 1970s will still give political participation a negative connotation, with the result that an active political participant is often regarded with deep suspicion.

THE INSTITUTIONAL FORMS OF SOCIALIST DEMOCRACY

Parties

On paper, China has provided for institutionalized democracy ever since it promulgated its first Party constitution in 1954. "Democratic parties" are permitted to function as independent organizations, have "political freedom," and "make their own decisions." It is, however, expressly stated that they must cooperate with and be under the leadership of the CCP. This leadership entails decisions on "the line, principles and policies" which the democratic parties must follow.[42] Such a broad definition of the power of the CCP to guide all the other parties really leaves few if any aspects of the guaranteed "political freedom" to the "democratic parties."

The activities of the half dozen democratic parties mesh with the CCP's goals. In accordance with the post-1978 "four modernizations" line, the democratic parties undertook special tasks to modernize science and technology. They have established spare-time schools, short-term lecture courses, nursery-kindergartens with accelerated programs for China's best and brightest, and even a university. But the average size of each of these parties ranges from under 10,000 to no more than 50,000. The CCP alone has over 40 million members![43] Although political reform to further democratize the leadership and electoral system has thus far done little to enhance the importance of the democratic parties,[44] the leaders of some of the democratic parties by the late 1980s privately voiced strong hopes that one day they would be able to gain control over the leadership through an electoral victory.

Almost by default, if intellectuals joined any political party before the 1980s, it would be a democratic party, for they were rarely accepted into the CCP. These parties have not, however, functioned as competing units for leadership in China, nor as channels for political dissidence. In fact, they provide little more than a supplement to, and expansion of, Communist Party policies into other sectors, and they draw together in their memberships certain select types of patriotic intellectuals. In this respect, they provide a thin gloss of "democratic" practice, but in no sense are they truly independent political parties. Their leaders, in fact, are always members of the Chinese Communist Party! There has never really been any question, then, of a multiparty system since 1949. The control of democratic parties by the CCP has been a settled issue in Chinese politics from the beginning.

China's pre-1949 legacy of political chaos and the continued existence of a strong Confucian tradition, which emphasizes harmony and discourages competition, may mean that the Chinese people do not find the Western practise of true multiparty competition appealing; for, out of fear that competition may disintegrate into chaos and disunity, they may far prefer a one-party system. The Chinese Communist conception of socialist democracy has itself rested on a noncompetitive and often authoritarian pattern of decisionmaking, but one cannot assume that the broad Chinese masses (if not the small intellectual minority) have felt uncomfortable with it. Indeed, since they have never really experienced true democracy, the Chinese people may not feel drawn to it, at least not in its Western form.

Political culture, especially the desire to avoid conflict, has affected the form socialist democracy has taken in China. Organizational means, such as elections or the separation of powers, to institutionalize social conflict have eluded the Chinese. "The Leninist vision identifies the Party with a moral truth that has the material force to triumph in history. This relegates conflict to issues of fundamental principle and denies it a positive role in the world of everyday politics."[45]

It is most unlikely that China will ever have a true multiparty system as long as it insists on adherence to the "four basic principles," particularly the principle of the Communist Party's infallibility. But what we may see is the opening up of the electoral system to greater participation by those who are not chosen from the top down by the old-guard Communist Party members. This, in turn, may mean an opening up of the political system to new political forces who accept the core of socialist values but differ on the fringes. The central leadership will not openly condone factionalism within the CCP, however, for it continues to live in fear of a "disloyal opposition." But as the leadership further consolidates its power and feels more secure, it is more likely to consider debate below the central level as beneficial to the formulation of better policy. Thus, it may countenance growing diversity within the Party itself. A realistic scenario for the future is two or more groups that represent different strategies and viewpoints actually functioning as de facto political parties within what is called the Communist Party. In fact, the existence since the mid 1980s of two groups of "reformers" in the central leadership may be seen as a step in this direction.

Elections

In a two-party or multiparty system, the electoral process is an important element of democracy. Parties must appeal to the voters on the basis of their proposed programs. Individual party candidates must make an additional appeal to the electorate based on their personal qualifications and previous performance. If either the candidates or the parties themselves disappoint or deceive the voters, the electorate may at a regularly scheduled time for elections be able to count on their right to vote in new candidates. This type of electoral system offers both the right to choose representatives and an opportunity for further inputs because of the representatives' desire to be reelected.

The electoral procedures in liberal democratic polities, then, tend to reflect the overall *purposes* of their political systems: the representation of the people's interests and the guarantee that those who hold office are responsible to the electorate. But China's one-party system has had different goals, although these have changed somewhat with the 1979 reforms of the 1953 electoral laws. As with most one-party systems, it was meaningless to discuss elections for the various levels of congresses in China as anything other than a formality for endorsing a slate of candidates chosen by the Chinese Communist Party. Without a truly multiparty system or, until 1980, a choice of candidates from the county level up in the countryside, and from the district level up in the cities, it was pointless for candidates to campaign for election.

More to the point, because the purposes of the Chinese electoral system differ from those in liberal democracies, its electoral procedures also differ. The electoral system's purpose is not to represent the people or ensure responsibility of the leadership to the electorate, but *to allow the Party to rule China*. The people "elect" individuals to the congresses who will serve as a communication link that unifies the center with the lower levels—the provinces, the autonomous regions, the independent municipalities, the counties, and the townships. On the basis of democratic centralism and the mass line, "elected" representatives at the various levels of congresses then return to explain state and Party policies to the people and ensure their correct implementation.

Impact of electoral reforms on centralized control

Unlike multiparty systems, where the party leadership may be ignored and party discipline is difficult to enforce, obedience to the Chinese Communist Party is strictly enforced. Candidates for congresses are chosen by the Party committees at each administrative level and approved by the next higher level. Until 1980, and even now at levels above the county, candidates are not chosen by members of their own constituencies. As a result, congress delegates are not concerned with representing their constituencies' local interests against the interests of the central Party and government. Rather, their best chance of nomination for reelection rests in obedience to Party directives. While 60 percent or more of all representatives to the congresses must be Party members, even those who are not must adhere closely to Party policy. Party members who act incorrectly may, of course, find themselves before the Party disciplinary commission, and they may ultimately be expelled from the Party by its leadership.

Thus, the party and electoral systems are linchpins of the most important tenet in Communist doctrine, namely the Communist Party's infallibility. They ensure that it is the *center* which adjusts the degree of democracy: how much, in what form, when, and for what purpose.

Once the reform leadership gained control over policy, however, it began to open up the electoral system. It did this in two ways. First, it issued a directive in December 1978 entitled "Regulations on the Work in the Rural People's Communes," or, "The New Sixty Articles." These regulations reaffirmed the earlier system of electing team (now replaced by "villagers' groups") cadres by secret ballots at team meetings every two years. Also every two years, peasants could elect delegates to the brigade and commune (now replaced by "township") congresses.[46] In addition, the "New Sixty Articles" abolished the policy of discriminating against landlords and rich peasants and their offspring, thus extending the scope of participation in local elections for the first time since 1949.[47] The reform leadership also promulgated a new Election Law for the National People's Congress, the Local People's Congresses, and the Local People's Government on July 1, 1979. In doing so, it potentially spawned a reopening of the unresolved issue concerning the balance between democracy and centralism by opening up the electoral system to democratizing forces. Although it undertook this risk for its own purposes, the leadership cannot dismiss the possibility that this new electoral system may eventually become an autonomous force with its own independent power base, the electorate, which may challenge the CCP's right to rule.

The Deng Xiaoping leadership believed it could safely involve the people to a greater degree in the electoral process because of the popularity of the "four modernizations" policies, especially in the countryside. The first new elections coincided with the new policy of the "responsibility system," in which individuals and households made production contracts. Although this new system greatly diminished the role of, and the need for, cadres, rapid economic modernization still required effective cadres. For this reason, the leadership saw a distinct advantage in giving more electoral power to the people, who would presumably choose to rid the system of inefficient or leftist cadres who frustrated their own ambitions for a better life. The old system of candidates being nominated from the top down would not be as useful for this purpose; for at least one-half of all middle- and lower-level government and party cadres were either "remnants from the Gang of Four," incompetent, or both. Had candidates to the congresses and local leaders continued to be chosen from the top down, then roughly one-half of all cadres would have continued to represent elements opposed to Deng's reforms. Consequently, putting greater electoral power into the hands of the people at the county and district level would serve to create a more efficient, competent, and pro-reform cadre system, as county and district congresses choose county and district governmental officials.

Greater legal and procedural safeguards

The 1979 Election Law offers the people far greater legal and procedural safeguards: more than one candidate per position,[48] the direct election of delegates up to the county people's congresses, the right of provincial congresses to pass local legislation, and a nominating process more open to popular participation. Further, the Election Law, in creating standing committees for the county congresses, added another safeguard. These committees operate throughout the year to oversee county governmental operations when the congresses are not in session. This is a marked improvement over the old system, under which the congresses as complete bodies could hardly supervise the local governments' adherence to the laws as they only met an average of seven to ten days per year.

Greater congressional autonomy and power advances the reform faction's objective of separating legislative from administrative functions, and state functions from Party functions. Allowing the people to select their own delegates to the congresses restricts the Party's ability to interfere in the nominating process. Although the people will presumably continue to elect many representatives who are Party members, this will only happen if the people see them as representing their interests. Manipulation of elections will become more difficult at the local level if there is more than one candidate per position; but in practise, the entrenched power of the Chinese Communist Party and the central role the election committee plays in the nomination process may afford Party candidates a decisive advantage over other candidates.[49]

One rather surprising result of the new electoral system is that *dozens* of individuals have been nominated, by themselves or by others, for each seat available. For example, in the 1984 election for the local people's congress in Peking, 375 representative seats were available, to be chosen from a Communist Party approved list of 600 candidates. But these 600 candidates had been selected from an original pool of several thousand nominees, who were then sifted through by the neighborhood or workplace caucuses to present a manageable number of candidates on the ballot.[50] By offering far too many candidates, however, the system gives the Communist Party leadership at various levels the power to syphon out those nominees it dislikes.

It is difficult to gauge the success of electoral reforms in shifting the balance between democracy and centralism. No national or provincial statistics are available to give comprehensive data on elections at the county level and below. The press and radio do, however, afford a glimpse into numerous cases of how the electoral system actually functions. At the lowest levels, namely the villagers' groups, it appears that as in the past, peasants have as little interest in village elections as have the Party and governmental cadres. Only if there are strong lineage or factional divisions in a village do elections become meaningful to the participants. "Village political culture values harmony and respect for authority. Raucous election meetings, campaigning, and standing for office are simply not a part of this tradition."[51]

The Chinese have reported both dramatic successes for the new election process at the county level, and instances of blatant refusal to implement the reforms correctly. In these cases they blame "local power holders" for obstructing justice. For example, candidates whom the people nominated "were sometimes arbitrarily crossed out or replaced," cadres from outside districts were placed on the ballots as candidates, and in some cases only one candidate per office was nominated. "In one case, the nomination process consisted of an enlarged CCP branch meeting to which only the heads of mass organizations were invited."[52] During the elections some cadres violated the requirement for secret ballots by watching the voters. One county's election results were discarded because "cadres had forged ballots and had added a representative to the congress who was not elected."[53] Unfortunately, the reform leadership has had little choice but to place power to implement the electoral system into the hands of these very people, the "local power holders," who have the most to lose if it is correctly implemented. In particular, if their ability to control the nomination and election process is eclipsed by the new system, their ability to use patronage and to develop a web of mutually interdependent relationships with other cadres will be restricted. Small wonder that lower-level cadres have hesitated in implementing the electoral reforms.

The case of Liang Heng, the non-Marxist student from Hunan Normal University who ran as a candidate for a seat in the Changsha county-level election, as well as the cases of students who contested the Party's control of certain district seats in Beijing, demonstrate that it has not just been "local power holders" who have obstructed the implementation of these political reforms. If candidates "do not love socialism" and do not uphold the "four basic principles," the Party at higher levels will obstruct their right to run for office by refusing to endorse them for election. Students from Beijing University, Beijing Normal University, and Beijing Normal Institute who dared to run against the CCP candidate in district-level elections in 1980 (and lost) were personally reprimanded by the Party's Director of Propaganda. He averred that they had gone beyond supporting modernization and the (intended) attack on "feudalism" to being "bourgeois liberals." Individuals may practice capitalism and democracy, but they cannot denounce socialism. Democratization must take place *within* socialism; it must enrich socialism, not replace it. The students' university Party branches claimed that they were idealistic youth who loved their country, and thereby protected them until they graduated in 1981. But at that time, all three discovered that they were assigned to work in distant Xinjiang Province.

Impact of electoral reforms on power of local cadres

From what we know thus far, then, electoral reforms have only been implemented to the extent they do not challenge those who are implementing them, nor the central Party leadership and its "four basic principles." Although in theory anyone may now run for election to the county congress, apparently few dare to run against the entrenched Party candidate lest they be accused of not loving socialism, or lest they offend the "local power-holders"; for the latter, who in the countryside control opportunities for work in factories, government contracts and the leasing of land, and in the cities control housing, educational and work opportunities, promotions, and much more, still hold considerable power over ordinary people's daily lives. Almost all of those the local election committees select as final candidates to be put on the ballots are either Party members or "model workers." The latter are, by definition, enthusiastic contributors to the "four modernizations" and loyal to the Party. Some articles in the Chinese press have, however, criticized the election committees' choice of so many Party members and "model workers," for they may not be the best representatives of their local constituencies. They are usually too involved with their own work to talk to their constituents about their concerns.[54]

If the new electoral process heightens the people's interest in who is elected to the congresses and the kinds of policies presented, if the people's congresses do not remain mere rubberstamp institutions for legislation formulated at the center, and if elected officials become more autonomous, then the people's congresses may become another channel for more representative "democracy." Thus far, the most significant inroad that the reformed congressional system has made on the prevailing system, in which the people seek special consideration from officials for their own specific problems in following the general policy, and the informal "back door" channels to satisfy individual or small group interests, is the deputies' right to submit motions concerning their constituents' interests to the congress. These motions, of which there may be several hundreds at each district or county level congressional meeting, usually address individual problems in need of an administrative remedy by the government. Deputies have made motions concerning, for example, the need for a construction company building a new building to replace the muddy walkways with finished sidewalks, the need for public restrooms to be regularly serviced by night-soil collectors, or the need for garbage collectors to wait long enough for residents to get their garbage to the curb before leaving. Although motions may have some broader policy pretensions, they still lack the force of law. Instead, a motion is submitted to a motion committee which, if it finds merit in the motion, submits it to the relevant department for action. Nevertheless, the power of congressional deputies to oversee local government and to represent their constituents' interests is growing. Eventually they may be able to seek broad changes in policies.[55]

Potential threat to Party's power

To the extent that the center actually loosens control over who runs as delegates to the congresses, it may be setting the stage for the Party relinquishing some of its power and authority to popularly elected officials. The central Party leaders see curbing patronage and other "feudalistic" forms of bureaucratic behavior as offsetting some of their own loss of central control over that political system that has accompanied greater democratization. If the people begin choosing congressional candidates on the basis of their policies, the elected delegates may become more responsive to their constituents' interests and more independent of Party control. This could lead to a challenge to the Party's leadership, which might result in a reversal of the electoral reforms. But if the Party's overall policies are successful, the Party should do well in elections.[56]

How the Party will cope with these potential threats to its right to rule is an unanswered question. But it is hard to imagine that the Party can resist a trend toward liberalism in politics while mandating freedom in the economic realm. An insistence on competency for economic officials, decentralized economic power, and individual autonomy in economic decision making does not mesh well with an insistence on loyalty to the "four basic principles" among political officials (who often *choose* the economic cadres) as a criterion for office, or with maintaining highly centralized political power. Over the long run such a contradictory policy may generate enough tensions to force the leadership to choose between more liberalization of the political realm, or a reassertion of centralized control in the economic sphere. This is all the more likely because the overlap of the political and economic systems means that economic decisions are inherently political decisions. Economic policies must be approved by the political system. And political leaders bear the blame for economic failures.

Perhaps the most important effect the electoral reforms may have is to move China one step closer to a system of checks and balances. The electoral reforms and related regulations augment the powers accorded to the congresses as state institutions, which will watch, investigate, and control the government's administrative operations. In this sense, they have helped institutionalize socialist democracy. Still, not all Chinese are in agreement that a separation of powers, or checks and balances à la bourgeois democracies, is desirable. Marxist scholars justify the people's congress system as "an historical leap past the bourgeois separation of legislative, judicial and executive functions of government." In their view, the separation of powers in bourgeois democracies "served the historically significant task of breaking up monarchical dictatorships," but it now simply indicates "the struggle for power amongst bourgeois cliques while the majority of people are excluded from power."[57] In China, the deputies to the people's congresses "represent the common interests of the people and are able to work with 'one heart and one mind' to achieve unanimity."[58]

For the immediate future, the broader participation of the people in the electoral system will probably continue to be manipulated by the leadership for its own ends. It is important to realize, however, that those may be "good" ends: Most likely, China's leaders desire greater democratic participation of the people because of their fear that if they do not speak out, bad cadres—cadres as unacceptable to the central leadership as to the ordinary citizen—will gain and maintain power at the expense of China's development. And, the leaders may have come to the conclusion that only the people's meaningful participation in the political system will permit the Party to keep its hands on the pulse of the country.[59]

The Press

As a major propaganda tool, the press is an instrument of state policy in the PRC. Its purpose is to convey information from the center to the lower levels, and to communicate the Party's goals and values. It serves, therefore, not as a forum for various opinions or for reporting news, but rather as an instrument for maintaining China's unity through a common understanding of what the Party's purpose and values are. Thus, statements by China's major Party leaders become the guidelines for determining newsworthy stories. The editorials run in the *People's Daily*, China's major newspaper (which is directly under the control of the Party's Central Committee through its Department of Propaganda),[60] indicate the Party's most recent interpretation of its own policies. As a result, all state and Party cadres must read these editorials to know the Party line.

Because the Party establishes and controls the value content of all the major instruments of propaganda, it is actually the Party, not the state, which controls the press. What kind of information flows to the press and what type of news is "fit to print," therefore, is almost entirely a Party decision. Except for foreign policy, state organs rarely distribute news or information. Party personnel also review all news stories before they are printed. The purpose of news stories is to stir up enthusiasm for the leadership's policies and to indicate how to approach problems in implementing those policies. It is not acceptable to print news items that indicate the inability of the leadership to cope with a failure in policy. Thus, although in the 1980s attacking official corruption became an important part of Party policy, the newspapers have usually only printed stories in which official corruption has been ferreted out and the culprits punished. If the implementation of the "four modernizations policy" is being hindered, the press will indicate who is obstructing it and how, and then will either indicate the course taken to correct the situation, the possible punishments for those found guilty of transgressing state policy, or what cadres might do to ensure that correct policy is followed.

As a result, the Chinese press is profoundly optimistic and upbeat. Problems are getting resolved, successes occur daily, and China is advancing. All problems can be overcome with perseverance and adherence to the Party line. Because of this orientation, the press does not operate as an outside force that, through its penetrating analysis and criticism, helps fine-tune Party policy, or keeps a watchful eye on the abuse of power and poor performance. Until China permits true freedom of the press, the Chinese people will learn from the press largely what the leadership wants it to learn, and nothing more. But the guarantee of a free press is itself dependent upon the development of the legal system to protect that freedom.

The press and the mass media have, however, gained considerable autonomy and power vis-à-vis the Party in the 1980s. This is in part because of the proliferation of magazines, journals, local newspapers, and news bulletins. In 1987, there were 1,574 newspapers and 5,248 magazines and 446 publishing houses. So many publishing houses sprang up, in fact, that it was virtually impossible for the Party to know what was being published. Further, since Party members have tended to be less educated than most intellectuals, they do not necessarily understand the political significance of those books, magazines, and journal articles which they review. This has made Party control over the mass media and even over publication of books increasingly difficult. The State Council in 1987 responded to what it perceived as a need to "unify management" in order to combat "bourgeois liberalization" by setting up a State Administration of News and Publications. It immediately moved to "consolidate" publishing by shutting down a number of newspapers and magazines.[61]

There can be little doubt that greater freedom of speech, which a truly free press ensures, would contribute dramatically to a realization of democracy. Further, a free press helps provide the accurate and timely information necessary for modernization. In the 1950s, when the PRC was a newly established government and desperately needed to control the entire country, a unified, instrumental press, conveying a single set of values and supportive of central policy, unquestionably contributed to the leadership's successes. But in the 1980s, the Chinese moved beyond these most basic needs, to needing the dynamism of a free press for support of both economic modernization and political reform. Yet even the Party's General Secretary, Hu Yaobang, eulogized as a champion of democracy since his precipitous removal in January 1987, insisted that the press act as the Party's mouthpiece.

SOCIALIST DEMOCRACY AND INDIVIDUAL FREEDOM

Cultural and Historical Constraints

The issue of how individual freedom and human rights fit into the larger picture of socialist democracy is intimately connected with two other important aspects of the Chinese polity: the role of intellectuals and the issue of order and control. Order and control are a constant challenge in a society that threatens to disintegrate at a dizzying speed if control is inadequate. As noted in Chapter Two, for at least one hundred years preceding the Chinese Communist victory in 1949, China suffered from international strife, provincial warlordism, civil war, and abject poverty. This profound disarray made the issue of order and control central to all Chinese governments, regardless of their ideological persuasion. Moreover, the leadership of this vast territory and population must always be wary of the re-emergence of centrifugal forces that would impede central control and resurrect provincialism.

At the level of the individual, the Chinese leadership is ever mindful of the historical role that influential and powerful individuals have played in sowing the seeds of discontent, alienation, and even rebellion. Liberal democratic polities tend to focus on individual freedom as the defining factor of true democracy. In China, however, even though many intellectuals have long wished for greater freedom of speech, or at least less censorship, the focus of the entire ideology and culture is on collective responsibility. The purpose of socialist democracy is not, after all, to validate pluralism, but to unify the people for the pursuit of common objectives. The Western concept of individual freedom, which in some countries may go beyond such rights as free speech and assembly, to include the right to emigrate freely and even to bear arms, is by no means universally accepted as an appropriate, necessary, or even wise component of democracy. Indeed, such a broad conceptualization of individual freedom is a luxury that few governments feel they can afford. That individual freedom may give rise to instability, even anarchy, before the government is firmly rooted and has gained popular support, is a concern not at all unique to the Chinese government. In any country, too much questioning of the government could lead to political instability, which in turn could result in a major disruption of economic development. Nevertheless, the invocation by power holders in China of social or national collective interests as a justification of their suppression of individual rights often has a hollow ring in the ears of the wider public.[62]

Policies to Enhance Individual Freedom of Expression

In China, as in most countries, it is usually those individuals who are well educated and have resolved the fundamental problem of economic security who become interested in higher levels of individual freedom. Further, there are few who would not want greater control over their own lives and even over the government were there no tradeoffs. But China's history, even its most recent past, has conditioned the Chinese to believe that democracy and freedom give rise to widespread chaos, and even to a greater tyranny perpetrated by those who manipulate democracy for their own ends.

Since 1949, a genuine concern for strengthening individual freedom has existed at different times in various intellectual circles, and even within the leadership. At such times as the "Hundred Flowers Movement" of 1956–1957, the Cultural Revolution, and the "democracy wall" movement of 1978–1979, the leadership has orchestrated a change in the balance between democracy and centralism, even encouraging individuals to speak out. In each case, the people were given more individual freedom because the leaders thought it would serve their own purposes well. But in each case, the practice of individual freedom spilled beyond tolerable bounds as individuals used their new rights to denounce the leadership, the Party, Marxism-Leninism, or even the socialist system. As a result, the leadership again restricted personal freedom and invariably blamed "rightists," "deviants," "counterrevolutionaries," or the influence of "bourgeois liberal" democracy for the excesses.

Most importantly, the Chinese people themselves sometimes became the victims of the new freedom, as happened during the Cultural Revolution, when certain revolutionary elements asserted their right to beat, loot, and smash, to enter homes at any time of night and day, to accuse people falsely, and to harangue people continuously—sometimes until they died. Innocent people were often falsely accused in "big character" posters and deprived of their democratic right to defend themselves. Because the authors of big character posters did not have to sign them, they had no need to take legal and moral responsibility for vilifying innocent people. This, of course, was the fault of the leftist leaders, who could have prohibited unsigned big character posters from being used as sources of factual truth to denounce individuals as "villains," "archenemies of socialism," "renegade scabs," "monsters," and "freaks."

The case of the "four big freedoms," put into the 1978 Constitution[63] by the reform leadership, illustrates again how China's leaders confer democracy on the people to serve their own interests. The reformers had hoped that the people, armed with the constitutional right to speak out freely and to write "big character" posters, would exercise their power to gain retribution against the reformers' leftist enemies. But those individuals who became involved in the 1978–1979 "democracy movement" went beyond this to attack the socialist system, and even the reform leadership itself.[64] As a result, the Party's Central Committee removed the "four bigs" from the 1978 Constitution, claiming that some people had abused these freedoms. In this case, the reformist leaders, like the leftist leaders before them, never mentioned their own failure to set ground rules and clearly defined boundaries for the exercise of those freedoms; nor that they would have been perfectly willing to let the abuse of the democratic rights of others continue had it served their interests. Instead, the reform leadership suggested that the "people's democratic rights" would be *better guaranteed* without the "four bigs."[65]

The West's translation of the loosening of controls over individual freedoms in China as "liberalization" has led to the wrong connotations. Although the Chinese use the term "liberalization," it does not mean opening one's mind to all ideas. Certain elements within the Party (which was deeply divided on the issue) seriously criticized those Chinese who mistakenly equated the "emancipate the minds" policy with "liberalization" in the "bourgeois liberal" democratic (Western) sense of the term.[66] Party theoreticians explained that the real meaning of "liberating the mind" was to free individuals from leftist mistakes and from acceptance of the "two whatevers" viewpoint.[67] The Party had not intended that the right to freely criticize leftism would confer the freedom to support bourgeois liberal ideas.

As a Party theoretician put it,

> Between emancipation of the mind and bourgeois liberalization there is a clear-cut demarcation line which should never be obscured. However, those who promote bourgeois liberalization always flaunt the banner of emancipating the mind. . . . In their point of view, to emancipate the mind means to smash the trammels of Marxism-Leninism-Mao Zedong Thought and break away from the restrictions of the four basic principles, so that they can say what they want to say. . . .[68]

The theoretician then quoted from Mao Zedong: "Democracy and freedom are not absolute, but relative. Both of them emerge and develop in the course of history."[69] Economic exploitation in capitalist societies is evidence that their working classes do not have real freedom. By contrast, socialist countries have used economically nonexploitative policies to expand both the range and degree of freedom. This is not "absolute freedom," but rather freedom restricted by socialist law and, for Party members, by Party discipline. It is freedom for "the broad masses," but not for "enemies of the people," because only those who abide by the law and Party discipline may exercise "freedom." Those Chinese who advocate "absolute freedom" are, of course, implying that freedom is limited in China. This is "slander on the socialist society and the people's democratic dictatorship," and is dangerous.[70] Were the "emancipation of the mind" policy permitted to lead to bourgeois liberalization, others would be able to condemn the reform leadership for tolerating unacceptable ideological principles. This would force the reform faction to end its political, economic, educational, and legal programs.[71] As it turned out this prognosis was correct, and the removal of Hu Yaobang and several key intellectuals in the Party in 1987 was the price the "radical" reformers had to pay to keep the support of more orthodox-minded Party leaders for reform.

It is clear, then, that the purpose of open debate and "freedom of thought" in China is to foster creative contributions to the four modernizations, not to permit "disloyal" dissent. Political dissent is not the only kind of individual freedom which the leadership restricts. It also has at various times limited such freedoms as the choice of where to live, where to work, whom to marry, the right to divorce,[72] to emigrate, and to do research on topics of one's choice without ideological constraints on the methods or conclusions. The leadership considers control over these areas as crucial for maintaining social order. Nevertheless, the leadership has left open the door to greater individual freedom, but how much and in what form is still an unresolved issue.

In stark contrast to the high level of political dissent in the Soviet Union, direct undisguised political dissent, and particularly the development of an "underground," is rare in the history of the PRC.[73] The spontaneous demonstration in Tiananmen Square in the spring of 1976 to protest the leftist leadership's limiting the people's right to express their grief over Premier Zhou Enlai's death was a watershed in part because public protest is so unusual. Moreover, the lack of factions operating *outside* the leadership in China suggests that effective opposition necessitates being an extension of the elite factions operating within the inner precincts of the political system.[74] The reasons for this rather remarkable situation[75] can only be speculated upon. Many would point to the fact that the Chinese, unlike the Russians, have no historical tradition of political protest, and that they lack a tradition of a "loyal opposition" acceptable to the ruler. As long ago as the Shang Dynasty (1520–1030 B.C.), Bi Gan "had protested 'loyally' only to be disemboweled and pickled by his exasperated monarch; yet, as others noted, 'to speak, knowing (one's words) will not be put to use, is stupid.'"[76] The Chinese Communist leadership itself has done little to dispel such historically and culturally embedded attitudes.

The absence of conspicuous political dissent could be attributed to overwhelming popular support for the government, or to a profound fear of the consequences of being labeled a dissident or "counterrevolutionary." Alternatively, its absence could be regarded as testimony to Chinese cultural support for obedience to authority, or to a culturally reinforced belief that ordinary individuals cannot influence politics. In the case of the "democracy movement" of 1978–1979, dissidents published "above ground."[77] Their open political dissent may well be attributed to their naive trust that the Party, which for its own purposes had originally condoned "democracy wall," would continue to tolerate and protect them, even when they went beyond attacking "leftist" authoritarianism to question the compatibility of democracy and socialism and to attack the concentration of power in the hands of any one leader, including Deng Xiaoping himself.[78]

The Role of the Intelligentsia

Historically, Chinese scholars and intellectuals were co-opted by the imperial house to become part of the ruling bureaucracy. They rarely functioned as an independent force in Chinese politics. Today, Chinese intellectuals are still a part of the state. The state pays their salaries and assigns them work. Those Chinese intellectuals most likely to criticize the government are in the social sciences and humanities and are usually assigned to work in the vast propaganda apparatus of the Party. They would include researchers in the Chinese Academy of Social Sciences, writers for television and radio, journalists, teachers, professors, playwrights, authors, and others. All are carefully supervised by the Party branches within their work units. Although they have held little real power since 1949, their influence is significant, and they compete with the Party for influence with the Chinese people whenever they dare to voice an independent opinion.

The Party's dilemma in deciding how much freedom to permit the intelligentsia arises in part from the leadership's need, on the one hand, to harness their creative force for China's successful development while not, on the other hand, permitting creative thought to evolve into critical thought. Members of the intelligentsia frequently possess perspectives on issues that are incompatible with the Party's orthodoxy, or challenge the authoritarian Party leadership.[79] From the policy of "emancipate the mind" in 1979 until 1988, there were only three major lapses in a more indulgent policy toward the intelligentsia: the 1980–1981 criticism of bourgeois liberalism, the 1983–1984 attack on spiritual pollution, and the attack on bourgeois liberalism again in early 1987. The fact that each of these campaigns was brief suggests a refusal on the part of both the intellectuals and the ordinary people to be drawn into another bitter political campaign. Concrete evidence of the power of the literati, and particularly of the Writers' Union, to stand up to the Party was the 1985 Writers' Conference. At that time, two writers known to be highly critical of the Party (Liu Binyan and Ba Jin) were elected to the conference's highest posts, whereas Party sycophants were not. The crackdown on bourgeois liberalism in 1986–1987 suggested, however, that China's intellectuals had gone too far in challenging socialism and Party rule, much to the detriment of the very people in the Party who could have protected them. Yet, the fact that in each of these cases more liberal policies rebounded, also indicates dissension over these reversals of liberal policies within the reform faction—and that the more liberal group of reformers supporting Deng was able to have its way. Many observers believe that China's intellectuals did not recover their expanded freedom to write and speak until that faction within the leadership which had sought to protect them regained its strength at the Thirteenth Party Congress in October 1987.[80]

In general, the Party has followed a two-tiered policy toward individual freedom. The first tier deals with political dissidence. Even if disguised as abstract discussions about "humanism," "alienation," "nihilism," "skepticism," or "existentialism," political dissidence is strictly curtailed. The second tier deals with all other forms of individual expression, whether through the fine arts, the humanities, the social sciences, teaching, research, and writing, management and economic activity or through personal life styles and fashions. In these areas, the Party is permitting far greater freedom of expression than at any time since 1949, even if the ideas are un-Marxist, and even if actual practices seem more capitalist than socialist. More artistic freedom is being permitted in part because the leadership no longer sees nonsocialist-realism in art forms as threatening to socialism. Still, the *content* must not challenge Party infallibility.

The unsettled problems within China's factionalized leadership mean, nevertheless, that even this level of permissiveness could end without warning. The tendency of the Party to reinterpret the past inhibits free expression. As the Chinese put it, "The difficulty . . . is not in predicting the future, it is in predicting the past."[81] For this reason, China's intellectuals still are reluctant to speak out or to be boldly creative, as the rewards have been limited, and the punishments severe.

SOCIALISM AS MAJOR OBSTACLE TO INSTITUTIONALIZING SOCIALIST DEMOCRACY

Leadership Struggles and Democratic Centralism

Socialist democracy's core organizational concept, namely democratic centralism, has not always operated as the Party envisioned. The struggle over the relative balance between democracy and centralism has, moreover, been at the core of many of the issues within the Party's central leadership since 1949. As a result, the emphasis placed on the democratic or centrist aspect has varied considerably over time. Regardless of how much "democracy" has been practiced within organizations, however, ultimately the Party has had the final say. The major exception was the Cultural Revolution, when the Party lost control. The result was not more democracy but anarchy. Further, an average of one major struggle within the top leadership every three years since 1949 suggests that the idea of *central control* should not be confused with the notion of a *unified center.* Ultimately, China's unstable central leadership has itself jeopardized Party control.

Democratic centralism's primary goal is not to guarantee democracy in the Western liberal sense but rather, to guarantee *Party discipline* for the purpose of ensuring the "Party's unity of action." Party discipline requires a Leninist modus operandi: The individual is subordinate to the majority, the lower level . . . to the higher level, and the entire Party . . . to the Central Committee." Within this process, democracy means settling "controversial issues among the people by the democratic method, that is, by the method of discussion, criticism, persuasion and education and not by the method of coercion or repression." Democracy does *not* mean that the people should have the final word, or make policy, or control the leadership, but merely that those in power "should take an enlightened attitude and refrain from coercion." The purpose of democratic centralism "*is to enable an organization to function effectively.*"[82]

Thus, from the Chinese Communist perspective, the problem of a lack of consistency and unanimity within the central Party is not its impact on democracy but on organizational effectiveness. "Struggle" at the center has meant struggle throughout the Party and all organizations, to the detriment of the Party's work and ability to implement policy. Given their view, we can conclude that the primary reason that democracy within the principle of democratic centralism has remained an unresolved issue is that China's leaders cannot agree on just how much democracy is necessary for organizational effectiveness.

Lack of a Democratic System

Access to any number of the *components* of democracy does not necessarily guarantee a democratic system. In turn, a system should have a philosophical grounding in democracy for any of its parts or procedures to be considered truly democratic.

Within a system of a proletarian dictatorship led by the Communist Party, it would be hard to say that China has anything in the political realm that is recognizable in any *systemic* sense as democracy. The Chinese people may experience far greater democracy in their daily lives than did the vast majority before 1949, especially in terms of interpreting and executing the policies handed down to them by the central leadership. But they have no guaranteed, institutionalized control over the formulation of that general policy. Those channels for inputs into policy formulation which the people possess may be ignored by the leadership. The PRC's history indicates, in fact, that even the collective voice of the central Party leadership itself may be ignored by powerful individuals within it.

What obstructs China from achieving democracy, even within the context of "socialist democracy," is the lack of a true separation of powers and the lack of legal and procedural controls. A system of "checks and balances" and a "separation of powers" among legislative, judicial, and executive branches would make it difficult for an individual or a minority within the central leadership to seize power. In theory, The National People's Congress (NPC), the legislative branch, represents the people, but thus far it has been a rubber stamp with no real power to legislate or to check executive power. Thus, the people have lacked control over the major policies that affect their lives.

At the executive level, China still lacks a careful delineation of each leader's particular functions and powers. As the system has operated since 1949, titles and positions have often been totally unrelated to the leaders' real powers. Positions are developed on the basis of factional power, without concern for legislative or constitutional restrictions.

Finally, there is no institutionalized procedure for transferring power democratically. The people have no say in choosing their leaders above the county/district level and no institutionalized procedure to get rid of bad leaders. Rather, those factions with the most power make the decisions.

Many Chinese believe, for example, that Hua Guofeng, who was responsible for ousting the Gang of Four, was shamefully treated by the Deng Xiaoping faction. They do not believe that a small group of individuals at the center should be able either to strip another leader of power, or to endow a person with power, at whim and without approval by the people. In any other political system that can legitimately be called "democratic," defeated government leaders step down from power once the electorate ousts them. They are not put in jail by their successors.

Inaccessibility of Democratic Channels

Although certain democratic channels to communicate criticisms, dissent, demands, and ideas do exist in the People's Republic of China, they are not really accessible to the ordinary person. It is rare for an individual (as opposed to a work unit) to directly question policy or the leadership. People are afraid of making a mistake if they speak out at a meeting or write a critical letter about a co-worker or cadre. In urban work units, where the leader holds all-encompassing powers to give or withhold benefits to employees, individuals who dare to question them risk discriminatory treatment, perhaps even black marks in their dossiers, which can be used against them in the next campaign or when promotions or Party membership are under consideration. Penalties range in severity, "from being asked to recant, to being required to undergo study, to being subjected to 'struggle,' or worse." In addition, "legitimate" participation is limited to a narrow range of problems that can be handled "within the framework of existing policy." Dialogue ends when state interests or state policy are at issue. In rural areas, the peasants could not have serious open debates over production and requisition quotas, and in urban areas, workers could not openly discuss industrial wages, although they "could gripe about them quietly."[83]

If individuals have little reason to expect that their units support their criticisms or requests, they have a few options. Depending on the style of the local leaders, and depending on each individual's own political status, age, class, education, occupation, and other factors, a person with complaints may say nothing, or try through informal channels, such as friends and coworkers, to determine in advance how much support he or she would have. Alternatively, the person may wait for a new "gust of wind"[84] from the center to present criticisms or requests. If an individual chooses to voice dissent to his or her group for discussion, the group's perspective, not the individual's will emerge in the end. The other alternative is to convey demands to immediate superiors, leaving it up to them to decide whether to forward the demands or drop them. Basically, those who have a request "have no independent means of expanding their audience and maintaining regular contact with those outside their own unit who might be interested."[85]

The history of the PRC indicates, however, that the leadership is foolish to ignore complaints, demands, and criticisms if they occur on a wide scale. As in any other system, workers who are dissatisfied with their working conditions and/or lives exhibit it through passive resistance or noncompliance. A high level of absenteeism, work slowdowns, violating work regulations that are not carefully monitored, taking advantage of loopholes or ambiguous policies—these are the weapons used against a nonresponsive leadership.[86] During the Cultural Revolution, Shanghai workers taught their compatriots another method of being perfectly obedient while bringing production virtually to a halt: "You just stop your job and assiduously study Mao Zedong Thought for weeks. Eventually someone figures out there is a grievance."[87] The "reform faction" may have realized from the low level of productivity how frustrated and angry the workers had become and concluded that democratizing the workplace to make it more responsive to workers' demands would help boost productivity. Here again, the central leadership sponsored democracy for its own purposes, not for the sake of democracy itself. Nevertheless, in cases such as this, the people are the beneficiaries whatever the central leadership's objectives.

Party Infallibility

When the major principle of a political system is that the Party leadership is perfect in its wisdom, and its right to lead may not be questioned, there is really not much room for discussion. Although since the Third Plenum the Party leadership has tried to end the practice of lower-level Party leaders demanding blind obedience from the people, it has not been easy. Both the Party cadres' reluctance to relinquish their power to make demands on people without having to submit to the tedious democratic process of discussion, and a deeply rooted tradition of obedience and respect for the authority of senior officials, obstruct such efforts.[88] To question authority, "to go against the tide," might, if it did not bring official retribution because of going against the *wrong* tide, trigger upheaval and chaos (*luan*). The chaotic "ten bad years," when Mao Zedong, as the "representative of the will of the people," could speak on behalf of the people and attack the Party, giving "democracy" full reign,[89] reinforced this deeply entrenched perspective, to the extent that the vast majority of the Chinese people fear the repercussions of their own political involvement.[90] Finally, there is the inherent problem of, on the one hand, formulating a correct line and mobilizing the enthusiastic support of the people for that line, and, on the other hand, encouraging "blooming and contending." The reform faction has not yet resolved this issue. So far, whenever "blooming and contending" have jeopardized the mobilization of support for the correct line, the leadership has usually demanded orthodoxy, even if it is really a *new* "orthodoxy."[91]

Deng Xiaoping chastised those who dared to suggest during the "democracy movement" that the right to free speech and political participation enabled individuals to correct the Party's mistakes: "Our Party has . . . made serious mistakes, but these were always corrected by the Party itself, not by any other force." Further, he said, "The whole Party must obey the Central Committee. . . . No one is allowed to resist the leadership of the Central Committee by using the Central Committee's mistakes as a pretext."[92] Such statements can leave little doubt in the minds of the Chinese people where democracy ends and centralism begins.

Elitist Assumptions

The belief that the ignorant Chinese masses need elite leadership existed from the time of the late-nineteenth-century reformers to the days of the twentieth-century revolutionaries, whether Nationalist or Communist. Marxism-Leninism merely provided a dogma for the Chinese Communists to explain what most of China's earlier reformers and revolutionaries accepted as a truth. The principles of "democratic centralism" and the "mass line" both call for face-to-face contact between the Party leadership and the masses, but both principles emphasize that the leaders have the last word. This is the core of socialist democracy. The Chinese have assiduously avoided imitating Western democratic processes. Mass participation at the lowest levels, education of the people in socialist principles, and Communist Party leadership, not representative democracy, separation of powers, and individual freedom, provide the core of socialist democracy. The Chinese Communists support the proposition that the people remain insufficiently educated as to what is in their own interests, and therefore they should be *ruled* by the Party, rather than represented. Thus, government is "from the masses, to the masses," but not "by the masses."

The degree to which the leaders have "listened to the masses" has varied considerably since 1949. Ever since the Third Plenum of the CCP's Central Committee in December 1978, the leadership has made great strides in institutionalizing democratic and legal procedures. These will more firmly guarantee at least the basics of socialist democracy to China's citizens. Yet, although democratic socialist practices are institutionalized, restrictions on what can be said and done *within* those institutionalized forms often leave them hollow. An optimistic assessment would suggest, however, that proper forms, procedures, and institutions are a major first step toward advancing democracy in a socialist system.

CONCLUSIONS

Several salient points emerge from an examination of China's socialist system of democracy. First, the leadership is still divided on how to resolve the key issues concerning democracy, namely freedom and control, centralization and democracy. Second, if not "democratic," China is also not "totalitarian." In part, the divided leadership has itself prevented the state from becoming totalitarian. Also, the many forces competing for scarce resources in China, and the diversity and vast size of China and its population, have obstructed totalitarian control. Moreover, there are simply too many loopholes in the socialist system as it has been implemented in China. As one Sinologist has commented,

> The most dangerous aspect of a totalitarian model applied to China is that it completely misconstrues the actual political experiences of daily life. Far from being swept over by a greased, smooth totalitarian machine, the Chinese citizen spends much of life figuring how to woo and win approval from a host of petty bureaucrats on the thousand little issues of daily life. China is a society where even the application for access to the city library is a bureaucratically controlled act.[93]

Of course, just because China is not totalitarian does not mean it is democratic. In fact, the commentary cited above would indicate that China really is a quite "feudal," patriarchal society.

The third point to be emphasized is that, although China may not possess the institutional plurality of Western liberal democracies, it appears to be moving in the direction of far greater *intraregime plurality*. That is, different institutions are developing power, which provides a form of "checks and balances" and may help prevent the reemergence of personal dictatorship. These institutions include: the Party's disciplinary inspection commissions, the court and legal system, the National People's Congress as well as lower-level congresses; the press; the expanded electoral system; and the development of powerful economic institutions and enterprises. Intraregime pluralism may provide "democracy with Chinese characteristics." Although it is hardly equivalent to Western institutional pluralism, it may be a form of democracy that can work in the People's Republic of China.[94]

The leadership tolerates and even encourages democratic forces to the extent that they serve the leadership's objectives—a point that should cause all to regard the emergence of "democracy" in China with suspicion. A related point is that individuals and groups in China who have something to offer to the leadership in return for more democratic rights are more likely to get them. Thus, the leadership has grown more concerned with democratizing the work environment for peasants and workers, who participate more enthusiastically in production when they are given greater control over the conditions of their daily work. Peasants and workers, in turn, have rarely taken advantage of their greater rights to challenge the Party's leadership. On the other hand, when intellectuals have been offered greater democratic rights, they have displayed a propensity to push beyond acceptable limits.

Even some of China's leading advocates of greater democracy, who are themselves deeply critical of the authoritarian aspects of China's socialist system, dismiss the liberal democratic vision of democracy. For example, they do not necessarily believe that the liberal democratic electoral system is crucial. Rather, they believe (along with many who have grown cynical within liberal democratic systems) that those elected may not represent the people's interests at all, and that many elected "representatives" have bought their positions, or misrepresented themselves to get elected. Some Chinese accept the Party's viewpoint that if the people are given a choice among candidates, it will not necessarily be good for the country. They can point to elections at the local (village) levels, where the largest clan or lineage or faction usually wins if simple majority (democratic) rule prevails without any intervention from the Party leadership.[95] In such cases, the majority may treat smaller clans, lineages, or factions very poorly, taking everything for themselves.

Many Chinese intellectuals seem quite willing to accept the concept of "enlightened" central direction and control. They are not entirely convinced that the right to vote guarantees a better government; that a choice among candidates prevents an evil and corrupt government (although they concede that a one-party system certainly has *fewer* barriers to corruption than a two-party or multiparty system); or that greater political participation means more democracy or better government.

Some Chinese feel that China needs several things in order to become more democratic within the context of socialism: first, a separation of powers with a system of checks and balances; second, the ability to get rid of bad leaders; third, government of law rather than of individuals; and fourth, greater tolerance of diversity and dissent. However, the obstacles to the development of even these democratic characteristics have their roots in a 2000-year-old tradition of absolute imperial rule. Chinese Communism has simply been grafted onto millenia-old Chinese traditions and attitudes. Becoming more democratic, then, means moving beyond not just Leninist principles of organization, the intolerant principle of Party infallibility, and the rigidity of the dichotomization in Mao's theory of contradictions, but also beyond Chinese history, culture, and tradition.[96] The limits of change, in China as elsewhere, are determined by culture. While political institutions can be imposed from above, and socialist doctrine can seemingly be modified at will, Chinese history and culture are not easily willed away. The Chinese Communists know this better than anyone else.

NOTES

[1]Harold J. Laski, "Democracy," *International Encyclopaedia of the Social Sciences*, Vol. 4 (New York: Macmillan Company and the Free Press, 1968), p. 76.

[2]"Authority and Democracy: Two Sides of Same Coin," taken from *Hongqi (Red Flag)*, in *China Daily (CD)* (November 1, 1984), p. 4.

[3]George H. Sabine, "The Two Democratic Traditions," *The Philosophical Review*, Vol. 61 (October 1952), p. 451.

[4]Sidney Verba, Norman H. Nie, and Jae-on Kim, *Participation and Political Equality: A Seven Nation Comparison* (Cambridge, England: Cambridge University Press, 1978), pp. 1 and 4.

[5]Laski, "Democracy," pp. 77, 80.

[6]De Tocqueville, as referred to in Samuel Huntington and Joan M. Nelson, *No Easy Choice: Political Participation in Developing Countries* (Cambridge, Mass.: Harvard University Press, 1976), pp. 65, 66.

[7]Laski, "Democracy," p. 83.

[8]Democracy and dictatorship are "two sides of the same coin," in Chinese Communist parlance. In the Chinese view, China's proletarian dictatorship only became undemocratic because, although China eliminated bourgeois influence, it ignored "feudal" influence.

[9]Laski, "Democracy," p. 84.

[10]Although a number of "unofficial" periodicals sprang up during the "democracy movement," they were officially tolerated until the Party leadership condemned them.

[11]David S. G. Goodman, *Beijing Street Voices: The Poetry and Politics of China's Democracy Movement* (London: Marion Boyars, 1981), pp. 7, 8. Emphasis added. Wei became the best-known spokesman for the democracy movement. He was then arrested, tried, and sentenced to fifteen years in prison—but not for his advocacy of "democracy." Rather, the government used the pretext that he sold state secrets to a foreign correspondent to silence him as a key leader of the democracy movement.

[12]The 1976 manifesto of Chen Erjin, a student during the Cultural Revolution, is a case in point. Chen believed that if China had *two* Communist parties and a separation of powers, China would have democracy. Chen Erjin, *China: Crossroad Socialism. An Unofficial Manifesto for Proletarian Democracy* (London: Verson Editions, 1984). The weakness of democratic theory among those in the democracy movement is also discussed in Andrew J. Nathan, *Chinese Democracy* (New York: Alfred A. Knopf, 1985).

[13]Based on discussions with PRC students in the United States in the early 1980s.

[14]Huntington and Nelson, *No Easy Choice*, pp. 36, 37.

[15]In Taiwan, the Chinese Nationalist leaders, of the same cultural and historical background as the CCP leaders, institutionalized a formal system of checks and balances among five separate institutions. But in spite of this effort to at least look democratic, and in spite of American influence, until the 1970s, one could hardly say that Taiwan was a democracy in any meaningful sense. This perhaps indicates the impact of China's history and culture for the practice of democracy.

[16]Until the late 1980s some of China's non-Party intellectuals argued that the reason China could not have democracy was because the educational level of the *Party leadership* was too low, and not because the educational level of the people was too low.

[17]Edward Friedman, "In Defense of China Studies: Review Article," *Pacific Affairs*, Vol. 55, No. 2 (Summer, 1982), p. 255.

[18]For Mao's own explanation of democratic centralism and the mass line, see his 1957 "Speech on the Correct Handling of Contradictions Among the People," in Anne Fremantle (ed), *Mao Tse-tung: An Anthology of His Writings* (New York: The New American Library, 1962), pp. 264–297; and his January 30, 1962 speech on democratic centralism: "Talk at an Enlarged Central Work Conference," in Stuart Schram (ed), *Chairman Mao Talks to the People, Talks and Letters: 1956–1971* (New York: Pantheon Books, 1974), pp. 158–187.

[19]James R. Townsend, *Political Participation in Communist China*, (Berkeley: University of California Press, 1969), pp. 33, 61, 153.

[20]Ibid., p. 72.

[21]Mao Zedong, "Rectify the Party's Style in Work," (1943), *Selected Works*, Vol. IV, p. 113, in Townsend, *Political Participation*, p. 57.

[22]Mao Zedong (1965), *Selected Works*, Vol. IV, p. 236, quoted in Marc Blecher, "Consensual Politics in Rural Chinese Communities: The Mass Line in Theory and Practice," *Modern China*, Vol. 5, No. 1 (January 1979), pp. 107, 108.

[23]James R. Townsend, *Politics in China*, 2nd edition (Boston: Little Brown, 1980), pp. 107, 108.

[24]Huntington and Nelson, *No Easy Choice*, p. 50.

[25]Blecher, "Consensual Politics," pp. 107, 108.

[26]Ibid., p. 109.

[27]Ibid., pp. 121–123.

[28]Ibid., p. 110.

[29]Ibid., pp. 111, 114.

[30]Ibid., p. 112.

[31]For vivid details about peasant democracy, and the efforts the Party has expended in discussing policies and their implementation with the peasants (and even bargaining with the peasants), see B. Michael Frolic, "A Foot of Mud and a Pile of Shit," *Mao's People* (Cambridge Mass.: Harvard University Press, 1980), pp. 24, 25, 35–38.

[32]In China, "there is no conflict of basic interest between the state, the enterprise and the individual. To defend their rights and interests, the workers can solve their problems through . . . democratic channels. . . . It is not necessary for them to go on strike." "Worker's Movement Enters a New Period," *Beijing Review (BR)*, No. 7 (February 13, 1984), pp. 19, 20.

[33]As of the mid-1980s, there were more than 50,000 workers' schools, with an enrollment of some 11 million students. In addition, an equal number attend radio and TV universities, correspondence colleges, and short-term courses.

[34]Trade unions have provoked Party retaliation three times since 1949: in 1951 and 1957 when the unions demanded some degree of independence from the Party, and in 1966–1967, when the trade unions supported the "Liuists" and resisted the Red Guards carrying out "revolution" in the factories—and the Party promptly cracked down on them. See Townsend, *Politics in China*, pp. 239–241. For a description of the struggle within the central leadership over the Red Guards entering the factories, see Michel Oksenberg, "Occupational Groups in Chinese Society and the Cultural Revolution," in Lenard J. Cohen and Jane P. Shapiro (eds), *Communist Systems in Comparative Perspective* (New York: Anchor Press, 1974), pp. 343–347. Note, however, that in the case of the Cultural Revolution, the workers *united with management* to resist the Party's directive to the Red Guards to "make revolution."

[35]"Workers' Movement Enters a New Period," *BR*, No. 7 (February 13, 1984), pp. 18, 19.

[36]"The Power to Increase Profits," *CD* (October 30, 1984), p. 4; and "Delegated Authority Improves Efficiency," *BR*, No. 26 (June 30, 1986), p. 23.

[37]Zhou Ping, "An Important Step Towards Democratic Management," *BR*, No. 36 (September 7, 1981), pp. 14, 15.

[38]"Provisional Regulations Concerning Congresses of Workers and Staff Members in State-Owned Industrial Enterprises" (June 15, 1981), Articles 5 and 7, in *BR*, No. 36 (September 7, 1981), p. 17.

[39]Zhou Ping, "Democratic Management," pp. 14, 15. Also see "Trade Union's Role to be Stressed," *Workers' Daily*, in *BR*, No. 13 (March 31, 1986), p. 27, which strongly implies that the recommendations of the trade unions and workers' congresses to reward and punish cadres are not being followed, and that their views on wage reforms and distribution programs are not being listened to.

[40]*People's Daily*, as excerpted in "Factory Mix-ups," *CD* (July 2, 1984), p. 4.

[41]Victor C. Falkenheim, "Political Participation in China," *Problems of Communism* (May-June 1978), Vol. XXVII, p. 21.

[42]"Democratic Parties Play Their Role," *BR*, No. 29 (July 20, 1981), pp. 5, 6.

[43]A student from the PRC indicated, however, that over half of all members of the democratic parties joined between 1976 and 1986, and that in 1984 alone, some 160,000 people joined them. He also stated that the democratic parties operate about 5,000 schools, with a total enrollment of 500,000 students. Further, although these parties after 1957 became primarily philanthropic in orientation, since 1976 they have been repoliticized and participate more actively in politics. Gu Weichun, New England China Seminar, Harvard University, Cambridge, Mass. (April 16, 1986), notes. Also see "Democratic Parties Play Their Role," *BR*, No. 29 (July 20, 1981), pp. 5, 6, and "Democratic League Runs University," *CD* (September 4, 1984), p. 3.

[44]As evidence of the continued unimportance of the "democratic parties," see "Political Reform Put on Agenda," *BR*, No. 31 (August 4, 1986), pp. 5, 6.

[45]Barrett L. McCormick, "Leninist Implementation: The Election Campaign," in David M. Lampton (ed), *Policy Implementation in Post-Mao China* (Berkeley, Calif.: University of California; 1987), pp. 392–393.

[46]Although the people already directly elected team cadres, the situation was confused.

Often no one wanted to be team leader. And often brigade leaders made it clear whom they wanted elected by the teams. The teams had little choice but to comply, partly because elections were carried out by a show of hands, and no one dared to go against the brigade leaders who watched. John P. Burns, "The Implementation of Sub-village Elections in South China, 1979–1982," p. 47 (draft). Paper prepared for ACLS-SSRC Workshop on Policy Implementation in the Post-Mao Era, Ohio State University (June 1983). Paper to be published in John P. Burns, *Political Participation in Rural China* (Berkeley, Calif.: University of California Press, forthcoming), Chapter 5.

⁴⁷Ibid. pp. 9, 49.

⁴⁸The new law requires that there be 50% to 100% more candidates than positions on the ballot for county-level delegates, but requires a smaller percentage of candidates for provincial-level congresses. McCormick, "Leninist Implementation," p. 391, note 30.

⁴⁹Brantly Womack, "The 1980 County-Level Elections in China: Experiment in Democratic Modernization," *Asian Survey*, Vol XXII, No. 3 (March 1982), p. 266.

⁵⁰Allen Abel, *Globe and Mail* (August 24, 1984), p. 14; and Womack, "County-Level Elections," p. 269.

⁵¹Burns, "Implementation of Elections," pp. 54–56.

⁵²Ibid., pp. 51, 52.

⁵³Womack, "County-Level Elections," p. 269.

⁵⁴McCormick, "Leninist Implementation," p. 399.

⁵⁵Ibid., pp. 407–410.

⁵⁶Womack, "County-Level Elections," pp. 261, 262, 270–273.

⁵⁷Lu Shilun, "Capitalist Separation of Three Powers and the People's Congress System" ("Zichang Jieji 'San Quan Fenli' He Renmin Daibiao Dahui Zhi"), *Studies and Explorations*, No. 2 (1980), pp. 4–10, as referenced in McCormick, "Leninist Implementation," p. 393.

⁵⁸Xu Chongde and Pi Chunxie, *Questions and Answers on the Election System* (Beijing: Qunzhong Publishing Co., 1980), p. 158, referenced in McCormick, "Leninist Implementation," p. 393.

⁵⁹McCormick, correspondence, May 1987.

⁶⁰Similarly, the provincial newspapers are under the control of their respective provincial Party committees.

⁶¹"Publishing: Unified Management," *BR*, No. 21 (May 25, 1987), pp. 14–15.

⁶²McCormick, correspondence, May 1987.

⁶³The "four bigs" or "sz da" in Article 45 of the 1978 Constitution were that citizens have the right to speak out freely, air their views fully, hold great debates, and write big character posters.

⁶⁴For excellent detail on the speeches and publications of the "democracy movement" from 1978 to 1979, see Nathan, *Chinese Democracy*, pp. 3–44; and Goodman, *Beijing Street Voices*.

⁶⁵See "Big-Character Posters Not Equivalent to Democracy," *BR*, No. 17 (April 28, 1980), pp. 3–5, for example of the kind of justification the Party offered for summarily removing the people's constitutionally guaranteed rights. Emphasis added. Also see "Hua Guofeng Answers Questions from Yugoslav Correspondent," *BR*, No. 33 (August 18, 1980), pp. 15, 16.

⁶⁶For example, when Hu Yaobang was removed from his position as Party General Secretary in 1987, he was accused of not upholding the "four basic principles."

⁶⁷The "two whatevers" viewpoint, held by Hua Guofeng and his supporters, was that whatever Mao instructed must be carried out, and whatever Mao said was correct. It implied a noncritical acceptance of leftist policies.

⁶⁸Yu Yiding, "On Emancipating the Mind and Opposing Bourgeois Liberalization," *Red Flag (Hongqi)*, No. 23 (December 1, 1981), pp. 23–28, translated in *Foreign Broadcasts Information Service*, China, No. 250 (December 30, 1981), p. K13.

⁶⁹Ibid., p. K13, quoting from "Selected Works of Mao Zedong," Vol. 5, p. 368.

⁷⁰Ibid., pp. K14–K16. Also see Jie Ji, "Whoever Enjoys Democracy Must Obey Law," in *Democracy and the Legal System (Minzu yu fazhi)*, No. 10 (October 1983), p. 39.

⁷¹"Notes from the Editor," *BR*, No. 43 (October 26, 1982), p. 3.

⁷²Although the Chinese have long held legal the right to marry freely and to divorce, in actual practice these rights were greatly constrained until the 1980s by the concern for class

background, and the Party's concern for upholding the sanctity of marriage, the better to serve socialism.

[73]For a "Democracy Movement" dissident's view of why no new theories have developed to challenge Marxism-Leninism and why no underground developed, see essay in Goodman, *Beijing Street Voices*, beginning on p. 131. Also see Peter R. Moody, *Opposition and Dissent in Contemporary China* (Stanford, Calif.: Hoover Institute, Stanford University Press, 1977).

[74]Huntington and Nelson, *No Easy Choice*, p. 30. Andrew Nathan makes the point that the Chinese democracy movement was unique among those in socialist countries because almost all the Chinese activists in it "saw themselves not as challenging the regime but as enlisting on the side of a faction within it." They saw themselves as loyal remonstrators, not dissenters. See Nathan, *Chinese Democracy*, p. 24.

[75]It is remarkable, of course, only if one believes that profound dissent exists in China that is unvocalized simply because it lacks a format for expression.

[76]Jonathan D. Spence, "China: How Much Dissent?" *The New York Review of Books* (August 13, 1981), p. 32.

[77]In fact, most of the journals of that movement were not underground at all. The editors' names and addresses were printed on them; and the editors tried to register their journals with the proper authorities and pay taxes. Some even sent copies to the top Party leadership and to libraries. See Nathan, *Chinese Democracy*, p. 16. China's democracy movement was, in any event, an unusual example of political dissidence in the PRC, for it was led by workers—sons and daughters of cadres who because of the Cultural Revolution lost their chance to be educated and to become officials themselves. The "intellectuals," on the other hand, who were afraid of losing their own newly gained rights to speak and write more freely, did not openly support them.

[78]According to David S. G. Goodman, the 1978–1979 democracy movement lost official support for three major reasons: the publication of "The Fifth Modernization: Democracy" by the editor and dissident Wei Jingsheng; the emergence of a human rights section in the democracy movement (which promoted the view that human rights is not a proletarian slogan); and a trend toward opposing Deng and his rapid modernization because Deng was too defensive of Mao. The dissidents also suggested that Deng was inadequately apprised of the dangers of modernization, most notably the inevitable appearance of a privileged class of bureaucrats. See Goodman, *Beijing Street Voices*, op. cit., pp. 140, 64, 65, 88, 89, 105, 106, 152. For examples of how far some of those who questioned the "four basic principles" went, see Ralph Croizier, "The Thorny Flowers of 1979: Political Cartoons and Liberalization in China," *Bulletin of Concerned Asian Scholars*, China Special, Part 2, Vol. 13, No. 3 (1981), pp. 50–59. For documents, see James D. Seymour (ed), *The Fifth Modernization: China's Human Rights Movement 1978–1979* (Stanfordville, N.Y.: Human Rights Publishing Group, 1981). In the opinion of another China specialist, the only reason intellectuals were protected during such a political movement, even when they expressed unpopular ideas and criticized the government, was because of "political disagreement and pressing economic needs." Because the right to dissent never rested on institutional or legal guarantees, however, when the power struggle among factions shifted its balance or its tactics, political dissidents would be attacked. Merle Goldman, *China's Intellectuals: Advise and Dissent* (Cambridge, Mass.: Harvard University Press, 1981), pp. 240, 244.

[79]The playwright Bai Hua, for example, sparked the Party's attack on bourgeois liberalism with his play "Unrequited Love." In this play, an overseas Chinese who returns to serve his country in the early 1950s continuously sacrifices for his country in spite of the repeated attacks on him. The theme is that he loved his country, but his country did not repay his love. The play implies that even the present leadership is guilty of destroying the very people who have loved China most deeply. The play was subsequently banned, and Bai Hua was forced to make a public self-criticism.

[80]Several important studies have affirmed the symbiotic relationship between intellectuals and central Party leaders, and even between dissidents (whether intellectuals, students, or workers) and central Party leaders. The studies presented in Carol Lee Hamrin and Timothy Cheek (eds), *China's Establishment Intellectuals* (Armonk, N.Y.: M. E. Sharpe, 1986), illustrate the cooptation of intellectuals by the bureaucratic elite. As John Israel writes in the Foreword," (p. x), "In contemporary China, if you are not some kind of establishment intellectual, you are not a legitimate intellectual at all." Other works that study this relationship

include Stanly Rosen, "Guangzhou's Democracy Movement in Cultural Revolution Perspective," *China Quarterly*, No. 101 (March 1985), pp. 1–31; Merle Goldman, *China's Intellectuals;* Peter R. Moody, *Opposition and Dissent in Contemporary China;* and Andrew Nathan, *Chinese Democracy.*

[81]Cyril Chihren Lin, "The Reinstatement of Economics in China Today," *China Quarterly*, No. 85 (March 1981), p. 46.

[82]Liu Chengyun, "Democracy and Democratic Centralism," referring to reports on revising the Party's Constitution at the eleventh Party Congress in August 1977 in Qi Xin, *China's New Democracy* (Hong Kong: Cosmos Books Ltd., 1979), p. 8.

[83]Falkenheim, "Political Participation in China," p. 26. Falkenheim's study indicates, however, that cadre reprisals were rare because they were illegitimate and could not, therefore, occur openly or directly.

[84]The Chinese see decisions as being made at the center, by a "gust of wind" (*yi zheng feng*).

[85]Townsend, *Politics in China*, op. cit., pp. 232–236; and Falkenheim, "Political Participation in China," pp. 27, 31, 32.

[86]Townsend, *Politics in China*, p. 237.

[87]John Fraser, *The Chinese*, (New York: Summit Books, 1980), p. 378.

[88]Qi Xin, "China 1978—From a New Power Struggle to the End of Class Struggle?" in Qi Xin, *China's New Democracy*, p. 144.

[89]For a commentary on the tension between leaders and led, see Maurice Meisner, "The Maoist Vision of the Future," in Maurice Meisner (ed), *Marxism, Maoism and Utopianism* (Madison: University of Wisconsin Press, 1982), p. 103.

[90]See Tom Gold, "Back to the City: The Return of Shanghai's Educated Youth," *China Quarterly*, No. 84 (December 1980), p. 762; and Roger Garside, *Coming Alive: China after Mao* (New York: McGraw-Hill Book Co., 1981), pp. 230–252.

[91]Lowell Dittmar, "China in 1980: Modernization and Its Discontents," *Asian Survey*, Vol. XXI, No. 1 (January 1981), pp. 41, 42.

[92]Deng Xiaoping, speech in January 1980, quoted in Nathan, *Chinese Democracy*, p. 37.

[93]Edward Friedman, "In Defense of China Studies. p. 259.

[94]See Andrew Nathan, *Chinese Democracy*, pp. 226–232.

[95]This viewpoint is substantiated by Falkenheim's study, which indicated that votes in elections at the production team (village) level tend to split among candidates along lineage lines. Falkenheim, "Political Participation in China," p. 25.

[96]This is not to deny the existence of any democratic or liberal forces whatsoever in imperial China. William Theodore De Bary, in his book *The Liberal Tradition in China* (New York: Columbia University Press, 1983), pp. 7, 8, indicates that one thread of Chinese culture in the Sung and Ming dynasties was quite liberal, at least in the sense in which he defines Confucian liberalism. But liberalism was only a thin strand within the dominant authoritarian tradition. Similarly, a certain school of scholarship during the Ming and Qing dynasties was "liberal" and reflected the imperial monarchy's tolerance for dissent; but it was again a minor part of the whole picture.

Chapter Six
SOCIALIST LEGALITY AND SOCIAL CONTROL

Schoolmaster Ho: You may have done *nothing wrong, but we still can look at what you say. If you don't say anything we can consider your thoughts. And how do we know your thoughts, if you don't say anything? This can be judged from outward appearances. In all these meetings we have held since 1956, you have said less than anyone. And with a background like yours, you almost* have *to have certain dissatisfactions with the Party and with socialism. How could we expect you to be pure? You can't possibly be. Yet you keep quiet, you won't come clean.*

OK, everybody, just take a look at what the problem is here. This is even worse, even more dangerous, than those who are willing to expose their erroneous ideas, and who are courageous enough to unburden their hearts to the Party. This man is set against the Party in the deepest recesses of his mind. If this isn't the most dangerous, most vicious form of anti-Party anti-socialist behavior, then what is it?[1]

INTRODUCTION

The interplay of the cultural, developmental, and ideological variables has significantly affected China's legal system. The developmental variable, which includes those limitations on legal development imposed by poverty and underdevelopment, is common to all developing countries. For China's unresolved legal issues, it is perhaps the least significant of the three variables, but it is nonetheless a part of the explanation. Because the post-1949 leadership rejected the legal structure inherited from the defeated Chinese Nationalists, China was put in the position, shared by many developing countries, of having to undertake the costly and difficult task of building a modern legal system from the ground up.

But developmental constraints pale in comparison with the constraints on modernizing the legal system set up by the interplay of cultural and ideological factors. Culturally, the Chinese Communist leaders inherited the traditional Chinese repugnance for the law and lawyers, which meshed nicely with their own preference for having the Party rather than the legal community make determinations of "right and "wrong." Moreover, the very effective informal mediation system of traditional China, which the Communists inherited and adapted, made the development of formal legal structures less urgent. As a result, China's leaders were culturally predisposed to construct a minimal legal system and were ideologically committed to developing socialist legality. As in so many other spheres, they formally adopted the Soviet model. This model established the preeminence of policy and politics over law and was not dedicated to the development of a truly autonomous legal system.

It is unfair to argue that the "problem" of China's legal system is that it is not the kind found in liberal democracies; but one can argue that the Chinese system of legality has failed to achieve its own objectives, precisely because socialist and ideological factors intervened. The reforms undertaken by the leadership since 1978 seek to address many of these obstacles to the development of a sound socialist legal system. Such reforms are not, however, easily implemented, since the legal system must continue to operate within the context of a socialist political system.

THE FORMAL STRUCTURE OF THE LEGAL SYSTEM: THE SOCIALIST VARIABLE

Because both the structure and process of the Chinese legal system were modelled on the Soviet legal system, it conforms closely to the imperatives of socialist ideology and policy: The legal system is explicitly meant to function as a tool of the state.

The Constitutional and Legal Basis of the Judicial System

The People's Republic of China (PRC) has had a series of constitutions. The constitution provides both the legal and policy basis for all other laws. From 1949 to 1954, China functioned under a provisional constitution, namely the Common Programme. Since then, China has had four state constitutions: the 1954 Constitution, an intentionally transitional constitution heavily influenced by the Soviet model;[2] the 1975 and 1978 Constitutions, heavily influenced by "leftism"; and the 1982 Constitution, a product of the "reforms". In theory, the National People's Congress (NPC) formulates the constitution and passes legislation that becomes law. In fact, the NPC was a rubber stamp until Peng Zhen became the head of it in 1981 and made it into both his own power base and, for the first time, an institution that seriously examined the proposed legislation that came before it. For the most part, however, laws continue to flow, as they always have, from the Party and the State Council; and the Standing Committee of the NPC may amend legislation and the Constitution without consultation with the NPC.

By the mid-1960s, the Chinese had ceased compiling regulations and decrees on civil matters. Those that existed were filed away and largely forgotten. Until the 1979 reforms, the bulk of all civil disputes were handled through mediation and administrative intervention by the state. Only since 1979 have institutions, procedures, and laws been formalized to address civil disputes. The Organic Law of the People's Courts, promulgated in 1979, stipulated that courts at each level have both civil and criminal divisions, and that all above the basic level have an economic division.

The following description of the Chinese legal system as it exists in the 1980s emphasizes criminal law and criminal procedures, but it also discusses the progress made in civil law. According to the Law of Criminal Procedure of 1979, there are three basic elements in the judicial system: the public security organs; the people's procuratorates (procuracies), and the people's courts. The 1978 Constitution and the many reforms emanating from the Third Plenum of the Eleventh Session of the Central Committee of the Party in December 1978 brought about a restoration of the centrality of the procuracy and the importance of courts as institutions.[3]

Public Security Organs: Legal and Social Control

Structurally, the public security organs, which exist at each level of government, are subordinate to the people's governments of the corresponding levels. In addition, special public security organs exist in such fields as water and railway transport. Each level is subordinate to the jurisdiction of the public security organs at the next higher level, and ultimately to the Ministry of Public Security, which is itself subordinate to the State Council. Moreover, each unit and enterprise has personnel who report to the public security organs on any suspicious individuals or activities within it. In 1986, of the 1.2 million public security personnel, half were armed police officers. Most of the others were cadres.[4]

In quiet, orderly periods, police usually maintain a low profile, a tribute to the effectiveness of the para-security network formed by neighborhood committees, the "granny police" (older, retired women who carefully watch their own neighborhoods), and other organizations. Those who participate in the para-security network are usually familiar with all the residents (and their problems) in their area. The police are stationed only where they expect trouble. Criminality tends to be higher in the factory and industrial workers' urban neighborhoods (and around construction sites or shut-down factories, which, if left unattended, are likely to be totally dismantled by people wanting building materials). In general, however, a pervasive presence of security forces has not been necessary, largely because as soon as there are any indications of a problem at the lower level, it is referred to local mediation committees. Additionally, the Chinese are reluctant to call in the police when a crime occurs or threatens to occur, for it may mean a very close investigation of the lives of everyone involved, including the victim's. Before the widespread ownership of consumer goods in the 1980s, for example, if a color television set was reported stolen from a house, questions could arise as to how the family acquired enough money to buy the television, or how it acquired a particularly scarce brand of television. Moreover, one's other personal belongings might also be perused, and questions raised that could eventually become the source of political problems. A formal police investigation would be recorded in either the household register, the work dossier, or both. To avoid these possibilities, and because of the average citizen's general sense of help-lessness vis-à-vis the police once they become involved, along with a cultur-ally embedded fear of "losing face" (by failing to resolve a dispute amica-bly), the police have generally been less involved in social control in the PRC than in most one-party socialist systems, and certainly less than in most right-wing dictatorships.

In 1983, however, the level of criminality had risen to such an intol-erably high level (by Chinese Communist standards), that the state consid-erably augmented the size of the public security system. Robberies, rapes, and murders had increased, but the bulk of the crimes were actually in the economic arena, and were addressed largely through investigatory com-mittees, the campaign against economic corruption, and improved ac-counting and inventory procedures, not through the police. In 1987, the Chinese created a Ministry of Supervision as a further effort to crack down on economic corruption within state-owned enterprises.

On a daily basis, the police work out of neighborhood stations, each of which is responsible for overseeing some 6,000 to 7,000 households. The 20 to 25 officers in each station are responsible for propagating the legal system, enforcing public security with foot patrols, overseeing the "re-habilitation through labor" (*laojiao*)[5] of those counterrevolutionaries and other criminals who are serving terms in prisons or labor camps, and for supervising criminals sentenced to "surveillance" while they remain in the community at large. Finally, the police are responsible for educating juve-niles who make "mistakes," for performing "good deeds," and for main-taining household registration records and census data.[6]

Household registers

Household registers (*hukouji*) have been used in one form or another ever since the Zhou Dynasty, well over 2,000 years ago. Since 1949, they have been legally required throughout China. They have functioned largely as a preventative control measure, allowing the authorities to main-tain social order by keeping track of the population, and particularly of any strangers in a community. Urban residence is difficult to change, and moving in or out of urban housing requires permission from the local police station. For this reason, until the more liberal policies toward migration began in the mid-1980s, household registers inhibited an even greater overcrowding of China's cities and the concomitant increase in urban poverty and criminality that usually accompanies overcrowding. The registers have also served to keep the various geographical areas in China separated. Until 1986, when the regulation was eliminated, those who stayed for even one night in urban areas where they were not residents were supposed to register with the local police. This rule was not always followed except during campaigns,[7] but those who failed to register risked being reported.

In urban areas after 1949, the household register also served as the necessary document for residents to obtain almost all necessities and services: for example, coupons for certain foodstuffs in limited supply, as well as grains, cotton cloth, housing, schooling, medical care, and employment. But the household registers' chief function, like that of the work units' dossiers, has been political control.[8] Although they record information that need not have any relevance to deviance control, when a mass campaign is begun, the registers are quickly dusted off to find out individuals' class backgrounds, information concerning black marks recorded there by the local residence committees, evidence that individuals have been targeted by previous deviance-control campaigns (a sure sign that they will be targeted in succeeding campaigns as well), and for potentially damaging information about a person's religion, education, and political activism. What would in other times seem innocuous, such as an individual's education level, dress style, or eating habits, could suddenly assume paramount importance if the latest campaign were meant to uncover "white experts," or socialists with the "hearts of capitalists."

Thus, although the major function of the members of public security organs is to maintain law and order, in China this means more than preventing criminal activities, providing safety for China's citizens, and protecting state institutions, enterprises, and social organizations. It means, in particular, combatting political deviants and counterrevolutionaries, those who whether by criminal actions, *or through political activities,* are potentially or actually subverting the state and its "four basic principles": the socialist system, the dictatorship of the proletariat, Party leadership, and Marxism-Leninism-Mao Zedong Thought. Public security organs, then, can and frequently do become involved in controlling, investigating, and arresting *political* criminals. The Party itself, of course, is also engaged in such control measures.

Dossiers(dang'an)

In each work unit, the Party Organization Department maintains personnel dossiers.[9] These record all important "life events," as well as housing, schooling, schedules for childbirth, work transfers, and, of course, work behavior. By their very existence, dossiers serve as a deterrent to deviance from traditional and socialist norms.

Dossiers accompany individuals throughout their work careers.[10] Dossier supervisors, highly trusted Party members with strong political credentials, keep these accounts of morality. Although dossier supervisors are not really "secret" police, they function as part of the internal public security apparatus, and the dossiers that they control are shrouded in secrecy. Thus, individuals can only surmise through the constant surveillance of their activities, the innuendoes and attacks on them during campaigns, and in other indirect ways, that damaging materials about them exist in their dossiers. For example, certain Chinese individuals who have in campaign after campaign been treated with great suspicion have sometimes, perhaps after 20 or 30 years of constant harassment, been called in by their supervisors and told, much to their amazement, that "we have cleared you of the charge against you of being a foreign spy," about which the subjects knew nothing.

Dossiers provide an account of people's politically related activities and performance. What is "political," however, may be very broad: Over-dedication to one's work at the expense of attendance at political meetings could, during periods of leftist dominance, be cited as evidence in a dossier that the person was too "expert" and not sufficiently "red." Inadequate political activism or friendship with a person under suspicion for deviance of some sort might also be noted in the dossier, and this could well become the basis for criticism during struggle sessions. Negative statements a person had made about individuals within the leadership or about the flaws of particular policies may also be entered and later, during the campaign, be used as evidence to indicate an anti-Party or antisocialist position.

Most dossier entries are made during campaigns targeted at controlling deviance. At these times, friends and colleagues within a unit are "encouraged" to write "unsolicited letters" (*jian ju xin*) that comment on a person's political character. Some colleagues will take this opportunity to disparage a person whom they particularly dislike or are jealous of. Because these letters will never be seen by the subject, the authors are free to be vindictive; they will not be held accountable for false statements. Under pressure from the leadership, even friends might submit critical letters to be filed in a person's dossier.

Many factors affect how information in a dossier is used. The most important seem to be the overall character, beliefs, temperament, and attitudes of the cadre in charge of the dossier, and the personal relationship of the dossier subject with that cadre. Other factors, such as whether someone who has been denounced can be connected with the subject of the dossier, and the political environment itself, are important. From the perspective of the subjects of the dossiers, their most distressing aspect is that they have no chance to refute what is included, even if they are gross untruths, precisely because they cannot know what the dossiers contain. A person may be told, after applying to transfer to another unit or to study abroad, that the application was denied because of a black mark in her dossier. But the nature of the "mistake" will not be revealed; and questioning the validity of the dossier's contents may cause a person even more problems.

It is all too easy to make mistakes in China because the criteria for *not* making mistakes are so narrow. Knowing the potential consequences of critical statements being placed in one's dossier, the average individual is likely to step gingerly to avoid them. Minimally, most people try to achieve at least outward conformity to the political value preferences of the person in charge of the dossiers. Adroit political maneuverers, by conforming to the political preferences of each of their successive bosses (even deviating from the center's dominant views precisely to the extent to which the bosses themselves do) will over their lifetime have relatively few negative inputs in their dossiers—in spite of their conspicuously vacillating values. Survivors, those who manage to escape severe victimization by any major campaign, have no doubt done just this.[11]

In addition to black marks, letters, and the supervisor's own comments, a dossier will also contain information about a person's class background, education, friends and relations (especially if they have bad class backgrounds or have lived abroad), and participation in political organizations. If a person has a bad class origin or has ever been labeled as one of the "five bad elements," that fact can haunt him for the rest of his life. For example, one man who before 1949 had joined the Kuomintang Youth League when he was only 12 years old was struggled against repeatedly for 20 years as being a "reactionary" and possibly a "foreign spy." When he finally discovered the reason he was victimized, he committed suicide. Another man, one of China's first college graduates in engineering and a "model worker," was in 1958 labeled an "historical counterrevolutionary" because he confessed to joining a "reactionary youth league" several years before liberation and remaining in it for one year. He appealed the Party's verdict, but the Party refused to lift his political "hat." Instead, it sentenced him to seven years' imprisonment. When he was later released, he went to work again, but his background destined him to repeated "struggle."[12]

Once errors or problems are recorded in the dossier during a particular campaign, they provide the "signal for re-recruitment in subsequent campaigns."[13] At various times, some Chinese have demanded that the Party eliminate the much detested dossiers; but those who spoke out against the dossiers during the 1956–1957 Hundred Flowers Campaign were subsequently denounced as "die-hard rightists" and punished harshly.

In the 1980s the reformist leadership again addressed the issue of the dossiers, not for the purpose of eliminating them, but rather to rescue "some potential leaders from political limbo" by purging the dossiers of allegedly unjust, false, duplicated, useless, and wrong documents from the Cultural Revolution. Because personnel dossiers are crucial to cadre recruitment, promotions, removals, and transfers, this is highly sensitive work. There may be hundreds or even thousands of documents, including countless handwritten notes and comments, in the dossiers of each cadre investigated during that period. It is also time-consuming as documents must first be examined and then approved for removal by the relevant Party committee.[14]

Dossiers appear to have contributed to a high degree of at least superficial conformity to prevailing political and societal norms, and for this reason they have served as a valuable control mechanism. Alternatively, perhaps the dossiers have simply made many people deceitful, by indirectly motivating them to learn how to hide carefully their profound differences in values with the regime. They have perhaps encouraged political sycophancy and superficial commitment to political values. And perhaps they have made it less likely that people will constructively criticize the leadership or its policies for fear that, although they may not be punished at the time, their words will be entered into the dossier for reference later on. In this respect, although the dossiers provide an organizational tool for controlling deviant thought and behavior, they also serve to inhibit constructive, creative ideas that could advance China's goals of modernization.

Thus, the public security organs function both as a part of the formal judicial system and as a part of the highly organized system of political and social control. For the former, the public security personnel are concerned largely with criminals who have broken the laws and with preventing criminality. For the latter, they are concerned with the broader control of the entire population, to ensure conformity to Party doctrine and political mores.

The People's Procuracies (Procuratorates)

The major function of the procuracy is to oversee the administration of justice in its role as an investigative and supervisory branch of the judicial system. Like the courts, the procuracies are state organs. They exist at every level of people's courts, with higher-level procuracies leading and controlling the work of lower-level ones. In theory, no other administrative organ is permitted to interfere with its procuratorial authority. In its investigatory role in particular, it is meant to serve as a check on police actions that have led to arrests, prosecutions, or exemptions from prosecution; and it assures that police investigations conform to correct legal process. Once a police action has been approved, however, the procuracy takes on a further investigatory role, which includes mustering evidence against criminals and acting as public prosecutors in criminal trials.

Once the procuracy issues an indictment, it indicates agreement with the police on the guilt of the suspect, and the suspect becomes a "defendant."[15] The court then has the right either to affirm the procuracy's decision (the usual case), to return it to the procuracy for further investigation, or even to request the procuracy to withdraw the case. The procuracies have direct authority over major criminal cases involving such crimes as embezzlement and malfeasance; and they, rather than the police, make the initial, and subsequent, investigations in such cases. Civil cases and light criminal cases, on the other hand, are handled directly by the people's courts.

The People's Courts

The people's courts exist at four levels: *basic* (at the level of counties, cities, and municipal districts); *intermediate* (at the level of prefectures, centrally administered large cities, and large cities under the direct administrative control of provinces or autonomous regions; *higher* (at the level of provinces, autonomous regions, and the centrally administered municipalities of Beijing, Shanghai, Tianjin, and Chongqing); and the *Supreme People's Court*. In addition there are *Special People's Courts*, which are functionally specific to certain types of organizations, such as military, railway transport, water transport, and forest courts. Courts at each level ordinarily handle cases of first instance from within their respective jurisdiction, as well as appeals made to them from the immediately lower level of court. Only one appeal (*shangsu*) is allowed, regardless of which court is the court of first instance. The Supreme People's Court may issue explanations of how certain laws and legal decrees should be interpreted or applied; but it has no power to determine the constitutionality of legislation or government policies.

People's Assessors

In all cases of first instance, people's assessors (jurors) sit in the people's courts, with the same power as that of the judges. The assessors are either elected for a three-year term by the people or are chosen by workers and staff in government institutions, social organizations, and enterprises. In practice, most tend to be Party members. They usually serve only a few weeks out of each year.

Adversary Tactics

Adversary tactics are not used in the Chinese legal system. This reflects the influence of the Soviet model and socialist ideology on the development of the legal process: The state's collective interests must take precedence over the individual's rights. Thus, just as both criminal and civil law serve the community and the state in keeping the public order, so too does a lawyer's primary responsibility lie with the collective interests of the people, not with the individual client. Lawyers must represent the facts and "seek the truth" in order to help the court arrive at correct conclusions.

The lawyer must not use tactics designed to muddle the evidence and confuse the judge and public prosecutors in order to win the case for the defendant, regardless of guilt, as Western lawyers often feel obliged to do. In fact, a lawyer will not and cannot represent a client in court if the lawyer believes that the client is guilty, except to plea for leniency if the defendant admits his or her guilt. Article 188 of the Criminal Law provides for punishment of any legal worker who "deliberately harbors a guilty person and saves him from prosecution or deliberately confuses right and wrong and perverts the law. . . ." If a case is appealed, a lawyer "must remain silent" if the lawyer believes the lower court's decision was correct.[16]

The effect of this practice is to limit the caseload of an inadequately staffed legal system. By quickly disposing of those cases of "proven" guilt the legal system may concentrate on those cases where guilt is not proven. This protects the system from drowning in cases where lawyers, anxious to make more money and establish good reputations, try to get their clients off on "technicalities" or "mitigating circumstances" such as a biased jury, insanity, incorrect procedure, illegally acquired evidence, or any of the other tactics used in courts in the West (all with the lawyer's full awareness that his client committed the crime). In any event, because lawyers do not enter the legal process until *after* the police and the procuracy have made an investigation and issued an indictment that indicates guilt, and because the trial is usually held within a week from the time the indictment is issued,[17] the role of the "defense" lawyer in China is greatly constricted.

From the Chinese perspective, allowing those found guilty of crimes to go free on the basis of a legal argument harms society in two ways: First, the person's freedom from punishment or reform suggests to others that they, too, may get away with crime. Second, the criminal is free to commit a crime against society again, before either labor reform or imprisonment has remolded the perpetrator. The Chinese do not accept the view that the dangers of letting a guilty person go free are outweighed by the importance attached to the correctness of the legal process itself.

In practice, however, the collective interest of the whole has often become identified with the interests of a political faction or local cadre. Especially during intense political campaigns such as the "ten bad years," guilt and innocence were arbitrarily defined by local leaders in accord with whether the accused was politically Right or Left. The mass line replaced correct legal procedure. Even if for different reasons, the Chinese legal process is no more immune to arbitrary manipulation than it is in the West.[18]

Presumption of Guilt

The Chinese presume innocence until the time of the trial, at which time they usually *know* that the person is guilty—or else the accused would not be on trial! Once a case reaches the court for trial, there is close to a 100 percent conviction rate. Thus, the purpose of the courts is not to determine guilt, which the procuracy has already decided, but to mete out punishments.

According to the Law on Criminal Procedure, however, if a substantial discrepancy appears during the trial "between the evidence gathered prior to trial and the testimony in court," the trial may be *suspended* until further investigation is undertaken. The courtroom trial is not, in short, the procedure by which to determine guilt or innocence; further, a defendant may not introduce new evidence or testimony suggesting his or her innocence without the court's permission.[19]

The real purpose of a court trial is to humiliate and ostracize the guilty from society, and to educate the public about right and wrong. Trial proceedings are frequently broadcast onto the streets, and a number of trials in the 1980s have been held in large stadiums so thousands could attend. In this respect, public trials are more like morality plays than they are trials in the Western sense. Thus, the trial process reinforces both the traditional Chinese and socialist predilection to view the moral and political domains as identical.

THE INFORMAL STRUCTURE: THE CULTURAL VARIABLE

Mediation

Although the structure and process of China's post-1949 legal system was consciously modelled after the Soviet Union's, the actual functioning of China's legal system has been heavily influenced by traditional Chinese legal and social values. One of the most conspicuous remnants of traditional Chinese culture is the continued reliance on mediation for handling civil disputes. In the context of a society in which socialist ideology has reinforced the Chinese cultural predisposition to sharply dichotomize everything and everyone into categories of "good" and "bad," "right" and "wrong," mediation represents compromise, another facet of a very complex traditional Chinese culture.[20] (This should not be overstated, however; for even mediators are obliged to criticize those who, in the course of mediation, persist in upholding wrong ideas, and to ensure that the results of mediation conform to "correct" Party policies.)[21]

Like their ancestors, today's Chinese favor mediation partly because they distrust the legal system, and partly because they want to avoid the bureaucratism that plagues it. They also believe that a mediator is more able than a judge to sort out the complexity of ambiguous rights and wrongs that arise in disputes, especially those among relatives and neighbors, and to find a solution satisfactory to all parties. As the Chinese say, "Even an upright official finds it difficult to settle a family quarrel."[22]

The Chinese believe, moreover, that mediation prevents criminality, for many crimes, including murder, start with unresolved civil conflicts over marriage or property.[23] For minor criminal offenses,[24] and for almost all civil cases, then, the Chinese prefer the informal process of mediation.

Several types of organizations may conduct mediation, including the litigants' own work units, but most mediation is conducted by people's mediation committees. These are "mass organizations," controlled by the people's government and people's court at the grass-roots level.[25] First established in 1954, by the mid-1980s, mediation committees totalled more than 900,000, with a staff of close to 6 million. These formally established committees handle almost eleven times more civil disputes than are handled by court mediation. Court mediation may occur before, or even during, a hearing. It is conducted by a judge or a collegiate bench. Concerned organizations, ordinary people, and even relatives may also be called in by the court to help in the mediation.[26]

The Low Level of Institutionalization

The informality and low level of institutionalization of the Chinese legal system may be seen as reflecting attitudes inherited from imperial China. The traditional ethical-moral order was based on relationships between people, not on laws. The rarity of legal intervention and the paucity of formal laws suggest that informal societal norms and procedures were effective in dealing with "legal" problems. But these aspects of the legal system may also have resulted from other factors. For example, failure to resolve a problem outside the formal legal system might lead to a loss of face for both the litigant and the litigant's family. In any event, most people were ignorant of what legal remedies existed, and few were able to finance formal legal actions. Finally, a general fear of authority combined with a belief that involving the state in any problem was likely to make things worse, and a recognition that China was governed more by individuals than by laws, were enough to make most Chinese reluctant to call upon the legal system for support.

The development of socialist legality has also been affected by the traditional Chinese belief that law is simply a legal codification of society's ethical norms, and that morality therefore takes precedence over law; but on paper the Communists have to some degree replaced traditional norms with socialist norms. As a result, the Party's interpretations of socialist doctrine take precedence over the formal legal codes. These interpretations are usually known to the people through the daily propaganda barrage and their study groups. In general, before 1979, the only formal documents that the people reviewed as a guide to action were policy speeches and proclamations issued by the Central Committee of the Party, or by the State Council. They rarely studied codified laws.

Both tradition and ideology contribute to making the Chinese far less litigious than most Westerners. But Chinese attitudes have also been shaped by reality: So few laws, courts, or lawyers have been available that disputes could be resolved more expeditiously through mediation. And, in light of its limited resources, the state has not really been able to afford a larger judicial system. In the early 1980s, China had only 5,500 full-time lawyers and 1,300 part-time lawyers to serve the legal needs of its one billion people.[27] Although much has been done since that time to address this situation, there are still few lawyers available to ordinary citizens.

Although barely institutionalized, the formal Chinese legal system functioned fairly effectively (given Chinese Communist Party objectives) until the 1957 anti-rightist campaign. Thereafter, the Party undercut the role of the courts and procuracies, and those with legal training were removed from positions of influence. The radical, Maoist faction, which was anti-legal and favored the mass-line method of handling conflict, gradually gained the upper hand in determining how the legal system would develop. After 1957, the Party and the police gradually assumed the major role in law enforcement and exceeded their prescribed roles.[28] The limitations of the informal legal system became apparent: The low level of institutionalized laws and legal procedures proved no match against the enhanced powers of the Party and the police.

In the course of the ten frightening years between 1966 and 1976, society was turned against itself. Armed warfare occurred between opposing Red Guard factions. Ten percent of the population (100 million people) were directly victimized, and almost everyone was a participant, either as an activist, or as an activist turned victim, as a relative of a victim, or as passive participants—those who were frightened into silence and stood by helplessly while their colleagues, friends, and relatives were brutalized.[29] In the process of this upheaval, society's adherence to standards of decent behavior disintegrated, and the Party's ability to guide policy and legislate morality deteriorated.

During the "ten bad years" the procuracy was completely dismantled and formal courts were replaced by ad hoc tribunals set up by the radicals and Party committees. In criminal cases, especially cases involving counterrevolutionaries, no prescribed judicial procedures were followed. Suspects were apprehended without any procedural protection. Led by the radicals, the "revolutionary masses" dragged people out of offices, homes, and factories, placed them under arrest on their own authority as representatives of the "people" or "radical" causes, and punished them in the name of "revolutionary justice." The leftists' mass line system of legal justice prevailed with no clear-cut guidelines for the determination of guilt and innocence. Formal legal institutions and processes were dispensed with. Trials by the masses bore no semblance to court trials as practiced before or after

1949. Countless individuals were unjustly charged with crimes and sentenced on the basis of "the arbitrary decisions of the masses."[30]

Within each unit, a "revolutionary three-in-one committee" (made up of a member of the People's Liberation Army (PLA), a revolutionary cadre, and a revolutionary rebel) was established to serve as the court for all the unit's members. This committee determined who was guilty of political crimes. Still, in many cases, the real decisions about a person's guilt were determined by announcements in the *dazi bao,* or "big character posters." Anyone claiming to be a "revolutionary rebel" could put up a big character poster and condemn a person for a political crime. This sometimes conflicted with the security bureau's own assessment, but often the security bureau itself gave a tip to the "revolutionary rebels" that they should put up big character posters about certain people, and indicated what crimes they should be accused of. The revolutionary three-in-one committee would then determine the punishment to be meted out.[31]

Law codifies ethics in order to ensure that the people will know what is expected of them, and it suggests the kinds of legal sanctions awaiting them if their behavior deviates from the law. In a society in which the inner, normative controls on behavior are adequate, and extrajudicial institutions and procedures are sufficient to cope with most of society's conflicts and problems, the laws remain at a distance. But when the society's own norms begin to disintegrate, law tends to play a more active role. The problem at this point was that when China's legal system failed, the cultural and ideological basis for order was also under siege. Even the highest Party and state leaders lacked recourse to legal protection. They too became victims of lawlessness.

This showed the limits of a system ruled by individuals. Law became an "auxiliary tactic" subordinate to Party leadership, Mao Thought, Party policies, and direction by the masses. Law proved inadequate to cope with the ordering of society and what were basically political questions. Had law, instead of Mao's "two categories of contradictions for our guidance," and "the Party policy on the question of suppression of counterrevolutionaries by fully mobilizing the masses," been used to address questions of criminality, political errors of "leftism" or "rightism" in legal judgments might not have occurred.[32] But the Cultural Revolution activists rarely bothered to refer to the law for justifying their behavior. Acting according to the "Thoughts of Mao Zedong" (as interpreted by themselves), "fomenting revolution" for the purpose of creating a "red" society, or attacking "revisionism" were the new, ad hoc methods to achieve justice. And socialist ethical doctrines, cynically manipulated for "revolutionary" ends, lost their credibility. As the Cultural Revolution raged on, such excesses gradually destroyed not only the legal system but also the traditional and socialist ethical systems. The Chinese people were compelled to attack the "four olds" (old Chinese habits, customs, ideas, and culture) and to question such traditional principles as filial piety and respect for age and authority. When the movement spilled out over its poorly defined edges, individuals and groups were incited to take authority into their own hands. Hapless victims, led by the political activists of the day, were dragged before "struggle meetings" and subjected to harangues, accusations, and even physical abuse. The accused had no recourse to traditional ethics, which were themselves the target of attack, nor to socialist ethics, which had become a matter of interpretation, nor to the law or standardized legal procedures.

By the early 1970s, the legal system developed before 1957 was almost nonexistent. The 1975 Constitution, strongly influenced by the Maoist line and the then-dominant "leftists," underscored the diminished role of the formal legal system: The number of articles dealing with the judicial system was reduced from the 12 of the 1954 Constitution to one. In addition to mandating the application of the mass line during trials, the abolition of the procuracies, and the transfer of their powers and functions to the police, the 1975 Constitution abolished the former constitutional guarantees of judicial independence, equality before the law, the right to a defense, and protection against arbitrary arrest.[33] Essentially, the 1975 Constitution simply codified current legal reality; for over the years, the 1954 Constitution's provisions for the judiciary had gradually come to be ignored.

The repercussions of this destruction of authority and the ethical basis for behavior, the absence of law, and the lack of clearly defined objectives magnified the inability of the system to curb criminal behavior. For example, labor camps used to be guarded without barbed-wire fences, flood lights, and security boxes because there was nowhere escapees could go without being turned in. But with the death of Mao, the arrest of the Gang of Four, and, in particular, the removal of Wang Dongxing, the head of Mao's secret police, escapees from labor camps could hide without fear of exposure.[34]

In the economic arena, mismanagement by the radicals and disorganization within enterprises fueled an upsurge in economic crimes. But major perpetrators of street crime were the urban educated youth who had been sent to the countryside upon the ad hoc authority of one group or another. Unable to endure the separation from their family and friends, miserable in their new role as peasants, disillusioned with the outcome of the Cultural Revolution, and distressed that the good urban life had suddenly vanished, they illegally returned to the cities, but without jobs or the residence permit necessary for access to ration coupons. Even in the late 1980s, a significant percentage of all crimes are being committed by unemployed youth. For the leadership, this has exacerbated the problem of controlling the country.

The reform leaders' response to "past injustices" has been to reintroduce a formalized legal system similar to the model in the early 1950s, one that includes more efficient law enforcement, stricter procedural controls, and a plethora of very specific laws. But in addition, China's leaders have tried to rebuild socialist ethics. Beginning with the campaign in the early 1980s to build a "spiritual civilization," they emphasized the need to restore socialist (political) ethics. They did not admit to the importance of restoring traditional *Chinese* ethics. To all appearances, many post-1949 policies were in fact aimed at destroying traditional values, part of a backward, "feudal" past that hindered socialist modernization. But these values provided much of the glue that held the new socialist fragments together in a cohesive entity. The leaders have consciously built on the strength of these traditional values since 1949, without ever admitting that *some* parts of Chinese culture were useful even in a socialist society. From their perspective, anything less than a totalistic denial of the value of traditional Chinese culture would have been counterproductive and might only have confused the people and detracted from socialist goals. But in their policies and campaigns since the late 1970s, the leadership has, again without giving them the label of "traditional Chinese values," attempted to revive those very values as the basis for rebuilding the fragmented Chinese social order. Thus, the "socialist education campaign" in 1980 (which bore a remarkable similarity to Chiang Kai-Shek's "New Life Movement" in the 1930s), to teach civility to the Chinese people through the "four things that should be made beautiful" (behavior, the environment, hygiene, and sanitation) and the "five things that should be paid attention to" (decorum, manners, hygiene, discipline, and morals) was an implicit recognition of the need to restore Chinese societal values. These slogans were later replaced by the slogans of being polite (*limao*) and "civilized" (*wenming*), no doubt because the Chinese seemed incapable of remembering what the uninspiring "four beautifuls" and "five attentions" referred to.

The Chinese leadership's belief that the erosion of socialist ethics, and implicitly the erosion of traditional social ethics, set the stage for criminality is undoubtedly accurate. Urban Chinese now look back on the period before 1957 as China's "golden age," when doors did not have to be locked, the streets were safe, people lined up in orderly fashion at bus stops and in markets, and the elderly were treated with great respect. Now, long after the "ten bad years," respect for the social order has not yet been restored. This reflects a troubling problem within Chinese society, which has manifested itself in deviance and criminality.

The leadership had chosen, however, to target the *manifestation* of the problem by trying to change people's behavior, when the actual *source* of the problem is cynicism about the socialist system and the tension in the workplace. At work, people have over the years been subjected to insults, shame, and humiliation, and they are frustrated with the low rewards for their hard work. But they cannot speak out against the system or against the personnel who they think are responsible. Some Chinese describe the societal situation as one in which "Everyone has eaten an atomic bomb." Since they cannot explode at work, they explode in situations where they are anonymous, such as first fights when someone breaks into a line, or swearing at people on buses. Unwilling to confront the basic cause of a breakdown in societal cohesiveness, the leadership hopes to improve the situation by encouraging socially acceptable behavior in the context of unacceptable societal and work conditions.

Law, Cultural Values, and Social Policy

The influence of political values on China's legal system is abundantly clear. But the codification of social values in China's laws has also affected the kinds of laws enacted and their applications. For example, in 1983 a mother was sentenced to eighteen months in prison for publicly slandering a young woman in an effort to prevent her from marrying her son.[35] In Shenyang a man was imprisoned for fifteen years for committing adultery.[36] Libel does not normally carry such a heavy sentence, and adultery is not even a crime in China, but in both these cases "serious consequences" followed the original act: The young woman drowned herself and the adultery also resulted in a suicide. In traditional Confucian law, suicide was regarded as a crime for which someone other than the victim was responsible. These values still seem to be influential. Thus, in 1984 when an old woman drowned herself in a pond, the daughter-in-law was arrested for driving her to such despair.[37]

The decisions in these cases also reflect the more general principle of traditional Chinese law that individuals are responsible for all the *consequences* of their acts, whether those acts are in themselves criminal or not, and should be punished if the consequences are serious. Negligence resulting in destruction of property, death, or injury is a crime, regardless of intention or whether the defendant acted "recklessly."[38] Thus, in a case in the early 1980s, workers went off and left their tools on the railroad track, and their negligence led to the derailment of a train and heavy property losses. Because the loss was considerable, the punishment of the workers was severe, even though the act itself was simply a minor oversight.[39] In another case in the mid-1980s, a foreigner who fell asleep while smoking in bed in a Chinese hotel allegedly caused a fire that led to several deaths and serious damage to the hotel. Although no formal law prohibits smoking in bed, the foreigner was nevertheless sentenced to 18 months in prison and required to pay the hotel $53,000 in damages.[40]

The explicit incorporation of such traditional social values, as, for example, the relevance of the effect of a person's actions on the community, forces individuals to take responsibility for the broader social consequences of their behavior. The Chinese cannot escape punishment when a deed triggers results that they could not have expected. In the libel and adultery cases cited above, it was essentially the reaction of the victim that determined the punishment of the perpetrator of the original misdeed. Tougher victims might not have committed suicide. If punishment depends on the unpredictable reactions of the victims, the law itself becomes unpredictable, making it difficult to know when one is breaking it.

One final example of the legal codification of traditional cultural values is the requirement that children support their parents, which appears in both the Marriage Law and the Criminal Law (Article 183). Few societies have specific laws regulating intrafamilial relations, or explicitly defined penalties for failure to conform to them. Traditional values are easily ignored and often disappear entirely under the pressures of modernization. China is using its legal system to defend such traditional cultural values as filial piety against these pressures. This illustrates a central dilemma that China, like other developing countries with deeply rooted cultures, faces when trying to modernize its legal system.

PROBLEMS IN DEVELOPMENT OF THE LEGAL SYSTEM

What follows are a number of issues that were not seen as problems for China's legal development in the years immediately following the 1949 Communist victory but later became obstacles to the implementation of an efficient, effective, and just legal system. Some of these issues are not publicly discussed, so it is difficult to ascertain to what degree the Chinese leadership perceives them as problems; but others have been subjects of open discourse since the late 1970s. Why they are now perceived as problems in the implementation of socialist justice, and were not so perceived before the late 1970s, will be examined.

Lack of Separation of Powers: Implication for an Independent Judiciary

"Socialist legality" and "socialist justice" have different objectives and priorities from legality and justice in a nonsocialist system. Among the differences has been the insistence that the judicial system be supportive of state and Party policies, with the result that the judicial system has been no more reliable than politics. Although certain cases tried in China in the 1980s suggest that new Party and state policies cannot overrule established laws and legal procedures, this is hardly common practice.

Party interference and the destruction of the judicial system

Direct Party interference in both the court and legal system began in the wake of the 1957 Anti-Rightist Campaign, when the legal system gradually came under the control of the Party and the Ministry of Public

Security. Any questioning of Party leadership on grounds of judicial independence became politically risky.[41] The formal judicial system was increasingly ignored as the institutional curbs on the powers of the Party and the policy declined.

Eventually, the police could, even without the approval of the procuracy, arrest, prosecute, and impose sentences upon political "deviants" and criminal suspects. The role of the court was limited to a virtual rubber stamp for sentences recommended by the Party. During the Cultural Revolution, however, when even the police and Party were attacked, law was condemned as a "bourgeois restraint" on the "revolutionary masses." Because members of the Party were themselves being removed from power, the Party's authority could not be sustained. Hence, the Party could no longer oversee the implementation of "socialist justice," and was replaced by revolutionary committees who created a "revolutionary" judicial system.[42]

The lack of an independent judiciary is in essence an issue of the political power structure. By the 1970s, China had almost no lawyers, judges rarely had legal training, and no significant legislation had been passed since the 1950s. The formal Chinese legal system was in shambles. In the early 1970s, the "leftist" leadership desperately tried to rebuild the Party and restore its power over every level of the policy process. As it slowly pieced both the judicial system and the Party back together, the Party limped back into its position of power over judicial processes and decisions, to ensure their conformity to the prevailing Party line.

The 1978 Constitution, although heavily influenced by leftism, called for a return to rule by law. Still, the "four freedoms" (the right to demonstrate, assemble, post character posters, and petition) embodied in the 1978 Constitution were not intended to protect individual rights in the Western sense, but rather to serve the political purposes of the reform faction: to permit greater freedom of speech so that the people could (and would) protest against the illegal and arbitrary rule of both the leftists during the "ten bad years" and of Deng Xiaoping's major competitor for power, Party Chairman and Premier Hua Guofeng. Since Hua's assumption of power was not constitutionally sanctioned, Deng's emphasis on legality was indirectly an attack on Hua's illegality, and on Hua's leftist followers who had a history of abusing the law.[43] When in late 1978, participants in China's democracy movement invoked the four freedoms to protect their right to speak out against the Party, however, they discovered that this was not the purpose that these constitutional provisions were intended to serve. As with the Hundred Flowers Campaign, the limits of those "law-based rights" became clear when critics of the Party laid claim to them. The leadership quickly eliminated any possibility that the four freedoms would be used as a legal, constitutional basis to challenge the Party's authority by "amending" the Constitution to delete them.

Yet, at the same time that individual rights were being curbed, legal writers and even high ranking officials were arguing for a clear distinction between the law of the state and Party policy. They maintained that laws should take precedence over policy and be revised only according to proper legal procedures, not at the whim of any individual leader.[44] It was at this time that the reform leadership began redefining the role of the Party, and limiting its functions to ideological supervision. Nevertheless, it also tried to ensure that the courts and procuracies made decisions that could conform both to Party policies and the law, in part by allowing the Party to select and educate the cadres for the courts and procuracies.[45] Further, the leadership in 1979 reestablished the Ministry of Justice (abolished in 1959), and an explosion of new laws and legal writing ensued.

Not until a new Criminal Law and a Law of Criminal Procedure were adopted in July 1979 were mass campaigns no longer sanctioned as a method of discovery and punishment. Article 136 of the Criminal Code specifically prohibits obtaining confessions through torture; Article 137 forbids the "gathering of crowds to beat, smash and loot"; Article 138 forbids "bringing false changes"; and Article 145 forbids the use of big character posters or other means to insult publicly or fabricate stories to defame another person. Nevertheless, in some cases these forbidden procedures continued. According to an official report from Guangdong Province, for example, even in ordinary cases, basic-level cadres were "still illegally detaining people, setting up clandestine tribunals, arbitrarily interrogating people and even tying them up and marching them around to be struggled against, extorting confessions by torture, illegally searching people's homes and humiliating them."[46]

After the promulgation of the Criminal Law, the people's courts began to reexamine criminal cases, mostly for the period from 1966 to 1976. By 1983, the courts had examined 1.2 million such cases and reversed the verdicts on 31,000 of them.[47] Although the Chinese leadership presented such figures with great pride and evidence that justice was carried out once the radical leftists were deposed from power, it is noteworthy that the reversal of verdicts occurred in less than 3 percent of the cases. Of course, these figures for "reversed verdicts" do not cover the large number of unjustly accused individuals who were released between the arrest of the Gang of Four in October 1976 and the courts' reexamination of earlier verdicts that began in 1979. Nor do they cover the tens of thousands who were in and out of prison and punished for political crimes in other non-institutional ways from 1966 to 1976.[48] But the figures nevertheless suggest the possibility that for those people still in jail in the early 1980s, whose cases the reformist leadership felt were questionable enough to invite further investigation, the results of the system of "revolutionary justice" of the preceding leftists were upheld.

In addition to the new criminal codes, there has also been a plethora of new legislation in the area of civil law. These laws affect foreigners as well as Chinese. However, it is difficult to get copies of the applicable laws; for the Chinese leadership worries that both foreigners and Chinese might use them to assert rights that the state does not want to grant, and that their actual application may redound to China's detriment. China's leaders therefore want to test them out first, to be sure their effects are as intended. Once publicized, laws that affect foreigners cannot be easily changed, so the Chinese have avoided publishing them until they feel confident about their consequences. However, they still feel free to change laws that apply solely to their own citizens whenever the effects might prove harmful to the state's interests.[49] Even in civil law, then, the Chinese continue to favor the decisions of the Party leadership and the exigencies of policy over law-based rights, precisely because they are able to ignore existing laws without penalty. Instead, they make policies that are then justified by *new* laws. Alternatively, they simply do not refer to laws at all. The prohibition (enacted January 1, 1980) against the practice of applying laws retroactively, is ignored at whim.

The post-facto rationalization of policy points to another element limiting the ability of the judicary to act independently: The judiciary lacks the ability to develop legal concepts that will guide policies. Instead, *policies guide legal development.* Although many Chinese are cognizant of the weakness of such a legal system, thus far they have had little success in making law a constraint on policy.

The four constitutions China has had since 1954 illustrate the pattern of rewriting laws to reflect and support the dominant leadership's political values and policies and the limited sentimentality the Chinese hold for constitutions or constitutionalism. Unlike Western constitutional democracies, the Chinese do not consider the constitution to be the "fundamental law of the land."[50] For example, the "radical" faction wrote the mass-line approach to legal problems into the 1975 Constitution (Article 25). Further, it provided that the police exercise the functions of the procuracy, thereby deleting the earlier constitutional safeguards of the people's rights. (They had long been ignored anyway.) The 1978 Constitution removed procuratorial power from the police and returned it to the procuracy and the people's courts, but fell short of a complete endorsement of the concept of "judicial independence": "procuratorial and judicial organizations must maintain their independence *as is appropriate.*"[51] "Independence" was thus left up to a subjective interpretation of the meaning of "appropriate." The 1982 Constitution (Articles 126, 131), however, specifically affirmed the independent judicial power of the courts and procuracies.

Article 15 of the 1978 Constitution again illustrates the pattern of rewriting laws to support political values and policies: "All state organs must constantly maintain a close relationship with the masses . . . stream-line administration, practice economy, raise efficiency and combat bureau-cracy." The 1982 Constitution emphasizes the duty of the Chinese people to practice family planning (Article 49). Such provisions are policy state-ments, not laws in any meaningful sense.

Two Incompatible Goals: Law as a Tool for the State and an Independent Judiciary

The unresolved problem of the role of law and the judiciary reflects the incompatibility of socialist values with the further development of an independent legal system. The thinking of Chinese Communist writers and leaders differs fundamentally from that underlying the dominant tradition of Western political and legal theory, which attempts to base general con-clusions on valid first principles (ontological and epistemological), so that the conclusions are universally true and applicable. The Chinese assume that the formulations of political and legal theory should be wholly subser-vient to the needs of the Chinese state. Whatever value these formulations have as "truth" derives from their foundation in Marxist doctrine. Their truth, however, is less important than their usefulness in justifying the Party's and state's objectives. These methodological assumptions pro-foundly affect their conclusions.[52]

In socialist legality, law is the tool of the state and its ruling class, the proletariat. Theoretically this constitutes 95 percent of the Chinese popula-tion, because the "property-less class" (the Chinese understanding of the term "proletariat") includes both workers and peasants. This means that 95 percent of the population forms a dictatorship over the 5 percent (50 million people) who are not to be trusted or who are "bad." For the Chinese reformers, however, the concern is with law sometimes becoming the tool of the rulers instead of the ruling class. When this happens, law serves the political whims of individuals, not the needs of the state. Thus, the reform-ers blamed the Gang of Four and Mao Zedong for seizing instruments of state power, without being bound by the collective leadership. They con-cluded that the equation of law with politics was dangerous. And yet, like their predecessors, they refused to relinquish their right to interpret the law according to their own political needs.

For the modern Chinese, as for their Confucian ancestors, the ques-tion is not whether to choose rule by law or rule by individuals, but rather, how to balance the two: At what point is the law autonomous and not subject to interpretation? In this respect, Chinese tradition continues to influence both legal values and structures today.[53] The dilemma at the heart of the problem of an independent judiciary is, then, how to ensure that the processes and decisions of the judicial system conform to Party policy while preventing individual Party leaders from intervening in the judicial process for self-serving purposes.

China's reformist leaders recognize the problems created by the lack of a clear and independent role for the judiciary. They have gone so far as to examine the experience of other countries for direction on how to redefine the role and structure of the judiciary,[54] insisted that the Party "conduct its activities within the limits permitted by the constitution and the laws of the state," and warned members of the Party against assuming "a special privilege mentality of ignoring the laws."[55] Yet, at the same time, China's leaders demand that the final decisions of the courts conform to Party policy. Thus, the courts still lack the right of judicial review of the legislation and laws passed by the National People's Congress (NPC), or the policies and regulations passed by the Party. China's legislative and administrative organs, such as the State Council, may still enact laws and promulgate administrative decrees that contravene existing laws or curtail citizens' constitutionally given rights. Because the laws flow directly from the pens of the top Party leadership, and even the NPC does not actively participate in formulating legislation, establishment of judicial autonomy is all the more difficult.[56]

But it is primarily the Party's interference with the police, the courts, and the procuracies that remains at the root of the problem. This interference has led to serious injustices and to a perversion even of "socialist legality." Both Party and governmental organs have repeatedly placed themselves above the law through the "back door," the use of bribery or political power to suppress evidence and intimidate those who might question their actions, and by the suppression of democratic rights. Usually, however, it is individual Party and state cadres who are actually at fault. Articles in the Chinese press indicate that many cadres are inhibited from implementing the new laws by their own superiors, as well as by fear of losing their own power over those subordinate to them. The leaders recognize that it is these culturally embedded attitudes, reinforced by the bureaucratic hierarchy of socialism, that must be eliminated by insistence on the principles of equality before the law and rule by law. At the same time, they ignore how the Party's stranglehold on the interpretation of laws contributes to these abuses. Local Party leaders with supervisory powers over the legal system rely on their highly subjective and arbitrary political preferences in determining justice. In this respect, then, the central Party itself loses control over the implementation of justice at the local level.

In the past, the arbitrary actions of cadres were encouraged by the lack of enforcement of the principle of legal equality.[57] Since the Third Plenum, however, stories abound of officials at all levels being exposed and punished—even executed—for their crimes in an effort to convince the people that all are truly equal before the law. Yet cases of official corruption continue to be dealt with by Party-conducted investigations, Party committees, the people's government organs, and people's work units, rather than by the formal judicial system. "Disciplinary" sanctions are most frequently substituted for legal sanctions when a Party member is involved, or when nonlegal administrative sanctions are more expedient, such as for employees of a factory. Thus, even if Party members are involved in a crime such as rape, embezzlement, or assault, fines, demotions, or disciplinary demerits, which may hurt their future chances in the Party, can be invoked against them through internal Party procedures; but they may entirely avoid such legal punishments as imprisonment.[58] To give an example: In December 1984, the Chinese press reported that in the preceding thirteen months, "279 Party officials in Tianjin had been subjected to disciplinary measures with 85 of them stripped of their party membership for 'crimes ranging from corruption to embezzlement.' "[59]

Although China's new laws have had only a limited effect on the practice of *circumventing* the legal system, they may be having a greater impact in addressing the issues of judicial autonomy when the legal system is actually involved. Still, although the Party as an institution may theoretically not be permitted to interfere in the judicial process, the Party's fingers remain in the pie: The Party still retains the right to determine whether actions by the courts and procuracies have conformed to Party policy; and the Party itself still trains all judges and most judicial personnel. The Party is, in short, *built into* the judicial system.

Lack of System of Judicial Precedent

The lack of a system of judicial precedent further illustrates the problem of political interference in the legal system. In 1957, one of China's leading legal theorists attempted to rationalize the Chinese leadership's viewpoint that Soviet intervention in Hungary was justifiable since it was "invited." In 1958 he was attacked as a "rightist" because this publicly stated legal rationale would likewise justify the Lebanese government's "invitation" to the United States to intervene. Policy had changed, and the principle of international law proposed by this theorist could not be allowed to serve as a precedent. This case illustrates the difficulties faced by any Chinese theorist hoping to develop a systematic "theory" of law and a concept of judicial precedent.[60]

Chinese courts do not formulate their own basis for legal decisions, such as common law in England or case law in the United States. Each decision is discrete and subject to being annulled if it transgresses the most recent policy preferences of the leadership. Lacking a system of judicial precedent, decisions made in one court are not available for reference by other courts, nor are the decisions of one court in any way binding on other courts. In fact, it is difficult even to gain access to the briefs of previous trials in the same court.[61]

This permits the laws to be applied arbitrarily, with nearly identical cases being treated differently even within the same court. This is the inevitable result of court decisions being post-facto attempts to rationalize policies or the local Party leader's politics. No concept of law as a process—an accumulation of legal and judicial precedents that as a body of values and procedures limits and determines actions—has developed in China. The Chinese seem to believe instead that if they have *a larger number of laws,* then they have more *law.* What they have in fact is a thoroughly un-systematized collection of decisions that do not add up to "legal theory."[62]

Like China's constitutions, the laws are always subject to revision without prior notification, and punishment for crimes may be changed. For example, when a sudden nationwide campaign to control crime was launched in the summer of 1983, the Chinese leaders, as in the past, simply amended the law in order to provide a legal basis for the execution of "broader categories of criminals than previously, including gang leaders, organizers of prostitution" and spies. This was in spite of the Criminal Law (Article 140), which provided that an organizer of prostitution "shall be sentenced to fixed-term imprisonment of not more than ten years." Certainly nothing in the Criminal Law informed the Chinese that economic corruption or robbing a Friendship store would bring the death penalty, as happened in 1983. In addition, hijackers of a Chinese airliner were summarily executed, even though the Criminal Law (Article 100) specifically states that the maximum punishment for airplane hijacking is life imprisonment. The Law of Criminal Procedures (Article 153), which required death sentences for violent crimes to be reviewed by the Supreme People's Court, was simply rescinded in 1983, so that a lower court could act without delay to execute those convicted of violent crimes. And in spite of the Law on Criminal Procedures (Article 155), which specifically prohibits the execution of criminals in public, this practice continued in the 1980s.[63]

Given the deterioration of the social order and the conspicuous need to control rampant crime, such *ad hoc* changes and the retroactivity of the laws might be seen as both realistic and effective. Crime plummeted some 30 percent after the 1983 anti-crime campaign began. Yet such changes have negatively affected the people's confidence in the leaders' commitment to rule by law. The people will continue to be insecure about future interpretations of their actions. China's reform leaders recognize the importance of guaranteeing the predictability of the laws when changes in leadership occur. But the Chinese Constitution and other laws continue to reflect policies and politics. As a result, the political-socialist variable seems to be the major source of China's difficulties in developing a more modern and independent legal system.

Shortage of Trained Legal Personnel

Ideology, traditional culture, and the problems of development have all interacted to create a shortage of adequately trained legal personnel in China. The traditional Chinese antipathy toward resorting to the formal legal process combined with post-1949 policies to circumscribe the role that legal personnel could play and eventually to subordinate the entire system first to the Party and then to citizen activists. This discouraged any growth in the numbers of lawyers. In fact, as long as the traditional system of mediation, modified by the intervention of the Party, was capable of handling the vast majority of civil and criminal cases, China's inadequately staffed legal system did not seem to be a pressing problem. On the contrary, the willingness of the people to rely on mediation, paralegal, and extrajudicial processes and institutions, and to resolve their disputes at the lowest possible level, served to confirm the strength of the Chinese legal system—and of the Chinese political-moral system.

However, as noted above, the legal system gradually broke down, as did the traditional social/ethical order's ability to exercise normative controls adequate to prevent criminality. The need to reexamine the system became particularly acute because the acceleration of the modernization process after 1978 was accompanied by greater legal complexity. By 1983, 700 new laws, decrees, and regulations were approved or enacted.[64] The fact that the Chinese chose to modernize with the help of foreign countries necessitated dealing with foreign legal systems, with foreigners in China, and with principles and practices that required going beyond the pat norms of a socialist moral and political order to concrete legal documents, processes, and institutions. Further, foreigners hesitated to invest in China not only because of the dearth of laws and legal protection but also because of the unpredictability of the law.

Under such pressures, the Chinese felt compelled to create a more formal and complex legal system. This, in turn, required trained legal personnel, first to draw up new laws and subsequently to interpret the meaning of the new laws for each enterprise, ministry, or unit. New principles of taxation, contract laws, civil procedures, corporate law, foreign-venture law, commercial law, and other legal principles have drawn Chinese work units deeper into the legal system. But the desire to attract foreigners to invest in China is clearly the greatest stimulus to training more legal personnel. Evidence of this is the assignment of most of China's lawyers to positions related to international business transactions, not to positions in which they could address the average citizen's or work unit's problems.[65]

In some respects, then, the shortage of legal personnel is a new problem of the 1980s, not an unresolved one; but in the cyclical manner in which problems evolve, it is now inhibiting the very legal development that made it a problem. By 1984, the Chinese government had increased the number of full-time lawyers to 9,701 and part-time lawyers to 5,770 to serve the legal need of its one billion people and its ministries, enterprises, offices, etc.[66] This averages out to about one lawyer per 100,000 people. The Ministry of Justice has announced a target of training one lawyer for every 10,000 urban inhabitants or every 50,000 rural inhabitants by the turn of the century. The numbers hardly begin to suggest the depth of the problem of inadequate legal training. In fact, so few lawyers are available to fulfill the provision for the defendant's right to defense that the Law of Criminal Procedure (Article 26) offers the accused recourse to other forms of defense: self-defense, a citizen recommended by either a people's organization or the unit to which the accused belongs, a citizen approved by the people's court, or a close relative or guardian. Further, due to a shortage of legal personnel to serve as judges and arbitrators, Party officials often assume those positions by default. Of course, in making their decisions, they rely on their only area of expertise: Party policy.[67]

Mediation inadequate in context of greater complexity

Mediation continues to be used in almost all cases calling for legal redress of economic disputes. Article 14 of the Law on Civil Procedure (1982) endorses mediation as the preferred method of settlement of a civil dispute. There is, in fact, much reluctance to rely on the new Law of Economic Contracts if it means going to court.[68] But as China becomes a technologically more complex society, and as its economy becomes further decentralized, with individuals, organs, and enterprises making contracts with each other[69] as well as with foreigners,[70] China is faced with increasingly complex legal issues.

Mediation is likely to prove inadequate for many of the situations arising out of China's new economic policies. First, mediation (especially by "superior organs") is a comparatively slow process. It is particularly susceptible to the influence of personal power and persuasion (and may often favor the more powerful rather than those who are legally correct). Further, mediation is not done by legally competent personnel. As more laws are codified, increasingly difficult legal problems will arise, which will require trained personnel. This may explain the tendency toward formalism among China's "specialized households" in the countryside: They want to have formal, written contracts to protect them against local officials and against more powerful state and collective units in case a dispute arises.[71] In other words, if a state unit responsible for supplying coal to a "specialized household" does not fulfill its part of the contract and, in the process, causes serious losses to the household, the only real protection it would have against the power of the state would be contract law, and a fair application of it by trained and neutral legal personnel.

Second, the increasingly complex commercial and economic links with other countries have pressured the Chinese to formalize their legal system and to permit lawyers to become independent professionals. Westerners entering into economic contracts with the Chinese, for example, are particularly distressed that the same bureaucracy or enterprise that provokes a problem may decide the merits of the dispute. And to protect

Western personnel who work in China, they want to know in advance the precise nature of "economic crimes," "negligence," and "fault," when a contract is "void," the kind of legal process that will determine fault, how compensation is determined, etc. The Law of Economic Contracts, which governs economic relationships between enterprises, is quite legalistic and moves far toward addressing these anxieties. Until lawyers act on behalf of their clients, rather than in defense of China's collective interest and loyalty to socialism,[72] however, their role in advancing China's legal system will remain sharply circumscribed. Although it reflects a value judgment, it appears that thus far the concern for protecting the state's interests above all else has severely hindered the development of the legal profession.

Merging of political and legal studies

Efforts to address the issue of quantity and quality of legal personnel has been hindered by the expense of legal training. Its cost puts the legal profession in competition with demands for the allocation of scarce resources to other urgent problems confronting a poor country. But the legal training that has been available has been limited by the injection of political concerns. In the 1950s, China had only four institutes and four university law departments for training lawyers, but these "law schools" were actually institutes of *politics and law*. Law was never seen as a discipline separate from the study of politics. Even journals on legal topics were actually journals on law *and* politics.

After 1957, when most professionally trained legal personnel were denounced as "rightists," guilty of trying to eliminate the state's control of law and advocating the adoption of certain Western legal institutions, they were removed from positions in which they could influence legal development. As a result, the attempt to codify laws or to develop new laws was essentially shelved. Law schools and the teaching of law were inseparable from the profession of politics. Almost all legal "experts" who managed to survive the anti-rightist campaigns of the late 1950s and early 1960s were victims of the Cultural Revolution because, by virtue of their advanced education, they fell into the "stinking ninth category" of intellectuals. Law schools, shut down during the Cultural Revolution, reopened in the early 1970s with a severely truncated curriculum.

Thus, the old-guard, the liberal retreads trained in Western institutions, or at least in Western legal principles before 1949, had by the 1980s either died off or seen their own legal abilities atrophy through nonuse. But they were the only source of trained legal personnel that China had as of the early 1980s. With the opening to the West after the Third Plenum, old, even if out-of-circulation, legal experts were suddenly rehabilitated politically and given an exam to see if they still maintained adequate legal expertise.[73] Those who passed became responsible for the training of a new generation of legal experts. In the three years from 1980 to 1983, a mere 300 legal experts compiled fifty-four textbooks and related reference books for teaching about law![74] In 1982, the Ministry of Justice made successful testing by a legal bar examination one of the requirements for law practice.

By 1985, China's Ministry of Education had jurisdiction over thirty-seven law departments, with an annual enrollment of well over 10,000 students. Some graduates will become lawyers, but most will work for governmental ministries or for state enterprises.[75] Further, the state is training large numbers of "judicial workers" who have only six months of training, but the state assigns them legal duties, including judgeships. These short-term courses resemble China's training programs for barefoot doctors, or the training for paralegals in the United States.

The curriculum still emphasizes law as a tool of the state, with policies and politics basic to the correct use of the law. Law schools remain more concerned with the performance of students on the political section of tests and their political behavior than on the legal section.[76] Moreover, the inadequacy of training given to legal workers either by restored former legal personnel or personnel who have taken crash courses in law themselves, hardly augurs well for the first generation of new legal workers. Foreign lawyers have contributed to raising the level of legal education by offering special seminars in China on such topics as commercial law, contracts, and taxation, and by consulting with various ministries and enterprises. Some Chinese who have done well in China's law schools further their legal education in the West. In the meantime, the Chinese in their dealings with foreigners are often learning from "eating bitterness": When they are in the wrong according to their own published laws, they are having to pay dearly for their mistakes.

Persecution of lawyers

The fact that China's lawyers and legal theorists were in the past subjected to persecution when policy changed has also hindered legal development. In 1980, the Chinese adopted special "Provisional Regulations" to define a lawyer's functions and to protect the lawyer's rights against outside interference.[77] That these regulations did not go into effect until 1982 suggests the debate surrounding them. They accorded lawyers immunity from prosecution for defending cases assigned to them by the state. Thus, if lawyers were assigned to defend "counterrevolutionaries" or anyone else, they could not be condemned for defending them. But in fact, many of them have been.[78] As state employees, lawyers are obligated by law to "propagate the socialist legal system" and "serve loyally the cause of socialism." The defendant's or plaintiff's legal fees for a lawyer's services are paid to the state, not to the lawyer directly, so that the latter's primary loyalty to the state, not to the client, will be assured. Thus, the protection for lawyers from the "Provisional Regulations on Lawyers" may in practice be removed if a lawyer defends a client too well against the state's interests.

As employees of the state, most matters assigned to lawyers are considered "state secrets." The definition of "state secrets" still relies on a 1951 statute that says, in essence, that anything not published is a state secret, and that divulging state secrets is a crime. Thus, if a lawyer, or any other legal worker, divulges the details of a case to another person, this individual may be accused of a criminal act.[79] According to the 1979 Criminal Law, "Any state functionary who betrays any important secret of the state in violation of state security regulations to a serious degree shall be [sent to prison] for not more than seven years, or to detention, or to deprivation of political rights."[80] Thus, those who would be lawyers must not only worry about their immunity from political persecution when policy changes, but also about violating the law on state secrets.

Finally, the discipline of law falls under the rubric of "social science;" and the social sciences, because of their role in inculcating political values and rationalizing the Party line, are an integral part of China's propaganda machine. As a result, most Chinese regard them with great disdain and believe that only the least talented of the 4 percent that go on to higher education will enter any field of the social sciences.[81] In the 1980s, however, the attitude toward legal studies has changed considerably. This may largely be attributed to the leadership's own new perception of the vital importance of lawyers and the legal system and, no doubt, to the enhanced opportunities that those trained as lawyers now have of coming into contact with foreigners—with all that implies for access to foreign goods and trips to the West.

Attitudes Toward Law

Attitudes toward law were as much the cause as they were the effect of the deterioration of the formal legal system from 1957 to 1976. Some police and judicial cadres actually viewed the law as a hindrance to their fight against "the enemy," and legal powers were frequently abused by bureaucrats and Party officials. Such abuses increased dramatically in the years after 1957, but it became increasingly dangerous for ordinary people or even lower-level officials to accuse anyone with power of breaking the law. It was power, not law, that guaranteed a person's rights and limited his or her actions. Just as in traditional China, access to patronage and the "back door" has offered protection from the objective application of the law. Thus, it is hardly surprising that the Chinese people have grown cynical about the ability of law to protect their rights or prevent the abuse of power.

Lack of respect for the law combines with the problems of a pervasive ignorance of the law to present major obstacles to the development of an effective legal system. It would be unfair to say that in the past, the people's ignorance of the law greatly detracted from the development of the Chinese legal system as there was not much of a legal system of which to be ignorant. Still, until the 1980s, the Chinese people have been generally uninformed about the laws in existence and about their legal rights vis-à-vis officials. This has permitted its abuse by those, usually officials, who pretend to know its content. The presumption today, though not necessarily correct, is that knowledge of the law will activate the people to dare to challenge officials.

Several steps have been taken to systematically educate the people about their legal rights and responsibilities. Some of China's newspapers now carry regular columns explaining various aspects of the law to the ordinary reader, thereby making the law seem less formidable and remote. A monthly periodical, *Democracy and the Legal System,* discusses legal questions. Television stations broadcast lectures on law. Since 1983, street clinics in the major cities have given citizens at least some access to legal personnel and enabled them to ask questions about their legal rights and problems. The one million legal personnel who took part in the "know the law" campaign in its first year were deluged with requests from long lines of people eager to know what legal recourse they might have in particular cases. In 1983 the city of Beijing, with a population of 8 million, established its first Legal Advisory Office."[82] These exemplify important steps in providing rudimentary legal services and legal knowledge to the people, who must understand the laws before they can effectively use a formalized legal system.

Equality Before the Law

The issue of equality before the law is related to judicial independence. If the Party is allowed to interfere with the judicial process, those who oppose its policies will have difficulty obtaining justice. Equality before the law also relates to two other questions. First, *who* is to be protected by the principle of "equality before the law"? Although the 1954 Constitution and the Organic Law of the People's Courts stated that citizens of China are equal before the law, this proposition was rejected after 1966 for lacking a class viewpoint and "allowing counter-revolutionaries to gain equality with revolutionaries."[83] Because treating all persons equally left open the possibility of giving legal protection to counterrevolutionaries, the leftists ignored the principle. Thus, once a person was labeled a counterrevolutionary, all recourse to the law was denied to that individual. The 1978 Constitution, still heavily influenced by leftist values, offered no statement concerning equality before the law. Article 18 stated the need to *punish* (not *protect* the legal or political rights of) "all traitors and counterrevolutionaries" and "new-born bourgeois elements and other bad elements"; and in accordance with the then-existing law, it deprived "landlords, rich peasants, and reactionary capitalists who have not yet been reformed" of political rights. Here again, the leadership's policies and politics determined who should actually receive the protection of the law.

The second questions is, does the principle of the equality of all citizens before the law mean only that they are equal in the judicial process, or does it also include equal treatment to all classes in the *legislation* that is formulated? Discussions among leaders in the legal field suggest that all citizens are equal in the *application* of the law (Article 4 of the Law on Criminal Procedure); but there is disagreement over whether equality is both a judicial and a legislative principle. In other words, if the principle of equality before the law were introduced in the legislative process, then even the "remnants" of the exploiting classes, counterrevolutionaries, and criminals would have their interests embodied in the law. Thus, according to one view, in the legislative process, the concept of "everyone is equal before the law" refers only to "the people" (acknowledged to be a political concept) and does not include the "enemies of the people."[84]

The Marxist belief that law has a class nature, one reflecting the ethics and interests of the ruling class, is at the heart of the issue of equality before the law. Were this principle incorporated in the legislative process, it would negate the class nature of laws. The logical conclusion of this argument is, therefore, that the principle of equality before the law cannot be incorporated into the legislative process until China becomes a classless society. The opposing viewpoint is that it should be embodied in both the legislative and judicial processes and, therefore, should even give rights to "enemies of the people"—at least until it is *proven* that they have committed a crime.[85]

The Laws on the Organization of the People's Courts and the People's Procuratorates, and the Law on Criminal Procedure upheld the principle of the equality of *all* citizens before the law; but it was not a constitutionally guaranteed right until the 1982 Constitution (Article 33). Article 34, in an attempt to eliminate the prevailing practice of depriving certain people of political rights according to nonlegal criteria, specifically dismisses reasons for deprivation of rights such as "family background," "education," and "property status." The 1982 Constitution really seems less concerned with the esoteric issues surrounding equality before the law, than with the use of political criteria and extralegal procedures and institutions to deprive those accused of "deviance" of their rights. It implicitly condemns this kind of extralegal persecution of people for political reasons. But there is still no consensus about how these articles should be interpreted.

Counterrevolutionaries and Political Criminals

Counterrevolutionary"[86] is a special type of label for a person who is in many instances no more than a political deviant. Counterrevolutionaries are those who attempt to subvert the state through criminal *or* political activities. These activities are actually banned by law, whereas other kinds of deviance are judged not by the law but by political authorities.

Over the years, there has been a wide range of interpretation and opinion as to the dividing line between lawful and counterrevolutionary actions and how a person's status or class background relates to such judgments. In the 1980s, the reform leaders' stance has been that the determination of whether an offense is counterrevolutionary depends on the actual deeds and whether the person's actions have a "counterrevolutionary purpose," and not, as in the past, on the person's class background, "thoughts," or personal habits.[87] This stance is a repudiation of the "leftist line," which from 1957 to 1976 condemned reliance upon law for determining criminality as a "bourgeois theory" opposed to the Party's principles and policies. Innocent people "were branded as 'counter-revolutionaries' solely on charges of 'viciously smearing party leaders,' though they did not harbour any counter-revolutionary motives."[88]

In spite of the reform leadership's repudiation of the nonlegal determination of criminality, in the 1980s any attack on the "four basic principles" has become the equivalent of "viciously smearing Party leaders" and is similarly condemned as counterrevolutionary. The present *legal* basis for determining counterrevolutionary criminality is, therefore, now neatly predicated upon upholding the four basic principles. Yet, the Chinese leadership has never explained why the same actions committed by "counterrevolutionaries" such as the Gang of Four, and those committed by "true Marxist revolutionaries" such as Mao Zedong, are treated differently. Did the Gang really commit "crimes" (and hence were tried on legally based criminal charges), whereas Mao just made "mistakes"? To treat them differently suggests that an individual's politics are still an integral part of the determination of counterrevolutionary guilt, even when the actual deeds and their outcomes are the same.

The Criminal Code leaves the door ajar for punishing political deviants under the category of "counterrevolutionary crimes."[89] Cases involving political dissidents indicate that the limits of dissent and the definition of the criminal category of counterrevolutionary remain murky. The Criminal Law defines a counterrevolutionary act as one aimed at overthrowing the dictatorship of the proletariat and socialism, but it does not indicate how it will be determined whether that was the true nature of the offense. Indeed, it in no way obstructs prosecuting people essentially for the political "crime" of opposing the leadership or its policies.

Because the government denies that the category of political criminal exists (as this might raise the issue of the denial of human rights and the blatant disregard of the rule of law), it need not recognize the rights of political criminals under the law. Hence, there is no need to arrest or detain them according to the Law of Criminal Procedure nor for the procuracy or courts to become involved to determine guilt or whether the punishment fits the crime: There was no "crime." Their acts offend the Party, not the law. For this reason, political criminals are usually punished by political or administrative authorities, the very same individuals who originally decided that something was "deviant" about their behavior.

Some Chinese believe that political criminals are treated far worse than ordinary criminals because in a broad sense they threaten the political system itself, whereas ordinary criminals only threaten a narrow part of the social order. Although political deviants are rarely imprisoned, they may be relentlessly subjected to political persecution, physical punishment, and psychological abuse through shunning, isolation, and humiliation. They are often required to have their thoughts corrected by a process termed "education through labor." Unlike "reform through labor," which is a punishment in accordance with Criminal Law and is handled by the judicial system, education through labor is an administrative measure handled by the "education through labor" committees that exist at all levels of the Chinese government. A representative of the public security department sits on this committee, and the committee makes a decision without reference to law. In 1986, the maximum amount of time for education through labor was four years.[90] When political criminals are imprisoned, they are not allowed to read, write, or talk to one another (unless they are in a labor camp) and are kept under surveillance—as if they might conspire while in prison to bring down the state.

In addition, political criminals may be denied opportunities to advance in the workplace, expelled from their work units (thereupon losing their urban residency permits), sent to a distant province to work, put under mass surveillance, or forced to undergo protracted political study and self-criticism. Even under the reform leadership in the 1980s, these kinds of actions have been taken against a number of individuals who were considered political deviants, all without recourse to the legal system. The severity of punishment for ordinary criminals is, on the other hand, determined by the judicial process. They may plea-bargain for reduced sentences, and they will retain their legal residence and the right to return to their job after serving their sentence.

In general, the reform leadership's attention in the 1980s has been far more absorbed with ordinary criminality and the threat this poses to its policies and the social fabric of China. Individuals such as the playwright Bai Hua, who in an earlier period would have been punished by the Party as if they were political criminals, are now criticized for specific antisocialist works and asked to make public recantations and self-criticisms. Similarly, in early 1987 the removal (in the name of "antibourgeois liberalism") of a number of prominent individuals from Party membership, notably Fang Lizhi, a well-known university leader, and Wang Ruowang and Liu Binyan, prominent writers (all three of whom had also been victims of the 1957 Anti-Rightist Campaign), did not result in their complete removal from positions of influence. They were removed from the Party, but all were allowed to continue writing and to deliver conference papers, albeit with a different "tone" than before. Their careers were not put on hold while they underwent thought reform.

BEYOND THE LEGAL SYSTEM: PROBLEMS IN CONTROLLING NONCRIMINAL DEVIANCE

Broad Definition of Deviance

Apart from counterrevolutionary behavior, most deviant behavior in the PRC today is not legally "criminal." Mao's theory of contradictions, which has yet to be repudiated, asserts that criminality is far more serious than deviance. Criminal cases are "contradictions between the people and the enemy," and they must be resolved with punishment according to the law. Counterevolutionaries have, therefore, at least some recourse to the law. Deviance, on the other hand, is merely a contradiction among the people, and can for this reason be resolved by the people through criticism/self-criticism sessions or by mass movements.[91]

Criminality in China has its sources in the tensions associated with economic development, unemployment, and societal breakdown, as it does in most underdeveloped countries. For criminality, the developmental variable may be the key one. Deviance is another matter. Because what is deviant is merely a matter of definition, it has its roots in ideology and China's traditional culture. The traditional Chinese intolerance for cultural nonconformity has provided the perfect milieu for post-1949 intolerance of political nonconformity. In a society that has from ancient times to the present required acceptance of a standard of absolute truth, with no alternative truths permissible, there has been little room for individual differences in behavior, thoughts, and attitudes.

The basis for this standard of absolute truth since 1949 has been Party diktat. These are "infallible" and contribute to a rigidity that permeates the entire socialist system. The built-in ideological intolerance for diversity and pluralism is precisely what makes it so easy for an ordinary Chinese citizen to fall into the deviant category. Socialist ideology in itself need not have been quite so narrowly defined; but extremist values, especially those of Mao Zedong and "leftists," constricted socialist ideology into a narrow spectrum of acceptable attitudes, thoughts, and behavior. The political leadership has, in short, repeatedly used ideology to draw a clear line between its enemies and its friends in an ever more restrictive manner. Thus, in a one-party socialist dictatorship such as China's, since diversity of opinion cannot be reflected in an electoral and legislative system, or protected by an adequate legal and judicial system, it necessarily surfaces in the interpretation of deviance.

Deviance in the PRC is thus quintessentially political. Although much of what is decried as deviant is decidedly cultural in the sense that it challenges traditional Chinese values, mores, social customs, or expectations, the Party normally casts deviance in political terms. Culturally embedded concepts of self-sacrifice, serving the collective, duty, rank, obedience, loyalty, and respect for authority are reformulated and stated in acceptable political vocabulary. To be acceptable in Chinese cultural terms, then, is fundamental to being acceptable in political terms.

Thought Reform

Thought reform serves both as a preventative control measure and a corrective to crime and deviance. The entire propaganda and educational machine produces a uniform normative framework in an effort to create a unified national will and objective. According to dissidents, such as a leader of one of the 1978–1979 democratic movement's key organs shortly before his arrest,

> China's youth has been taught that not only must the activities and movements of people be unified but that so must their souls and innermost thoughts be similarly united. . . . From the cradle to the grave, people are only allowed to believe—indeed must believe—in one "ism." All else is criminal except to read the one type of "philosophy," to laud one type of system, to fawn on one leader and to curry favour with one political party.[92]

The following describes some of the institutions and processes used to control deviance in thought.

Small groups (xiaozu) and mass mobilization (yundong)

Small groups are organized in neighborhoods, factories, mines, government offices, schools, and the military. In urban China, and to a lesser extent among the peasantry, everyone belongs to a small group of about eight to fifteen people. Small groups are created by the state for its own purposes. They do not emerge spontaneously or determine their own agenda for action. Members of a small group do regular work and activities together. This affords them an opportunity to become familiar with each other's personal strengths and weaknesses in a "nonthreatening" environment, but their main function is control. For "preventative" control purposes, these groups engage in political study, including both the study of Marxism-Leninism-Mao Zedong Thought, and the most recent state and Party directives on everything from the heroism of the single-child family, and the correct attitude toward foreign values, to public sanitation, production, and the laws. In this way, the participants are informed about what they are supposed to believe at any given time.[93] Those whose thoughts are flowing, even if unconsciously, in the wrong direction are criticized and pressured to think correctly; whereas those whose actual behavior has degenerated into the deviant category are subjected to highly punitive processes, without recourse to the legal system.

Small-group mobilization for the purpose of shunning and shaming deviants during the most intense periods of *mass mobilization campaigns* (ad hoc organizational measures to control deviance and criminality) provides a means "to absorb deviants into the very institutions where they are discovered." The rationale of this process of "struggle" is again based on the idea of "educability" and the belief that "curing" political deviance warrants "the risks involved in sometimes prolonged disruptions of productive and administrative routines."[94] For example, in the case of high-level KMT military personnel (not low-level—they were often shot) captured during the civil war from 1945 to 1949, the Communist Party expended enormous resources after 1949 to indoctrinate and "reeducate" them, and to force them to admit their "wrong" deeds, after which they were usually released back into Chinese society.[95] Similarly, during the "Five-Antis Campaign" of 1951–1952, "tiger beating teams," composed of worker activists, were organized to find and harass errant capitalists until they confessed their crimes and paid their debts to the state and the people. While imprisoned in their offices or homes for prolonged periods, outside their doors "tiger-beaters" shouted accusations against them. A rash of suicides resulted from this form of humiliation. The 1957 Anti-Rightist Campaign also hoped to reform through reeducation: The "sending down" (*xiafang*), initially used to inculcate rural values into urbanites and to reduce the size of urban bureaucracies, became a method to reeducate "rightist" and "right-tending" cadres and intellectuals by sending them to the countryside to participate in labor with the peasants. Some 300,000 to 400,000 young intellectuals were "sent down" as a result of the Anti-Rightist Campaign and remained there for the next twenty years. But bureaucrats usually only remained in the countryside until they could prove they had reformed their thoughts, a process which on the average took nine months. Figures available indicate that as many as 60 million people actively participated in *xiafang* deviance-control campaigns carried out between 1949 and 1965.[96]

The Chinese clearly view *thoughts* as the point at which control must begin, for in their view bad thoughts inevitably lead to bad actions, including criminality.[97] The Cultural Revolution provides a frightening commentary on the extent to which the leadership successfully inculcated the importance, and the possibility, of reforming people's thoughts: Red Guards (and others) acted on this conviction by putting dunce caps on individuals and parading them in an excruciatingly painful hand-cuffed "airplane" position through hostile crowds that denounced them, spit on them, hit them. They beat those who resisted thought reform, locked alleged deviants in bathrooms, small dark rooms ("cow pens"), and forced highly placed officials and intellectuals to engage full-time in such demeaning labor as cleaning latrines. Most of these things were done out of the conviction that deviants would thereby realize the need to reform their thoughts.[98]

Small groups have used extremist tactics against actual or even potential deviance; for in the absence of the rule of law, those holding power within these groups determined the definition of a "rightist," "revisionist," "counterrevolutionary," or "renegade scab." It appears that the definition of "deviance" has varied even *within* work units, and has depended on who held power. One study indicates that a minority of activists can dominate an entire organization, such as a factory or school, through the small-group network, largely by mobilizing group pressure against individual group members. Those who are more emotionally tied into the group are naturally more susceptible to group pressures. By emphasizing group solidarity, and playing upon the traditional Chinese fear of ostracism, the Party hopes that people will attempt to earn praise and avoid criticism.[99]

An alternative to haranguing, torturing, and ostracizing the enemies of the dominant faction in any given work unit could easily have been *removing* them from positions of power. But, except for the deviant intellectuals in universities and the Academy of Sciences sent out to the border regions repeatedly since 1957, this has not been the preferred remedy. In short, simply *getting rid of* deviants or criminals (or one's political enemies), either by incarceration or execution, does not fit in with the Chinese view of how to tackle the problems of the human condition.

> [I]t is only the tiny handful of criminal elements guilty of serious crimes whom we punish without delay to the full extent of the law; *all criminals, other than those sentenced to death and immediately executed, must be subjected to education and remolding and the great majority of them made into new persons.*[100]

Executions, however, are as much for the purpose of educating the public about the consequences of misbehavior as for punishing the criminal. Thus, executions in 1983 again took place in stadiums so that thousands of people could attend—and think about the dire consequences of bad behavior.[101] For the time being, however, international condemnation of the Chinese for this practice appears to have ended it.

Alternatives to normative deviance-control measures

From a short-run perspective, deviance-control measures seemingly provided the necessary environment for social order and political consciousness. But from the long-run perspective, they have been counterproductive. Because China's leaders have defined deviance too broadly, altered their definition of deviance too frequently, and punished alleged deviants too severely, each successive assault on deviance proved short lived. Alienation deepened as campaigns became increasingly shrill, while at the same time they accomplished less in terms of desired economic and production goals.[102] The long-run results have been cynicism among the youth, who have for this reason become increasingly passive politically;[103] the questioning of the wisdom of a leadership that punished its most talented people, and which cannot decide once and for all what is "right" and what is "wrong;" a deep-seated hatred of the Party for encouraging behavior disruptive to the participants' personal lives; and a population generally hesitant to contribute toward China's development for fear of political repercussions.

In the 1980s, normative control measures have succeeded in controlling some criminal elements and combatting political deviance, but they have simultaneously intimidated ordinary citizens, rendering them compliant and passive. China's leaders have turned, therefore, to a combination of coercive and legal measures to control criminal elements, and remunerative measures to reward and stimulate the rest of the population to support and contribute more positively to their policy objectives. Although remuneration and coercion are, in the short run, far more costly methods of social control, the results by the late 1980s indicated that they are far cheaper than the quasi-coercive normative measures (such as struggle sessions and campaigns) previously used.

Efforts to control political deviance have taken new forms: an emphasis on recuitment of talented and educated individuals, "get rich" policies in the economic arena (to undercut "leftist deviance"), and political liberalization, which would benefit all intellectuals who did not challenge the "four basic principles." Officials condemn the "kind and honest"—but idle, tea-drinking—cadres who lack the boldness to contribute to China's modernization efforts. "People are afraid of doing work and committing mistakes, but not afraid of remaining idle." Enterprising individuals who dare "to explore new and challenge old ways" may sometimes err; but if they are punished, they will tend to remain idle and play it safe, which leads to bureaucratism and lethargy. As one manager put it, "Cadres possessing both ability and faults are preferable to those who have neither."[104]

Nevertheless, even the reform leaders feel compelled to reeducate both deviants and criminals, this in spite of the fact that many of these leaders were themselves the victims of reeducation during the "ten bad years." For example, in 1983 the public security sector was reprimanded for its "outmoded concepts, ways of thinking, theoretical viewpoints and work styles," because public security organs thought their work was limited to law enforcement, when in fact they are also "educational agencies." They must "educate the masses . . . so that they know the law, obey it, . . . and become moral human beings with ideals and a sense of discipline."[105]

From the perspective of national unity, strict deviance control may be considered a positive factor that has contributed to fairly narrow parameters of behavior and a high level of conformity to the state's values and objectives. To the extent that *control* over the population must be considered a central issue for *any* Chinese government, control of deviance is absolutely vital. The real issue is how much control, over which people, for what purpose, and the relative centrality of deviance control compared to other vital goals. Over the years, China's leaders have failed to resolve the issue of how much control is necessary, and at what point the advantages of control outweigh the disadvantages. In any event, control has been difficult to achieve, precisely because the standards for deviance are broad, abstract, and ill-defined, and because they, like the laws, change whenever the leaders or policies change.

Structures That Permit Deviation and Crime

Some structures allow, or even encourage, deviance,[106] including criminality. For example, in the 1980s, we can point to new capitalist-style market schemes, decentralization of decision making, changes in the supply system, and modifications in production units in China that purposefully encourage the pursuit of profit. The mind-set of materialism, in turn, usually accompanies the pursuit of profits and often leads to both deviance and criminality.

Because the PRC had previously prohibited a market economy, it lacked experience in addressing the general spectrum of problems that it tends to spawn, especially one caught halfway between being a centrally orchestrated command economy and a free market economy. The Chinese leadership has repeatedly acknowledged that the rapid changes in structure in the 1980s, combined with inadequate supervision by the Party or administrative leaders over those new structures, has permitted economic corruption. Further, economic liberalization policies and the focus on competitiveness and self-enrichment have put a premium on behavior that is effective in increasing productivity, seemingly by any method. The issue for the leaders is where to draw the line. How far, for example, can individuals go to obtain necessary raw materials for production before they have broken the law? How much profit can middlemen make and through what kind of dealings before they have engaged in criminal actions?

The conditions of China's mixed socialist-capitalist system have permitted the emergence of individuals who are willing to bring together the conflicting demands of the mixed economy. To illustrate, under the new orders of the early 1980s for enterprises to "get rich," efficient productive enterprises quickly grew frustrated. On the one hand, they could produce more and higher quality goods than less efficient, less productive enterprises. On the other hand, when they tried to expand their productive capacity to make greater profits, they came up against the fact that the necessary supplies were still being uniformly allocated by the center in disregard of factors of profitability, efficiency, and so on. What to do? Either the management itself could manipulate the administrative apparatus to gain greater profits, or it could find a "middleman" who would, for a price, be willing to *get* additional necessary supplies for the enterprise. The means used—blackmail, extortion, theft—were his business. The enterprise simply paid him for delivering.

According to a report on economic crimes by the Party's Central Commission for Discipline Inspection, some criminality has resulted from the "indiscriminate hiring of inveterate criminals by state and collectively run enterprises in the belief that they are good at making money."[107] Obviously it has not been in the self-interest of enterprises to take notice of possibly criminal actions, as often it is precisely such behavior that helped advance their profits.

Thus, in addition to economic criminality, China is facing a peculiarly socialist form of corruption: criminality carried out to benefit collective units, even if it is at the expense of other units' productivity, or at the cost of wasting national resources. Many enterprises try to hide their profits to avoid turning over a larger percentage of profits to the state. Some production units have underreported production, engaged in other forms of collectively corrupt behavior, or simply not carried out state policies. China's leaders have openly commented on the need to halt what had become common practices as a result of this loyalty to the collectivity: the illegal acquisition of raw materials by enterprises; the illegal sale of their products; falsified names on the accounts of enterprises depositing funds in banks; the illegal transfer of bank credits; paying commissions to middlemen to acquire materials or find markets for their products; and outright bribery.[108] The effort to ferret out economic corruption and malpractices by cadres steadily escalated after 1981, with the major three-and-a-half-year Party rectification campaign (1983–1987) and criminal investigations as part of the overall effort.

The development in China of "collective bodies" (*jiti*), which are large, even enormous bodies that command substantial resources, and are quintessentially competitive units (competing for the state's limited resources against all other units) has placed an intermediate unit for loyalty between the individual and the state. Most individuals are linked primarily to their work "unit" (*danwei*) or *jiti*, whether it be an enterprise, a ministry, university, or a factory, which can provide or withhold all things the individual wants or needs. The individual's interest is, therefore, in having his or her unit do well. In the past, the same was true of agricultural team or brigade members, whose major link was with their production unit, and the resources they received as members of a production unit could be used to resist the powers of the state, just as villages in traditional China did.[109]

The fundamental question that the Chinese government continues to face is how much deviance, whether collectively or individually oriented, can be tolerated at any given time. The answer must take into account at what point the social-political-economic order is truly threatened, and how much of a challenge is actually healthy for the system. But what seems obvious is that a minimalist legal system as a form of social-political control has been supplemented by a maximalist system of deviance control; and that the unpredictability and intrusion of politics into both forms of control have greatly impaired their effectiveness.

CONCLUSIONS

The Third Plenum of December 1978 launched the beginning of a new era in China's legal development, with China's leaders boldly promoting a new legal order. But the legal system is still in a state of becoming because China's leaders are concerned about the unknown consequences of having laws, rather than the Party, as the reference point for what is right and wrong. The underlying objectives, institutional underpinnings, and ideological principles of socialism continue to limit the direction and speed of China's legal development.

In spite of this overriding concern for socialism's fate, China's leaders feel that the potential benefits of a comprehensive legal system outweigh the potential disadvantages. Their sudden embrace of the law may, of course, be seen as highly utilitarian, a response to the new demands on the legal system that China's "open door" policy introduced. Foreign trade, foreign investments, joint ventures, and tourism had by 1978 made China's existing laws and regulations inadequate. The numerous laws written since 1979 seem to have arisen less out of an awareness of the need for such laws than from a reluctant recognition that greater foreign business and commerce would be stymied without them. These laws have, however, also profoundly influenced Chinese enterpreneurs' legal relationships with each other.

The Third Plenum was a watershed because it marked the demise of "leftist" influence on legal development. Further, the destruction of traditional Chinese values, a crisis of faith in Marxism-Leninism-Mao Zedong Thought, and disenchantment with the Party's role as a model of social virtues and values led to a moral vacuum, which in turn led to criminality and a challenge to law and order. For this reason, the Chinese leadership resorted anew to the law to reestablish a legal basis for ethical order, a task which as a first step seemed far less formidable than restoring the concept of "Party infallibility" or the sanctity of Marxism-Leninism-Mao Zedong Thought. Because the Chinese people see the protection of their individual rights as having far less to do with laws and constitutions than with the government's morality and efficiency,[110] however, formal constitutional and legal provisions matter little to them.

Deng Xiaoping, was, however, committed to eliminating opportunities for officials to abuse power. The Law on Criminal Procedure carefully delineates the legal process for the detention or arrest of an individual, and it prohibits arbitrary detentions or arrests and convictions
based on such subjective factors as political viewpoint, and class and educational background. Yet, because the Party retains its own independent
"disciplinary inspection commissions" for searching out and taking disciplinary measures against deviants, anti-Party elements and counterrevolutionaries, the formal legal protection offered by the laws can easily be
rendered meaningless.

Since late 1978, the Chinese legal system has undergone dramatic
development in order to address societal crisis, foreign pressures, and issues concerning the power structure. If the legal system is respected, the
plethora of new laws, rules, and regulations will eventually envelop the
Chinese in a legal web that will effectively inhibit the abuse of power by
officials.

In spite of the many limitations to the new system of socialist legality,
the problems it is still unable to resolve, and the new problems it is creating,
it must be viewed as a positive step forward. This advance may, in closing,
be attributed to the leadership's success in resolving the tensions among the
relevant cultural, ideological, and developmental factors, a success made
possible largely by limiting the influence of the political-ideological factor.

NOTES

[1]Liu Binyan, "The Fifth Man in the Overcoat," in Perry Link (ed), *People or Monsters?*
(Bloomington: Indiana University Press, 1983), pp. 90, 91.

[2]For an in-depth examination of China's history of constitutionalism, see Jerome Alan
Cohen, "China's Changing Constitution," *China Quarterly* (December 1978), pp. 794–841.

[3]Except where otherwise noted, information on the formal structure of the Chinese
legal system is derived from *China: Facts and Figures, the Legal System* (Beijing: Foreign Languages Press, November 1982), pp. 2, 3; and from *China Reconstructs* (June 1980).

[4]"Minister on Social Order in China," *Beijing Review (BR)*, No. 34 (August 25, 1986), p.
13.

[5]*Laojiao* is a "noncriminal" sanction, determined solely by an administrative decision,
under which a person may be confined for up to four years in what is virtually a labor camp,
without access to any of the rights prescribed by the legal system. See "Supplementary Regulations of the State Council and Rehabilitation through Labor" (Promulgated November 29,
1979), as commented on in Jerome Alan Cohen, "Foreword—China's Criminal Codes," *Journal of Criminal Law and Criminology*, Vol. 73, No. 1 (1982) (Northwestern University School of
Law), pp. 136, 137. Harvard East Asian Legal Studies reprint, No. 29.

[6]George T. Felkenes, "Criminal Justice in the People's Republic of China: A System of
Contradictions," *Judicature*, Vol. 69 (April–May 1986), cited in Donald Wilson, "An Overview
of China's Legal System," graduate seminar paper (December 1986), Northeastern University,
Department of Political Science.

[7]Lynn T. White, III, "Deviance, Modernization, Rations, and Household Registers in
Urban China," in Amy A. Wilson, Sidney L. Greenblatt, and Richard W. Wilson (eds), *Deviance
and Social Control in Chinese Society* (New York: Praeger Special Studies, 1977), p. 155.

⁸Ibid., pp. 151–171.

⁹A. Doak Barnett's sudy in the 1960s indicated that the Party Organization Department was responsible only for Party cadres' dossiers, whereas the personnel department kept non-Party members' dossiers. But the 1983 Handbook of the Party's Central Organization Department drew no such distinction. See Melanie Manion, "The Cadre Management System, Post-Mao: The Appointment, Promotion, Transfer, and Removal of Party and State Leaders," *China Quarterly*, No. 102 (June 1985) p. 224, note 69.

¹⁰Much of the information below on dossier content comes from discussion with Chinese scholars studying in the United States who had themselves been tormented because of undisclosed information available in their dossiers.

¹¹The key to such rapid fluctuations in one's values is, according to some Chinese, simply never to be very deeply committed to any values, and not to analyze what the Party says very closely. This results in fewer difficulties in adjusting one's thoughts when the Party announces a change. That so many Chinese do just this no doubt reflects the widespread cynicism and nihilism that has developed.

¹²"Ex-prisoner Becomes Vice-Governor," *China Daily (CD)* (February 6, 1984), p. 6.

¹³Sidney L. Greenblatt, "Campaigns and the Manufacture of Deviance," Greenblatt, Wilson, and Wilson (eds), *Deviance and Social Control*, p. 112.

¹⁴Manion, "Cadre Management System," pp. 224, 225.

¹⁵Stanley Lubman and Gregory C. Wajnowski, "Criminal Justice and the Foreigner," *The China Business Review* (November–December 1985), p. 28.

¹⁶Paul A. Allen and Marc S. Palay, "China Law: Economic Courts," *The China Business Review* (November–December 1981), p. 48.

¹⁷Lubman and Wajnowski, "Criminal Justice," p. 28.

¹⁸Allen and Palay, "China Law," p. 45.

¹⁹Lubman and Wajnowski, "Criminal Justice," pp. 28, 29.

²⁰James Feinerman, Georgetown University Law School, correspondence, 1984.

²¹Donald Clarke, School of Oriental and African Studies, University of London, correspondence, 1987. On Mediation, see Stanley Lubman, "Mao and Mediation," *California Law Review*, Vol. 55 (1967), pp. 1284ff; and Jerome Alan Cohen, "Chinese Mediation on the Eve of Modernization," *California Law Review*, Vol. 54 (1966), pp. 1201ff.

²²"Mediation Committees," *BR*, No. 41 (October 12, 1981), p. 8.

²³"How China Handles Civil Disputes," *BR*, No. 7 (February 13, 1984), pp. 24, 25.

²⁴Minor civil disputes would include those "involving neighborhood relations, housing, debts, marriage, family, compensation for losses, inheritance, division of family property, provision of livelihood for aged parents, support of children after divorce, etc. Minor criminal cases involve such matters as physical injury of a minor type, maltreatment, petty larceny, encroachments, scuffles or fist fights, and slandering." *China: Facts*, p. 2.

²⁵"Mediation Committees," p. 8.

²⁶"How China Handles Civil Disputes," pp. 24, 25.

²⁷By contrast, the United States has 565,000 lawyers to protect the rights of 231 million people. This works out to one lawyer per *409* people. New York City alone has 42,000 lawyers! Christopher Wren, "China Moves to Resurrect a Credible Legal System," *The New York Times* (December 5, 1982), p. 22.

²⁸Leng Shao-chuan, "The Chinese Judicial System: A New Direction," in Sidney Greenblatt, Richard Wilson, and Amy Wilson (eds), *Organizational Behavior in Chinese Society* (New York: Praeger, 1981), p. 113. For an analysis of the PRC's judicial development before the Cultural Revolution, see Jerome A. Cohen, *The Criminal Process in the People's Republic of China* (Cambridge, Mass.: Harvard University Press, 1968) and Leng Shao-chuan, *Justice in Communist China* (Dobbs Ferry, N.Y.: Oceana, 1967).

²⁹Anne F. Thurston, "Victims of China's Cultural Revolution: The Invisible Wounds," Parts I and II, in *Pacific Affairs* (Winter 1984–1985, pp. 599–620, and Spring 1985, pp. 5–27, respectively).

³⁰*China: Facts*, pp. 1, 2.

³¹Jerome Alan Cohen, "Will China Have a Formal Legal System?" *American Bar Association Journal (ABAJ)*, (October 1978), Vol. 64, p. 1511.

³²Wang Jiafu, "Certain Problems in the Compiling and Writing of The Theory of the State and Law," in *Political and Legal Studies (Zhengfa Yanjiu)*, No. 1 (1962), pp. 35–40.

[33]Leng, "Chinese Judicial System," p. 113.

[34]*China News Analysis*, No. 1215 (September 11, 1981), pp. 3, 7.

[35]Zhang Zhiye, "Legislative and Judicial Work in China," *BR*, No. 33 (August 15, 1983), p. 20.

[36]Prison in Shenyang, August 1979. Case described to our delegation while visiting the prison and after having met the prisoner.

[37]"Mistreatment," *CD* (July 26, 1984), p. 3. This was an announcement of the woman's arrest. The outcome of the case is unknown to author.

[38]Lubman and Wajnowski, "Criminal Justice," p. 27.

[39]On the issue of negligence and criminal intent, see Jiang Rentian, "On Indirect, Intentional Crime and Motives," *Political and Legal Studies*, No. 2 (1983), pp. 18–20.

[40]Fortunately for this American businessman, it was later discovered that the hotel's fire doors were locked and that the night security guards were off in the ballroom enjoying the music. The fate of those guards is unknown.

[41]Leng, "Chinese Judicial System," p. 126.

[42]Cohen, "Will China Have a Formal Legal System?" p. 1511.

[43]Dorothy Fontana, "Background to the Fall of Hua Guofeng," *Asian Survey* (March 1982), pp. 252, 253.

[44]Sun Guohua, "Relationship Between Party Policy and the Law," *Faxue Yanjiu*, (December 1978) pp. 29, 30, and *FBIS, Daily Report: PRC* (July 2, 1979), pp. L4, L5; *RMRB* (July 29, 1979), p. 1; as referenced in Leng, "Chinese Judicial System," p. 126; and "Constitutional Safeguards," *CD* (May 26, 1984), p. 3.

[45]Leng, "Chinese Judicial System," p. 126. Reference is to Peng Zhen's statement in *People's Daily* (July 29, 1979), p. 1, and to others.

[46]*Guangdong Provincial Broadcast* (October 27, 1980), as quoted in Cohen, "Foreword—China's Criminal Codes," p. 36.

[47]Zhang Zhiye, "Legislative and Judicial Work in China," p. 20.

[48]The New China News Agency estimated that 60% of the "counterrevolutionary" charges made during the Cultural Revolution had no other basis than that the Gang of Four found certain people and their actions to their distaste. They arbitrarily determined what was right and wrong, and no laws protected the people from false charges. Kathryn Cronin, "The Changing Face of Justice," *U.S.-China Review* (May–June 1980), p. 12. If we accept this figure to cover those people who were found guilty of crimes and punished, but had their punishments ended or their labels removed before 1978, this perhaps gets us closer to the truth about the degree of fairness in the system of mass justice. It is nevertheless still surprising that even 40% of the charges were considered accurate by the post-1976 leadership.

[49]Civil law and economic laws are not necessarily published even if they only affect Chinese citizens. Many of the economic "crimes" committed in the 1980s, for example, could be attributed to the fact that those individuals involved did not know what legal limits existed. Thus, in such cases as those Hainan Island officials wheeling and dealing in motorcycle and auto imports and their resale to make a profit, there was nothing in the existing published laws stating that these activities were illegal. In fact, in a capitalist country their behavior (with some exceptions) would have been considered quite legal.

[50]James Feinerman, "Constitutionalism in China," lecture given at New England China Seminar, Harvard University, March 15, 1984.

[51]"Communique of the Third Plenary Session of the 11th Central Committee of the Communist Party of China," *BR* (December 29, 1978), p. 14, as quoted in Leng, "Chinese Judicial System," pp. 117, 120. For further comparisons of the 1954, 1975, and 1978 Constitutions on legal provisions, see Leng, pp. 115, 116.

[52]Suzanne Ogden, "China and International Law: Implications for Foreign Policy," *Pacific Affairs*, Vol. 49, No. 1 (Spring 1976), p. 28.

[53]Feinerman, "Constitutionalism in China."

[54]"Trends in Chinese Jurisprudence," *BR*, No. 14 (April 6, 1981), p. 14.

[55]"The Party Must Conduct Its Activities Within the Limits Permitted by the Constitution and the Laws of the State," from *Red Flag*, No. 4 (February 1983), pp. 36–38, in *JPRS*, No. 83314 (April 22, 1983), *China Report*, pp. 61, 62.

[56]Leng, "Chinese Judicial System," p. 118; and Hungdah Chiu, "China's Legal Reforms," *Current History* (September 1985), p. 270.

[57]"Whoever Enjoys Democracy Must Obey the Laws," *Democracy and the Legal System (Minzhu yu fazhi)* (October 1983), p. 39.

[58]Donald C. Clarke, "Concepts of Law in the Chinese Anti-Crime Campaign," *Harvard Law Review*, Vol. 98, No. 8 (June 1985), p. 1898.

[59]"Party Officials Sacked for Crimes," *CD* (December 7, 1984), p. 3, as referenced in Clarke, "Concepts of Law," p. 1899, note 43. Also see An Zhiguo, "More on Improving the Party's Style of Work" *BR*, No. 34 (August 25, 1986), p. 4.

[60]This theorist, Chen Tiqiang, was attacked because he was a "pure legalist" and "did not recognize that international law is simply one instrument for serving China, socialism, and peace, to be used when useful but discarded and replaced by a new instrument when disadvantageous." See Ogden, "China and International Law," note 4.

[61]Wren, "Credible Legal System," *The New York Times*, (December 5, 1982), p. 22.

[62]Stanley Lubman, Lecture at Fairbank Center, Harvard University, November 5, 1982.

[63]Colin Campbell, "China Suddenly Taking a Tougher Line on Crime," *The New York Times* (September 13, 1983), p. 2. Also see such cases as "Timber Tigress Executed," *CD* (August 28, 1984), p. 3, in which a purchasing agent for a construction co-operative was executed for fraudulently purchasing some 8,000 cubic metres of timber and taking graft payments worth $70,000 (143,000 yuan).

[64]Zhang Zhiye, "Legislative and Judiciary," p. 19.

[65]Wren, "Credible Legal System," p. 22.

[66]"Expanding Role for Lawyers," *CD* (May 26, 1984), p. 4.

[67]Clarke, "Concepts of Law, pp. 1903, 1904.

[68]Lubman, lecture at Fairbank Center, Harvard University, November 5, 1982.

[69]If each of China's 400,000 industrial etnerprises and 600,000 commercial and trade enterprises were to hire a lawyer to protect its interests, that alone would require China to train one million additional lawyers. "Expanding Role for Lawyers," p. 4.

[70]"Of 12,000 noncourt cases resolved in 1983, 6,808 involved foreign parties," "Expanding Role for Lawyers," p. 4.

[71]James Feinerman and Kathleen Hartford, "The Influence of the Legal System on the Rural Economy in 1985," Fairbank Center Seminar, Harvard University, December 1985.

[72]According to Article III of the Provisional Regulations for Lawyers of the PRC, "In their legal practice, lawyers must base their cases on facts, be guided by the law and be *loyal to the cause of socialism* and the interests of the people." "Expanding Role for Lawyers," p. 4. Emphasis added.

[73]Suzanne Ogden, Meeting with Deputy Director of Management Committee of Lawyers, Hangzhou, China, August 8, 1981.

[74]Zhang Zhiye, "Legislative and Judiciary," pp. 20–22.

[75]James Feinerman, Fairbank Center Seminar, January 18, 1985. Hungdah Chiu's figures differ somewhat. According to Chiu, the total enrollment of law students in 1985 was 13,000, and there were "29 universities with law departments, 4 political-legal institutes, and a political-legal university," which includes a school for training cadres. Hungdah Chiu, "China's Legal Reforms," p. 268. For an in-depth article on the revival of legal education, see Timothy A. Gelatt and Frederick E. Snyder, "Legal Education in China: Training for New Era," *China Law Reporter*, Vol. 1, No. 2 (Fall 1980), pp. 41–60.

[76]James Feinerman, Fairbank Center Seminar, January 18, 1985.

[77]Article 3 of "Provisional Regulations," translated in Owen D. Nee, Franklin D. Chu, and Michael J. Moser (eds), *Commercial, Business and Trade Laws, The People's Republic of China* (Dobbs Ferry, N.Y.: Oceana, 1982).

[78]According to the Chinese press, one defense lawyer was erroneously charged with "conspiring with the accused," for which crime the county authorities in Hainan Island jailed him. He was released after the local lawyers protested. The error resulted, according to the Minister of Justice, because some "officials had no knowledge of the role of the legal profession." "Lawyers Defend Business Interests," *CD* (December 18, 1984), p. 3.

[79]Ogden, Meeting with Deputy Director of Management Committee of Lawyers, Hangzhou, August 8, 1981.

[80]Is divulging the time, place, and agenda of the meeting of the Plenary Session of the

Party's Central Committee "equivalent to divulging a state secret"? The official line is that since the Party's Central Committee leads the Chinese people in their work, all the Party's private activities are *state* secrets prior to the time at which they are officially made public. See "Notes from the Editor," *BR*, No. 20 (May 17, 1982), p. 3.

[81]Suzanne Ogden, "China's Social Sciences: Prospects for Teaching and Research in the 1980s," *Asian Survey*, Vol. XXII, No. 7 (July 1982), p. 582.

[82]"Police, Courts Join in Bettering Legal Work," *CD* (February 7, 1984), p. 4; *BR*, No. 23 (June 6, 1983), p. 26; and "China Builds up its Legal System," *CD* (October 15, 1984), p. 4.

[83]"Trends in Chinese Jurisprudence," p. 15.

[84]Ibid., p. 15.

[85]"Equality Before the Law," *BR*, No. 41 (October 12, 1981), pp. 26, 27, excerpted from *RMRB* (August 31, 1981).

[86]The term "political criminals" was used by the Kuomintang (KMT) and the CCP before 1949. The Chinese Communists no longer use this term, although the KMT in Taiwan still does. Of course, those executed before 1949 by the KMT for being "political criminals" became heroes for the Communists. China today insists that there are only criminals, not political criminals, in its jails. See "Minister on Social Order in China," *BR*, No. 34 (April 25, 1986), p. 15.

[87]Leng, "Chinese Judicial System," p. 127.

[88]"Trends in Chinese Jurisprudence," p. 16.

[89]Articles 90–104 in the Criminal Code are related to counterrevolutionary crimes. Article 102 provides the largest loophole to catch political deviants.

[90]"Minister on Social Order in China," *BR*, No. 34 (August 25, 1986), p. 16.

[91]"On the Correct Handling of Contradictions Among the People" (July, 1957), in Anne Fremantle (ed), *Mao Tse-tung: An Anthology of His Writings* (New York: The New American Library, 1962), pp. 264–267.

[92]An essay written by a leader of the democracy movement shortly before his arrest in May 1979, "What Are the Implications of China's Democracy Movement?" in D. S. G. Goodman, *Beijing Street Voices* (Boston: Marion Boyars, 1981), pp. 131, 134.

[93]Martin K. Whyte, *Small Groups and Political Rituals in China* (Berkeley: University of California Press, 1974), pp. 2, 3.

[94]Greenblatt, "Campaigns and the Manufacture," p. 95.

[95]T. A. Fyfield, *Re-educating Chinese Anti-Communists* (New York: St. Martin's Press, 1982), p. 83.

[96]Greenblatt, "Campaigns and the Manufacture," pp. 96, 97.

[97]For an elaboration of the importance of the thinking-acting connection for the Chinese, see Donald J. Munro, "Belief Control: The Psychological and Ethical Foundations," in Wilson, Greenblatt, and Wilson, *Deviance and Social Control*, pp. 23–25.

[98]The author's own discussion with former Red Guards (1983, 1984).

[99]Whyte, *Groups and Rituals*, pp. 9–11, 52.

[100]*People's Daily* (May 29, 1983), translated in *Inside Mainland China* (July 1983), p. 3. Emphasis added.

[101]For example, Associated Press report, "Five Executed in Peking for Murder or Rape," *The New York Times* (July 19, 1983) in which a young man was sentenced to death before a rally of 18,000 people.

[102]See Charles P. Cell, "The Utility of Mass Mobilization Campaigns in China: A Partial Test of the Skinner-Winckler Compliance Model," in Greenblatt, Wilson, and Wilson, *Organizational Behavior in Chinese Society*, p. 27, referring to G. William Skinner and Edward A. Winckler, "Compliance Succession in Rural Communist China: A Cyclical Theory," in Amitai Etzioni (ed), *A Sociological Reader on Complex Organizations*, 2nd edition (New York: Holt, Rinehart & Winston, 1969), p. 41.

[103]Gordon Bennett, "China's Mass Campaign and Social Control," in Wilson, Greenblatt, and Wilson, *Deviance and Social Control*, p. 132.

[104]On the limitations of "good" and "honest" cadres, see such articles as "Break-up 'Net' of Ill Practices in Party" (from the Party's magazine, *Hongqi (Red Flag)*, in *CD* (January 27, 1984), p. 4; "Criteria of Cadres," *CD* (June 8, 1984), p. 4; and "Honesty Is Not All," *CD* (June 16, 1984), p. 4.

[105]*People's Daily* (May 29, 1983), op. cit. p. 30.

[106]Parsons, as referenced in White, "Deviance, Modernization, Rations," op. cit., p. 152.

[107]"Crackdown on Economic Crimes," *BR*, No. 33 (August 15, 1983), p. 7.

[108]*People's Daily* (July 17, 1981), p. 1, referenced in *China News Analysis*, No. 1218 (October 23, 1981), p. 2. For article on collective corruption, see Commentator, "Is It Impermissible to Blackmail the State?" *Renmin Ribao* (December 11, 1981), and "Hunan Ribao Letter on Year-end State Revenue," *FBIS*, No. 243 (December 18, 1981), p. P3, in which it exposes the attempts of state-owned enterprises to falsify enterprise accounts in order to cheat the state out of revenues. On this topic, also see *Fujian Daily* (May 29, 1983); and on tax evasion by state factories and corporations, see *Tianjin Daily* (September 5, 1981); and *Anhui PBS* (October 6, 1981). All are referenced in *China News Analysis*, No. 1218 (October 23, 1981), p. 3.

[109]Elizabeth Perry, seminar discussion, Fairbank Center Seminar, Harvard University, September 25, 1982.

[110]Feinerman, "Constitutionalism in China."

Chapter Seven
CLASS AND CLASS STRUGGLE: IS CHINA UNITED OR DIVIDED?

Classes are large groups of people which differ from each other by the place they occupy in a historically determined system of social production, by their relation (in most cases fixed and formulated in law) to the means of production, by their role in the social organization of labor, and consequently, by the dimensions and mode of acquiring the share of social wealth of which they dispose.[1]

Classes . . . never rule, any more than nations. The rulers are always certain persons. And, whatever class they may have once belonged to, once they are rulers they belong to the ruling class.[2]

THE IDEOLOGICAL AND CULTURAL ROOTS OF THE SEARCH FOR INEQUALITY

The definition of "class" has been profoundly important in shaping China's social, political, and economic development. To achieve the utopian classless society Marxism envisioned, the Chinese Communists carried out both revolution and reform to eliminate classes. With their victory in 1949, class background became a key determinant of the distribution of China's scarce resources, particularly land, but also of limited opportunities to gain power and influence through education, work, and admission to the Communist Party. It also became the major determinant of who would be "struggled" in class struggle campaigns.

If the Chinese leadership had held onto the classical Marxist conception of class—that class was determined by the economic yardstick of a person's relationship to the means of production—then the issue of eliminating class and class struggle would have been ended by 1956. But in 1957, Mao Zedong reopened the question of the meaning of class and how to determine each person's class. As far back as the 1930s, Mao had expanded on Marx's economic definition of class to include behavioral and attitudinal aspects. In 1957, Mao returned to this analysis to explain why class struggle in socialist China had to continue. From this point on, the definition of class and class struggle became weapons to use against the dominant leadership faction's enemies. They also became tools for resolving China's most fundamental problems. By directing the government's attention toward the *wrong* issues, however, the sources of China's problems were left unresolved.

It is one of the supreme ironies of a country under the guidance of an ideology with the objective of equality that its citizens expend endless efforts searching for inequality: qualities or things that will differentiate them from their fellow citizens and give them greater status, power, or privileges. This search for inequality has both strong ideological and cultural roots, which accentuate the importance the Chinese attribute to social, political, and occupational stratification. An obsession with rank and status may, in fact, be traced at least as far back as the Qin (Ch'in) Dynasty (221– 207 B.C.) and even the Shang Dynasty, and it continues to this very day; for in the present Chinese cultural and ideological context, rank may be all-important to a person's opportunities. This reinforces the importance of class designation in socialist ideology as interpreted in China: Until the 1980s, although class and status differentiation were often distinct from each other, class was the broadest category for determining who would have greater access to society's scarce resources and opportunities and who would have no access at all. Hence the importance of class struggle as a process determining one's relative ranking within Chinese society.

Through repeated class struggles, the Chinese Communist leadership easily manipulated the cultural predisposition toward ranking individuals to accommodate its own politics. It was Mao Zedong's own ideology and political concerns, more than socialist ideology per se, however, which shaped the issue of class and class struggle. Thus, in an assessment of the relative importance of cultural, ideological, and developmental variables as they affected the evolution of class-related issues, the ideological-political variable unquestionably provides the richest source of explanation. But the reason for its importance was precisely because it fit so comfortably into a Chinese context predisposed by culture and history to categorize and label people, and to draw sharp distinctions between "good" and "evil" individuals.

The developmental variable, on the other hand, explains little about class conflict until the late 1970s. An analysis of societal histories throughout the world suggests, in fact, that class *collaboration* and alliances across classes for the survival of both classes were as common as class conflict in developing societies. After 1978, however, the reformist leadership specifically used the necessity for developing China's productive forces as the rationale for dropping class and class struggle in favor of economic construction as the major tool. In this respect, the reform leadership consciously *chose* to make the developmental variable the key variable and to reduce the significance of the ideological-political variable; for with economic reforms, individuals were encouraged to "get rich" in the process of contributing to China's development, even if it meant the reestablishment of classes by a Marxist economic definition. It would have, therefore, been counterproductive to threaten those who moved into higher economic classes with class struggle.

HISTORY OF CLASS AND CLASS STRUGGLE

Historically, the Chinese have had a penchant for ranking individuals by placing each one into a hierarchy of categories. During the Qin Dynasty, a person's rank was based upon how many enemy heads he had cut off in battle. A person could inherit the rank of his father.[3] Everyone was ranked, but those who did *not* participate in battle (like women) were only categorized as "rank and file."

Ranking of Chinese people according to complicated formulae, whether in the bureaucracy, the military, or in the general Confucian terms used for ranking all the people, became a deeply rooted cultural element reinforced by continued historical practice. While Confucianism as a state ideology ended with the fall of the Qing (Ch'ing) Dynasty in 1911, the entrenched habit of ranking people continued. The Chinese Communists considered this traditional form of ranking pernicious; but they themselves proceeded to set up a highly complex system for both social stratification and class differentiation.[4] Although the Chinese Communists tried to eliminate the very existence of different classes by eliminating private ownership of property, they constructed at the same time strict workgrade categories for differentiating people along scales that measured their earning power, prestige, and authority. This careful delineation of individuals according to noneconomic categories contributed significantly to keeping the issue of class alive. Further, it contributed to the ability of various leadership factions to manipulate class definitions to serve their own political ends by confusing class with status, with stratification, and even with governmental and other socioeconomic categories that cut across simple class labels. The result was the creation after 1949 of some sixty "class designations,"[5] hardly what Lenin had in mind when he discussed "class."

Land Reform and Redistribution of Property, 1949–1956

The history of class struggle after 1949 (Chapter Three), underscores the importance class played in determining the distribution of life's opportunities, and property, among the Chinese. Its history also indicates the leadership's belief that class struggle would serve as a psychological and political process for creating unity by mobilizing class hatred against a targeted group of individuals. The definition of a Chinese person's own goodness was his or her willingness to struggle actively against bad class elements. Failure to struggle could be used as evidence of one's complicity with the enemy class. But class struggle did not unify people. Rather, it turned them against each other in an enduring hatred. Class struggle proved to be the most socially fragmentizing policy the Chinese Communists ever adopted.

During rural land reform (1949–1952), and the redistribution of property in the cities (1949–1956), the definition of each individual's class was important in determining who received what. But class labels also served to draw distinctions between "the enemy" and "the people," or "exploiter" and "exploited."[6] From the Communist leaders' perspective, this broad division of all people into two opposing categories based on the classes to which they belonged in the three years before 1949 was essential for creating the political foundation for the "democratic dictatorship" of the laboring class and for carrying out the "united front" policy. Both during the civil war with the Kuomintang, and when the Communists were consolidating their control over China, the purpose of the united front policy was to unite as many people as possible to face "the enemy." By isolating "the enemy" into as narrow a category as possible, it could easily be vanquished, and in a salami-cutting-type tactic, the next level of enemy could be isolated from "the people" and vanquished. Designation of each person's class was the first step in determining who would be the targets of class struggle. By 1956, the redistribution of property in both the cities and the countryside was done, and the Party could claim that "socialist transformation" had been completed.

The One Hundred Flowers Campaign and Renewed Class Struggle, 1956–1965

Although exploitative economic classes had been eliminated by 1956, the issues of class and class struggle were renewed for reasons totally unrelated to the issue of the capitalist (property-owning) class exploiting the propertyless classes. This reason was the "One Hundred Flowers" Campaign (1956–1957) and Mao's interpretation of its consequences. The unexpectedly harsh criticism by China's intellectuals of the Party's policies and even the socialist system during that campaign led Mao to conclude that class conflict was a long-term issue. China's intellectuals and experts for the most part had capitalist class roots, and so even though the property basis for their class had been eliminated, Mao could reason that the remnant exploitative and antisocialist attitudes of their class remained in their thoughts. Further, as far back as the 1930s, Mao had created the rationale for a behavioral-attitudinal component to class: Classes shifted in relationship to the principal contradiction, and *how* individuals responded to the principal contradiction determined their class standpoint (*lichang*).[7] Therefore, class struggle would continue even under socialism, but as a struggle between class ideologies rather than between actual social classes. And class struggle was still viewed as an appropriate technique to instill a new class standpoint different from that of an individual's class origin. After all, Marx had not been a proletarian, and Mao had been a rich peasant's son; yet both acquired a revolutionary class standpoint.[8] Thus, the One Hundred Flowers Campaign was followed by the Anti-Rightist Movement, whose major victims were intellectuals from capitalist class backgrounds.

Mao again reassessed the meaning of class after his veteran party colleagues meted out severe criticism of his Great Leap Forward policies at the Lushan Plenum in 1959. In spite of their impeccable class backgrounds and outstanding contributions to the victory of communism, Mao was offended by their criticisms, and he sought a rationale for retribution in class analysis: His critics were bureaucrats who, within the context of *socialist* institutions (the People's Liberation Army, the Party, and state organizations), had gained power and privilege that they used to exploit the people. Mao blamed their antisocialist behavior not on socialism, but on influence of remnant bourgeois elements, and even on Soviet revisionism. The standard that Mao now embraced for determining the new class enemies was not property ownership but political behavior: They *acted* as if they opposed socialism.[9]

In 1957, Mao had said that class struggle would never be enlarged or harsh again. Further, in the "three bad years" that followed the disastrous Great Leap Forward policies, the Chinese people had cooperated together to get the economy moving, and had little thought of "class" as a divisive issue. So the people were stunned when in 1962 Mao announced his new slogan, "Never Forget Class Struggle."[10] Class struggle was again renewed, this time in the Socialist Education Movement.

Mao's repeated campaigns calling for struggle against the same "black elements" suggest that in spite of overwhelming evidence to the contrary, Mao remained convinced that class struggle, thought reform, and rectification worked. But recognizing that 80 percent of China's university graduates were still from the wrong class background, Mao was determined to train a new generation of experts whose loyalty to socialist goals and revolutionary values ("redness") could not be in doubt.[11] An alternative and more cynical interpretation is that by 1957 the Communists had consolidated their control over the cities and, thereafter, believed they could dispense with industrialists, technocrats, or intellectuals with bad class backgrounds. The result was endless class struggle in the cities from the Anti-Rightist Campaign of 1957 to the arrest of the Gang of Four in 1976.[12]

The Cultural Revolution and the Ten Bad Years: 1966–1976

The possibility that Mao's insistence on intensified class struggle had less to do with class issues than with his political rivals and his belief that the Soviet leaders (first Khrushchev and then Brezhnev) were "revisionists taking the capitalist road" can hardly be dismissed. Regardless, the key point is that even if it were a power struggle for control of both the CCP *and* the international Communist movement, it was approached *as if* it were a class struggle. Mao now claimed that the capitalist class was *inside* the Party. Socialist bureaucrats had formed a new class, which acted like an exploiting capitalist class with interests sharply antagonistic to those of the peasants and workers. These bureaucrats had usurped the power of the Party and used their authority as capitalists would use capital, to exploit the people and advance their own interests. Thus, policy and ideological conflicts within the Party were now viewed as class conflicts, and individual Party leaders took on the label of the class they represented. Mao, Lin Biao, and others represented the proletariat, whereas Liu Shaoqi, Deng Xiaoping, and others represented the new bureaucratic class, the bourgeoisie or "capitalist roaders" within the Party. Thus, the Party itself became the arena for the class struggle between the proletariat and the bourgeoisie.[13] Ironically, the elite now under attack owed much of its power to the fact that its members, or their parents, had belonged to the right class in 1949!

Cultural Revolution policies, however, also focused on the children of the former bourgeoisie; for although some children with proletarian roots managed to gain access to higher education, far more youth from the "exploiting classes" did.[14] In spite of social and job discrimination against the capitalist class, then, the fact that urban class struggle and the labeling of the urban bourgeoisie before 1956 had been rather lax, and that the school examination system in practice favored "experts" over those with the correct political background, allowed capitalist class families to achieve positions of significant influence.

Thus, the previously "resolved" issue of class conflict became an ongoing issue because of Mao's changing definition of class and interpretation of politics: Instead of seeing as legitimate and necessary to the health of the polity and the economy either the criticism offered by the intellectuals in the "One Hundred Flowers Campaign," or the criticism by veteran cadres in the aftermath of the disastrous failures of the Great Leap Forward policies, Mao chose to see them as a reflection of unresolved *class* problems. Mao interpreted his colleagues' lip service to his policies in the early 1960s, and their bureaucratization of the Party and state apparatus, as a class issue, not an organizational one. He ignored the possibility that all organizations tend toward certain bureaucratic pathologies, and that these issues might best be addressed through organizational procedures and controls.

Shortly before Mao's death in 1976, his final reanalysis of class acknowledged that it was precisely those institutional structures which the Communist revolution had established in order to reshape society that had provided the power basis for new exploiting groups. Structural inequalities existed before liberation, but were unavoidably perpetuated in China's socialist institutions after 1949. In fact, it was the state apparatus itself that permitted a new bourgeoisie, based on unequal access to power, to arise.[15] Yet Mao never concluded that either socialism as an organizational theory, or organization as such, was the source of the problem.

The old "bloodlines theory," which doomed people to the economic class into which they were born, together with the new subjective and vague political criteria that permitted individuals to escape their ascribed class status through good behavior, or receive a bad class label through "bad" behavior, played into the hands of all those who wished to seize power for themselves. Enemies were labeled as "rightists," "bad elements," "counter-revolutionaries," "revisionists," "ultra-leftists," "ultra-rightists," and "newborn bourgeois elements." Class struggle served as a moral cloak to be used by any and by all to criticize one's own *political* enemies as if they were *class* enemies.[16] A bad class background could be the basis for eliminating access to the valued goods in a socialist society (education, membership in the Party, a good job, entry into the People's Liberation Army, etc.) or for social ostracism. Those with bad labels were treated as political and social pariahs. The precise determination of class backgound grew so complicated and so pivotal to a person's status and opportunities that the investigation and determination of class background took on "a role similar to the profession of law in the West. People's University in Beijing even established a separate academic department specifically devoted to teaching the criteria and methods for settling class status cases. University students who were of sufficiently good class background and political behavior could 'major' in this subject and make it their life's career."[17]

Class labels (even "earned" ones) were passed down from parents to children, and thence to grandchildren. Denigrating moral connotations accompanied the class labels ascribed to the children of parents with bad class labels. Individuals with bad class labels were even discriminated against socially (for example, when they wanted to get married),[18] and were considered "politically backward, *bad* people." This was the source of much bitterness during class struggle campaigns.[19]

Post-Gang of Four Policies, 1976 to Present

The "leftist line" in policy, which took class struggle as a tool for ferreting out enemies of socialism and remolding people's thoughts, held sway in the political realm from 1957 to 1976, the period which some Chinese now refer to as "the twenty bad years." With Mao's death in September 1976, and the subsequent arrest of the Gang of Four in October, the leftist line was challenged, but not entirely refuted. Only after the reform faction in the leadership gained control over the Party leadership at the December 1978 Third Party Plenum, at the expense of Hua Guofeng and the "whatever" faction, was the reliance on class struggle undermined.

Thus, the 1978 Constitution, written before Deng Xiaoping gained the upper hand, reflected the leftist line and reaffirmed the need for continuing the "dictatorship of the proletariat" over people with labels of "reactionary capitalists," "landlords," and "rich peasants," even though nearly thirty years had elapsed since these labels were originally imposed. The "dictatorship" would also remain over "counterrevolutionaries," "bad elements," and "newborn bourgeois elements" (the latter being defined as "persons of good class status who, because of their opposition to the Party line, remove themselves from 'the people' and become the enemy.")[20]

Only with a major policy change in early 1979 did the Party eliminate the class labels of "landlords" and "rich peasants," labels still attached to more than 4 million people in the countryside, in a process almost as complicated as when they assigned them. Even then, it did not remove these labels from about 50,000 "rather bad" people. But the removal of class labels was seen as confirming, not refuting, the value of class struggle, "the actual fruit of many years of struggle against the exploiting classes in the countryside, the result of being remolded."[21] As a result, only "enlarged class struggle" and mass movements were dispensed with.

Labels were also removed from those branded "enemies of the people" after 1957. They regained political, civil, and legal rights which they had not had since the day their labels were applied. The new policy emphasized, moreover, that they were no longer to be discriminated against in job assignments, in obtaining marriage partners, in the educational system, or in any other way. "Remnants" of exploiting classes could continue to exist under socialism and new exploiters might even emerge under socialism, but they could never form an exploiting *class* as long as China maintained a socialist political and economic system.[22]

Class struggle continued into the 1980s with no assurances that it would not occur at levels short of "massive." The possibility, and even the need for class struggle to "intensify," always loomed in the backgound. This was because "bad elements" (such as counterrevolutionaries, enemy agents, spies, and criminals) still existed; and "new exploiters"—embezzlers, robbers, speculators—were appearing because of the "historical influences of the system of exploitation and exploiting classes," and because of the influence of capitalist exploiters from abroad. Nevertheless, the political and economic bases of the exploiting classes were so thoroughly decimated, that whatever class struggle occurred could not be "between two full-fledged antagonistic classes." Instead it would be "the remnant of class struggle left behind by history," which is "a peculiar form of the class struggle under socialism."[23]

The Deng Xiaoping leadership, moreover, redefined class in the early 1980s according to classical Marxism-Leninism by asserting that people should be divided into classes "on the basis of their relationship to the means of production," not their behavior: Class would be based on persons' "position in the production process, on whether they possess the means of production, and *how they have acquired these productive means.*" In other words, if they got rich without exploiting others' labor, then they were still members of the working class. In this way the leadership tried to impart a "scientific" meaning to class. And because ideology and political attitudes could not provide a scientific basis and "differ over time,"[24] they could not form a yardstick for determining class.

Further, bureaucrats *could not* form a class because they were paid wages by the state, and they owned none of the means of production. Nor could bureaucrats become "the principal contradiction which decides or changes the nature of society and affects the orientation of social development." Even "new exploiters" who were cadres could not form a class. As a result, "normal procedures," laws, and Party discipline could be used to correct their improper behavior.[25]

But Deng Xiaoping's return to the economic yardstick for measuring class does give pause; for his most ardent supporters of the 1980s were those in China who, by the economic yardstick, had managed to move into what verge on being "rich peasant," "landlord," and "national capitalist" classes. In fact, in the 1980s, the best way to prove one's loyalty to the Party and commitment to socialism was to "get rich!" Thus, a return to an economic definition of class based solely on ownership of property, together with an emphasis on class struggle, would endanger those very individuals who had most enthusiastically carried out the Party's policy. And a return to the definition of class in a bureaucratic society as being based on *control* (not ownership) of property would endanger the very leaders whom the reformers had restored to power.[26]

In spite of these new interpretations of class, the Party insisted that class struggle must continue. In the early 1980s, the Chinese officially designated the campaign against economic crimes as a manifestation of class struggle: Socialist ideology was used to combat corruption caused by bourgeois ideology, the remaining influence of the "remnants of exploiting classes," and foreign influence. "Some of today's exploiters, degenerates and criminals are waverers in the ranks of workers, peasants, intellectuals and cadres who have succumbed to the corrosion of the exploiting classes ideology."[27] Although China's leaders assured the people that they would not repeat their past mistake of "enlarging the scope of class struggle" because class contradictions had ceased to be the "principal contradiction," class struggle was still necessary, and could "become acute under certain circumstances."[28]

If class conflict was no longer the "principal contradiction," what, then, had taken its place? China's new principal contradiction, or major problem, was *the tension between the rising expectations of the Chinese people, and an underdeveloped economy that was incapable of meeting those expectations.*[29]

This new principal contradiction necessitated a change in both ends and means. The new end was economic construction: to meet the "people's increasing demands for material and cultural well-being" by developing "backward social productive forces." And the means were the tools of economic development. Class struggle was now only a "subordinate" means to achieve economic construction, whereas Mao and the radical leftists had believed it was critical even for economic development. They had believed that changes in the relations of production (the ownership of the means of production) would promote economic development. These conflicting perspectives on the role of class struggle in economic development had been at the heart of leadership struggles from 1956 to 1978.

Some of China's reform leaders suggested that even limited class struggle was unnecessary. Instead, the legal system could be used as a means to punish people who committed crimes, and other instruments could serve as means to control deviance. These were far more suitable because China no longer had antagonistic contradictions between "the people" and "the enemy." Class struggle was inappropriate for resolving either "nonantagonistic" contradictions *among* the people, or nonclass contradictions "between right and wrong and between advanced and backward thinking."[30]

By the mid-1980s, the reform leaders no longer referred to class struggle. Deng Xiaoping called for pragmatic methods to pursue the "four modernizations" in order to address the principal contradiction created by the revolution of rising expectations and China's poverty. His unstated objective was to stabilize Chinese politics, in part by fulfilling the demands of the Chinese people for a better life and in part by eliminating the specter of more class struggle. Toward this end Deng rephrased the issues and redefined "class conflict" as "class competition."[31] Obviously, this reinterpretation served well the reformers' policies; for many Chinese exhibited extreme caution and concern about implementing the "get rich" policies initiated in the early 1980s. After all, if class struggle were to recur after they had become rich, they would become its primary targets. More to the point, the reform leaders' message was, and is, that class is irrelevant. This attitude may contain within itself the best chance for burying the issue of class, as long as "leftists" do not regain power.

The reform leaders remain concerned about the "red" aspect of a person's character, as determined in a negative sense: *nonopposition* to the "four basic principles" (namely, support of the democratic dictatorship, Marxism-Leninism-Mao Zedong Thought, the socialist system, and Party infallibility). A person's political credentials must remain intact, but a "correct" perspective on the four basic principles, not class background, appears to be the only true political requirement. Of those four principles, the only one which the Party really insists on in practice is obedience to Party leadership. Out of concern for its own survival, the Party is adamant about a person's willingness to obey Party leadership by supporting Party policies—whether or not those policies actually support socialism, Marxism-Leninism-Mao Zedong Thought, or the dictatorship of the people! This concern for "redness," however, is the same sort of attitudinal evaluation used in class analysis. In this respect, it is really just another name for the same thing: Whether class attitude or attitude toward the four principles, the dominant leaders have a powerful weapon for attacking anyone who does not carry out their policies.

The reform leaders' most important message, however, is that a person's opportunities for getting ahead in the People's Republic of China will depend on his or her *contribution* to China's modernization. This emphasis changes the whole conceptualization of what is at stake. It moves away from a concern for class background, class standpoint, and even "redness" to a concern for expertise and hard work. A person's willingness and ability to carry out the Party's policies are the new criteria for determining whether a person has "correct" attitudes and behavior. Undoubtedly those who dare to oppose Party policy openly will continue, if the leadership considers it convenient, to be vulnerable to the charge of being class enemies, criminals, or "deviants." Nevertheless, political activism and a good class background have temporarily bowed out to expertise and hard work as the means to succeed.

OBSTACLES TO THE RESOLUTION OF THE ISSUES OF CLASS AND CLASS STRUGGLE

Although the history of the conceptual development of class by the Chinese is itself revealing as to how class and class struggle became and remained issues, other cultural and ideological aspects of these issues suggest some of the obstacles to sweeping away class-related issues.

Obsession with Rank

The combination of a deeply rooted cultural-historical practice of ranking individuals in a Confucian hierarchy, together with the Leninist emphasis on ranking in a hierarchical leadership, contributed to a continued obsession with rank after 1949. China, in its attempt to make everyone equal through the equalization of property and to submerge individuality within the collective, has bred citizens who want nothing more than to give themselves an edge over others. China seems to be fighting against a "human" tendency to want to be distinct and *unequal*—more equal than others. Even Mao Zedong reputedly lamented that "Humanity left to its own devices does not necessarily reestablish capitalism . . . but it does reestablish inequality. The forces tending toward the creation of new classes are powerful."[32]

The result is that the average Chinese seizes upon even the slightest opportunity to advance his or her position in the social or political hierarchy through acquisition of scarce commodities, through influence or power, and through rank and status; for in the Chinese cultural and ideological context, rank is all-important to a person's life opportunities. Within Chinese society, many privileges are available only to specific persons. Ranks do not apply just to cadres. Workers, soldiers, professors, researchers, technicians, writers, and others in the fine arts and elsewhere also have specific ranks. *Neibu* (internal) documents can only be read by people above a certain cadre rank (*jibie*), of which there are between twenty and thirty.[33] Access to certain resort areas, overnight nurseries, better housing, the right to travel on an airplane, shop in specified stores, or be chauffeured in the unit's automobile are all privileges reserved for those with the proper rank. Foreigners who have visited China in delegations are all too aware of the extreme discomfort the Chinese suffer until they have ranked the members of the delegation and can thereby better determine how to treat them in a manner appropriate to their status. The penchant of members of delegations from Western Europe and the United States to insist that all members are "equal" meshes poorly with the Chinese predisposition to believe they are not. It is this search for inequality, with its strong ideological *and* cultural roots, that accentuates the importance the Chinese attribute to social, political, and occupational stratification, and that leads to a near obsession with rank and status.

This obsession reinforced the importance of class designation to the Chinese. Until the 1980s, although class, status and rank differentiations were often different, class was one of the broadest categories for determining who would have greater access to society's scarce resources and opportunities—and who would have no access at all. Hence, the desirability of class struggle for those who thought they could advance their position through it.

Mao's Theory of Contradiction

Mao's view on the dialectical progression of "contradictions," which was based on Marxist dialectics, played an important role in laying the theoretical foundations for justifying continuous class conflict. Mao argued that the world is fueled by contradictions and there is no such thing as perfect harmony (or perfection), because all things carry within them inherent contradictions. Just at the point at which people believe there is unity, the point at which the preceding contradiction has been resolved, a new contradiction is formed that must be resolved. Mao's theory of contradictions divides everything into good and evil, right and wrong, forces in conflict with each other. Thus it provides an intellectual rationale for polarizing Chinese society by putting everyone into a category of "the people" or "the enemy." Because there is always a contradiction within a society, just when the society thinks there is class harmony, a new enemy class will form. The leftist radicals of the 1960s, who supported Mao's theory that "one divides into two," labeled as reactionaries those such as Liu Shaoqi and Deng Xiaoping, who argued that class struggle had died out, that "two had united into one."

As long as the Chinese leadership continued to use the concept of contradiction as one of its central analytical constructs, it dichotomized everything into two opposing forces. Positive and negative forces confronted each other. When the leadership concluded that "antagonistic contradictions" had developed, they used class struggle to resolve the contradiction. Put more cynically, if certain elements in society challenged the leadership's policy, the leadership could always point to an "antagonistic contradiction," and use class struggle to silence or eliminate it.

Although the reform leadership has moved away from a theory of contradictions as its analytical foundation and relegated class conflict to history for the time being, it has not eliminated the tendency, entrenched in Chinese culture, to dichotomize everything into polar opposites of good and evil, right and wrong. But rather than reflecting Mao's theory of contradictions, this is a natural product of the insistence on Party infallibility, with all its authoritarian implications: Whoever follows the Party leadership is good and acts correctly; whoever does not is bad and acts incorrectly. There is still little room for accepting the possibility that individuals are more complex than a simple black-and-white characterization acknowledges.

Inconsistent Definition of Class

Mao's personal subjective interpretation of politics and who was *his* enemy (not *the* enemy) led to an inconsistent definition of class after 1949. The issue of class and class struggle could have been resolved in 1956, when China became "socially transformed" and all enemy classes had had their economic basis eliminated. It was Mao, China's preeminent leader, who chose to reopen the case and to interpret opposition as a sign of "class conflict." Mao's political enemies became "class enemies," not according to Marxist economic criteria, but according to behavioral-attitudinal criteria. First he argued that the descendants of enemy classes *inherited* bad class characteristics; then, that the new class conflict was in the form of competing class *ideologies*, which managed to survive the demise of the very classes that formulated them; then, that socialist leaders and bureaucrats, after acquiring political power under socialism, *acted* in antisocialist ways.

In short, Mao opened up the possibility of a multitude of subjective political interpretations of class. Combined with the officially advocated view that the Chinese polity was imminently threatened by enemy classes, the definition of class became a critical issue that lent itself to endless interpretation—and abuse. Class lines changed as quickly as politics changed. The various definitions and descriptions of class were available to any leader who chose to attack his or her enemies through class struggle.[34] At the local level, interpersonal disputes were translated into class disputes to justify getting even.[35] Such blurred criteria for class designations evolved that ordinary citizens could not even determine what their own class label ought to be.[36] As with "deviance," the Party wavered on the issue of class and used the weapon of class struggle to attack whoever were the enemies of the Party leadership of the day. Ultimately, the Communist Party's inability to resolve the issue of class, and to end disruptive class struggle campaigns once and for all, led to hostility, tension, and cynicism concerning the wisdom of the Party.

Almost all Chinese people have felt victimized by the shifting interpretations of class, or the irrelevance of good class designations to certain policies, which discriminated against them based on their worst feature. If people were from a bad class background, they felt class labels were used to discriminate against them in education and occupational mobility, regardless of their expertise, achievement, or political activism. If they were from the right class background, such as worker or poor peasant, they felt that policy discriminated against them in spite of class, since poverty kept them from educational advancement adequate to compete against the expertise of those from the wrong (but better educated) class background. It was, in fact, because of the claim of so many segments of the population to have suffered from discrimination in favor of another class that the Red Guards clashed so bitterly during the Cultural Revolution.[37] When the reformers gained power, those from the "good" classes of the preceding leftist period either discovered that they no longer belonged to a good class (because their behavior condemned them to "ultra-leftism"), or that their good class background no longer gave them preference in advancement. Instead, those from the wrong class backgrounds of the 1950s (descendants of the bourgeoisie) and the wrong class *standpoint* of the 1960s (the "capitalist roaders" in the leadership) were again advancing.

Because the Party never established a reliable and consistent standard for defining "class enemies," and because it wavered on the need for class struggle as a tool to resolve problems of various sorts, the Chinese people display a general distrust of the reliability of the Party's policies in *any* area. The unsettled nature of class designations and class struggle has thereby bred an even more serious issue: a crisis of leadership—a crisis in the people's faith in the Communist Party's ability and right to lead.

Class Analysis and the Misdiagnosis of China's Problems

Whatever might be said in defense of either the validity of Marxist class analysis, or its usefulness as a diagnostic and prescriptive tool for treating China's problems until 1956, it appears to have done more harm than good since that time. Rigid ideological class analysis, whatever the criteria for "class," directed the Chinese government's attention toward the wrong issue, so that the real issues were not addressed. Because of their presumed need to take arguments about class and class struggle seriously, and to justify all changes in policies by defending their adherence to Marxism-Leninism or Mao Zedong Thought, the leadership dissipated much of its energy for dealing directly with what were really nonideological, and certainly nonclass, issues. Further, the focus on class accentuated the Chinese Communists' proclivity for finding scapegoats rather than searching for the real source of their problems. Even if China's problems, such as local leaders openly flaunting their power over the peasants, or bureaucrats using their official power to exploit the people, could have been interpreted as manifestations of class problems, repeated class struggle was ineffective in resolving them. Further, it left in its wake a legacy of bitterness, distrust, and hatred, shattered China's fragile social unity, and exposed the incompatibility of communist values with concepts of class and class struggle:

> Communists say that you must have mutual help, serve the people and sacrifice yourself for others, put other people ahead of yourself (*xian ren, hou ji*). Of course, if this really worked, China would be an ideal society. But in reality it doesn't work because of the idea of class struggle. The idea of class line and class struggle is in contradiction with the idea of "put other people ahead of yourself." This is because according to the class line, one class—the proletariat—is *not* supposed to give way to other classes; it is supposed to struggle with other classes and try to keep its dominant position. If classes are supposed to be struggling, how are people from different classes going to behave according to the principle of "put other people ahead of yourself"? It clearly is a contradiction. And class struggle comes first.[38]

Through class analysis, which provided the dynamic framework of the Cultural Revolution, Mao Zedong suggested that a "bourgeoisie" had arisen in the Communist Party itself. "Soviet revisionism" (a codeword for antisocialism within a socialist system) and the lingering influence of capitalism were responsible for this phenomenon. Mao concluded that this new bureaucratic "class," which acted like a capitalist class, was formed in part because bad class ideology influenced how officials used their control over the means of production—the land, resources, labor, and equipment.

The more likely reason that bureaucratized social relations developed, however, may be found in the socialist system itself. The bureaucracy functioned in a rigidly centralized socialist system that had purposefully built up an enormous Leninist-style state and Party bureaucracy after 1949. In this situation, the bureaucrats gained inordinate power because they, rather than impersonal market mechanisms or achievement criteria, determined the allocation of resources. In the strictly hierarchical bureaucracy that had developed, persons at each level within the bureaucracy were beholden to the persons above them, but had power over all the persons beneath them, and all those outside the bureaucracy who needed it for even routine matters. The power of bureaucrats to dispense or withhold access, permission, allocation of scarce resources, or simply to stonewall, became a weapon by which they could gain greater privilege and access for themselves, while denying it to those who would not offer them something in return. This type of bureaucratic abuse of powers appears to be endemic to socialist systems, not just to China.

Thus, an alternative interpretation of China's issues, which could have led before the 1980s to more efficacious solutions, is that the over-centralization of power and bureaucratic pathologies, not class struggle, were the real issues and should have been addressed through political reform. Greater organizational, not ideological, discipline might have corrected many of the abuses, without creating "struggle" victims. Changing the method of recruitment or work assignment to limit nepotism; relying on formal legal procedures and the law; democratizing managerial and administrative practices, formal regulations, accounting procedures, inventory control—such kinds of organizational or procedural reforms would have removed much power from individual cadres and "objectified" the allocation of privilege.

Yet even in the early 1980s campaign against economic crimes, the reform leaders termed smuggling, graft, and corruption as "manifestations of class struggle." They blamed rampant economic crime on *remnant* exploiting classes. They used class analysis, however, not as a weapon of the state, but rather as a rationale, a political ploy to undermine the criticism of their political opponents that economic liberalization and China's opening to the outside world had created *new* classes. The reform leaders hardly dared to suggest that a certain level of economic crime was a necessary evil that accompanied rapid modernization and could perhaps be best dealt with by regulations, organizational reforms, and readjusting economic controls (for example, on the distribution of resources, on profits, wages, contracts, markets, banking regulations, and so on). But class struggle campaigns sidetracked attention away from the real source of economic crime: the mixture of capitalist market mechanisms with a highly centralized socialist system. With this mixing of systems, there were bound to be people taking advantage of the loopholes.

By the mid-1980s, however, the more liberal or "radical" of the reformers confronted the real issues head on, perhaps because they had gained the upper hand in the leadership and no longer needed to rely on a class struggle analysis in order to satisfy their opponents. They became brutally frank in criticizing the shortcomings of the socialist system in the context of a very poor country in which people still have "feudal" relationships. They even criticized the socialist system as contributing, along with feudal attitudes, to the many problems in the relations between cadres and the people. And they ignored class struggle in favor of organizational, economic, and political reforms as the appropriate methods to address the problems created by a socialist system attempting to modernize.

Perhaps most importantly, by elevating the importance of law over politics as the measure of who is "right" and who is "wrong," the reform leaders moved away from a subjective political interpretation toward a legal basis for assessing behavior. Class enemies and political deviants have, by definition, grown rare, while *criminals,* guilty according to state laws, have taken their place.

Although the more liberal wing of the reform leadership quietly shelved class analysis and class struggle by saying classes no longer existed, and that socialist bureaucrats in a socialist society cannot form a class, they have not openly repudiated the possibility of class struggle if classes reassert themselves. Perhaps it may once again prove useful as a weapon to isolate and attack their enemies. But they have other tools to use for the same purpose, and with fewer bad side effects, notably, an emphasis on expertise, education, and competence. At least for the time being, then, the more liberal of the reform leaders have succeeded in shifting the policy focus away from class to competence, and away from class struggle to competition as the driving force of development.

> By denying the force of competition, and by exaggerating instead the importance of class struggle, we regarded the normal phenomenon of competition between individuals as being class struggle. Those who excelled in their studies and work or those who made a fortune through their labor were criticized as capitalist roaders or capitalist experts wanting to make a name for themselves. This was one reason why class struggle was magnified. At the same time, we denied that competition existed under socialist conditions and we unrealistically exaggerated cooperation. This provided the theoretical

basis for the tendency to effect the transition to communism prematurely and for the egalitarian practice of "eating from the same big rice pot," and thus hindered the development of productive forces.[39]

CONCLUSIONS

A Cost-Benefit Analysis of China's Focus on Class and Class Struggle

Those who espouse a liberal-democratic philosophy are unlikely to see any benefits in a classic Marxist class analysis, or in class struggle. But the Chinese Communists necessarily upheld the principle that class struggle was an integral part of the revolution. In the first phase of socialist development, the Chinese leadership was in agreement on means and ends: the determination of each person's class background, especially in the countryside; the confiscation and subsequent redistribution of property; and "struggle" against the "enemy" classes as a part of that redistribution in an effort to reshape the attitudes of the Chinese masses toward exploitative authorities. The latter was an integral part of Mao's view that in the revolutionary process the masses must be *involved* emotionally, by speaking bitterness against the enemy classes, and by participating in the process of economic redistribution. Finally, the designation of class served the useful purpose of distinguishing "friends" from "enemies."

The real problems for the Chinese began when the leadership went beyond the goal of eliminating classes to using class as an evaluative scheme for the distribution of social values. Mao's renewal of class struggle in 1957 with the Anti-Rightist Campaign sowed seeds of bitter dissent. The explosive leadership conflicts in the 1960s and 1970s were the fruits of those seeds.[40] The issues of class and class struggle became weapons used by factions within the leadership to advance their own power bases. For the years from 1965 to 1976, and perhaps through the early 1980s, class labels, when to use class struggle and against whom were some of the principal issues that preoccupied China's leaders and its people. The reasons were simple. First, the leadership could not agree on who should have the right to rule, manage, and succeed in socialist China. Second, they differed over what should be done and who should be blamed if a policy failed. The concept of class antagonisms fulfilled their objective of finding a scapegoat.

Like the unresolved issue of deviance and control, which intersects with the issue of class at so many points, the constant struggle campaigns against enemy classes, or enemy-class ideologies, long after there was an objectively identifiable enemy, had a wearing effect on the Chinese people. Never knowing when the definition of the enemy class might change, or when their class background might be used against them, the Chinese people grew jittery, tired, and annoyed at their leadership for not being able to settle the issue. Class struggle ultimately undermined the concept of "infallibility," for if the bourgeoisie was *in* the Party, then the Party itself had grown corrupt. If the bourgeoisie was *not* within the Party, then liars and dissemblers of truth must have gained control of the Party. In either case, a Party that could not agree who was in the enemy class was hardly infallible. Deng Xiaoping, who desperately wanted to restore trust in the Party's ability to lead, tried to bury the class issue, even while keeping alive the importance of correct political thought. But it is a hard balance to strike, precisely because in the process of redefining China's real issues, the leadership feels compelled to explain why these issues make class and class struggle irrelevant. It seems that the leadership cannot just ignore the issue and hope it will disappear.

The careful designation of each person's class at the outset could have ended the issue had there been agreement that, given the goal of attaining a Communist utopia, it was best to have China run by those from the right class background. These "red" leaders would be better than trained "experts" of questionable class background and dubious political commitment. If such agreement had existed, it would have been useful to maintain a record of proper class background. But once socialist transformation had been completed and a new generation was indoctrinated solely in socialist values, who was to say that one person was more "red" than another, regardless of their parents' values or class background? Expertise could be measured, but revolutionary commitment could be faked. Thus, designation of class was ineffective because it was subjectively determined, and hence easily abused by those using it as a tool to achieve their own goals.

The combination of the varying criteria of "class" after 1956, the distribution of so many of the privileges, positions, benefits, and opportunities on the basis of "class," in addition to the fact that one's career and even one's personal life could be ruined with the wrong class label, created an environment of hostility, tension, cynicism, and struggle. Over time, class struggle alienated the Chinese people from each other and thereby hindered the very cooperation that socialism sought. All Chinese are the victims of the resulting insecurity, but so is the Chinese Communist Party. By being so inconsistent, the Party lost its right to unquestionable authority.

During the 1980s, the Chinese people have seriously questioned the reliance upon class struggle to rid China of its "black elements." One of the reasons the campaign against "spiritual pollution" in 1983–1984 was so short lived was undoubtedly that, when the opponents of reform tried to expand the campaign's targets and turn it into another quintessential class struggle campaign, many people simply refused to participate.

In effect, the use of class designations and class struggle were not effective tools to achieve China's objectives because neither the "remnants of the exploiting class" nor the influence of bourgeois ideology was the problem. The problem was first, the Party's own persistent abuse of its power after 1957, and second, policies that were ineffective in achieving their goals within a socialist system. The result is that many Chinese people are now acting in their own self-interests, selfishly. They are, in the 1980s, behaving in the same way as any people do who have witnessed the general breakdown of authority: Grab while you can! They didn't learn this from capitalist ideology, but from the environment created within China.

Finally, even if the problem actually were the influence of capitalist ideology, the heart of the problem lies in the vulnerability of China to such influence. Chinese culture and the polity have been too vulnerable in the 1980s to resist successfully this alleged cultural subversion by capitalist values from abroad, values such as materialism, individualism, and freedom. Ironically, the reform leadership has implicitly sponsored these bourgeois values in its own policies as the best way to get the Chinese economy moving!

Prognosis

As long ago as the Third Plenum of the Communist Party in December 1978, the Deng Xiaoping leadership group officially recognized that Mao Zedong and Mao Thought had incorrectly analyzed the issue of class, and that the "leftist line" had incorrectly used and expanded class struggle in a socialist society. And yet, the class issue was not thoroughly eliminated. If Deng's blatant use of capitalist methods of development is successful in achieving development, it will undoubtedly mean the continued growth of inequality within Chinese society. The reform leadership became convinced that "all eating out of the same pot," all receiving equal rewards regardless of their contribution, was an idea whose time had not yet come; and that greater rewards for those who contributed more, regardless of class background, would advance modernization more rapidly. The price of a rebirth of true economic inequality, and hence of new economically defined classes, seems to be a price the leadership is willing to pay.

As impersonal market mechanisms assume more and more of the power formerly held by bureaucrats, new classes, whose primary distinction will be their control and even their ownership of the means of production, will undoubtedly require continuous ideological justification by a leadership that hopes to maintain at least the pretense of being socialist. Thus far the Chinese have kept up the administrative formality of collectives still owning land: Collectives simply "contract" their land out to farmers, for perhaps as long as thirty years. During this time, they may use it, their children may inherit it, and, if they so choose, they may subcontract it to other families. Although the Chinese leadership can still maintain that land is not private property in any ultimate sense, even if it is used as if it were private, the other means of production are unquestionably becoming privatized. Peasants who "get rich" may, for example, choose to buy trucks, harvesters, ditch diggers, ploughs, carts, and tools, all of which are their own private property. Urban workers who "get rich" may also purchase the machinery and material for a shop. They may even buy stock in certain companies and put their money in the bank that pays the highest rate of interest. These means of production all belong to them as individuals, not to a collective.

Classes, measured by an economic yardstick, are rapidly being re-formed. If the now dominant reform leadership successfully consolidates its control, and manages to bury the issues of class and class struggle and rephrase the issues as those of competition and modernization; and if the importance of expertise rather than class becomes the critical factor in individual advancement, then China is likely to stay away from class as a central political issue.

Finally, the leadership's concern for the future relationship of the mainland with Taiwan and Hong Kong may also be a factor affecting the fate of the issues of class and class struggle. Were these to remain unre-solved issues, there is no doubt that the people of Hong Kong and Taiwan would be reluctant to become a part of the Chinese polity; for on *no* grounds would the class background or political behavior of most of the people in Hong Kong and Taiwan be acceptable according to either Marx-ist economic categories or the shifting class criteria offered over time by China's various leaders. The continuing efforts to bring Hong Kong and Taiwan peaceably into the framework of the PRC's government may, in fact, contribute to the permanent resolution of the issues of class and class struggle.

NOTES

[1]V. I. Lenin, "A Great Beginning," *Selected Works,* Vol. II (Moscow: Foreign Languages Publishing House, 1952), p. 224, in Richard C. Kraus, *Class Conflict in Chinese Socialism* (New York: Columbia University Press, 1981), p. 21, note 4. The Chinese have frequently quoted Lenin's definition of class.

[2]Karl Popper, *Conjectures and Refutations* (New York: Harper & Row, 1968), p. 345.

[3]Michael Loewi, "The Order of Aristocratic Rank of Han China," *T'oung Pao,* Vol. 48, Nos. 1–3 (1960), pp. 97–174.

[4]The distinction between social stratification and class differentiation is dealt with by Kraus, *Class Conflict in Chinese Socialism,* chapter 2.

[5]Examples of these could be the distinction between skilled and nonskilled workers, and between professionals and organizational bureaucrats. See Chalmers Johnson, "What's Wrong with Chinese Studies?" *Asian Survey,* No. 10 (October 1982), pp. 924, 925.

[6]See Mao's view on contradictions between the enemy and the people, and contradic-tions among the people, in his essay written just months before the Anti-Rightist Campaign of 1957, in "On the Correct Handling of Contradictions Among the People" (July 1957), in

Anne Fremantle (ed), *Mao Tse-Tung: An Anthology of His Writings* (New York: The New American Library, A Mentor Book, 1962), pp. 264–297, especially pp. 265–267, 272–274.

[7]Mao Zedong, "On Contradiction" (August 1937), in Fremantle (ed), *Mao Tse-tung: An Anthology of His Writings*, pp. 214–241; also see Mao, "On the Correct Handling," pp. 264–297.

[8]Kraus, *Class Conflict in Chinese Socialism*, p. 21.

[9]Kraus, *Class Conflict in Chinese Socialism*, pp. 14–17.

[10]Mao Zedong, "Never Forget Class Struggle," speech to Tenth Plenum of Central Committee of the Chinese Communist Party (September 1962).

[11]Stuart R. Schram, "Classes, Old and New, in Mao Zedong's Thought, 1970–1976," in James L. Watson (ed), *Class and Social Stratification in Post-Revolution China* (Cambridge, U.K.: Cambridge University Press, 1984), pp. 30–38.

[12]James L. Watson, "Introduction: Class and Class Formation in Chinese Society," in Watson (ed), *Class and Social Stratification* p. 13.

[13]Maurice Meisner, "The Maoist Vision of the Future," in Maurice Meisner (ed), *Marxism, Maoism and Utopianism* (Madison: University of Wisconsin Press, 1982), pp. 103, 104.

[14]Susan L. Shirk, *Competitive Comrades: Career Incentives and Student Strategies in China* (Berkeley: University of California Press, 1982), p. 50.

[15]Kraus, *Class Conflict in Chinese Socialism*, pp. 16, 17.

[16]Kraus, *Class Conflict in Chinese Socialism*, p. 9. Also see George Ginsburgs, "Soviet Critique of the Maoist Political Model," in James C. Hsiung (ed), *The Logic of 'Maoism'* (New York: Praeger, 1974), pp. 137–162.

[17]Jonathan Unger, *Education Under Mao: Class and Competition in Canton Schools, 1960–1980* (New York: Columbia University Press, 1982), p. 13.

[18]"What Happened after Ma Fengchun's Marriage," *Comrade Editor: Letters to the People's Daily*, translated by Hugh Thomas, (Hong Kong: Joint Publishing Company, 1980), pp. 126, 127.

[19]Shirk, *Competitive Comrades*, p. 76.

[20]Jerome A. Cohen, "Will China Have a Formal Legal System?" in *American Bar Association Journal* Vol. 64 (October 1978), p. 1515.

[21]"Class Status in the Countryside: Changes Over Three Decades," *BR*, No. 3 (January 21, 1980), p. 14. A concrete sign that class labels were deemphasized was the conduct of a countywide registration drive as a component of the 1980–1981 election campaign, run under the new (1980) Election Laws. During the registration, all but a few individuals had their class labels removed, which meant that their voting rights were restored and that they were even eligible for local leadership positions. See John P. Burns, *Political Participation in Rural China* (Berkeley: University of California Press, forthcoming).

[22]Shi Zhongquan, "The 'Cultural Revolution'," *BR*, No. 49 (December 7, 1981), p. 18.

[23]Xi Xuan (a "theoretician"), "Why Should a Theory Be Discarded? An Analysis of the Theory of 'Continuing the Revolution under the Dictatorship of the Proletariat'," *BR*, No. 44 (November 2, 1981), p. 22.

[24]Xi Xuan, "Why Should a Theory Be Discarded?" p. 25. Emphasis added. Also see Shi Zhongquan, "The 'Cultural Revolution'," p. 18. The introduction of this new principle, of how productive means were acquired, was made necessary by two conditions. First, the "redemption" program in the 1950s for members of the former "national bourgeoisie" had resulted in the state giving a large amount of money to a number of people when their property was nationalized. Many of these former capitalists have been active leaders in economic modernization in the 1980s. Second, this definition of class paved the way for the Party's programs for the people to "get rich."

[25]Shi Zhongquan, "The 'Cultural Revolution'," p. 18. Both Djilas and Dahrendorf have extensively studied class in postrevolutionary regimes. The issue of ownership *or* control, rather than ownership *and* control of the means of production, is fully examined in Djilas' work in particular. See Milovan Djilas, *The New Class: An Analysis of The Communist System* (San Diego: Harcourt Brace Jovanovich, 1982); and Ralf Dahrendorf, *Class and Class Conflict in Industrial Society* (Stanford: Stanford University Press, 1959).

[26]For the view that the definition of class must change in a bureaucratic society away from Mao's emphasis on ownership *and* control to mere control of property, see the works of Dahrendorf and Djilas, ibid.

[27]Zhou Yan (staff writer), "On China's Current Class Struggle," *BR*, No. 33 (August 16, 1982) p. 18.

[28]An Zhiguo (Political Editor), "Current Class Struggle," *BR*, No. 17 (April 26, 1982), p. 3.

[29]Zhou Yan, "China's Current Class Struggle," p. 19.

[30]Ibid.

[31]"Looking at Competition Between Individuals," *BR*, No. 49 (December 5, 1983), p. 28.

[32]Mao Zedong, a remark made to French Minister of Culture Andre Malraux in Beijing, 1965, in Kraus, *Class Conflict in Chinese Socialism*, p. 1. See note 1.

[33]This, incidentally, is not the same as "classified documents," available only to a few hundred people. *Neibu* materials usually circulate among several tens of thousands of cadres with a specified rank.

[34]This was certainly the Soviet view of Mao's adoption of "a vague hybrid conception," designed to give himself "maximum freedom and flexibility in internal political maneuvers." See Ginsburgs, "Soviet Critique of the Maoist Political Model," in Hsiung (ed), *The Logic of 'Maoism'*, p. 150.

[35]As examples, see Gu Hua, *A Small Town Called Hibiscus*, translated by Gladys Yang (Beijing: Panda Books, 1983); and Anita Chan, Richard Madsen, and Jonathan Unger, *Chen Village* (Berkeley: University of California Press, 1984).

[36]See letters to the editors in *Comrade Editor*, chapter 5, on "How Do I Declare My Class Origins?" (pp. 120–122) as examples of pervasive befuddlement.

[37]Shirk, *Competitive Comrades*, pp. 52, 53.

[38]From an interview with a Hong Kong refugee from the PRC, in Shirk, *Competitive Comrades*, p. 168.

[39]"Opinion: Looking for Competition Between Individuals," *Shanghai Journal*, Issue No. 4, in *Beijing Review*, No. 49 (December 5, 1982), p. 28.

[40]For the "seeds" that were planted from 1956 to 1960, see Roderick MacFarquhar, *The Origins of the Cultural Revolution*, Vol. I, *Contradictions Among the People 1956–1957*, and Vol. II, *The Great Leap Forward 1958–1960* (New York: Columbia University Press, 1974, 1983, respectively).

Chapter Eight
ECONOMIC DEVELOPMENT: THE CONFLICT BETWEEN SOCIALlST AND DEVELOPMENTAL OBJECTIVES

ECONOMY A HOSTAGE TO POLITICS AND IDEOLOGY

Many of the obstacles to China successfully resolving issues of economic development are the obstacles all less developed countries (LDCs) face: They are poor and must try to develop within the context of a scarcity economy. But a country either does or does not overcome factors of underdevelopment at some point. If poverty always kept a country poor, then economic development would never occur. In this sense, even though the developmental variable is very important for understanding problems in China's economy, it is at the same time inadequate as an explanatory variable.

Although China's underdevelopment has posed many obstacles, the evidence available indicates that ideological and political factors have even more severely hampered China's economic development. Specifically, the Chinese Communist Party leaders set a trap for themselves by insisting on ideological purity. They stepped into a box called the "socialist economic system," the boundaries of which they defined themselves during political struggles, and then discovered they could not escape it when it did not work. Ideological values and policies worked well in the economy in some years, but did not work at all well in other years. Yet each time the leaders tried to escape from being a hostage to ideology, they found their political enemies confronting them with "ideological backsliding," "selling out the revolution," or "revisionism." Those who had benefitted from China's form of socialism had vested interests in the system not changing. Further, a centralized planned economy offered only a limited number of options, especially in the context of a factious political environment and scarcity economy. Those who wanted to escape the trap of their own definition of a socialist economy had to do ideological somersaults in order to maintain their socialist credentials.

After China stepped partially outside of its socialist ideological box in 1978, its development accelerated, and many of the obstacles to growth that were inherent in its underdeveloped state were overcome. This is persuasive evidence that political-ideological factors, in the *context* of China's poverty and culture, were the major impediments to China's growth.

In essence, the Chinese leadership after 1949 translated the demands of a socialist ideology into economic processes and structures that could comfortably be labeled "socialist." If economic failures occurred, however, the leadership did not blame the socialist system. Rather, they searched for political causes; and that inevitably meant that *people,* not the system, were still considered the major cause of problems.

Unfortunately, the Chinese pitted socialist values and a socialist system (as interpreted by Mao Zedong) *against* developmental values. This was not intentional, of course, as the socialist model can be effective for economic development. But when it proved ineffective in China, the leftist leadership proved incapable of modifying it significantly. It may well be argued that the Stalinist form of a socialist economic model was the only one the Chinese understood from experience, and that they were ideologically blinded from understanding nonsocialist models of development. Further, the political and ideological constraints of the Chinese socialist system could not be eliminated without endangering both socialism and the leaders' own political careers.

Members of the reform faction who emerged as the dominant leaders in 1978 were determined to put aside those aspects of socialist ideology that they considered detrimental to development and modernization, while pretending they had not. They used the escape clause that the methods for achieving socialism must be suitable to Chinese conditions. They call this "socialism with Chinese characteristics," and combine it with methods to neutralize, if not eliminate, the political opposition to their economic reforms. The result has been a dramatic change of course in economic development since 1978. In the process, China's leaders have resolved many of the problems that are developmental issues for LDCs.

MAJOR UNRESOLVED ISSUES IN CHINA'S ECONOMIC DEVELOPMENT

Ever since 1949 the Chinese Communists have faced six broad issues of economic development.

First, *the structural element:* the level of centralizing and decision making—the proper balance between control and independence, between "directing" and "releasing" human energy;[1] between direct or indirect control; the optimal size of organization; and the problems endemic to a socialist economic system operating in a Chinese culture.

Second, *the human element:* the kinds of incentives to motivate people; egalitarianism as an incentive or disincentive; and the role of political consciousness in increasing production.

Third, *the role of politics and the Party:* the degree to which Communist Party personnel and political goals promote or interfere with economic goals; and the role of economic experts.

Fourth, *competing objectives:* the importance of pursuing socialism's political and social objectives, even at the expense of more rapid economic development.

Fifth, *the issue of the balance in investments between heavy industry, light industry, and agriculture.*

And sixth, *the role of foreign investment, trade, and finance in the development of the economy.*

These are the key issues with which China's leaders have been absorbed in the economic arena. In addressing each issue, the Chinese have been constrained by ideology, culture, and developmental level. The tension among these three factors in confronting economic problems has been enormous; and yet it is in the economic arena that China, in comparison with most LDCs, has witnessed its greatest successes in resolving issues.

HOW A CENTRALLY PLANNED ECONOMY FUNCTIONS

Like other socialist countries, until the 1980s, China had a centrally planned economy. Within it, the function of the market in determining prices, plans, allocation, and distribution of goods varied over time, but was generally minimal in the period from 1957 to 1979.[2] In the vast countryside, peasants could take produce from their private plots (after 1956 this usually amounted to no more than 5 percent of the sown acreage) and sell it in free markets (except during the Great Leap Forward and Cultural Revolution, when both private plots and free markets were restricted or banned). In the urban industrial sector, however, as of the late 1980s, China's state-owned enterprises still had virtually no independence from state decisions: "The state sets targets for them, distributes their products, assigns their personnel, allocates their equipment, takes over their profit, and covers all their deficits."[3]

In China's centrally planned economy, such serious concerns for a Western capitalist economy as profits and efficiency were not major considerations when distributing resources (including land, labor, capital, and raw materials) and assigning production quotas to each farm and factory.[4] Further, because those who set policies were not and are not those who implement them, it is understandable that with over 90,000 state enterprises, central planners cannot be familiar with their day-to-day problems. Much wastage occurs because of the difficulties of administratively coordinating the distribution of goods, first to the production units, and then among the production units. Some enterprises may overstock either resources or producer products, while others suffer from a shortage. Rarely are one enterprise's inventories transferred to another enterprise that needs them, since neither an incentive nor a mechanism for doing so exists. In fact, as long as the centrally planned portion of the economy continues to set production targets, the system will positively encourage a manager "to produce inefficiently, requesting more inputs than are really needed and producing less output than is actually possible, to avoid having the production targets raised in future periods."[5] After all, in a shortage economy in which there is centralized control and allocation, the key concern is the availability of necessary inputs, not their price.

The state's central administrative organs fix prices for most important consumer and producer goods. Local economic bureaucrats will, however, set the price and control the supply of locally distributed products.[6] Prices of food, clothing, housing, trucks, glass, cement and thousands of other products have little to do with their actual cost and more to do with what the government believes are "necessities" and what type of consumption pattern it wants to encourage. Further, the products from an inefficient factory in which unit production costs are high will be priced the same as products from a highly efficient factory.

For this reason, in a centrally planned economy, although prices affect consumption patterns, they neither encourage nor discourage production; for the objective of enterprises is not to make profits but to fulfill quotas. Managers do not make decisions based on price. If an enterprise does make profits, the bulk of them are turned over to the central planning authority. If the enterprise loses money, the state authorities may blame the manager but will subsidize the losses. Therefore, if money for investment projects is available, a manager is more likely to invest in a "safe but not very profitable" project than in a risky one that might yield a high profit.[7]

In the case of producer goods (goods to be used by other producers), central administrators determine how many producer goods ought to be manufactured on the basis of past production figures and centrally determined production goals. They are also responsible for distributing 70 percent to 90 percent of all producer goods to other enterprises. They do not do market studies to determine whether the centrally determined production quotas are appropriate, but of course they are trying to make the best estimate possible. The problem is one of calculating, through administrative rather than market mechanisms, precisely what those needs are. Since there are, on the one hand, over one billion consumers, and on the other hand, over 90,000 state owned enterprises (and still over 700 million individual producers in the rural economy), it is a monumental task for a centralized state organ to determine each unit's (and individual's) production needs, which products it should manufacture, how many inputs it requires, and how many outputs it will produce. To attempt to do so, the central economic organs must collect an enormous amount of information. Given the size of the Chinese economy, this requires a huge administrative bureaucracy of educated personnel. The less that politics and objectives other than economic ones intrude in these economic calculations, the easier is the determination of the best distribution of resources, goods, services, and personnel.

In the case of consumer goods, the administrators divide them into *rationed* and *nonrationed* goods. Rationed products have in the past included cotton cloth, food grain, vegetable oil, sugar, meat, soap, and a few other products that are considered basic essentials which, if not rationed, might not be widely available.[8] Each month each person receives a fixed number of ration coupons for these goods. These must be presented, together with cash, in order to purchase them.[9]

Nonrationed goods may be bought whenever they are available and in unlimited quantity. The state has determined that they are not essential consumer goods, but this does not mean that these products are available on the market for purchase. Umbrellas, better-made televisions and tape recorders, plate glass, beer, washing machines, and many other products in great demand are not rationed, have low fixed prices established by the central administration with no concern for market demand, and are for these reasons only sporadically available in the stores—unless, of course, one knows someone who can get these products through "the back door." The following description of a centrally planned economy helps illustrate the kinds of burdens that fall upon its administrative apparatus:

> Consumer goods flow from producers to consumers. Labor services flow from consumers to producers. Material inputs and capital goods flow from producers to producers. In a market economy all flows go through markets. In a centrally planned economy all flows are controlled by the planning authority. It orders the producers to produce certain consumer goods and distribute them to the consumers. It assigns laborers to work in various production units. It orders producers to produce material inputs and distribute them to other producers. It also directs the production of capital goods and the construction of investment projects.[10]

THE HISTORY OF CHINA'S ECONOMIC POLICIES

As in any economy, the optimal solution to one set of problems may have negative repercussions for other issues. The history of China's economic development after 1949 illustrates the conflicts generated by each shift in economic policies. Below is a brief summary, first of the overall policy trends after 1949, and then more specifically of the economic policies officially followed since the landmark Third Party Plenum of December 1978. One caveat: Just because these are the policies does not mean they are being implemented uniformly throughout China, nor that when they are implemented, they are having the intended effects.

The Maoist Model of Economic Development and the Importance of the Ideological Variable

In the West it is generally held that economic development encompasses a growing complexity, diversity, and specialization, that investment increases as per capita income increases, and that consumerism and materialism accompany growth. Profit and efficiency are measures of economic development. In China, the "Maoist" view of economic development was the prevailing view in most of the years from 1950 to 1978 (as described in Chapter Three), although much of the actual structure of the economy was modeled on the Soviet centralized "command" economy.

In contrast to the Western view, the Maoist conceptualization was that economic development was a step-by-step resolution of contradictions. Each resolution would move China toward a higher mode of production in a Marxian economic progression until it reached communism. Resolving the "contradiction" between landlords and landless or poor peasants by land redistribution was, according to Mao, one step toward economic development. Further, Mao saw economic development as a series of steps moving toward ever-larger production units, with the level of ownership also progressing steadily higher, until the "whole people" owned everything. Rather than becoming more complex, the economy would be composed of large "self-reliant" units. In the countryside, these units were the communes, and they were to meet all the needs of their members: agricultural and industrial goods, health maintenance and medical services, education, cultural and sports facilities, etc. Rather than increased specialization and diversity according to "comparative advantage" (by which regions or communes specialize in providing products or services they do best, and leave everything else to be produced by other regions or communes), then, all communes would perform identical tasks and be self-sufficient. Further, those in charge would not be increasingly specialized, but rather, increasingly politicized. Armed with correct political thought, they could administer the economy better than economic specialists.

A related Maoist perspective was that economic development entails the gradual elimination of the "three great differences," the gaps between rural and urban life, between industrial and agricultural sectors, and between mental and manual labor. In eliminating these gaps, any distinctions of material wealth or social status deriving from property or roles are also eliminated. The Maoist model of economic development did not, however, take into consideration the possibility that locking peasants into agricultural production in the countryside, even while closing the "gaps," would limit growth. The experience of most countries that have successfully developed suggests, in fact, that the percentage of the labor force in the agricultural sector must be greatly reduced for growth to continue. Because the marginal product of agricultural labor in underdeveloped countries is virtually nil, the impact on total agricultural output of transferring labor out of the agricultural sector is negligible, and average farm worker output actually increases. But China's policy did not *permit* mobility to the cities, or even within the countryside. Thus, although economic development seems to require a reduction of the agricultural labor force to about 20 percent to 30 percent of the population, as of 1979, it was still 83 percent, just as it had been in 1952.[11]

The Maoist model of economic development did not entirely ignore issues of efficiency and quality, but its priority was to increase output rapidly by meeting ever-larger production quotas. More output, especially of heavy industrial producer goods was thought to mean more "development." After 1956, the issue of whether or not there was a need for specific heavy industrial products was less important than was their very production.[12] It was assumed that all products would eventually be used, a viewpoint that did not take into account the effect the production quota system had on enterprise managers: They would hoard or stockpile goods in warehouses for a rainy day. End-users were a secondary concern. The production of consumer goods was discouraged, as it was assumed that the purchase of consumer goods would simply siphon the people's savings into industries that would not benefit China's economic growth. The result was an appallingly low quality of consumer goods and services.

The Maoist view of how to accomplish economic development was through a "revolutionary" process entailing rapid, massive, and often violent change. (As Deng Xiaoping was later to note when assessing China's economic development, it was precisely because China tried to go so fast that it developed so slowly!) To attain rapid change, politically conscious masses and dedicated cadres loyal to the Communist Party's vision were essential. Mao believed that changes in people's minds, and hence in their behavior, could be willed through thought reform. In turn, the underdeveloped material "substructure," the economy, could be willed into economic development by the "superstructure" of thought and values. Mao Zedong Thought, a "spiritual atomic bomb," would stimulate greater productivity. The Red Guards' attempts during the Cultural Revolution to remold people's thoughts through various physical forms of brutalization, shunning, or political discussion groups are only the most stunning examples of the leadership's efforts at political consciousness-raising and the belief that correct political thought could enhance production. For workers, time taken away from productive work for political education would make the few remaining hours of work more effective.

Finally, the Soviet model of a highly centralized command economy served, even in the Maoist radical model, as the organizing principle for achieving economic development: Central state economic planning agencies would determine what would be produced, who would produce it, and how services, raw materials, and finished products would be distributed.

From 1956 until 1978, Mao's view of economic development dominated, but another vision of economic development within the Chinese leadership, which for the purpose of distinguishing it from the Maoist view will be called the "rightist" view, coincided more with the Western vision. It was less utopian, favored consolidation of gains, and saw increased materialism and consumerism, hence greater material incentives, as necessary ingredients of economic growth. This view preferred nonviolent, incremental gains guided by economic specialists and economic reality. The "rightist" view, which also embraced the hope of achieving communism some time in the distant future, had guiding principles no more radical than those of America's New Deal of the 1930s. These "rightist" economic policies were advocated by Liu Shaoqi and later were condemned by leftists as "revisionist;" but they subsequently became the basis of the reforms that began in December 1978.

The Actual Economic Policies of 1949–1978

The history of China's economic policies (outlined in Chapter Three) indicates that China's centrally planned economy performed erratically after 1949. Further, the degree of centralized economic planning and its effectiveness varied with political conditions. The general procedure was that the Party determined overall policy, and then the State Planning Commission and the State Economic Commission decided how to carry out policy through specific administrative programs. State commissions, ministries, and bureaus then allocated China's resources in accord with economic objectives.

In this sense, China had a "command economy": Central planners would issue production quotas and policy directives to be implemented by administrators at the middle and lower levels. But unless the lower levels of administrators had special ties right up to the central leadership and so would be protected from middle-level bureaucrats by the center when they implemented new policies, they were unlikely to depart from old policies. All kinds of pushing and tugging would occur along the way to full implementation. The fact that the press would be full of stories about middle-level bureaucrats hampering their implementation for months after each new policy was announced suggests how "uncommanding" central directives really were.[13]

China's central planners managed most of the economy as if it were "a single big enterprise," with just one set of needs and problems to address. Because of the complexity, diversity, and immensity of China, however, over time this highly centralized economy proved inefficient and even a hindrance to economic productivity.

Further, policy decisions that merged Party and governmental/administrative work led to continual political interference in economic work. Decisions affecting economic development were often made for political reasons. Politics frequently disrupted the planning process to such an extent that plans were sometimes announced after they had been completed.[14] (The First Five-Year Plan, 1953 to 1957, was, for example, announced in 1955.) Although the immediate impact of political education campaigns on economic production may certainly be debated, the repeated class struggles and purges of Party and administrative cadres throughout the economic system had decidedly negative long-term repercussions for economic growth. And there can be little doubt about the effect of constant mobilization and rectification campaigns on the behavior of cadres. With political concerns of utmost importance, cadres became more interested in enhancing their own political authority, or even just in protecting themselves, than in economic development. Particularly in the countryside, cadres in the intensely political environment of the 1960s and 1970s were more likely to make economic decisions for political than for economic reasons. In fact, they frequently ignored, or found it politically dangerous to pay attention to, the damage that inappropriate policies for local conditions would cause. In their search for political correctness, for example, they "learned from Dazhai," the national agricultural model brigade, by terracing their fields as Dazhai did, even though the costs of terracing in their own localities were far greater than the economic returns. In one village, peasants every winter dug new canals that would predictably be washed out by the following spring rain. "They were responding to a quota which fixed the amount of earth they had to dig."[15]

Another example of the damaging consequences of China's style of centralized planning is the leftists' "self-sufficiency in grain" campaign that began in 1965. It illustrates how a few Party politicians in a highly centralized political system could manipulate China's centralized economic system. In this case, the leftist leadership forced the entire country to "grow grain" in order to make China self-sufficient in grain. There was not the slightest regard for the dictates of comparative advantage. Similarly, the leftists' self-reliance model for industry required each enterprise to be "small but complete:" Each factory would do everything necessary in the production cycle to produce a final manufactured product. Again, scant regard was paid to the costs of having one enterprise perform all stages of manufacturing a product. One of the major reasons for the growth of small (or large) and complete enterprises after 1965 was inherent in the system of central allocation in a shortage economy: These self-reliant enterprises were organized *vertically* in order to guarantee the necessary supplies for production. Thus, the suppliers of raw materials or producer goods became part of a vertically integrated enterprise.

The steady decline in efficiency, or total "factor productivity" after 1957, illustrates the opportunity costs the Chinese incurred under the Maoist model: They poured raw materials, capital, and labor ("factors") into the economy at rates higher than the output growth rates. In other words, better economic policies combined with these same resources and labor could have bought a much higher rate of economic growth.[16] The growth of the gross national product in spite of the decline in factor growth rates in the 1980s illustrates the possibility that, with a different economic model and less political interference, the Chinese could have achieved higher growth rates in earlier years.

The Reformers' Model of Economic Development and the Importance of the Developmental Variable, 1978 to 1988

In the 1980s, the reform or pragmatist policies have gone much further than the policies Liu Shaoqi envisioned in the 1950s and 1960s. The reformers have reworked the ideas of socialist political economy to accommodate new methods for resolving China's economic problems. Their viewpoint is that socialism is more than an ideology: It is a promise of both a better spiritual and material life. The purpose of economic development is not to achieve larger and larger production units, nor to produce more goods with no specific objective beyond meeting production quotas, but rather to increase the level of technology, production, and management abilities so that the material needs of the people will be satisfied.[17] Consumerism would provide the stimulus to economic development, which would one day lead to communism.

In the mean time, the reformers urge the people to "Seek truth from facts," that is, to look at the reality of China's developmental conditions and to address the problems of underdevelopment with economic, not political, strategies, including some of the successful methods used in the developed countries. In contrast to the Maoist model, the reformers' pragmatic model tries to play down political-ideological issues in the economic realm. With "economics in command," the developmental variable takes precedence to the point of almost excluding the ideological variable.

The reformers feel they can ideologically rationalize some people becoming wealthier than others as long as those who "get rich" do not trample on the socialist principle of nonexploitation of labor. (In practice, exploitation of labor is condoned through a policy of benign neglect.) After all, socialism is a "new-born system," so that the methods to achieve and maintain it are still subject to change until "practice," in the context of Chinese conditions, indicates that the methods are correct.[18] With the reformers, "socialism with Chinese characteristics" has become the most appropriate guiding principle for China's economic development. The system remains, however, a far cry from "market socialism," for plans are still far more important than markets in resource allocation.

Economic Policies from 1978 to 1988

With the Third Party Plenum in 1978, the Chinese witnessed a massive reversal of the vestigial leftist economic policies still remaining after the death of Mao and the arrest of the Gang of Four in 1976. They also witnessed both a questioning of the Soviet centralized model of development and a repudiation of Premier Hua Guofeng's expansionist economic policies, which had been based on a major miscalculation of petroleum production. Some reform leaders believed the Soviet model was inappropriate for China's level of economic development, in part because it assumed that a high level of economic development already existed, and in part because it relied on administrative control rather than marketplace instruments to direct the economy. They fought to escape the Soviet economic model of a centrally planned economy in order to address issues of inefficiency, poor quality, suppressed inflation, bureaucracy, and political interference. Whether it is called "socialism with Chinese characteristics" or "a socialist commodity economy," economic policies since 1978 have emphasized profits and efficiency more than any policy since 1949. Yet the fear of more "conservative" reform leaders that China will acquire problems endemic to a liberalized economy, and the resistance of those with a vested interest in the socialist economic model, have continued to limit both the options and the speed of reform.

Rural production "responsibility system" since 1978

Decentralization and Contracts.   Ever since the Third Party Plenum announced that collectivized agriculture would be replaced with the "household responsibility system," in most cases the household has determined its own production plans and functioned as both the basic production and accounting unit. Decision making was, therefore, decentralized to the lowest level possible. Virtually any "responsibility system" form has been permissible as long as it meets two requirements: collective ownership of the land and fulfillment of state production quotas.[19] In most parts of China, the "responsibility system" has evolved from the more collectivist "household quotas" (*bao chan dao hu*) to the more individualistic one in which the households have "contracts with fixed levies" (*bao gan dao hu*). The key elements of most forms of "responsibility system" are the clear linkage between income and output and the contract between the peasant producers and the production team. The team collects the grain or produce contracted for, and the peasants may keep any surplus, most of which is food for themselves. Peasant producers are free to market any surplus in the flourishing rural free markets, although the market price of grain may be below the state purchasing price.[20] Households are encouraged to produce whatever crops grow best in their area, a mandate limited, however, by planned quotas imposed on each production unit and by the forces of market demand.

The previous policy for developing rural industries, which encouraged localities to become self-sufficient by producing goods for all their needs instead of specializing in what they did best, has been replaced by a policy of rural industrialization that takes into account local resources, transportation, costs, and markets for the finished products.[21] For this reason, state purchasing departments must compete with 33,000 peasant markets in commune-towns for products that are not subject to any quotas (Class III) *and* for goods *above* quota in the Class II category (goods that can legally be sold in the market once the quota is met).[22]

Free Markets and Deregulation of Prices.   With greater attention to a market system of supply and demand, and less interference from a centralized administration, peasants have moved into production of those crops that command the highest prices. "Politics in command" and Dazhai Brigade's mass-movement methods for increasing production have been replaced with the slogan of "economics" or "production in command" and exhortations to "get rich." Finally, the introduction of contractual work tasks allows peasant producers to allocate their time between collective and private work. Permitting the peasants to make many of their own economic decisions, then, addresses the problem of peasant resentment caused by the alleged inept or corrupt leadership of team and brigade cadres.[23]

Assignment of Land and Specialized Households.   Although households are merely "assigned" land for their use under the "responsibility system" (technically, the villages contract the land out), they are able to act as if they *own* the land. They have freedom to plant it as they choose for up to fifteen (and in some areas even thirty) years. Further, rural reforms since 1984 have encouraged those who are less successful at farming to lease and even *sell*[24] their land to others and leave farming for work in rural industries, or to start up services sorely needed in the countryside, such as food processing, irrigation, and transportation services. They are to leave farming, but stay in the small towns.

The combination of free markets, the household contract system, and the commercialization of the agricultural economy is meant to encourage peasants to enrich and develop the land, something they were not inclined to do when it was collectively run. The far larger "private" farm will, it is hoped, have the same economies of scale that China's leaders had originally hoped for in the large commune structure. It is thought that the longer time span of land assignment and the right of peasants to will their assigned land to their heirs (even if a team still "owns" the land) will also encourage the development of agriculture.

The state is aiming to get up to 70 percent of all peasants off the land and working in rural towns to develop the commercial and industrial sector by 1995. As of late 1987, over 70 million farmers had already left farming. Crucial to these efforts is the "sparking program." Started in 1985, its purpose is to transfer advanced science and technology from abroad to the rural areas of China. Some of the "sparking program's" key goals are: (1) to develop a better technology to store and transport, and especially to preserve and process, farm and special local products *at the place they are produced;* (2) to construct villages, towns, and building-material industries; (3) to improve mining and primary processing in small mines; (4) to popularize and apply new technologies and materials; (5) to exploit regions comprehensively; (6) to develop small production equipment; and (7) to train technical and managerial personnel for township enterprises.[25] In addition, free markets, the ability to buy tractors and other agricultural machinery that can be turned into transportation and hauling vehicles, the elimination of some regulations that thwarted the integration of the rural and urban economy, and new financial arrangements to encourage the development of "specialized households" have led many former peasants to develop new products for sideline industries, services, and commercial links to the cities. The bulk of the peasantry has, as a result, appeared content to remain in the countryside, although a small percentage of peasants with specialized skills or products and with their own grain rations are moving into the cities.

"Economics in Command."   Overall, the series of rural reforms initiated since 1978 have had a remarkably beneficial impact on the economy, namely: a greater variety of crops; higher quality goods and services in the countryside; greater agricultural productivity; increased output in spite of a significant decrease in the percentage of sown areas; and a remarkable "leap forward" in integrating the rural and urban economies. Because China's leaders have so frequently failed in implementing policies, or have successfully implemented policies that have had bad results, students of China inevitably ask why the reformist leaders succeeded this time. The best and most general answer seems to be that, apart from adroitly disposing of opposition within the leadership, careful planning, continuous innovation and persistence, the reformist leaders permitted peasants to experiment locally. Further, they interpreted the Maoist slogan of "Seek truth from facts" (which had under the leftists come to mean seek truth from

whatever Mao said), to mean that the criteria of policy evaluation would be "facts," that is, economic results. By replacing the former criterion of policy evaluation, namely political orientation, with the criterion of economic results, the reform leaders were able to play down the political content of policies and emphasize their economic content.[26]

Finally, the policy on the responsibility system and other rural reforms was not "commanded" to all areas at once. They were first tested and implemented in a few areas, then in others. Whole regions of China did not even test out the responsibility system until 1983 or 1984. Policy formation was incremental, allowing an environment to develop that was favorable to the introduction of still further reforms.[27] Still although the leadership adopted a more flexible system of policy formation and implementation in the formulation of rural policies, it did not completely eliminate a socialist "command" economy.

Urban industrial policy since 1978

Decentralization of Economic Decision Making. After the Third Party Plenum, decentralization occurred in some ministries, such as transportation and communication, in the service and banking sectors, and in some industries. The central government still sets economic policy guidelines, but it no longer attempts to administer policy. Decision-making power has been delegated downward to the regions, the major cities and even to the industrial enterprises.[28] This has provided a stimulus to growth of a *collectively owned* sector to compete with the state-owned enterprises and transportation, not only in production, but also in services. Independent tailors, shoe repairers, carpenters, and haulers now successfully compete with state-offered services. Taxi drivers in some cities actually cruise the streets looking for customers, rather than sitting for countless hours ensconced in a few locations smoking cigarettes and waiting for a central dispatch system to call them. Small family-run restaurants have sprung up all over China's cities, offering food and service superior to state-run restaurants. The now decentralized trucking, airline, and tourist industries offer better and more diverse services.

Nevertheless, the majority of enterprises still remain under state control. For all the talk about decentralization, only 3 percent of the nonrural economy in 1985 (13 million employees in 9.3 million small enterprises, which generate a $16-billion turnover annually) was in the hands of private enterpreneurs.[29] Central planners continue to assign production targets to agricultural and industrial production units, supply their inputs, control many of their products' prices, regulate the wages of most workers in urban state enterprises, and operate a rationing system (reduced in significance because the rationed goods are often now available in free markets). Many enterprises still have materials bureaus supply them under unified purchase plans, which insulate them from market signals.[30] As a result, urban industrial enterprises have not responded to the reforms with the increased productivity that the agrarian sector has. Although reforms are on paper, many problems have arisen in their implementation. Industrial enterprises still try to "socialize losses" (meaning the state subsidizes the losses) and "privatize profits" (meaning the enterprises keep the profits).

Deregulation of Prices on Most Nonessential Products. The law of supply and demand now determines prices on most nonessential products. After 1979 the state decontrolled prices, which had been held stable for twenty-two years on more than 10,000 products.[31] The state still determines prices on a broad range of essential products, notably energy, producer goods, and raw materials.

New Accounting Procedures and Bankruptcy. New accounting procedures emphasize costs per unit and profits to measure efficiency. Closing down inefficient or unprofitable enterprises is now considered acceptable under "socialism with Chinese characteristics." But it is still only possible in sectors where competitive enterprises have sprung up. State-run enterprises in most key areas, such as energy, raw materials, and heavy industries, are kept running regardless of their inefficiency. Even factories flooding the market with unwanted consumer goods resist being shut down.

Although the reforms are still rather rudimentary, the introduction of both a partial market economy and market-based pricing has allowed those enterprises with the lowest costs (and highest quality) to capture the market and threatened less efficient enterprises with bankruptcy. As of 1988, however, there was just one bankruptcy, a collectively owned factory in Shenyang. The bankruptcy law for state enterprises was only appended to the Constitution. Bankruptcy now is a more plausible threat, one that may encourage greater efficiency in the Chinese economy.

Decentralization of Job Allocation. Some degree of decentralization has occurred in the allocation of jobs to high school and university graduates. This is in conjunction with efforts to pressure enterprise managers to show profits or face removal. In this new context, it is unfair to force managers to accept state-allocated personnel who are either redundant or incompetent. Certain enterprises are now free to advertise and recruit directly, but the state continues to allocate most jobs. However, the state no longer guarantees employment, especially for youth. This is part of the effort to cut the costs of subsidizing the wages of unnecessary employees in state-controlled enterprises. It has resulted, on the one hand, in massive numbers of unemployed youth, but has led, on the other hand, to the creation of thousands of collective enterprises, with start-up funds provided either by the state or by the youths' families. Many of these have apparently become highly successful Horatio Alger stories.

Contracts.   The establishment of a contract system, whereby one enterprise contracts to buy or sell goods to another enterprise, or to the state, is gradually replacing the system of all enterprises fulfilling production quotas to the state, which would in turn allocate the products according to plan. The contract system permits enterprises to reject goods that do not meet contract specifications, and to insert penalties for poor performance (such as late deliveries).

Material Incentives.   In the 1980s, the Chinese leadership has explicitly noted the need to reward the Chinese for their decades of hard work and forced savings by raising the standard of living, rather than simply ploughing all available funds into ever-greater industrial growth. Reforms therefore encouraged people to work harder in order to get monetary bonuses. By 1986, 15 percent of all workers in state enterprises were being paid according to a "responsibility system," in which income was tied to job responsibilities and output, instead of seniority. The result was a dramatic increase in revenues from state enterprises.[32]

The reforms also encouraged the production of higher quality consumer goods to give the people a reason for earning more money. This was accomplished in part by providing larger investments for light industry, the source of consumer goods. Measures to develop the urban light-industrial economy have benefitted from managerial reforms and an expansion of opportunities for obtaining greater investment from and trade links with the West.[33] Managerial reforms include separating an enterprise's ownership from its management: The state continues to own the enterprise, but turns over managerial power to the enterprise. The enterprise then receives a share of the profits it makes. And under the "director responsibility system" introduced in 1987, the factory director, not the Party Committee secretary, assumes full responsibility for production.[34] These are, of course, only the intentions of the reforms, not their actual results. To what degree these reforms are successfully implemented will only be known several years from now.

THE DEVELOPMENTAL VARIABLE

China shares with other less developed countries certain characteristics that have impaired economic development. But China also has certain strengths that most LDCs do not have, strengths that have helped China develop economically. As the following analysis indicates, those characteristics that China shares with other LDCs tend to relate to scarcity and poverty. These, in turn, have formed the context in which China has tried to resolve its structural, human, and political issues.

The impact of China's "underdeveloped" characteristics on its post-1949 economic development has been substantial. The reform leaders now suggest that China's backwardness has *not* been because China was "feudal" or "capitalistic," but rather because it was poor and under-developed. Although somewhat tautological (and not necessarily entirely correct), this is a stunning indictment by the Chinese leadership of mass movements, rectifications, and class struggles as methods to eliminate the obstacles to China's economic development, and it suggests the profound importance of the developmental variable.

Nevertheless, we can observe more successes in the economic sphere in dealing with the unresolved issues of the past than in any other major issue area. In light of China's sustained growth rates, we can hardly con-clude that China has failed to confront problems of economic develop-ment.[35] In fact, China's economic performance measured on the combined basis of growth, stability, and equal distribution of the benefits of growth suggests a more than acceptable performance.

Measuring China's Economic Development

GNP, per capita income, and growth

China's economy is massive and complex. It has the sixth largest gross national product (GNP) in the world (about $300 billion in 1986) with a per capita income averaging over $300. This puts it in the top third of all developing countries. Further, in spite of the "three bad years" (1959 to 1961) for the economy, and the "ten bad years" (1966 to 1976), China's industrial production value grew, from 1949 to 1976, at an annual average rate of 13.5 percent. Its agricultural production value grew at an annual average rate of 4.2 percent. The overall GNP had a long-term growth rate from 1949 to 1984 of about 6 percent per annum. Other data could be presented, but they would no doubt be just as misleading as these un-qualified figures. For example, apart from everything else, China's popula-tion in this same period grew from 540 million to 940 million, a 75 percent increase. Although this reduces the actual annual percentage increase in the GNP per capita to just about 4 percent, compared to most developing countries, this still is quite good.[36] Yet, with the world's largest population and third largest territory, to generate only the sixth largest GNP is not in itself an outstanding achievement.

Per capita income figures are far more revealing as to China's level of economic development; but for comparative purposes, the measurement of the value of one U.S. dollar in terms of its purchasing power in a society where housing, energy, and raw materials are vastly underpriced, is far from an exact science.[37] Further, much of what China's peasantry (80 percent of the population) consumes is a product of home production. As such it is difficult to calculate as a part of per capita or GNP figures. A crude estimate is that average rural per capita income is about 400 yuan, urban income about 800 yuan.

Equitable distribution of income

Per capita figures do not reveal how equitable the distribution of income is. We know that China has done better than most developing countries in distributing wealth equitably, but we also know that the disparities in China between urban and rural incomes and living conditions are large. So are the disparities among regions within the countryside. Those peasants living on river deltas, along the coast, on major transportation routes, and on the outskirts of cities may well show per capita incomes ten or even twenty times greater than the incomes of peasants in remote or poorly endowed areas of China. China's open appeal for international aid in the late 1970s because 100 million of its people were on the verge of starvation does not permit an optimistic assessment of the strength of China's economy. Having "just enough" leaves little leeway for errors or bad weather.

Nevertheless, the economic reforms begun in 1979 have shown stunning results. The annual rate of rural per capita income growth from 1979 through 1984, for example, averaged 18.4 percent.[38] Although this growth rate has slowed down considerably, unless political instability disrupts China's economy, it is hard to imagine that it will not continue to grow at an acceptable pace. In fact, as this chapter shows, some of the primary hindrances to China's rural economic development in the past have recently been, or appear about to be, eliminated. The annual rate of *urban* industrial growth since 1979 has, on the other hand, not been nearly as impressive because of certain structural limitations in the socialist model as heretofore implemented in China.

Constraints of Low Level of Development

Underdevelopment is itself a hindrance to escaping underdevelopment; and poverty is an obstacle to achieving wealth. Not to belabor this point, let us examine some of the characteristics that China has in common with many other LDCs.

A large population-to-land ratio

Alone, a large population-to-land ratio cannot be considered a major cause of underdevelopment. When combined with a low level of scientific and technological development, however, it can cause serious obstacles to development. Not the least of these is the diversion of resources otherwise available for development into feeding the population. This hindrance to development could have been controlled through a population control program, but because Mao insisted that human labor was China's greatest resource, the government did not take population control seriously until 1979. Before that time, it even encouraged population growth.

A low level of scientific and technological development

This factor exacerbates the problem of a large population-to-land ratio. Although China's output per acre is in any case quite high by international standards, far less land could support a larger population if farming were scientific and used advanced technology.[39] The level of technological development may, in fact, outweigh the importance of investment capital for economic development. Studies indicate, for example, that small amounts of land and natural resources per person need not be an obstacle to development. If China were able to use whatever resources it has *in a different way*, development would be enhanced:

> The pertinent fact is that . . . the present level of living is being obtained from them with primitive techniques and instruments. With improved technology, the same resources will yield greater output—higher yields per acre, more water power, more tons of coal per manyear, more raw materials for industry per year.[40]

This, of course, does not exclude the possibility that better economic policies and managerial practices might also enhance economic development for the same reason: The same resources would be used in a better way. The fact that economic reforms since 1978 have permitted a significant percentage of the rural population to switch from farming the land to other occupations, and that agricultural production *increased* with a diminished percentage of the population actually farming, supports this hypothesis.

Technological development itself requires several other conditions. First, it requires investment in research and development. In China's case, one cannot argue that its poverty was so extreme that it could not afford the costs of scientific-technological development. Rather, China's leaders made a policy decision, influenced by their reliance in the 1950s on the Soviet model, to invest most of its available resources in the development of heavy industry, and in the development of science and technology related to military defense. While the capital investment in heavy industry had the immediate effect of building up the industrial infrastructure and contributing to China's defense, it did not generate the long-term benefits for all dimensions of the economy that research and development in the intermediate and lower levels of technology would have done.

Second, a value system that rewards expertise and education, and thereby contributes to the formation of "human capital," advances technological development. But from 1957 to the 1980s, expertise and education were not rewarded. Here again, China's leaders made a policy decision, based on ideological values, to reward those who were "red" and politically active, and not to reward (even to punish) those who were educated.[41] Mao's distrust of the educated class, encapsulated in Communist Party policies, discouraged many from becoming highly educated.

The combination of the political environment with limited material incentives further discouraged technological experimentation. China's highly centralized economic system was too concerned with meeting quotas to invest in risky innovations. Even those technological innovations that did not risk an enterprise's production targets reaped no economic rewards. Central agencies had to approve technological changes but were reluctant to do so if changes would generate imbalances among production units in the tightly planned economic system. Further, although the central authorities wanted to encourage the transfer of new technologies among enterprises, the production quota system actually inhibited such transfers: Advanced enterprises *concealed* their advanced technologies because they "feared that widespread knowledge of their improved capabilities would result in the setting of higher output targets."[42] In short, the technologically successful believed they would be punished for their success.

Third, by the 1960s, the Party had decided to favor mass education over elite education. Although generally literacy is important for scientific and technological innovation, it also requires a high level of technical training and elitist institutions of higher education. Further, China's misallocation of technically qualified individuals to jobs outside their field of knowledge rendered their expertise rather useless. To wit, many highly educated individuals were assigned administrative jobs that did not permit them to continue to develop their expertise. Finally, the U.S. policy of isolation and containment of China, and China's practice of autarky (functioning as an isolated, independent economy and society), had the effect of cutting China and its technological scientific community off from international scientific and technological development.

Even though China's technological and scientific development since 1949 witnessed advances that far exceeded those of most LDCs, these were largely due to China's immense GNP. The dedication of just a small percentage of China's GNP to scientific and technological development can buy far more than a larger percentage of the small GNP of most LDCs. Still, China lags anywhere from ten to thirty years behind the developed states in advanced sciences and technology.[43] Political and ideological considerations that diverted the allocation of resources away from the educational and research establishments must shoulder much of the blame for this.

Underdeveloped infrastructure

Like most LDCs, China lacks such fundamental requisites for development as an adequate transportation and communication network. Inadequate transportation has in turn led to bottlenecks that impede the transport of the essential ingredients of economic growth: industrial raw materials and energy resources. The result is an inability to get goods to both markets and consumers in time, frequent electrical power shortages, and the consequent inability of industries to operate at more than 60 percent to 70 percent capacity. Hence the need for round-the-clock, seven-day-week work schedules in China's major cities.

China's underdeveloped infrastructure has less to do with funds than with planning. Economic planners consistently ignored the importance of the transportation and communication system for economic integration and development. This was affected by Mao's conception of self-contained, self-sufficient work units or regions. In spite of centralized planning, and allocating goods as if China were "one big enterprise," shaping China into an integrated economic totality was not the overarching idea of China's planners.

Few economic laws and regulations

As discussed in Chapter Six, unlikely many LDCs, China's economic planners did not formulate written economic laws and regulations to guide economic transactions. At a macro level, planners in a centrally controlled economy see no need for laws concerning contracts, commerce, legal entities, etc. Because most of the Chinese economy was under central control until the 1980s, with enterprises fulfilling mandated production quotas, there was seemingly no need for a law of contracts to regulate the behavior of two enterprises contracting with each other, or of enterprises contracting with the state. At the micro level, however, the reality was that the production of one enterprise often depended upon services or products of another enterprise. If these were not provided on time (or at all), an enterprise might incur severe losses. Although losses would be subsidized by the state, the enterprise and its management would be penalized in other ways, such as by fines. But the enterprise had no recourse to the law to recover its losses from those who had not fulfilled their part of planned production.

When the economy was almost totally centralized, state planners decided when to expand. With the introduction of collective and individual enterprises, and joint ventures with foreigners, adequate economic laws became essential to promote economic expansion. Although literally hundreds of laws have been written since 1979, China will continue to receive only a modest level of foreign investment until adequate legal protection of economic activities in ensured.

China as an Uncharacteristic LDC

Other features common to both China and other LDCs serve as constraints on China's economic development. But the more interesting question is, which features does China have in common with *developed* countries? The answer suggests that China has faced far fewer development-related obstacles than most LDCs, and that explanations for China's problems in successfully resolving issues of economic development are, therefore, more likely to be found in the political/ideological realm.

What follows is a discussion of some of the hindrances to economic development faced by most LDCs that China has largely avoided.

Squandering of public funds in luxury consumption by a small elite

Although China has not been immune to officials squandering public funds, the proportions are much smaller than in most LDCs. The puritanical values of the Chinese Communist leaders, who insisted on at least the superficial appearance of equality between officials and the people, and on the creation of an egalitarian and "classless" society, go far in explaining the low level of abuse of official power in this respect. But it may also be explained by the fact that the Chinese have, since 1949, neither produced nor imported many consumer goods for anyone to buy. Added to this is the fact that until the late 1970s, Chinese officials were rarely able to travel abroad or to send their children abroad for education. In short, Chinese officials simply did not have access to the goods, services, and travel that would have invited their indulgence in private luxury at public expense. With the opening of China since 1979, however, high-ranking Chinese have far greater access than before to foreign goods and travel. The day may not be far off when Chinese officials are flying around in their own Lear jets and Bell helicopters. They are already making sure their children get educated abroad, at public expense.

Investment abroad and export of hard currency

Because of strict currency controls, and because China's currency is not internationally convertible, China's officials have not been able to take personal funds, or whatever state funds they might embezzle, and invest them abroad. Nor have members of China's preliberation capitalist class, who were compensated when their property was nationalized, been able to export their capital. We have yet to hear of a Chinese Communist official with a Swiss bank account (although by now they may exist).

Nor was a significant amount of China's scarce hard currency invested abroad until the mid-1980s. Even then, it was controlled investment.

Individuals may still not invest abroad. The result of such strict limitations on currency and investment abroad is that the Chinese government has had available for investment a higher percentage of national savings than almost any developing country.

Small, undiversified economy

China's economy is so large and diversified that it is one of the few national economies which can choose, and has chosen, to be totally self-contained, isolated from the devastating fluctuations of the world economy. Although it may not have been in the PRC's long-run interest to remain so isolated after 1949 (nor its own choice), it could be argued that it suffered less than most LDCs, which found their one- or two-crop economies totally at the whim of the forces of the international market. When China finally did enter the world economy in the 1970s, it was able to protect itself better than most developing countries by offering a variety of products, both primary (resources) and secondary (manufactured products).

On the other hand, one could argue that the phase of the world development cycle at which the PRC entered the world market is too advanced for what China has to offer. China cannot export enough of the type of goods, such as light industrial goods (textiles, electronics, and the assembly of consumer products), that helped spur on economic growth for places such as Korea, Taiwan, Japan, the Philippines, Singapore, and Hong Kong. They jumped into the world developmental cycle earlier and have already flooded the markets with their goods, leaving little space to squeeze in Chinese products. The wealthier industrialized countries believe that they can no longer afford to function as the export markets for these kinds of goods without further weakening their own manufacturers. One need only review U.S. import restrictions on textiles, which effectively exclude 80 percent of China's textiles, to confirm this perspective. (Even in giving China a small market share, the United States took that share away from other nations who exported textiles to the U.S. market.) To break into the export market, China needs a special product that other "newly industrialized countries" (NICs) have not already used as their own entree into the world market. The problem is that China at this time has no such product. Only Chinese labor, one-third cheaper than the cheapest labor heretofore available, is an attractive commodity. And yet the Chinese insist on overpricing even this commodity for those investing in China.

Low life expenctancy, high mortality

In 1949, the Chinese Communist regime faced seemingly insurmountable problems of disease, poor health and sanitation, and high mortality rates. If anything, the wars and invasions that shaped Chinese history for the 100 years preceding the Chinese Communist victory made these problems far greater for China than for most LDCs. Yet within a decade of their victory, the Communists had made significant progress in fighting many life-threatening diseases: shistosomiasis, malaria, smallpox, measles, mumps, and diphtheria. Further, the government endorsed preventative medicine, resulting in better health care and lower levels of mortality.

The very fact that this potential hindrance to economic development was eliminated is a tribute not to the lesser magnitude of the problem, nor to the amount of resources available to cope with the problem, but to the ideology and politics of the Chinese Communists. The eradication of disease and improved sanitation and preventative health care were established as government priorities from the beginning. Fly-swatting and rat-killing campaigns may have appeared to the outside world to be too "totalitarian" in their organization, but they were the very stuff of which effective health care and sanitation were made.

Lack of sense of national identity, unity, and commitment to the state

Many LDCs suffer from a fragmented polity, one shattered by ethnic, racial, religious, and regional conflicts. The Chinese Communists began with a fragmented, war-torn society lacking any sense of national cohesion; but in less than a decade they had integrated the society to a level where fragmentation was no longer an obstacle to economic development. Although centrifugal forces have continued to threaten national cohesion ever since 1949, they have basically been kept under control. There is no way to measure the influence of culture and history, but perhaps the existence for some 2,000 years of a cultural (and political) entity called "China" contributed to this coherence.

Low level of institutional development

With China's 2,000 years of bureaucratic development and practice, the PRC had a far stronger institutional structure than most LDCs. This bureaucratic institutionalized structure (reinforced by the Soviet model of institution building) was essential to organizing the economy, carrying out centrally mandated policies, controlling the people, and establishing a stable political environment conducive to economic development. China's strong central leadership and well-developed bureaucracy have created some of the most important ingredients for centrally planned economic development, even though "bureaucratism" is simultaneously one of the greatest obstacles to development.

POLITICAL AND IDEOLOGICAL CONSTRAINTS ON
ECONOMIC DEVELOPMENT

Although developmental factors are fundamental to understanding China's unresolved economic issues, it is political-ideological factors that have determined whether or not China could successfully modernize under such developmental constraints. As mentioned earlier, the Chinese under Mao's influence pitted socialist values and the socialist system *against* developmental values, rather than building on them. The following analysis will look at some characteristics of a typical Western liberal model of economic development and compare it to the Chinese model. This will highlight some aspects of the political/ideological variable that have operated in the context of China's developmental conditions and culture while the country pursued economic modernization.

Economic Experts and Political Generalists

A Western liberal model of economic development usually relies upon the collection of comprehensive economic data, with trained economists and statisticians to analyze the data's significance. Their conclusions, distilled from a large data base, are used by economic planners to formulate economic policy. Presumably these policies, while compatible with the leaders' politics, will also provide a rational strategy for economic development. Otherwise, the political leaders' terms in office will be limited by a citizenry dissatisfied with the country's economic performance.

China's leaders have functioned under an entirely different set of assumptions. Whether their economic policies were motivated largely by economic or political considerations, and regardless of how their objectives differed from those of a capitalist model, the means utilized to attain their objectives were not necessarily "rational." Although the Chinese have continuously collected economic information, after 1957 the leadership did not give the economists a meaningful role in the decision-making process.[44] China's economists, like its lawyers, provided a source of ex post facto rationalization for economic decisions already reached by the central leaders on the basis of their best guesstimates. The role of the State Statistical Bureau was steadily undermined. Those who could analyze and make comprehensible the implications of economic data were not asked to do so. Moreover, they were often denied *access* to that information.

Those leaders who treated economic development as a political issue and who desperately wanted the economy to conform to their own interpretation of socialist economic development apparently did not realize the importance of grounding policy on solid economic data. When the leadership became divided over the best course of economic development after 1957, Mao ignored economic data that indicated the potential pitfalls in his economic model and apparently hid it from other leaders. No systematic economic data were published for the next twenty years. A lack of data is, of course, even more of a problem for a centrally planned economy like China's than for a market system, for the former relies on a comprehensive planning process which requires comprehensive data.

Under the slogans "politics in command" and "red over expert," politically active or "revolutionary" cadres took charge of formulating and implementing economic policy. Diminished respect for economic experts meant that few of China's "best and brightest" were willing to become economists. Thus, the leaders were cut off from the very information and expertise necessary to formulate policies compatible with their own socialist economic objectives. Party bureaucrats untrained in economics or management soon came to interfere even with policy implementation to further their own political ambitions. Party personnel overlapped with state cadres in charge of implementing economic policies, and political constraints interfered with effective management.

Bureaucratism and Corruption

With the merging of Party and managerial cadres after 1957, the bureaucracy involved in economic planning and implementation nearly doubled in size. Excessive bureaucratization led to all the ills associated with "bureaucratism," notably inefficiency and corruption. Changes occurred because bureaucrats legislated change, not in response to market forces. Bureaucrats set prices, determined which crops to plant and which products to manufacture, distributed resources, and decided which products would be shipped where and when. The hoarding of resources in short supply exacerbated the problem of shortages and thereby put even more control into the hands of bureaucrats. This in turn led to the "back door," the use of connections with other bureaucrats to get what was not available from central allocations.

Inevitably, the combination of a shortage economy, with cadres empowered to open or close doors in the economy at will, bred bureaucratic corruption. Bureaucrats offered access to scarce commodities, services, and resources in exchange for favors. In turn, black markets, profiteering, thievery, and smuggling arose in response to demands to satisfy the needs of those who lacked access to the "back door."

Yet the Chinese definition of the socialist model, which excluded a free market economy, meant that the very same leaders who were most concerned about excessive bureaucratization and corruption were unable to use the market place as a tool to combat it. Although the marketplace in a capitalist system does introduce opportunities for corruption, a state-controlled economy generates its own brand of corruption. In a market economy, market forces of supply and demand determine the pricing and availability of goods. The market diminishes opportunities for a bureaucratic stranglehold over scarce resources. Control comes to rest, instead, in the hands of those with sufficient capital. Thus, productive, energetic, skilled, and educated entrepreneurs, as well as ordinary consumers, benefit more in a market economy, whereas well-placed bureaucrats benefit more in a centrally administered economy. For socialists, the problems associated with market forces are, first, inflation in the prices of scarce goods; second, social and economic inequities because some prosper more than others; and third, the poor may not necessarily benefit by overall economic growth.

Economic liberalization policies within the context of a system that still centrally allocates most resources and services are bound to produce corruption; for in a mixed economy, whatever the centrally administered economy does not provide will be provided by entrepreneurial middlemen. Production units benefitting, on the one hand, from expansive economic liberalization are trapped, on the other hand, by the inability of the state to provide sufficient services or resources for expansion. They will pay middlemen handsomely for supplying their necessities, and they will not ask questions about how the middlemen obtain them.[45]

Equity Versus Equality

Generally speaking, a Western liberal model of economic development permits, and even encourages, the formation of hierarchies, elites, expertise, and material incentives. Inequality is expected, but the model is not static. Those at the bottom are not locked into poverty. The presumption is that material incentives inspire greater productivity and creativity. Moreover, fairness, or "equity," requires that people be rewarded for the work they have done. Thus, equity does not mean equality, for to reward all workers equally, regardless of their work, would be inequitable.

In the early years of Communist rule, wages for urban workers varied considerably. The industry, the plant, and the region in which the industry was located could be the cause of significant variations in wages. Wages tended, for example, to be higher in heavy industrial enterprises than in light consumer enterprises, and higher in Shanghai and the three industrial provinces of northeast China than in other industrial centers. Large differentials in wages were due primarily to piece-work rates.[46] But in 1956, the Ministry of Labor established an eight-grade wage scale based on "skill, experience, and performance." As a result, the spread between the highest and lowest paid workers was reduced to 3:1. Wage policy combined incentives for working harder and attaining higher skills while at the same time moving pay toward a more egalitarian basis.[47]

After 1958, additional steps toward greater egalitarianism were undertaken as the "leftist line" became more dominant. The premise of the Maoist egalitarian or "redistributive" model was that a society cannot and need not sacrifice the socialist goal of equal wealth for short-term economic development. Indeed, Maoists considered an egalitarian approach the faster road to development; for a market system would, in their view, give rise to classes based on economic inequalities and would inhibit long-term economic growth. Further, Maoists assumed that inequalities led to exploitation. Thus the Maoist model, which required the redistribution of wealth and the tightening up of wage differentials, rewarded those who worked harder with political rewards: recognition by their work units, a big red ribbon, and perhaps a promotion. For individuals to be willing to contribute with only normative incentives, however, required the raising of their political consciousness.

The Maoist model of development actually did much to transform traditional and backward societal habits, behavior, and institutions in a way that enhanced economic development. In particular, it modified and even eliminated many of the structural inequalities of traditional Chinese society:

> In the villages, literacy, clock-watching, awareness of the outside world, female emancipation, adoption of modern technology and organizational forms—all this is evidence of the inexorable march towards the modernization of the Chinese countryside. The temple and household gods are no longer visible; landlords with their long manicured fingernails have departed; the brutal terror of the gentry's personal thugs and enforcers is gone from the villages. . . .[48]

In the long run, however, the extreme form of the egalitarian model proved detrimental to economic growth. Attempts to eliminate the "three great differences" by "sending down" intellectuals, bureaucrats, and specialists to rural areas, and sending some 15 million young students "up to the mountains and down to the countryside" led to some "leveling upward" of culture in the countryside; but it also wasted the talents of those most capable of contributing to economic development. Further, Maoist political consciousness-raising proved inadequate to overcome the preference for material incentives. During the Cultural Revolution, those dissatisfied with the "equalization of poverty" relied on personal connections and the "back door" to improve their material lot. All could "eat out of the same pot," but there was hardly anything in the pot. The result was some of the worst corruption since 1949.

Finally, although China's peasants bore the cost of industrialization, the Maoist search for egalitarianism maintained an anti-urban bias. This was particularly evident during the "ten bad years," when the leftist government redistributed most of the hard-won profits of Shanghai and other coastal cities to the hinterland. There was, in fact, almost *no* investment in China's coastal cities between 1966 and 1975.[49] Investing in the hinterland's industrialization reflected the leftists' preference for egalitarianism and balanced social change; but because the investments were poorly made, the hinterland remains poor today. Many resources were allocated to areas that had no real chance of raising outputs to a higher level than inputs. Departing from the practice of most LDCs, the Maoist model dictated an investment of capital in areas that could offer only a poor return in the short run because of their poor geographical location vis-à-vis both resources and markets.[50]

Political Campaigns and Class Struggle as Remedies for Corruption

In a Western liberal economy it is assumed that there will be abuses of a free-market economic system, but that if limited, these are acceptable costs for the greater developmental gains. This model also assumes that the most effective responses to economic corruption are, first, tight economic regulations and laws that clearly delineate the limits of acceptable activities and punish those who deviate from them according to the law; and second, economic reforms that improve the institutional structure and process of the economy so that corruption is more difficult. Better accounting, auditing, and managerial procedures not only help control attempts to cheat the government out of its fair share of an enterprise's profits but also help limit bureaucratic corruption.

In its more extreme leftist form, the Chinese Communist model assumed that mass political campaigns, purges of the elite, and class struggle would provide the most effective means to control economic deviance. Much evidence indicates that class struggle, political-education campaigns, and purges of bureaucrats and Party officials have had a positive impact on the control of economic corruption, but only in the short run. As one campaign ran into another, people became inured to them and participated in a mechanical, apathetic way. When political campaigns were heightened after 1965 so that participation could not so easily be feigned, the campaigns interfered with economic productivity. In terms of lost productivity, the costs of these campaigns undoubtedly outweighed the benefits. They were time-consuming and bred an air of unpredictability, which was highly destabilizing and inimicable to production. The leftists had presumed that if they transferred power out of the hands of the bureaucratic elites and into the hands of the masses, politically based economic corruption would be eliminated. Instead, corruption grew rife. Unwilling to resort to a free market, the leftists lacked truly effective instruments to limit corruption.[51]

The Rigidity of Centralized National Planning

One style for all

A central economic question for any country is the role of the government in directing the economy, particularly the relationship between governmental intervention and market forces. Put differently, the issue is the balance between control and autonomy, between centralism and decentralism. A market model of development allows for fluidity and flexibility within the context of an integrated and unified economy. It assumes that diversity is healthy and that local conditions should affect the choice of products to produce and the best methods for economic development. For these reasons, the state cannot be overly rigid when it formulates broad economic policies.

The Chinese Communist system of centralized national planning made no such assumptions. It became increasingly rigid and unresponsive to local differences after 1956, in part out of a concern for the centrifugal forces again threatening to pull China apart into myriad fragments. China's leaders opted for centralization, not a decentralized but integrated economy based on diversity, to keep China unified. But, this highly centralized model interacted with a political and cultural environment that at times negatively affected economic development. For example, ideology, political education, and class struggle frequently took precedence over production. Centralized plans also had to be implemented within certain pre-established economic patterns, such as traditional marketing systems that did not lend themselves to centralism, and within an economic environment of enormous diversity, one that could not simply be mandated to follow one single road toward socialism. If only for these reasons, rigid centralized planning seems to have been particularly inappropriate as a long-term policy for agricultural production. Policies for China's amazing variety of climatic, topographical, and soil conditions could best be formulated by those most familiar with local conditions, conditions unknown to tea-sipping bureaucrats in Beijing.

Following orders

The rigidity of a centrally planned "command economy" creates problems in part because it does not respond to economic forces.

Following orders is different from trying to make a factory economically efficient. Although profit may be one of the targets, managers cannot operate efficiently because they are asked to fulfill other targets as well. Maximizing profit requires taking one's own initiative, or "doing one's own thing." If managers are ordered to produce specified quantities of different output, are given the supplies of different inputs at specified prices, are assigned the laborers and the capital equipment to be used in production, and so on, they have no opportunity to become efficient. *They cannot then be criticized for being inefficient, because they are simply following orders.*[52]

In China's command economy, managers, workers and consumers are unable to participate in the determination of primary goals and allocation of resources. Precisely because the economy is neither democratic nor capitalist, it lacks built-in "independent and entrepreneurial sensors" that could *automatically* signal, without receiving specific orders, "utility-maximizing and cost-minimizing opportunities." Thus, the burden of making all these decisions goes by default to the "top political leadership, acting through the planners and served by the bureaucratic establishment." This often leads to a divergence between what the planners perceive must be done on behalf of the "macro interests of society," and what the enterprise managers feel would be the best approach to benefit the "micro interests" of their own enterprises. The center wants to achieve high output targets with minimum inputs, whereas the managers argue for the reverse.

> Managers will supply faulty information on past performance. They will hoard labor and capital so as to fulfill more easily the assigned tasks and anticipate the frequent upward adjustments in those tasks. Since capital is free, and is helpful in emergencies, they will ask for more of it than they need. Together with the planners' preoccupation with growth achievable through additions to the capital stock, this leads to inflated demand for capital—a permanently high rate of investment, a good part of it unnecessary. . . . Managers will try to maximize their personal and their enterprises' bonuses by fulfilling the major planner-set norms, but in the ways that suit them best— mainly by violating the less easily quantifiable and verifiable dimensions of the plan, especially product assortment and quality.[53]

China's leaders have, since 1978, tried to introduce greater flexibility and efficiency through a certain amount of decentralization in production decisions. The government has relinquished many of its central planning and allocation functions in the agricultural and service sectors, but rigidities remain. For example, in promoting the "household responsibility system" and "household contracts," the government made it almost mandatory for cadres to redistribute the collective property and tools of the brigades and teams. Although household contracting may offer great benefits, to *force* people to function as household units is not really "flexibility." Even in those localities where brigades or teams were highly productive, and in spite of the many other social benefits derived from them as collectives, they still had to be disbanded. Once again, the leadership in charge of economic policies mandated institutional change throughout China on the basis of an untested assumption: "Smaller is better" came to replace its predecessor "bigger is better."

For the time being, the dramatic improvement in the service sector and the greater quantity and variety of goods indicate that decentralization is working. There are, however, signs of resistance and discontent. Not only are the less talented, less entrepreneurial rural residents benefitting little from the new system, but also long-term damage to the medical and educational systems, which were brigade- or even commune-based, may be occurring. The single-minded pursuit of economic growth seems to have temporarily blinded officials in Beijing to the impact of economic policies on other sectors.

The issue of "how much central control" has been a choice between centralization and *levels* of decentralization. In the 1958 Great Leap Forward, for example, control was only decentralized to the level of the provinces. The commune controlled the economic and political affairs of the units under it; but economic *plans* were made at the provincial level, even if with tight control from the center. Since 1978, decentralization has moved down to *enterprise* level. That is, about 6,000 state enterprises out of 96,000[54] make their own policies and determine output. Their major responsibility to the state is to return to it a certain share of its total production or profits (originally in the form of "quotas" but now in the form of taxes).

In the past, the Chinese economy has suffered from "a recurring cycle in which centralization leads to rigidity, rigidity leads to complaints, complaints lead to decentralization, decentralization leads to disorder, and disorder leads back to centralization."[55] How successfully the Chinese leadership can address the problems emanating from decentralized authority in the 1980s will determine the future balance between centralization and decentralization.

Waste and Disproportionate Allocation of Resources

The costs of economic development in the now-industrialized countries were often borne by the peasantry. Peasant farmers were heavily taxed, with a disproportionate amount of the profits from agricultural production flowing into industry. Furthermore, the prices of agricultural goods were kept artificially low. China's disproportionate allocation of resources to heavy industry is, therefore, nothing new in the history of economic development. The assumption of both the Soviet and Maoist models was that heavy industrilization would bring overall economic development. Producing lathes that produce lathes that produce lathes would form the basis for growth. The emphasis on heavy industry seems to have been somewhat purposeless and derived from the view that if China had *more* large, heavy industries, it would be "industrialized."

Many analysts argue that the state leadership simply stepped into the landlords' role of taxing the peasants to the point where they retained only enough for a minimal standard of living. The Maoist model, in particular, seemed to assume that mere organizational *restructuring* would increase agricultural production, while state *investment* was required to increase industrial production.[56] China's leaders further assumed that any money siphoned off into the production and purchase of consumer goods (light industrial goods) would mean less money for capital investment, thus slowing down capital construction and overall economic growth. In the thirty years from 1949 to 1979, China's heavy industry received 76 percent of all investment and expanded to ninety-one times its original size, whereas light industry expanded only by twenty times its size.[57] The result was imbalanced development, and development at a slower pace than in countries where proportional development occurred.

Further, although China had a very high level of capital investment, in some years as high as 22 percent of the GNP (a percentage that far exceeds the investment rate of most developed countries), the inefficiencies of China's centralized economy led to enormous waste: for example, duplicated projects, products of such poor quality that they had to be discarded, and excessive energy consumption. The Chinese have estimated that the "ratio of consumption of standard fuel to national income is 1.3 to 6 times that of some developed countries and twice the average level of developing countries." Even when compared to its own past record, the Chinese economy in the 1980s is consuming roughly twice as much fuel per dollar of national income as it did during the First Five-Year Plan.[58] The fact that in a socialist economy prices are determined by an administrative bureaucracy goes far in explaining why China's resources are vastly underpriced, and hence, wasted with impunity.[59] The state system of setting production quotas without marketing surveys to determine end-users results in massive stockpiling of unwanted heavy industrial goods. In addition, because the government has been unwilling or unable to standardize parts, even heavy industrialization does not serve to integrate the economy: Trucks or machines that are produced in the north but break down while in the south can not be repaired with parts produced in the south.

Economic policy since the early 1950s had also required that an enterprise's profits be plowed back into capital investment, mostly in fixed assets. From 1953 to 1980, fixed capital investment increased by more than 10 percent per year, about 1.7 times the rate of growth of national income. In other words, for every 1.7 units of investment input, the economy only grew by one unit. China's leaders in the 1980s point to mismanagement, wasted energy, unfinished and redundant construction, investment in obsolete industries, and a disproportionate investment in heavy industry as the major causes of this poor rate of return on investment.[60]

Thus, China's socialist economic model has led to a far lower rate of growth than its high level of investment could have produced. No doubt the poor economic performance of the Soviet Union in the 1970s, juxtaposed to the extraordinary growth of the NICs, such as South Korea,

Taiwan, Singapore, and Hong Kong, that emphasize light industry, the service sector, and technology, influenced China's reform leaders to pursue a more balanced approach to economic development and to open its doors to foreign technology and investment.

SOCIALISM'S OBJECTIVES IN TENSION WITH ECONOMIC GROWTH

In a Western liberal model of economic development, efficiency is basic to making profits, which is the primary objective of enterpreneurial efforts. Reinvested profits, in turn, fuel economic growth. If enterprises are not subject to state regulations, they are likely to subordinate, or ignore completely, any objective that interferes with profit-making. In fact, the relatively recent development of the concept of "corporate social responsibility"[61] in the West is still viewed by many managers of enterprises as something that interferes with profits.

In the PRC, it was the state, not the corporation, which demonstrated an enlightened sense of "social responsibility" by using the "profits" from individual enterprises to support social programs. But in the initial stages of industrialization, this slowed down China's economic development. Most of China's leaders would still argue, however, that in the long run, the diversion of scarce resources to societal objectives (which are inherently political) makes for a far stronger economy, precisely because the society is healthier. The purpose of economic development is to increase the GNP for the purpose of improving the people's livelihood.

What follows are a few of the major social objectives to which the Chinese leadership has been committed since 1949, objectives which necessarily interfered with rapid economic growth. The key social objective, an egalitarian distribution of wealth in an effort to eliminate class differences, was considered above.

Full Employment

Until the 1980s, the Chinese leadership was committed to full employment and the realization of the social worth of each individual through work. Maintaining full employment at almost any cost, however, proved detrimental in overall development terms. Full employment has meant vast underemployment. In some industrial, commercial, and service enterprises, there are as many as three or four workers for every worker needed.[62] In state-run stores and restaurants, for example, the underemployed stand around most of the day with nothing to do. This greatly undermines morale and causes resentment: Each worker wants to have as much idle time as the other. As in agriculture, the marginal productivity of every extra worker is practically zero. Redundant officials in government ministries come in even larger numbers. Thus the state is paying for both underutilization of labor and for inefficiency. The "extras" in the cast, in short, interfere with smooth operations.

Further, Chinese socialist values support the idea that "to work is glorious" and that an American-style welfare system for the unemployed is immoral. Although the reforms in the 1980s endorse firing a person on the grounds of inability, laziness, or redundancy, few enterprises have actually done so. This is in part because of the structure of the system: If a unit dismisses an employee, it then must either find that person alternative work or continue to provide the discharged employee with housing and an adequate if substantially reduced living wage. This type of problem may be somewhat mitigated by efforts begun in 1987 to introduce unemployment insurance in a number of enterprises. Still, managers derive some of their power from the size of their work force, and therefore do not necessarily support efforts to eliminate jobs. "Collective" enterprises supported by government through start-up loans have absorbed well over 100 million of the unemployed or underemployed in both the rural and urban sectors. Although there is still no way to force redundant personnel to relinquish the security of a state enterprise in favor of a collective, the fact that an individual has the potential to make far higher wages in a collective provides its own appeal.

A Welfare State's Benefits

In most respects, China has functioned as a welfare state, ideologically committed to certain welfare functions: state subsidized education, child care, housing, medical care, food, and social security for the old and disabled. Further, it attempts to supply a "safety net" for those people locked into poor rural areas who are unable to sustain an acceptable standard of living by their own labor power. Funding these societal objectives siphons off capital that might otherwise be used to stimulate economic growth directly. Only very wealthy states can usually fulfill such broad welfare functions, and even they find it financially burdensome to do so. Thus, it is no surprise that the Chinese, in the grips of underdevelopment and with a far lower per capita income available, have found that the costs of such welfare functions have taken their toll on economic growth. Further, they have required high levels of taxation. Taxes (by way of fulfilling production quotas) have generally been set so high that little has been left for enterprises to reinvest in their own growth.

Controlled Inflation

The post-1949 Chinese leadership determined that low inflation, or even no inflation, was an important social objective. Unlike the capitalist countries, which have seen mildly inflationary policies as one of the costs of economic growth, China has not. In part, this comes from China's historical experience in the war years directly preceding the Communists' victory in 1949. Inflationary pressures were, in fact, one of the major contributing causes to the Nationalists' loss of popular support. China's leaders after 1949 were, therefore, obsessed with controlling inflation out of fear that it could reignite economic and political instability.

In part, however, anti-inflationary policy arises naturally in a centrally administered economy: Without the automatic mechanism of a free-market system, it is extremely difficult to know what inputs and outputs are actually worth. The value of land, labor, and resources is arbitrarily determined by state bureaucrats. Because the budgeting process is such that the state simply allocates whatever money and materials are necessary for keeping key enterprises running, these enterprises simply pass the additional costs of extra inputs and inefficient production back up to the state or along to other enterprises in the form of increased prices. These, in turn, become input prices for producer goods subsidized by the state. This means that the state must provide an even larger budget to enterprises and subsidize prices to consumers, so they will not feel the inflationary squeeze. By the early 1980s, subsidies (representing repressed inflation) had risen to one-third of the state budget.[63]

Low inflation rates were possible until the 1980s because the prices of goods in short supply were kept artificially low by centrally administered stable pricing policies. The resulting suppressed inflation manifested itself in increased bank savings, long lines for products in short supply, long waiting periods for products ordered, and ultimately black markets, smuggling, thievery, and extreme pressures on the "back door" to supply the goods needed. Thus, although a product such as plate glass is cheap, little is available to the ordinary consumer. When the glass comes into the store, the clerk will hold it for "back door" customers, while others stand in line for whatever is left.

Price reforms in the 1980s have gone far in addressing the problems created by artificial state pricing of goods: Permitting the market to determine the prices of most consumer goods has removed much of the motivation for corruption, black markets, and hoarding. Goods in short supply are priced higher, but at least those who are willing to pay for them can, in most cases, get them without standing in long lines or using the "back door." On the other hand, inflation has been inevitable, as urbanites, most of whom are still tied into the state-controlled pattern of wages, have insisted that their wages be raised to compensate for the increased cost of agricultural products. The state nevertheless continues to dole out an enormous proportion of the state budget to subsidize the prices of basic agricultural goods.[64] Although it is a painful transition from a state-controlled to a partially market based economy, so far the overall benefits of these changes seem to outweigh the problems, and they have resulted in a spurt of growth in the economy.

CULTURAL CONSTRAINTS ON ECONOMIC DEVELOPMENT

Important areas of the Chinese economy, including commerce, industry, and water control, were under central government regulation as long ago as the Qin Dynasty. Many of the traditional Chinese values and practices that constrain economic development, some of which emanated from the continuation of this centralized system into the Communist period, are discussed elsewhere in this book. Two other aspects of cultural influence will be analyzed.

Networks

Networks of relationships have traditionally been basic to business relationships among the Chinese. Under a state-controlled economy, however, Chinese did not do business with each other as independent actors, but with the state. Since the economic reforms of 1978 and after, China has seen a revitalization of these old networks, in which trust in business relationships is based on family, clan, or regional ties. Thus, in Shanghai, it is said, businesspeople from Ningpo dominate the commercial economy; and they will only do business with other Ningpo businesspeople. Not to belabor this point, it is at least worth noting that this creates a far different business environment than one in which political ties are dominant. And, it may be argued, business ties premised on culturally based networks may be a positive contribution to, rather than a constraint on, economic development.[65]

Historical Resistance to Foreign Trade and Investment

The PRC's preference for a self-reliant national policy has powerful cultural roots. China's tribute system, which had provided the basis of its relationships with all "barbarians" until the nineteenth century, was not really a concept of foreign trade but of national security. The treaty port system, which grew up in response to China's defeat in war with the Western powers in the nineteenth century, exemplified China's sense of cultural superiority: The purpose of this system was to keep the materially superior but "spiritually inferior" Western countries confined to treaty ports, thereby protecting Chinese civilization from cultural pollution. In the Chinese view, it was a way to limit foreign trade, not to expand it.

Although foreign exploitation embittered all Chinese, and a desire to rid China of foreign control was a point that Chinese of every political persuasion could agree upon, the Communists after their victory in October 1949 desperately needed foreign capital for development. But only the Soviets and their socialist allies were willing to engage in trade and investment in China. The Soviets' limited economic aid came to a crashing halt in 1959–1960 as a result of Khrushchev's belief that Mao's Great Leap Forward policies and his risky policies toward Taiwan were "irrational." This embittered the Chinese and spurred them further down the road toward national autarky.

In a sense, traditionally autarkic policies and a repudiation of foreign values, ideas, and even technology reemerged as a rationalization of the complete isolation imposed on China by the international community. The leadership presumed that China could develop economically *without* foreign trade, aid, investment, and technology. Of all the PRC's missed opportunities, this may prove to have been one of the most costly. Self-reliance and xenophobia emerged in extreme form in 1965 and thereafter, when China shut down its embassies abroad and recalled virtually its entire diplomatic corps. Chinese who had *any* kind of foreign connection, whether in their education, work, or through relatives (even if they had never seen them), or who showed any interest in the West were, at best, only harassed.

Although in some respects national autarky benefited China's economic development, and although China was thereby spared the foreign exploitation suffered by many LDCs, the foreign connection need not have been exploitative. Certainly the Chinese insistence on writing their own medical and scentific textbooks, even when superb textbooks were already available outside China, and on recreating technologies that already existed abroad, contributed little, if anything, to China's overall economic development. Once again, the central political leadership had objectives other than economic development to which they gave priority, and not the least of these was the protection of Chinese culture from foreign threats.

Efforts to open up China in the early 1970s quickly vanished as power struggles at the political center made those calling for expanded contacts with the West vulnerable to the charge of antisocialism. After the Third Plenum in 1978, and even more so after further economic reforms in 1984, however, China's door swung open to foreign aid, trade, and investment. The Chinese believe that investments, if made in the form of joint ventures, leave them in control of the situation. Most seem to view foreigners as valuable for what they can contribute to China's modernization, but they still want to confine their role and influence. Although this attitude may in part be attributed to a very pragmatic protectionism not uncommon to developing countries, it is still so extreme in the Chinese case as to warrant a cultural explanation: a fear of the power of Western values to overwhelm Chinese values.

The final words on the impact of foreign technology, science, ideas, trade, aid, and investment are not yet written. The Chinese have fitfully opened and closed doors with various countries. They are not sure how to control the corruption and exposure to foreign ideas antithetical to Communist ideals that have accompanied this opening and the introduction of a market economy. Much of the problem seems to relate to unscrupulous Chinese (ordinary workers and peasants, factory managers, highly placed Party officials, and state cadres) who perhaps took advantage of the former centrally controlled economy as well. In the new situation of a partially decentralized system, and particularly in the "special economic zones," China's cadres seem able (once again) to take advantage of their position in the economic/administrative network to arrange "deals" with foreigners. Many such deals have been at the expense of the national treasury. They have used up China's hard currency at an alarming rate, not to import beneficial foreign technology, but to import consumer goods: tape recorders, televisions, motorcycles, cars, and, if we are to believe Chinese reports, mountains of pornographic materials. Moreover, enterprises have used China's hard currency in excessive capital investment.

Although there have been several partial reversals of the open door policy, there has in general been a trend toward greater openness to foreign investment. The new problem China faces is, ironically, that the level of foreign investment is much lower than it had hoped for. The foreign business community has been leary of the political risk of investment in China. It has also been unwilling or unable to do business in a country where many necessary items for doing business (land, labor, raw materials) cannot be bought by a foreigner in a free market, but must instead be negotiated for through local and provincial suppliers in what remains a predominantly centrally controlled and planned economy, in which having connections is all; where the infrastructure of roads, ports, railroads, and communications are inadequately developed; where commercial and tax codes are still being written; and where legal protection is limited. In 1987, U.S. investment in China declined by almost 50 percent. The Chinese have, in fact, temporarily run out of foreign investors who are willing to pay any price to get a foothold in China, and they have found, much to their regret, that foreign investors will no longer tolerate price gouging. Beijing has become more expensive than Paris to do business in! In response, China's leaders have tried to price labor, land, resources, and services more competitively. But they seem determined to control the situation: For example, "friendship" prices will only be given to those foreign investors who agree to export the bulk of everything they produce in order to earn foreign currency for China; and to those foreign investors who, although they sell their products within China, agree to reinvest a significant percentage of all their profits.

Whether or not this change of strategy will attract greater foreign investment remains to be seen. In the meantime, it is an ironic twist of events that the Chinese are now trying to make their country an attractive investment opportunity rather than viewing foreigners as a potentially destabilizing force threatening both Chinese culture and socialist ideology. At this point, the greatest concern of China's leaders appears to be development. Perhaps they now believe that a developed, wealthier China will be better prepared to defend its culture and political values.

PROBLEMS ARISING FROM ECONOMIC REFORMS

Abandonment of Social Objectives

China's reformist leaders have encountered significant opposition to their reforms. For example, their efforts to close down inefficient state enterprises, upgrade the work force's level of education and expertise, and eliminate incompetent or redundant workers and managerial personnel have proceeded at a snail's pace. Moreover, although in terms of efficiency, quality, and economic growth the reforms seem to be paying off, their social costs have not been acceptable to all Chinese. Indeed, the new forces set in motion by the economic reforms could in the future hinder both developmental and political objectives. For example, changes in the pricing and procurement policies of agricultural products have contributed to a high rate of inflation. Permitting a high unemployment rate among urban youth will necessarily lead to wide socioeconomic disparities. In fact, the reemergence of a class society as a result of the broad-ranging economic reforms seems inevitable, in spite of regulations to control the purchase and sale of property and taxes on personal incomes.

Nevertheless, no clear relationship exists between a market system and increasing inequality, unless the market system generates millionaire-enterpreneurs—and chances of this happening in China seem remote. In any event, the pre-1978 economic system itself actually perpetuated regional inequality and urban–rural inequality by prohibiting mobility from one area to another. In short, although new forms of inequality may arise, *vast economic inequalities already existed under socialist economic policies.* Inequalities will simply be shifted to new groups.

Inefficiencies of a Mixed Economy

The state introduction of a partial market economy has created a situation in which households, collectives, and state-owned enterprises are all competing furiously for limited resources. State-owned enterprises, because the state allocates inputs at no cost to the enterprises, tend to make more than they need and to overexpand capital construction at the state's expense. This leaves the state with fewer resources to allocate to collectives and private enterprises. On the other hand, efficient state enterprises, which under the new policies are encouraged to expand, cannot get extra resources for expansion through state allocation. Like households and collectives, they too have responded to this situation by creating networks outside the state for acquiring supplies. This in turn further strains the state's available resources. Finally, many newly formed enterprises are smaller and less efficient than the existing state-run ones in the larger cities, and this has led to outcries against "overdecentralization."[66]

Tax Evasion

In October 1984 the Party Central Committee further decentralized control over state enterprises and their after-tax profits. Instead of remitting profits to the state, a medium or large state-owned enterprise now pays taxes on its profits. This was intended to encourage higher productivity and efficiency in enterprises, while at the same time siphoning off a percentage of that higher productivity to the state. But this reform has not worked out as intended. Enterprises take advantage of greater control over their own management, accounting, and after-tax net income to sequester their profits. Tax evasion has become widespread. In 1985 the Ministry of Finance reported that more than 50 percent of all state- and collectively-owned enterprises and individual businesses were cheating on their taxes.[67] The state continues to allocate underpriced inputs to enterprises, but enterprise management, rather than turn over profits to the state, plows them back into the enterprise in the form of higher wages and bonuses for workers (and management), or in the form of further capital investment.[68] As a result, the state is actually losing money.

Corruption in a Mixed Economy

The economic reforms introduced since 1978 have generated their own form of corruption. Whether it is more or less than before is difficult to judge. The many new, changing, and unsettled conditions offer many opportunities for corruption. For example, local cadres can distort the meaning of central directives permitting free enterprise, or at least make life difficult for entrepreneurs trying to "get rich:" Bureaucrats from a number of different work units may demand extra fees from peddlers, sidewalk stall operators, or peasants selling in free markets, alleging that they are required to pay for sewage, sidewalks, or local government. Alternatively, they may pressure individuals to make "contributions" for new schools, fire houses, or other items. This is even more likely to happen to "10,000 yuan" households than to itinerant peddlers or shopkeepers in the cities, for the former are visible members of a small distinct community, and their sudden wealth is conspicuous—and envied by many. In addition, local cadres may use their still considerable state power to deny peasants necessary licenses for business, block legal attempts of peasants to leave the villages to pursue nonagricultural work, force peasants to make them partners in enterprises without their contributing their fair share, or confiscate their goods in the free market on the pretext that they are unsanitary.[69]

Thus, although the introduction of the contractual household responsibility system and free markets markedly reduces the power of local cadres, many have held onto some of their old power because the economic system is still partly state controlled. The continuing need for peasants to turn over a portion of their produce to the state, for example, still permits cadres to use their power to cheat the peasant when the produce is weighed; and the continued state allocation of chemical fertilizers still allows cadres to distribute it unequally. In addition, the price differential on goods that are both state-priced and market-priced permits cadres and peasants to cut lucrative deals. Similarly, the state's agreement until 1985 to purchase all grain produced at high set prices resulted in overproduction of grain to sell to the state. Then, faced with a massive surplus beyond the capacity of its storehouses, the state agreed to pay peasants to store the grain—even without the grain ever having been delivered to the state first.[70] Nevertheless, the liberalizing economic reforms at least provide urban and rural entrepreneurs with *alternatives* that were formerly lacking, alternatives that legitimize the fulfillment of their needs outside the framework of a centrally led state economy.

Distortions From Lopsided Emphasis on Profits

The Chinese understanding of the meaning of "modernization" has come to be equated with increased productivity, higher profits, and advanced science and technology. Because in earlier periods all of these elements were played down (or even ignored) in pursuit of other, noneconomic objectives, this new understanding of modernization has led to a reordering of priorities to favor economic objectives. However, the new emphasis on profits, in the context of a mixed economy, distorts an appropriate assessment of efficiency among enterprises and lopsidedly encourages the production of certain goods. For example, because the state continues to fix prices on many goods, those goods assigned high prices may well yield high profits, whereas those to which the state assigns low prices may yield low profits. Arbitrarily determined tax rates that differ according to the product, rather than the profit, also favor certain enterprises over others. Although the government has tried using highly complicated formulae to balance out the advantages and disadvantages to various enterprises, many enterprises now try to shift over into high profit products, even if they are in excess supply. This is happening not only in industry but also in agriculture, with peasants preferring to plant high-profit cash crops rather than low-profit grains and vegetables.[71]

The new emphasis in the 1980s on profits and efficiency has benefitted productivity in many cases. Guest houses affiliated with some state organizations, for example, used to prefer to keep their guest rooms empty because staff salaries remained the same regardless of how many guests were served. However, once they could share in the profits, efforts were made to fill all rooms.[72] In other cases, a distorted emphasis on profits, productivity, and efficiency may well be creating new problems. New profit incentives for doctors serving in clinics and hospitals, for example, now tie wages to the number of patients seen and/or operated on. The preceding system offered few material benefits to reward efficiency and hard work and resulted in long lines of patients while doctors and medical aids smoked cigarettes and chatted. But now evidence suggests that medical staff, in a quest for higher wages, rush through patients rather than giving them thorough medical examinations and careful advice. And, of course, the problem plaguing other health-care systems (such as health insurance companies in the United States) may arise, with doctors submitting fraudulent claims to the state for reimbursement of services that were never performed.

A final problem arising from a lopsided emphasis on profits is the emergence (or reemergence) of questionable business practices. Although China's business practices in the past may have suffered from inefficiencies, mismanagement, and attempts to embezzle money and defraud the state, the post-1979 reforms' emphasis on profit criteria has spawned new kinds of ethical issues.[73] Until such time as the Chinese have a complete commercial code and adequate business regulations to govern business practices, and until severe punishments are incurred by those who engage in unethical business practices, the emphasis on profits will probably raise a host of new problems associated with outright human greed. Many of these problems are at this time being attributed to the influence of "bourgeois ideology," but they are, in fact, endemic to any economic system that lacks clear-cut ethical, legal, and commercial codes.

CONCLUSIONS

The decentralization of many economic and administrative decision-making powers and the introduction of a market system after 1978 may have created an irreversible momentum. These reforms have done much to address the problems inherent in a highly centralized socialist economy, and to move China outside the constraints of the socialist economic model adopted from the Soviets.

This is not to suggest that economic liberalism and decentralization are the solutions to China's economic issues. What, in fact, are the solutions will be quite dependent on the kinds of structures and values that take shape outside the economic sphere, notably in the political and cultural arenas. Both political reform and reform of the governmental structure are crucial to the success of economic reforms. Still, in the short run, economic liberalism and decentralization have contributed significantly to addressing many of the problems a socialist economy has faced operating in the Chinese context of a web of personal connections and strong traditional Chinese values. Although it may be going too far to suggest that what we are witnessing in the 1980s is a throwback to the pre-1949 economic system, it is certainly the case that the Chinese have not had this much freedom in the economic sphere since 1949.

With freedom to succeed economically, however, comes the freedom to fail. China is too large for us to draw grandiose conclusions for the whole country. Economic policies since 1978 have brought success to some areas and individuals, failure to others. Given our limited access to China, it is still difficult to know anything but the composite figures. The question in the end may be who has more *power* within the central leadership to get their way in determining the kind of economic structure and values China will pursue, rather than whether or not China is really benefitting in developmental terms. Political reforms that encourage the central leadership to make decisions reflective of the popular will may provide an essential underpinning to maintain support for successful economic reforms. Finally, once the Chinese leaders make up their minds where they are going in the economic sector, it will make policy formulation much easier and more predictable.

NOTES

[1]Victor Falkenheim, "Autonomy and Control in Chinese Organization: Dilemmas of Rural Administrative Reform," in Sidney Greenblatt, Richard Wilson, and Amy Wilson (eds), *Organizational Behavior in Chinese Society* (New York: Praeger Special Studies, 1981), pp. 190, 201, 204, 205. As Falkenheim notes, while in *theory* these values may be kept in "creative tension," in *practice*, usually one value has become subordinate to the other, "with periods of overcontrol succeeded by excessive autonomy."

[2]For a detailed study of this topic, see Dorothy J. Solinger, *Chinese Business Under Socialism: The Politics of Domestic Commerce, 1949–1980* (Berkeley: University of California Press, 1984).

[3]Jiang Yiwei, "Enterprise-Based Economy," *Social Sciences in China*, No. 1 (March 1980), p. 57.

[4]Ibid., p. 64.

[5]Gregory C. Chow, *The Chinese Economy* (New York: Harper & Row, 1985), pp. 50, 145. This is because the manager is judged by how well he can fulfill production quotas, not by his efficiency.

[6]Ibid., pp. 52, 53.

[7]For an excellent explanation of this and other issues that arise in a centrally planned economy, see Chow, *Chinese Economy*, p. 45.

[8]The rationing of grain even after adequate grain became available is interpreted by many scholars as one way for the state to control population movements. Without grain certificates, this reasoning goes, a person cannot survive in a city. But since the mid-1980s, the surplus of grain as well as a variety of other goods that diminish the significance of grain in the diet, and their availability for purchase in the free markets, invalidate this interpretation of the rationale for continuing to ration grain. Actually, the amount of grain supplied to an urban dweller has usually been far more than an individual needed, and the surplus could easily be passed on to a friend or family member trying to escape rural life for the city.

[9]Some goods are rationed out to work units. For example, a particular work unit might

be given ten coupons to purchase sewing machines, refrigerators, or bicycles. The unit's management would then distribute these coupons within the work unit.

[10]Chow, *Chinese Economy*, p. 43.

[11]Ibid., pp. 95, 96.

[12]"Communique on Fulfillment of China's 1981 National Economic Plan," *Beijing Review (BR)*, No. 20 (May 17, 1982), p. 18.

[13]Thomas Gottschang (Holy Cross), Seminar at Fairbank Seminar, Harvard University, April 11, 1986, notes.

[14]Chow, *Chinese Economy*, p. 53.

[15]David Zweig, *China's Agricultural Reform: Background and Prospects* (New York: The China Council of the Asia Society, 1985), p. 6.

[16]An example of the earlier and more successful economic policies is in the highly productive period of 1952–1957. Total factor productivity in the machine-building industry "rose 7.3 percent and accounted for 25 percent of the growth of total output." Further, there are strong indications that in China, as in other LDCs, increased mechanization has disguised lower labor productivity. Gilbert Rozman (ed), *The Modernization of China* (New York: Free Press, 1981), p. 328. This helps explain how during the "ten bad years," overall productivity could increase even if people were working much less, or less effectively, as "politics took command."

[17]Yuan Baohua, "Advancement of Industrial Enterprises Amidst Consolidation," in Xue Muqiao (ed), *Almanac of China's Economy: 1981* (Hong Kong: Modern Cultural Company, 1982), p. 340.

[18]Jiang Yiwei, "Enterprise-Based Economy," pp. 66, 67.

[19]There are at least six major varieties of responsibility system, each one attempting to attain the right balance between collective ownership and individual or group incentives. The team's wealth, the quality of its leadership, and the attitudes of the peasants seem to be the key variables in determining what type of "responsibility system" an area adopted. For details, see Gregory O'Leary and Andrew Watson, "The Production Responsibility and the Future of Collective Farming," *Australian Journal of Chinese Affairs*, No. 8 (1982), pp. 11–16.

[20]For excellent detail on this topic, see Jean C. Oi, "Peasant Grain Marketing and State Procurement: China's Grain Contracting System," *China Quarterly*, No. 106 (June 1986), pp. 272–290. Also see "Opening Markets for Rural Products," *BR*, No. 19 (May 11, 1987), pp. 14, 15.

[21]Falkenheim, "Autonomy and Control in Chinese Organization," p. 195.

[22]Anita Chan and Jonathan Unger, "Grey and Black: The Hidden Economy of Rural China," *Pacific Affairs*, Vol. 55, No. 3 (Fall 1982), p. 456.

[23]O'Leary and Watson, "Production Responsibility," pp. 4, 29.

[24]Edward A. Gargan, "China Considering Letting Farmers Sell Land Rights," *New York Times* (October 27, 1987), pp. A1, A6.

[25]"Technology Transfer to Rural Areas," *BR*, No. 25 (June 22, 1987), pp. 15, 16.

[26]David Zweig, "Context and Content in Policy Implementation: Household Contracts in China, 1977–1983," in David M. Lampton, *Policy Implementation in Post-Mao China* (Berkeley: University of California Press, 1987), pp. 280–281.

[27]Gottschang, April 11, 1986, notes. Also Daniel Kellaher, Seminar for Government Department, Harvard University, April 1987, notes.

[28]"Decision of the Central Committee of the Communist Party of China on Reform of the Economic Structure," *BR*, No. 44 (October 29, 1984), special supplement pp. I–XVI.

[29]Pico Iyer, "The Second Revolution," *Time* (September 23, 1985), p. 45.

[30]"Efforts Must be Made to Raise State Revenues," *China Daily*, (April 5, 1984), p. 4.

[31]Jan S. Prybyla, "Economic Problems of Communism: A Case Study of China," *Asian Survey*, Vol. xxii, No. 12 (December 1982), p. 1211.

[32]"Labour, Wage Reform to Develop in Depth," *BR*, No. 21 (May 26, 1986), p. 9. This, of course, is a conclusion that the Chinese have given, not one known to be true from data available to Western economists.

[33]"Decision of the Central Committee of the Communist Party of China on Reform of the Economic Structure," *BR*, No. 44 (October 29, 1984), special supplement pp. I–XVI.

[34]An Zhiguo (Political Editor), "Reform Deepens in 1987," *BR*, No. 20 (May 18, 1987), p. 4.

[35]China's average annual rate of growth in gross domestic product (GDP) compares quite favorably with other populous countries, developed and underdeveloped, and even with Japan, the "economic miracle":

COUNTRY	AVERAGE ANNUAL RATE OF GROWTH OF GDP (IN %)	
	1960–1970	1970–1979
China	5.2	6.0
India	3.4	3.4
Indonesia	3.9	7.6
Brazil	5.4	8.7
USSR	5.2	5.1
Japan	10.5	5.0
US	4.3	3.1

Maruyama Nobuo, "The Mechanism of China's Industrial Development: Background to the Shift in Development Strategy," *The Developing Economies* (Tokyo) Vol. xx, No. 4 (December 1982), p. 438.

[36]Christopher Johnson, "Economic Reform in China," *The World Today* (March 1985), p. 55.

[37]For example, a Chinese who earns the equivalent of $400 per annum might well live better than an American who earns $4,000 per annum. In the mid-1980s, the Chinese government indicated that the "poverty line" for China's peasants was 100 Renminbi ("People's Currency") or, in terms of 1987 U.S. dollars, about $35. The Chinese government has stated that some 70 million peasants live below this poverty line; but the government's ever optimistic assessment of this is that this is less than 10% of all peasants.

[38]Figures are from China's State Statistical Bureau, quoted in "Peasants' Successful Climb to Prosperity," *China Daily* (September 7, 1984), p. 4. We do not know whether this accounts for inflation or other mitigating factors, however.

[39]According to Louis Putterman, however, most developmental economists do not agree that scientific and mechanized agricultural production produces greater output. In any event, mechanization is not necessarily appropriate for China as long as labor is abundant and machines very costly. Louis Putterman (Brown University), correspondence, May 1987.

[40]Ernest E. Hagen, *On the Theory of Social Change: How Economic Growth Begins* (Cambridge, Mass.: M.I.T. Press, 1962), p. 49.

[41]Members of the scientific community, especially the Academy of Sciences, however, were immune to punishments arising from political movements until the Cultural Revolution.

[42]Rudi Volti, *Technology, Politics, and Society in China* (Boulder, Colo.: Westview Press, 1982), pp. 105, 106, 226.

[43]Liang Xiufeng, "China's Economic Achievements," *BR*, No. 40 (October 5, 1981), p. 20.

[44]Nina Halperin's study of the role of economists in economic decision making suggests that, although economists may always have been part of the decision-making process, they were often not *meaningful* participants, especially during leftist periods. Nina Halperin, "The Role of Economists in Policy-Making, 1955–1983," paper presented at New England China Seminar, Harvard University, April 16, 1986.

[45]In a centrally planned economy, there is also good reason for rural production teams and industries to engage in corruption. Forced to fulfill state-determined production quotas for food and industrial raw materials at low prices set by the state, they are likely to hide a part of their production from the state. Keeping their reported production figures lower than they really are means in effect that they will pay a lower tax to the state and retain more for themselves. Illegal and semi-illegal practices among rural teams include not reporting the

locations of mountain fields, reporting "good grain as having been spoiled," turning over wet (heavy) grain for fulfilling quota weight; falsifying account books; and a host of other imaginative but fraudulent activities. For detail on the hidden ecnomy of rural China, including group conspiracies to defraud the state, blackmarketing, and criminal activities, see Chan and Unger, "Grey and Black," pp. 452–470.

[46]In 1956, 42% of workers in state enterprises were paid according to piece rates. Eckstein, p. 151.

[47]Alexander Eckstein, *China's Economic Revolution* (Cambridge, U.K.: Cambridge University Press, 1977), pp. 150–152.

[48]B. Michael Frolic, "Reflections on the Chinese Model of Development," *Social Forces*, Vol. 57, No. 2 (December 1978), p. 393.

[49]Ibid., pp. 395–397, 400–402.

[50]Rozman, *Modernization of China*, p. 338. Perhaps somewhat ironically, in the context of the post-1979 reforms which have permitted the coastal cities to retain a far greater share of profits for reinvestment, Shanghai's growth rates have fallen behind those of the rest of the country. (This, no doubt, is due largely to the existence of a very old infrastructure.) The result was that, in 1985, the government castigated Shanghai's municipal leaders and removed its mayor.

[51]Nicholas R. Lardy, *Agriculture in China's Modern Economic Development*, (Cambridge, U.K.: Cambridge University Press, 1983), p. xi.

[52]Chow, *Chinese Economy*, p. 45. Emphasis added.

[53]Prybyla, "Economic Problems of Communism," pp. 1222–1223.

[54]Despite the fact that 6,000 state enterprises represent only 16% of the total number of state enterprises, in 1986 they accounted for 60% of the total value of output and 70% of the total profits from state-owned enterprises. "China Grants 6,000 Enterprises Extended Power," *BR*, No. 14 (April 6, 1986), p. 23. It is not clear whether this total value reflects the impact of autonomy or whether they were simply 6,000 of the largest industrial enterprises to begin with.

[55]Jiang Yiwei, "Enterprise-Based Economy," p. 55.

[56]Lardy, *Agriculture*, p. 144.

[57]"On the Basic Economic Law of Socialism," *BR*, No. 41 (October 13, 1980), p. 19, referenced in Volti, *Technology, Politics, and Society in China*, p. 223.

[58]"Hongqi Comments on Zhao Ziyang Report," *China Daily* (CD) (December 25, 1981), p. 4.

[59]The Chinese have, for example, priced coal at about one-fifth of its world price. See Johnson, "Economic Reform in China," p. 56.

[60]"Growth of National Income Slow," *CD* (February 8, 1984), p. 4.

[61]The idea that corporations should pay attention to the social costs of their productive activities rather than single-mindedly pursuing profits.

[62]According to the Shanghai Labor Bureau, "One worker out of every eight in China's state-owned industries is not needed. . . and this is too much by ten million or more." Jonathan Sharp, "Surplus Workers and Shirkers but No Sackings," *South China Morning Post* (February 2, 1982), referenced in Michel Chossudorsky, *Towards Capitalist Restoration? Chinese Socialism After Mao* (New York: St. Martin's Press, 1986), p. 113.

[63]Christine Wong, "The Economics of Shortage: Why China's Economic Reforms Will Fail," New England China Seminar, November 3, 1982, p. 6 of reporter's notes.

[64]For a detailed analysis of the strain that the agricultural surplus has put on the state budget, see Jean C. Oi, "Peasant Grain Marketing and State Procurement," pp. 272–290; and Nicholas R. Lardy, "Consumption and Living Standards in China, 1978–83," in *China Quarterly*, No. 100 (December 1984), pp. 849–865.

[65]David Zweig, correspondence, June 1987.

[66]Zhao Ziyang, "Report on the Work of the Government," Report to the National People's Congress (June 6, 1983), in *BR*, No. 27 (July 4, 1983), p. xii.

[67]"Financial Picture Satisfactory," *BR*, No. 32 (August 12, 1985), p. 8.

[68]Zhao Ziyang, "Report on the Work of the Government," p. xi and xii; and *GMRB*, September 11, 1983, p. 3.

[69]Jean C. Oi, "Commercializing China's Rural Cadres," *Problems of Communism* (September–October 1986), pp. 1–15; and Jean C. Oi, "Peasant Households Between Plan and

Market: Cadre Control Over Agricultural Inputs, *Modern China*, Vol. 12, No. 2 (April 1986), pp. 230–251.

[70]See Jean C. Oi, "Peasant Grain Marketing," pp. 272–290. Oi points out that, although the state was the main victim of cadre corruption before 1979, now the peasants as individuals are also victims.

[71]Martin Weil, "Tightening Up," *The China Business Review* (May–June 1982), p. 33; and Liu Guoguang, "Price Reform Essential to Growth," *BR*, No. 33 (August 18, 1986), pp. 14–17, in which the author discusses the "block-double-track" system of pricing that is being implemented in China.

[72]"Staff Services Should be Socialized," *Economic Daily* excerpted in *CD* (July 6, 1984), p. 4.

[73]False claims and promises, "lying," not honoring their word, attempts to cheat customers or other enterprises, price gouging, denying resources to competitors through various techniques (including bribing suppliers or middlemen, hoarding, etc.).

Chapter Nine
EDUCATION
AND SOCIALIST
POLITICAL CULTURE

Complex personal relationships, built of layer upon layer of interlocking connections, formed a dense net. Any Marxist-Leninist principle, any Party plan or policy that came into contact with this net would be struck dead, as if electrocuted. When an enterprise got entangled in the net, its socialist design would come undone; when a legal case fell into the net, the dictatorship of the proletariat would get twisted out of shape. Right and wrong became thoroughly confused, reward and punishment turned upside-down. Truth yielded to falsity; the good-hearted were ruled by the vicious.[1]

SOCIALIST CULTURE

The Chinese Communist Party has tried to define and create socialist culture ever since its founding in 1921. It has been crucial for it to do so because the CCP has taken upon itself the task of engineering a major change of political, social, and cultural values in China. The task has not been a simple one, and the approaches to it have varied immensely depending on the time, the dominant political leaders, and the other policies being pursued.

Questions concerning the development of cultural values have assumed far more importance for China than they have for most other countries. These questions have consumed the time and passion of China's central leadership and have not been subsidiary questions that evolved gracefully out of other larger issues. The issue of culture has been critical because it affects all areas of Chinese life: the content of education, the role of intellectuals,[2] the type of person recruited into the Communist Party, the issue of "red and expert," rectification campaigns and purges, the role of the Party in conveying values, and the content of movies, plays, music, art, newspaper, magazines, radio, and television. The content of socialist culture has, therefore, shaped if not controlled the minds and behavior of hundreds of millions of Chinese.

The crucial dilemma the Chinese leaders confront on the issue of culture echoes their dilemmas elsewhere: the proper mix of Chinese traditional culture, socialist culture, and modern culture. The problems are manifold: If Chinese culture is destroyed, what will remain of Chinese national identity? How can China confront the outside world forcefully if it has no cultural identity to defend? How can China modernize unless it can build on the strengths of Chinese culture (even if it must come to terms with its weaknesses)? How can Chinese traditional culture be appropriately merged with socialist culture? What aspects of traditional culture are useful in a modern, socialist polity? And how can China adopt modern values without seeming to adopt Western values that threaten to subvert both Chinese traditional and socialist values?

China's leaders have attempted to combine rapid economic development with egalitarianism, all the while maintaining China's sense of national identity, but the ideological variable has made this difficult. Socialist culture, validating and prescribing a socialist system through propagation of Marxism, Leninism, and Mao "Thought," has found itself in tension with both Chinese traditional culture and the values of modernization. On the one hand, socialist ideology deplores many traditional Chinese cultural values because they are unscientific, feudal, antimodern, and hence, antisocialist. On the other hand, while averring to be modern, socialist values have proven too rigid, and perhaps too egalitarian, to tolerate the Western liberalism implicit in so many values associated with modernization. Socialism in China has, in short, been uncomfortably situated between Chinese cultural and modern developmental values.

China's search for a new definition of "socialism," which takes these dilemmas into account, will be dealt with more fully in the concluding chapter. Here we will examine how the educational system promotes what the leadership sees as a modern socialist culture. The educational system illustrates the conflict between the three sets of values and objectives the Chinese pursue concurrently and how the leaders have manipulated it, just as they have manipulated the economic system, for the purpose of redistributing opportunities in a manner compatible with these changing values and objectives.

THE BALANCE BETWEEN IDEOLOGICAL AND DEVELOPMENTAL VALUES: 'RED AND EXPERT'

The "red and expert" (*hong yu zhuan*) issue could readily serve as a lens through which to view the vicissitudes of post-1949 Chinese politics and the leaders' efforts to reshape Chinese culture in a manner consistent with the pursuit of both ideological and developmental objectives. Underlying the leaders' orientation toward the balance between red and expert is whether rapid development should be favored at the expense of socialist objectives, or whether, as the leftist line posits, the adoption of red values provides both for the attainment of socialist objectives and the faster road to development.

The issue of the proper mix of "redness" and expertise" has not been a simple matter of tinkering with a basically sound system in which there is a consensus, of deciding that a moment of silence or a five-minute reading from the works of Marx are an appropriate way to begin the day. Rather, decisions on the balance between red and expert have been explosive in their repercussions. Because the leaders have taken an all-or-nothing approach, they have had great difficulty finding an appropriate balance in the educational system as elsewhere; for the correct development of youth is all-important in determining the value matrix of China's future workers and leaders. Had the leadership not repeatedly insisted on dichotomizing red and expert into polar opposites for the purpose of recruiting China's leaders, it no doubt would have disappeared as an issue in the educational system and political culture long ago.

Although in theory China's policies are supposed to hold the values of red and expert in creative tension (as with democratic centralism), in practice, China's overall policies tend to reflect an extreme emphasis on one characteristic or the other. Further, it is difficult for most individuals truly to be both red and expert. Whichever of the two values is emphasized, *both* have led to elitism and inegalitarianism: redness to an elite based on political qualities, expertise to one based on education. Yet, because in periods emphasizing redness those with better political credentials were the ones recruited into the educational system to begin with, it was possible for a "red" to become an expert.

One cannot dismiss the "red and expert" issue as a mere reflection of more basic policy decisions, nor as a crass political decision by a dominant central leadership faction to get rid of all those who gained power under the preceding leadership's policies. It is an important issue in itself precisely because it addresses the question of how China may best move toward two goals simultaneously: socialism and modernization. Honest individuals, whether leftists or rightists within the leadership, have differed honestly in their assessment of the best means for achieving these goals. Thus, policies emphasizing rapid modernization cannot necessarily be associated with the leadership group favoring the "expert" over the "red" element.

'Red' Policies

When "redness" is ascendant, as it has usually been during China's numerous mass campaigns and periods of class struggle, then "politics" are "in command." This has generally been a central element in "red" policies promoted by the leftist leadership under Mao Zedong. Political credentials—political activism, political education, ideology, and class background—have been of primary importance for recruitment to leadership positions, to Party membership, for promotion, and for educational advancement. In many respects, this policy has emphasized political *form* at the expense of content (knowledge and skills). When politics are "in command," those who are inadequately "red" are often seen as "white," a terminology borrowed from the Russian Bolshevik Revolution to describe counterrevolutionaries. That is, expertise is important, but "white experts" (*bai zhuan*) may use their knowledge and technical skills to oppose revolution and suppress mass movements. At the minimum, insufficiently red "experts" put technological progress ahead of value orientation and sacrifice socialist values in order to accelerate modernization.

'Expert' Policies

Policies emphasizing "expertise" take on quite different characteristics. These characteristics are diametrically opposite to "red" ones if policies are extreme, or simply modify the emphasis on "redness" if expertise is only relatively ascendant. However, although the Maoist model was anti-expert, there is really no period since 1949 when experts have been entirely excluded from participation in decision making. The issue is whether that participation was *meaningful* or not. Under Maoist policies, it was more likely that economic and legal experts would be included in the decision-making process solely for the purpose of justifying Mao's policies. Under "expert" policies, the participation of experts has been more meaningful because they have been encouraged to propose policies and identify alternative policies and strategies.[3]

Policies that give priority to "expertise" usually bear the following characteristics:

1. *Achievement criteria:* Cadres are recruited and promoted primarily on the basis of achievement criteria: competence, education, and/or skills. In education, students must score high on tests in order to enter the better schools. For cadres as for students, their political attitudes must be correct but provide a backdrop to their expertise. Unfortunate class background may well be ignored under expert policies.

2. *Need for expert advice:* Policies favoring expertise have, with the exception of the brief "One Hundred Flowers" interlude, tended to be remedial policies, that is, policies aimed at rectifying unacceptable, if not disastrous, situations caused by eclipsing the role of experts. Further, policies favoring expertise tend to dismiss mass movements as the proper method for modernization and prefer limited experiments before broad policies are executed.

Policies favoring expertise illustrate the Party's long-standing ambivalence toward intellectuals: the need to harness their creative energies for modernization, and the fear of the consequences of their greater involvement in decision making. Because the Party has never really trusted the educated class, its role in policy formulation has been limited. Most experts in the PRC have suffered from the stigma of a bad class background. Many had studied abroad, or in educational institutions in China run by foreigners, so their "red" credentials were always suspect. Whenever they suggested policies that challenged the prevailing truths of Marxism-Leninism-Mao Thought or socialism, it confirmed suspicions that they were truly "white experts." The relative weight accorded to expertise in policies provides guideposts to how "intellectuals" are to be treated. (According to Mao's standard, anyone with a high school education may be called an "intellectual" (*zhishi fenze*), but those with more education are termed "big" (*da*) intellectuals, and those with less "small" (*xiao*) intellectuals.)

Intellectuals concerned with matters of the mind and ideas are a particular kind of expert. Frequently, the change in the balance of the line on "red and expert" reflected a change in the regime's view of China's writers and thinkers, as opposed to the more general category of "experts." Unfortunately, when intellectuals in the arts, humanities, or social sciences have crossed the boundaries of political acceptability, all those with "expert" qualifications, even in apolitical technical roles, have tended to suffer from a renewed emphasis on "politics in command." Thus, when in 1956 Premier Zhou Enlai and the director of the Party's Department of Propaganda, Lu Dingyi, urged China to "march toward science," they prescribed better treatment of China's intellectuals. They were to be put into high positions and their advice heeded. Intellectuals were suddenly China's invaluable property. For a few months in 1956, the Chinese went to extremes in favoring "high-ranking intellectuals" (*gaoji zhishi fenze*), a category based on an intellectual's rank (usually associate professor and above). Suddenly, those who could claim status in this category received extraordinary benefits, even while those with high political rank did not. Chinese tell of such typically absurd situations as professors entering barber shops and announcing that they were "high-ranking intellectuals." They were immediately seated in the barber chairs, ahead of all those waiting! When the "One Hundred Flowers" policy was cut short by the "anti-rightist" campaign of 1957, however, both China's literati and experts again came under suspicion as rightists.

With the Third Plenum in 1978, the reform faction rejected the methods but not the goals of "continuing the revolution." "Class struggle" was an incorrect method to continue the revolution, which during this stage of China's development was redefined to mean "the ongoing drive . . . for socialist modernization."[4] "Good" and "honest" cadres who always did "the right thing" and never made "mistakes" by following the correct Party line, but who were incapable of promoting production and efficient management, would therefore be replaced by competent cadres. The latter might occasionally make mistakes, but at least they would be competent and willing to take risks and work hard for the purpose of promoting modernization. Perhaps more a reflection of a leadership struggle than of an assessment of the need for expertise in the modernization process, claims of political superiority and honesty were dismissed as the cry of the politically conservative and incompetent. As the writer of one article lamented, "honesty" varies according to one's perspective.

> For some, honesty is the synonym for obedience, taciturnity and meekness. Therefore, a person who is hard-working but eloquent can hardly be ranked among honest people. And many reformers who are full of fresh ideas . . . can never be considered qualified candidates for promotion if judged by this standard of honesty . . . the arduous task of modernizing China demands capable comrades who are not only honest but bold in innovation as well. . . . The simple truth is: not all good comrades can be qualified cadres.[5]

Another article commented that a stereotypical "good cadre" is a person who is both "faultless" and incapable of achieving anything. But this type of cadre is hardly "faultless" if judged by criteria measuring competence and their contributions to modernization.

> They stick to old rules and resent any changes. Their slow working style often delays urgent matters. Good suggestions are often pigeonholed, becoming outdated and useless. . . . Economic reforms require capable, industrious, specialized people. The "big pot" system and not-so-good "good cadres" must be eliminated for China to modernize.[6]

The suggestion that "redness" is not enough is actually good Leninism. Lenin evinced far greater concern for the professionalism and organizational expertise of Communist revolutionaries than for their revolutionary virtues. Said Lenin, "We . . . do not need saintliness but efficient management."[7] Even Mao, who stressed the primacy of politics over education, derided those without practical knowledge as "'pseudo-red, empty headed politicos.'"[8] As is evident, however, *who* is an expert, *how* to become an expert, and what *role* to play as an expert were more crucial matters for Mao and the leftists than they are for the reformers.

Today's Party reformers participate in a vast cover-up operation to protect the Party's legitimacy against detractors: They have desperately tried to *immerse* experts in redness by recruiting experts, intellectuals, and students into the Party. This is a reversal of earlier leftist policies, which tried to make Party cadres into experts. However, Party cadre schools and specialized cadre schools, of which there were more than 8,000 in the early 1980s, do try to increase the level of expertise of cadres who are already employed, even though there is still a strong emphasis on political and economic doctrine. Graduates of cadre schools then compete with university graduates for control of policy in state organs and enterprises,[9] so the Party is hardly eclipsing redness in its entirety.

Finally, reforms that have favored experts have proven double-edged. In fact, Deng Xiaoping's emphasis on expertise had caused many (the leadership in work units as well as educators and students) to ignore political education and ideology completely, and to challenge Party leadership. Deng's political enemies within the central leadership may possibly have threatened to undo his reforms and usurp power unless greater attention was paid to political education and the importance of politics in recruitment criteria. The result is that those in the more radical wing of the reformers have had to repeatedly readjust the balance between "red" and "expert." It must be said, however, that in the political environment of the late 1980s, only a thin facade of redness masks the efforts of most Chinese to get ahead on the basis of their expertise (and their connections).

THE SYSTEM OF EDUCATION: CENTRALIZED CONTROL

Except for the decade from 1966 to 1976, the Ministry of Education centrally administered the educational system until 1985. It determined the curriculum and the textbooks to be used in state-run (predominantly urban) primary and secondary schools, and in many but not all institutions of higher education under its authority.[10] Centralized control enabled the government to control the values communicated in the schools. When, for example, the Party viewed the United States as an aggressive war-mongering imperialist state and China's major enemy, then the Ministry of Education required all textbooks to reflect this message. Textbooks would glorify science when science was in ascendancy, and political thought when politics were "in command." When "class struggle" raged, textbooks disparaged those in "bad classes" and praised those in the "good classes."

This does not mean that individual teachers necessarily communicated only those values approved of by the Ministry of Education in the classroom. It was, in fact, the propensity of many teachers to deviate from the texts that caused them political problems during such tumultuous periods as the Cultural Revolution. (The result was that many teachers thereafter took up the practice of simply reading from the assigned texts.) Nor have the schools necessarily adhered to the centrally directed curriculum, as will be noted below in the discussion of the competitive schooling system that has evolved in the 1980s.

Generally speaking, however, the Party's values have been taught in the schools. And the high level of school attendance means that most children learn those values. As a result, the schools function as a system for "secondary socialization." Although the family, as the agent for "primary socialization," may continue to inculcate traditional Chinese cultural values in children, the school system supplements this with the socialist and "modern" values designated by the Party. When one considers that China was plagued for more than a hundred years before 1949 by centrifugal forces that thoroughly fragmented China, the contribution which a unified educational system made to a unified value structure, and hence a unified polity, cannot be dismissed. The problem is that since 1949 the Party itself has repeatedly *shifted* its value orientation, with profound implications for the value content and structure of Chinese education.

Herein lies one source of the problems in the Chinese educational system: The role of education in China's modernization process and in the development of socialism was not settled, largely because the political situation was not settled. Without a stable administration, the systematic building of educational institutions and consistent policies concerning curriculum, texts, exams, and qualifications has been greatly constrained. Educators have, as a result, spent as much time worrying about the direction of politics as about academic issues.

In 1985, the State Council replaced the Ministry of Education with a State Commission of Education. This is one step *above* all the other ministries and represents an effort to establish firm central control over the educational system. The problem faced by the former Ministry of Education was that it could not direct educational policy for the numerous educational institutions that fell under the jurisdiction of other ministries, provinces, municipalities, and enterprises. In response to Mao's pronouncement that the whole country should be involved in education, they had established their own independent educational systems, including sometimes even their own technical institutions or universities (although even if called "universities" they might in reality offer only a secondary-school curriculum). These "small but complete" schools suffered from inadequate staff, libraries, and laboratories, and a limited curriculum. Each was capable of producing only a small number of narrowly educated technicians. The new State Commission of Education, initially under the direction of the then Vice-Premier, Li Peng, is at least in principle now able to legislate policy for all schools and universities, regardless of where they fall on the organizational chart. In practice, the State Commission's real power is limited by the degree to which the various ministries and provinces are willing to relinquish their independent control over their own schools.

THE LEADERSHIP OF THE EDUCATIONAL SYSTEM: THE ISSUE OF PARTY CONTROL

1949 to 1978

Although the Ministry of Education was originally just an instrument for executing policy decisions made largely by the Communist Party, it was nevertheless a bureaucracy comprised of professionals in the realm of education. But with the Anti-Rightist Campaign of 1957, the educational bureaucracy became increasingly politicized. Party secretaries, whose main qualification was their understanding of and obedience to the Party line, not only kept tabs on the educational sphere, but actually administered educational policy. Incumbent administrators remained but lost power relative to Party personnel. The Party's control over daily administration grew steadily until 1965. During the Cultural Revolution, Mao attacked the Ministry of Education and destroyed the system of centralized educational planning. His rationale was that this ministry, like all bureaucracies, was staffed by "experts" who, by dint of their high level of education, were themselves inherently elitist, conservative, and hence, against revolution. As a result, Mao preferred that changes be initiated from below, from the masses.

Mao's destruction of centralized education was soon followed by attacks on the Party. Education was turned over to an interim "work group" for cultural and educational affairs, which functioned under the aegis of the State Council.[11] Those in charge of it were Mao's quintessential political animals. Revolutionary "three-in-one" committees, whose members were chosen for symbolic reasons,[12] administered the schools and universities when they reopened. The educational administrators who survived the Cultural Revolution had spent most of it in struggle sessions and humiliating manual labor. Mass campaigns and class struggle substituted for effective administration as instruments for solving basic problems in the educational system.[13]

1978 to the Present

By 1978, when educational reforms began to be implemented, former educational administrators had returned to their positions; but they fell under the control of Party or ex-military personnel who had earlier been reassigned by the leftists to administer schools. The leftists had viewed schools as if they were any other institution to be administered according to the correct Party line. Neither administrative skills nor knowledge of education were considered relevant. The vice-presidents and lower-level administrators were the professional educators, while university presidents and school principals were usually Party cadres or former military personnel. The State Council continued to appoint university presidents, who in turn appointed department heads and vice-chairmen.[14]

The post-1978 reforms, therefore, attempted to get the military and the Party out of educational administration. But the reforms had to be rationalized carefully. Thus the reformers maintained that the Party's *primary* task, namely political and ideological work, had been impaired by its involvement with administration. Removing the Party from administration would free it to pursue its proper work more vigorously. The Party would, in any event, retain its supervisory role in the educational system.[15] The Education Ministry also demanded that at least 80 percent of presidents, vice-presidents, and even Party secretaries in institutions of higher education be university graduates, and that no more cadres with a low level of education or who had not specialized in education would be hired.[16]

Although these reforms were frustrated at every step by incumbents, efforts to get the Party and ex-military personnel out of administration had made substantial progress by the mid-1980s. This policy has been furthered by the emphasis on the new criterion for redness: To be truly red, a person must now be expert. In fact, the term "socialist culture" has become synonymous with the term "expert," that is, skilled or educated. The term "culture" (*wenhua*), which used to represent history, traditions, language, customs, and habits, now connotes a level of education or skill. Further, through a cynical manipulation of Marxism, integral components of the new definition of culture (education, science, and technology) are no longer viewed as part of the "superstructure." Instead, they belong to the "latent productive forces," and not to the economically determined superstructure.[17] Education, formerly viewed as a "consumer enterprise," and even a "means of class struggle," is now seen "as a tool for the development of production," and investing in education is synonymous with investing in production.[18] Undertaking further education thereby has become the measure of a person's commitment to promoting socialism.

POPULISM AND EGALITARIANISM VERSUS ELITISM: LITERACY, KEY SCHOOLS, AND UNIVERSITIES

1949 to 1978

Literacy

A major principle upon which all Chinese leaders could agree immediately after victory in 1949 was the importance of literacy to the attainment of modernization. But the allocation of sufficient revenues and the implementation of appropriate policies did not flow out of this consensus. Instead, the scarce resources for the educational sector went to schools preparing students for college and to the development of the system of higher education. Further, until the mid-1980s, although all youngsters were supposed to attend schools for eight to nine years, they were not compelled to do so for two reasons. First, because education was not free, the Chinese leadership worried that parents would view fees for compulsory education as an additional compulsory tax burden. Moreover, such fees would cause further hardship to the very poor.[19]

Second, the state was unwilling to disperse its limited funds for the educational sector to finance schools in the rural areas. Instead, it encouraged rural localities to set up their own "people-managed" (*minban*) schools, financed and managed by rural collective units. This was in effect a restoration of a Chinese traditional practice: Rural communities were made responsible for the support of village schools, while the Chinese government supported urban schools. As the State Council phrased it in 1953, the state would develop education in cities, but in the countryside, "the principle of voluntarism and need should be the basis upon which to promote the operation of primary schools by the people." Considering that 85 percent of the population lived in the countryside, the state was casting a significant part of the peasantry into a state of permanent illiteracy; for many areas of China were too poor to siphon off enough funds even to build a schoolhouse, much less to hire a teacher. More to the point, the poorest areas often could not produce a person competent to teach primary school (a problem addressed in the mid-1960s by the policy of sending urban educated youth to teach in the *minban* schools). And, of course, China suffered from the kind of problem that plagues so many developing countries: Peasants often preferred to have their children earn extra income and to help them during the peak seasons rather than to send them to school. The most positive statement that can be made about the *minban* schools is that, although qualitatively they suffered in comparison to state-run schools in the cities, they offered a flexibility and simplicity that permitted them to respond to rural needs and represented "a form of adaptation to rural backwardness."[20]

Nevertheless, by the mid-1960s the Chinese managed to attain a significant level of literacy for a developing country, with literacy being defined as an ability to read 1,500, or about 75 percent, of the 2,000 characters that the Chinese Communist regime established as the core characters[21] for all printed media (including Party and governmental reports).[22] Further, school attendance had risen appreciably from 1949 to 1965: in 1949, 25 percent of all school-age children attended primary school. By 1965, 70 percent attended. The completion of primary school was, however, the end of the educational road for most children: In 1949, 2 percent of all school-age children attended secondary school, whereas the proportion had risen to only 16 percent by 1965.[23]

Advancement in the educational hierarchy

Of those fortunate enough to go on to secondary schools, many focused on getting into the best lower-middle schools, and then the best upper-middle schools. In general terms, the "key" schools, which the state rewarded for their excellence with better teachers, more equipment, and better teaching materials, were the best schools. The measure of their excellence was the ability of their students to get the highest test scores for entering the next level of education. Academic achievement was primary. A Chinese Communist version of "affirmative action" attempted, however, to favor those from the less-educated groups but "good" class backgrounds of workers, peasants, and families of Communist Party cadres. Nevertheless, as long as achievement test scores were the primary determinant for advancement to the next level of education, those with "bad" class backgrounds or questionable origins (that is, those from the dispossessed middle class or intellectual backgrounds), still tended to get the better placements. Therein lay the rub, not only for the more "leftist" or Maoist leadership, but also for those students with "red" credentials based on activism, behavior, and good class background.

During the 1950s there were few worker-peasant children eligible to attend institutions of higher education since only a small percentage had yet attended senior high school. This, combined with the fact that the university system had itself expanded, meant that even children with a bad class background were permitted to attend universities. In fact, until 1960, virtually all students in the academic track in senior high school could be certain they would be eligible to attend a university. In 1960, the government "went so far as to instruct employers to deny jobs to all new senior-high graduates, in order to force even the reluctant amongst them to sign up for the university entrance examinations."[24] But soon the rapid growth of primary and secondary school education had produced a far larger number of students eligible for university admission than universities could absorb. As a result, university admissions suddenly became very competitive.

This competitiveness emerged in the context of a political conflict between the Maoists and Liuists over the issues of who should lead, whom should education serve, the purpose of education, the values communicated in schools, and the role of education in influencing the form of the societal structure. If, after all, the educational system was a tool to redistribute opportunities as an affirmation of the redistribution performed by the socialist economic system, it could hardly reconfirm the previously existing class structure by permitting the children of the former middle class or intellectual "class" to rise to the top. On the other hand, if the purpose of education was, as in the Liuist view, rapid modernization, then perhaps certain aspects of the formerly unequal class structure, should be left intact; for the educational superiority of certain classes would contribute substantially to the building of a rich material basis. And, with a greater pie to divide up, the poorer classes would benefit more.

The Maoist line

In spite of serious setbacks after the failure of the Great Leap Forward, the Maoist line prevailed in the educational sector and in culture generally from 1958 to 1976. Maoist policies sought to close the gap between urban and rural education, and between key schools and nonkey schools in the cities. To remedy urban–rural inequality, educated middle school youth were sent for increasingly lengthy periods to the countryside to educate peasant youth. To remedy key versus nonkey school inequality, Maoist policies promoted technical, agricultural, and vocational schools, as well as work-study programs. Schools from the universities down to the elementary levels would set up their own factories or farms, or perform labor in some other way, such as tree planting, rope-making, gathering wild grasses and manure, sweeping the streets, and the like.[25] At first, students only labored during their vacations; but by the mid-1960s, students in many schools were devoting fully six months of each year or half of each school day to manual labor. In turn, work units set up their own schools to educate workers during the work day.

Until 1963, the socialist values communicated in educational materials glorified the peasant, the worker, and manual labor, but the system of greater rewards and more prestigious jobs for those with more education implicitly glorified the intellectual, the expert, and technician. In effect, then, educational policies undermined the Maoist objective of using the educational system to spread social equality. Educational elitism was, in the Maoist view, at cross-purposes with the goal of destroying classes. In fact, it was creating an educated "expert" class, not leaders who were both "red and expert," to become the new ruling class.

The educational system itself thus became the target of the leaders' efforts to reshape Chinese political culture. As Mao slowly gained the upper hand over policy in the cultural realm in 1963, the educational system shifted away from encouraging rapid economic development to redistributing status and opportunities. Class labels and political behavior became more important than educational achievement, and egalitarianism more important than short-term rapid growth. Admissions policies had to "draw the line" between "the enemy" and "the people." Achievement tests were, accordingly, denigrated in value. Class labels assumed paramount importance, with ironic results: Children of cadres were favored more than the children of ordinary workers and peasants. Workers and peasants were, after all, not the "originators" of the revolution. Thus, they were less "revolutionary" than cadres. "Reddest by birth [the children of cadres] had the easiest access to the better high schools and universities. Banking on their 'political capital,' most of them easily [became] even 'redder' by joining the Youth League."[26] The officially designated class boundaries thereby served to favor the creation of an elite made up of cadres' children, even though they rarely worked as hard in school as the children of the former middle class, and even though they had never suffered from the deprived lifestyle of the children of workers and peasants.

When the Cultural Revolution erupted, the children of Party cadres and those of the middle-class intelligentsia found themselves on the same side of the fence, fighting to maintain their privileged access to the best schools against the inroads of children of workers and peasants. But the emphasis on political criteria necessarily had different effects on the children of cadres than on those of the intelligentsia. As a result, some of the most brutal struggles during the Cultural Revolution occurred in China's best schools between these two achievement-oriented groups of students.[27] This conflict was greatly exacerbated by working-class children who took advantage of the call for "continuous revolution" and the denunciation of the new "capitalist workers" inside the Party to redress their grievances against the previously favored cadres' children.

By the time of the Cultural Revolution, Mao's educational policies were in control. Those policies focused on developing the relatively simple skills that were appropriate to China's low level of technological development and labor-intensive economy. Study was to be integrated with practice. Urban schools set up their own factories and farms. Students' elitist viewpoints were to be modified by manual labor and "learning from the masses." Resources and policy favored a basic education for the masses and an increased emphasis on the political content of education, class struggle, and anti-elitism. The hierarchical and elite-building system of education of the 1950s was slowly dismantled. To serve the dual purpose of closing the rural–urban gap, and inculcating pretentious urban school students with mass values, the leadership sent them to work in factories or to the countryside to educate peasants. By 1966, students were working six months out of every year in order to combine "theory with practice," and to learn the "mass-line work style." Then schools were completely shut down for two years, and the students were to make the entire country their classroom.

China's socialist educational system was reshaped to communicate the Maoist interpretation of socialist orthodoxy. Tests, if they were used at all, became a means of learning, not the basis for advancement. Mao endorsed the concept of students copying the answers to test questions from others as a way of learning. The important thing was to discover the right answer, not to prove who had learned more than others. As Mao put it,

> In examinations, students should be allowed to whisper to each other and to hire others to take the examinations for them. If your answer is right, I copy yours. Copying is good too. . . . When I cannot do what you have done, then let me copy. . . . Teachers giving lectures should allow the students to fall asleep. If the lecture is no good, it makes no sense to force others to listen. . . . Sleeping may help one to recover from fatigue.[28]

The objective of the leftist line in education, therefore, was to take the competition to get ahead in China out of the realm of academic achievement and into the realm of political struggle. Theoretically, this would socialize Chinese students in egalitarian values. In practice, it socialized them in competitive political values.

Key schools were abolished and most institutions of higher education were shut down for several years. Even when some universities reopened in the early 1970s, no distinct high school curriculum existed to prepare students for a university education. Moreover, few qualified teachers were left in the classrooms. As the guardians and communicators of "culture," teachers had been most vulnerable to attacks by student Red Guards during the Cultural Revolution. They were accused of perpetrating a traditional Chinese and elitist culture. Many were driven from the schools, beaten up, humiliated, even murdered, by the Red Guards. Unclear mandates from the top and ill-defined societal values had left students free to determine how much their desire for retribution toward teachers who had given them poor grades should enter into denunciations of them. No limits were imposed by responsible people in authority, for they were themselves the victims of denunciations and violence, and were powerless to control the youth.

Thus, the chastised teachers who returned to their posts hardly dared to say a word not written in the textbooks. The teachers could not consider themselves superior to the students, so classes were often taught either by students or factory workers, who by dint of their proletarian roots and manual labor were more attuned to "mass-line" politics and could better convey the appropriate political message to the students. But they were poorly equipped to turn out well-educated individuals.

In any event, when the high schools and universities reopened, students were ill-prepared for coping with intellectual messages more complex than those provided by Mao "thought." Chosen on the basis of their worker-peasant-soldier roots, political behavior,[29] and having met the criterion of working for two years in the countryside or in a factory, these students could absorb little in the way of sophisticated knowledge. They had graduated from school systems where the curriculum had been compressed to the bare minimum. The time spent in primary and secondary schools had been reduced to five instead of six years each. Only the most basic courses in the sciences and mathematics had been taught. The rest was considered too abstract and theoretical, irrelevant to the needs of a developing country. Implementing theory in practice, scientific experiments in the countryside and in factories had replaced experimentation in laboratories. The 120 research institutes of the Chinese Academy of Sciences, the pacesetters for scientific research and theory, had virtually been dismantled during the Cultural Revolution. And all the social sciences and humanities had become the study of one man's thought, that of Mao Zedong.

The universities offered a telescoped curriculum, requiring three instead of four years of study. Students at all levels spent much of their time putting "theory into practice" in school-run enterprises. Workers, students, and teachers collaborated to write the new textbooks. Even science texts had to have a correct political content. Although more up-to-date and better texts had been written elsewhere and could have been translated into Chinese, in its autarkic mood, China insisted on starting from scratch and writing its own texts. These texts ignored new developments in science, for even China's leaders in science knew little of theories and discoveries abroad. No one outside the Academy of Sciences dared to read foreign periodicals. And, in any event, China has always been too poor to purchase many foreign books and periodicals. Many of those that existed were destroyed by rampaging Red Guards, and the few that survived dated from the 1950s. Moreover, ever since the deterioration of China's relationship with the Soviet Union in the early 1960s, China had lacked access to Soviet books on science and technology. By 1976, therefore, China's scientific texts were largely limited to those Soviet texts remaining from the 1950s.

Educational materials were unavailable to students, teachers, and college professors alike. Further, of the surviving faculty members and teachers in 1976, those with a Western graduate education had usually received it no later than the early 1950s; and those with a Soviet or Eastern European education no later than the early 1960s. After 1949, few Chinese received the equivalent of a graduate eduation within China. As a result, barely literate students were graduating from middle schools; and universities served more as a completion of a middle-school education than as a training ground for professionals and experts. In any event, it was the People's Liberation Army, not education, that provided access to position, privilege, and power after 1966.

Most important, the Maoist line declared that education should serve the working class. Children of worker-peasant-soldier[30] backgrounds, not children of cadres, intellectuals, or the former bourgeoisie, gained admission to institutions of higher education.[31] Revolutionary committees located in work enterprises or communes determined which children could go on with their education, although a university revolutionary committee could reject students who were clearly unqualified academically.[32]

Although policies concerning admissions, curriculum, textbooks, and teachers changed after 1976, the policies of the preceding decade left indelible marks. First, the continued emphasis on mass education meant that the lower rungs of the educational system were bulging. Figures available for 1979, the year when major educational reforms were implemented, indicate that primary school enrollments had grown from 70 percent in 1965 to 93 percent of all children in the eligible age category. Secondary school enrollments (albeit predominantly in junior high or specialized technical and vocational senior highs) had grown from 16 percent to 46 percent. In the meantime, enrollment of eligible students in institutions of higher education had only risen from 1.4 percent to 1.6 percent of the total population of students in that age group.[33] In absolute numbers, there were nineteen times as many senior-high-school graduates in 1979 as there were in 1965; but the enrollment *ratio* in the university system, which had not been expanded at a rate commensurate with the expansion of the high school system, had dropped from 45.56 percent of eligible senior-high-school graduates in 1965 to 4.08 percent in 1979.[34] Thus, the large percentage of children eligible to go on to secondary school, and thence on to higher education, increased the competitive pressures to get into the best secondary schools. This was even more the case after the educational reforms began.

Second, while the quality of primary and secondary education had deteriorated greatly, the fact that such a large percentage of all eligible children had received even a rudimentary education contributed significantly to raising the educational level of the people. This fact cannot be discounted in evaluating the rural peasantry's success in taking advantage of the economic reforms instituted in the countryside after 1978, for much of their success was predicated upon functional literacy: their ability to read scientific, technical, and economic literature, and, of course, to do mathematical calculations.

Finally, although the popularization of education has been an important element in inculcating new cultural and political values, the virtual destruction of elite education left China in 1976 with few professionals and experts to contribute to rapid modernization. The quality and integrity of China's comprehensive system of provincial and national research institutes under the aegis of the Academy of Sciences fell apart as scientists were sent to farm in the countryside and the entire system of higher education was destroyed. This left students inadequately trained to funnel into postgraduate work in the research institutes.[35]

Although leftists believe that the egalitarian approach *is* the fastest route to development, the experience of developing countries indicates otherwise. Efforts in the initial stages of development to universalize education at the lower levels at the expense of education at higher levels is the slower road. Certainly illiteracy holds any country back from modernization; but without an educated elite, a country faces formidable obstacles to developing the scientific and technical knowledge necessary for modernization.[36] Even more to the point, it is almost impossible to adequately educate the teachers themselves. As of the early 1980s, only half of China's primary school teachers had graduated from a secondary teachers' school or a higher secondary school.[37] In a short time, the egalitarian approach thus led to a dead end in the educational system as a whole, and thereby impeded rapid economic development.

1978 to the Present

Power struggle affects educational policies

With the death of Mao Zedong and the fall of the Gang of Four in 1976, education policies did not change immediately. Education was so central to conveying proper values, to distributing and redistributing opportunities and benefits, and to laying the basis for modernization, that its future structure became the focal point of much debate among Party leaders who were themselves embroiled in a power struggle. Educational policies reflected the values that each leadership faction espoused. The reformers associated with Deng Xiaoping pushed for a quality-oriented, elitist educational system, which would reintroduce examinations for grades and placement, tracking of superior students into key schools, and a first-rate system of universities and research institutes. Those associated with Hua Guofeng, at that time the Premier and Party Chairman, deplored such elitism and continued to support mass education and the importance of manual labor in the curriculum. Even when the Ministry of Education reintroduced key schools on a trial basis in 1978, the leadership's divergent goals were evident. On the one hand, the key schools would take the lead in raising academic standards, and would allegedly contribute through their own excellence to the improvement of ordinary schools. On the other hand, the key schools would "popularize" education, and class struggle would be "the main course" throughout the educational system. "Ideological remolding" remained of primary importance.[38]

Until the jockeying for power stabilized, the educational system remained in a state of "struggle, criticism, and transformation." As the reform leadership further consolidated its control, class struggle and mass movements faded into the background in favor of scientific experiments as the best means to achieve "great leaps forward" in production. The "four modernizations" program challenged the linkage between education and labor. Most schools and universities eagerly responded by divesting themselves of their school-run factories and farms and returned to their pre-1957 pattern of spending the school day solely in the classroom. Both primary and secondary schools returned to a full six-year curriculum, and universities returned to a four-year curriculum. Many subjects such as law, sociology, and psychology, abolished during the Cultural Revolution, were restored to the curriculum.[39]

The educational reforms of 1978–1979 set the tone and direction of education, but debate continued to rage on many of the specifics. The reforms did reestablish the centrality of the educational system in rapid modernization, the importance of advanced knowledge, and the formation of an educated elite; but the popularization of education was to continue.

Reform leaders favor modernization values

The reform leaders' solution to the conflict among the values of traditional Chinese culture, socialist culture, and modernization is to favor modernization values largely at the expense of the other two. The leaders justify their policies by arguing that if China is ever to have the financial resources to support high-quality mass education, it must first modernize;

and just as a capitalist economic system must precede a socialist one, a hierarchical elitist educational system must precede a socialist, egalitarian educational system. Of course, those with a vested interest in egalitarian and mass educational policies, notably the teachers and students already produced under these policies, continue to press for a reversal of educational policies that emphasize quality and the development of an educational elite. At the moment, they appear to be losing the battle.

The attempt to increase literacy[40] and basic knowledge through mass education is not being jettisoned, however, as shown by the 1985 edict requiring nine years of compulsory education for all children.[41] In fact, the reformers' setting of minimum standards for mass education surpasses the previous efforts even of the Maoists. For example, in 1983 the Ministry of Education established a set of minimum requirements for a school to operate: no dangerous buildings, classrooms for all classes, tables and chairs for all students. But many rural primary schools are unable to meet such minimal requirements, and many primary and secondary schools lack the simplest of teaching equipment or even qualified teachers.[42] Thus, in spite of good policies for advancing education, and even if all significant opposition to educational reforms is overcome, the Chinese still face the very real limitation of a low level of development as a starting point.

CURRICULUM

Politics Versus Substance

The reforms instituted since 1979 have stressed the importance of substance over politics; but politics cannot be entirely eclipsed. Inevitably, the subject matter taught in the secondary schools has continued to reflect the political issues and power struggles within the central leadership, such as the "antispiritual pollution" and "antibourgeois liberalism" policies, and economic reforms. But, "politics" at the elementary school level has turned into a combination of basic moral education, manners, and training in good speech, discipline, and hygiene, a reflection of the reformers' efforts to support modernizing values taught in schools with a traditional sense of ethics and morality.[43] Better to teach elementary school children to observe public order, dress neatly, be honest, and not spit than to teach them that the Gang of Four was evil.

Reforms that diminished the role of politics in education have, however, been double-edged from the Party's point of view. The emphasis on expertise, scientific method, and "seeking truth from facts" has spilled over from its intended application in science and technology to a questioning of Party leadership and socialism. When middle schools and universities began eliminating political theory classes from the curriculum, after the leadership encouraged all scientists, academicians, and other experts to devote 90 percent of their time to their professional work, it stripped Party leaders in the educational sector of their central role. Students refused to attend political theory classes, except to cram for exams on theory; and the schools allocated classrooms originally set aside for these classes to academic subjects. Teachers had as little enthusiasm as the students.[44] The cancellation of political theory classes was subsequently denounced as an exaggerated response or a misinterpretation of the meaning of educational reforms.

The Party condemned the neglect of political education as unsocialist, a result of "bourgeois liberalization" and "spiritual pollution." The reassertion of Party control over these "erroneous trends" was brief, however, limited to little more than restoration of political theory classes, which were still sharply curtailed in both length and breadth. Chinese educators continued to complain of the deterioration in the character traits of university students. Students enrolled in the late 1970s, who had suffered the agonies of the Cultural Revolution and received a poor education, were, according to Chinese educators, highly motivated, unselfish, and mature. But those who entered later, on the basis of scores on achievement tests, were self-indulgent, refused to work hard, were attracted to "decadent ideologies," found manual labor loathsome, and were only interested in pursuing pleasure, leisure, and getting rich.[45]

Statements by top Party officials in 1984, to the effect that Marxism did not provide *all* (if any) of the answers to China's developmental problems, contributed further to the verbal haze surrounding the issue of how much time schools should allocate to political study. Those with a vested interest in a continued emphasis on political study are, for the time being, politically powerless to get their way. Still, there is obviously continued resistance throughout the Party structure to the wholesale jettisoning of political theory and socialist ethics classes.[46]

The Party apparatus has continued to exercise considerable control over Party branches in universities and the school system, but not necessarily over educational administrators and teachers. In the 1980s both the students' and the schools' rewards have come by ignoring Party directions. Students who concentrate on their academic achievements, even if they ignore political study, are more likely to move up the present ladder of success. Schools reap the rewards of key school status if their students do well, and are only reprimanded if they are found to be breaking regulations on preparing students for exams. They do not lose their key school status and their larger share of the pie.[47]

The fact that schools could get away with ignoring Ministry of Education (and later, the State Commission of Education) directives demonstrates not only the weakness of centralized control over the educational system at its basic levels, but also the pressure from the leadership to produce results. Because promotion rates from secondary schools to universities have thus far been the only truly measurable standards of performance, schools have poured their limited financial resources into achieving high rates, even when it means violating guidelines on education.[48] Provinces, prefectures, municipalities, and districts have found it easiest to rank schools under their jurisdiction according to their promotion rates. They were censured for doing this, as well as for issuing promotion rate quotas to the schools. The schools themselves were criticized "for abandoning the educational plan and study outline in order to ready their students for the entrance examinations, for concentrating only on promising students, and for ignoring moral and physical education."[49] The result, according to official Chinese statements, has been students mechanically memorizing everything, poor Chinese grammar, lack of breadth in education, exhausted, sickly, and near-sighted students, and the lack of a spirit of collectivism.[50]

Nevertheless, as the reputation of the Party continues to gain ground in the 1980s, and as membership in the China Youth League, and thence the Party itself, is reestablished as a significant factor for success, those who cannot risk all on academic competition alone choose the dual track of "red and expert" in the hopes of establishing a political record that will compensate to some degree for their less than equal academic record.

Traditional Versus Modern Value Content and Pedagogy

In addition to the concern for the balance between politics and academic subjects in the curriculum, some Chinese educators have begun to question the continued reliance upon China's traditional approach to teaching, as well as traditional ideas conveyed in the curriculum. Much of this pedagogy and value content dates back to the period of imperial rule before 1911. After the Communists gained power in 1949, they built on the traditional emphasis on academic and moral education, merely substituting Communist morals for Confucian morals, and infusing academic subjects with moral lessons. In most other respects, the traditional system and its pedagogy were left untouched. Educators in post-1949 China have continued to stress the learning of factual knowledge and academic skills without giving equal attention to conceptualization, thinking, and analysis (except Marxist analysis). They believe that the best way for students to learn is through rote memorization of the teachers' lectures, not independent thinking, or reading of materials beyond the classroom text. Classroom instruction remains the main form of teaching and learning. Permissible subject matter is still limited, and teachers in primary and secondary schools must rigidly follow the texts approved by the State Commission of Education. Students are not encouraged to ask questions, and they busily copy down whatever the teacher says in class.[51]

Nor do educators pay attention to the importance of independent study and research. In universities and throughout the Academy of Social Sciences, most research continues to be *assigned,* either by governmental ministries and agencies or by the Party. Rarely do researchers, especially in the social sciences or humanities, present their own proposals for research. Instead, researchers continue to serve largely as ex post facto rationalizers of governmental or Party policies, and as propagators of values endorsed by the Party. While it would be an exaggeration to say that no independent thinking goes on in Chinese education, or in research done in the social sciences and humanities, it would certainly be fair to argue that until the mid-1980s it was rare. Even in the late 1980s, China appears unprepared for the challenges its values and political system would have to undergo from truly "emancipated" minds. Thus, the Western model of education, while appealing in many of its structural components, is still unacceptable to many Chinese in its endorsement of liberal scholarship.

Chinese educators have been considering how to modernize their pedagogical techniques, curriculum content, and research system in ways that will encourage creative thought and greater knowledge. But it is not easy to abandon a style of education that is so deeply entrenched in Chinese ways of thinking: a cultural predisposition to think what one is told to think by people in positions of authority (reinforced in the Communist period by an awareness of the dangers of thinking independently).

The Soviet model of education, which the Chinese Communists copied after 1949, stressed specialization as early as possible, and separated teaching from research by establishing a system of scientific research institutes separate from the universities. Although China's exposure to some Western practices—namely the importance of a broad education before specializing, the combination of research and teaching in universities, and the flexibility offered to college students to change majors—has caused much discussion in academic circles, the Chinese hesitate to adopt such practices. Much of their reluctance to change may be attributed to developmental factors: Given China's limited financial resources, it seems cheaper to train a specialist than a generalist, and the earlier a person specializes, the better. Hence, the reluctance also to let students switch majors or take courses outside their majors, and the desire to concentrate funds for research in research institutes.

Some of China's key universities and key primary and secondary schools are eagerly adopting Western pedagogical techniques, curriculum, and institutional practices; but the vast majority of schools have not yet, and may not ever, decide that these practices are the most appropriate ones for them. In any event, as long as school entrance examinations continue to value rote memorization of facts over an ability to think, it is unlikely that the Chinese will rush into a Western style of education.

UNRESOLVED ISSUES IN THE EDUCATIONAL SECTOR

Whom to Educate?

Children of the intelligentsia

Educational policy has reflected the values established by the central political leadership. As the leadership became increasingly consumed with political issues after 1957, the educational system became engrossed with issues of the class background and political activism of students. The 1978–1979 educational reforms diminished the attention to students' class background and other political values, and promoted changes that would contribute more to developmental objectives. Examinations were restored as an allegedly "class-neutral" instrument for determining promotion within the educational system. In fact, exams have again favored the children of the educated, formerly "bourgeois," class. This has raised the ire of all those, including the children of Party members, who lack the advantages of the children from intellectually privileged backgrounds, and who under a leadership dedicated first and foremost to developmental values are most likely to lose out.

Adults

The expansion of the system of adult education in the 1980s offers another dimension of the issue of whom to educate. This expansion was in response to the emphasis after 1978 on educational level or technical skills as the basis for promotion of both workers and cadres. All younger workers and staff members who could not meet the educational standards of a junior middle school, and almost all workers who attended middle school during the Cultural Revolution and were in the bottom three wage grades, were required to take courses (with full pay) in order to catch up.[52] Teachers at every level were required to upgrade their educational skills through in-service training in courses offered by special institutions, teachers' schools and universities, summer courses, correspondence courses, or radio and television courses. And university professors who had graduated from universities during the Cultural Revolution had to pass examinations in order to keep their positions.[53]

A multitude of radio and television colleges, correspondence schools, night schools, county-run peasant universities, and "spare-time schools" have sprung up. Hundreds of thousands of adults are attending them each year. If they complete the course of study, they receive diplomas and may enroll in the next level of schooling. Thus, young workers and staff members who reach the appropriate level may enroll in spare-time classes of junior or senior middle schools or secondary technical schools. Those lacking elementary school education may enroll in spare-time classes at the elementary technical school level. The growth of this "nonconventional sector" is, the Chinese believe, both more rapid and more cost-effective than expanding the existing conventional educational institutions.[54]

Workers who wish to attend a TV college or take courses in a spare-time school, face one problem: They must receive approval from their leaders to be released from work (while continuing to receive wages) in order to watch the classes on television and study. Perhaps this is a relatively insignificant problem in the context of policies that promote expertise, and exterprises that are vastly overstaffed. Work units do, in fact, set up their own study classes, and often provide funding for the face-to-face teaching and printed materials to supplement the lectures transmitted on television. Major problems remain, however, for graduates of these non-conventional schools are not necessarily allocated jobs by the state. Further, for those educated in their own work units' schools, although they have their degrees in hand, there is often nowhere to promote them, and they are assigned to, or remain in, jobs inappropriate to their training.[55] Nevertheless, judging by the large number of those receiving diplomas, the Chinese "spare-time" students, who squeeze in their academic study after a six-day work week and endless time-consuming domestic chores, seem undaunted by the constraints on their time, the lack of a place to study in their cramped homes, or a lack of job mobility.

Chinese educational authorities are expanding enrollments in other ways. For example, some established colleges and universities are creating satellite campuses, and tens of thousands of cadres are testing to be qualified in a single field of study after being "self-taught."[56] All these efforts are designed to make education more accessible to people who have missed an opportunity for it in the past, or who are unable to enter a regular school or university because their age exceeds the permissible limit, or because university facilities are inadequate. In this respect, the expansion of higher education meets the dual objectives of both popularizing education and increasing the level of scientific and technical expertise.

But there are those in China who believe that better university education means expanded research facilities, not expanded size. They argue that only in this way can institutions of higher education become centers of both teaching and research, institutions that can train graduate students who will become leaders in their respective fields. Otherwise, China will remain dependent on foreign universities to train its graduate students. In general, this school of thought seems to have lost out, if for no other reason than inadequate funding. Few universities have yet established graduate training. China's universities largely remain teaching, not research, institutions.

Women

Finally, the issue of whom to educate must address the position of women in the educational system. It has, of course, been difficult to release

Chinese women from the shackles of powerful Chinese traditional values concerning the inferiority of women and their need to be subordinate to men. The Communists have made concerted efforts to break the hold of traditional values in their efforts both to develop China and to be orthodox Communists. Yet ironically, in spite of their commitment to egalitarianism in the treatment of women, they discriminate against them in most of the same ways and for most of the same reasons as nonsocialists do. In fact, urban educated Chinese are generally at the same level of thinking and policy discussions concerning women as the developed capitalist states of the West were some twenty to twenty-five years ago. This, however, should be seen as considerable progress: At least a more "modern" sexism has replaced a sexism based on traditional societal values.

In the educational sector, there has been unrelenting discrimination against women on the basis of their alleged sexual attributes. Young women who want to enter key schools, universities, and even technician schools must achieve a higher entrance examination score than young men.[57] In discussions with numerous Chinese educational officials, and even with those outside the eduational sector, the reasons offered for this higher requirement for women were invariably sexist: Girls mature faster than boys, but boys will in the end be the ones who are more talented. Therefore, schools must compensate for boys' slower maturation by accepting for admission a larger percentage of boys than an equal treatment of male–female test scores would justify. In addition to boys' slower maturation, girls' intellectual capabilities start to *decline* after they reach puberty. This is because they become interested in boys and because their brain cells begin to deteriorate. Chinese university officials further justify discrimination against female applicants with higher test scores because, although females may be the majority of "A" students upon graduation from high school, by the time they graduate from college four years later, they will only be the "B" students. (This, of course, contradicts the secondary school officials' rationale for discriminatory policies based on an assumption that girls will have fallen behind boys long before the end of high school.) Women university students, although very solid performers, will not be able to match male students in creativity and genius, not only for the reasons of their mating-nurturing instinct and brain deterioration, but also because they are too conservative. Male students, being more adventurous, will make the scientific and technological breakthroughs. It is no surprise, therefore, to find that most leaders and individuals assigned to the best positions in enterprises and units throughout China are male.

Thus, the educational system still contributes to a self-fulfilling prophecy: Because men will be the future innovators and leaders, it is pointless to take the education of women after elementary school too seriously. Reforms thus far have done virtually nothing to address this type of sexual inequality.

State Assignment of Graduates

The continuation of the system established in the first years of Communist rule, namely the assignment of high school and university graduates by the state, is not really a long-term unresolved issue, for it was not until the 1980s that the Chinese seriously considered it an issue that needed to be addressed. Nevertheless, as the reforms in the economic, educational, and leadership sectors are enacted, the system of a centralized assignment of jobs to graduates is increasingly at odds with many of the leaders' developmental objectives.

One particularly serious problem with China's state allocation of jobs is the all too frequent inappropriate assignment of graduates: Those trained in a speciality are assigned to a job in an unrelated area. One paper reported in 1984, for example, that for the preceding few years, 12.3 percent of all college graduates were assigned jobs unrelated to their specialities. History majors were given jobs in business while specialists in electronics became archive keepers. The article attributed the problem partially to the involvement of so many departments in the assignment of jobs: "Graduates are first assigned to bureaus, then reassigned to companies run by the bureaus, and then to factories run by the companies, and so on."[58]

The Chinese recognize the need to change the system of job allocation in order to address this misallocation of China's small number of educated individuals. They have made some limited progress in setting up a system in which various enterprises and state organs contract institutions of higher education to provide them graduates with a particular type of training. The continued implementation of China's economic reforms, which require enterprises to take responsibility for their profits and losses, makes it particularly unfair to assign them inappropriate personnel. As the imperatives of a market system become more apparent, China's leaders will no longer be able to ignore the personnel demands of work units.

This, of course, will also provide graduates greater flexibility in selecting their future employment, and it will make schools and universities more sensitive in their curriculum to the demands of the marketplace. Inevitably, these changes in the system of assigning high school and university graduates will lead—and has led—to some unanticipated new problems for the Chinese reform leaders. For example, well-educated students whom the state has assigned to teach in less desirable locations, such as in the countryside or distant provinces, have in recent years often simply not shown up for work. Because work units now have some leeway in hiring new employees, they have been able to "steal" talent from the state. Individuals, given an opportunity to work in a better location with potentially greater salaries, have chosen to ignore their state assignments to teach in the hinterland. Sichuan Province was, for example, assigned 1,593 graduates by the state to work in educational posts in 1985, but 360 of them never showed up. Many were allegedly lured away by other units, which promised them higher salaries, air-conditioned housing, and gifts of leather suitcases and money.[59] The educational sector as a whole may, in fact, be hurt by increased freedom to graduates to choose their own jobs, unless social status, political security, and salaries for teachers in the primary and secondary school system match what is elsewhere available.

SIDE EFFECTS OF REFORMS

The resolution of the conflict between the values of rapid development and quality on the one hand and slower development but greater equality on the other hand has, for the time being, been settled in favor of the former. The reform leaders unquestionably suspected the kinds of unpleasant side effects that this choice would have, and how it would detract from their objective of a socialist, egalitarian state by fostering the development of a new elitist social and political hierarchy. The possibility of educational reform leading to a new division of society into classes, especially when combined with the economic reforms, was also anticipated. But other side effects no doubt came as an unpleasant surprise. Some of these effects seem to be the product of the overall political and economic environment in which the educational system must function.

Tracking, Elitism, and Classes

One unanticipated consequence of the educational reforms is that the "tracking" of superior students into the "key schools" to prepare for college has had deleterious effects on those left out of this selection for elite status. The latter feel demoralized and suffer from diminished opportunities to learn from their brighter peers. The more desperate among the ordinary schools have, in some cases, resorted to extreme measures to prevent this from happening. For example, teachers and administrators in some nonkey junior middle schools have tried, through promises to give and threats to remove privileged treatment,[60] to block their best students from applying to keypoint senior highs. Teachers left behind in the nonkey schools have only the less talented students to teach. The best teachers are also often reassigned to keypoint schools. Because students in nonkey schools will almost surely not go on to college, students at an early age lower their vision. An alarming proportion of students in ordinary primary and secondary schools drop out or fail. Further, because there may or may not be jobs for those who graduate from technical and vocational schools, and because many opportunities exist to get wealthy in both the urban and rural sectors without any secondary schooling or specialized training, many potential students are leaving the school system to seek their fortunes. Thus, in the context of the economic reforms since 1978, the educational reforms have fostered two distinct types of youth: those who believe they can advance their careers and fortunes best through formal education, and those who seek easy opportunities to make money without advanced education.[61]

The State Council responded to these unintended consequences of the 1979 reforms with a new set of policies calling for (1) a drastic cut in the number of key schools and an improvement in the quality of those remaining, and (2) "a drastic reduction in the number of regular secondary schools and a gradual increase in the number of specialist, technical, and vocational schools."[62] The first point was obviously intended to channel limited resources to the very best schools, so that they could better prepare students to attend college. Increasing the number of specialist, technical, and vocational schools was intended to direct students into a curriculum that would provide technical and vocational skills for the workplace, as only a handful of students could realistically expect to attend an institution of higher education. But the educational administrators of ordinary secondary schools with even the slightest chance of achieving or regaining key-school status are reluctant to change over to a nonuniversity-oriented curriculum.[63]

Various efforts to ensure that the regular curriculum not be disrupted by preparation for college entrance examinations have had limited effects. The problem remains that the political and economic context of employment for the educated has affected the students', and their parents', approach to education. A university education has become the new path to success in the 1980s, and it is virtually impossible to convince the Chinese that a solid high school education is good enough. The result is for China, as for many developing countries, what has become known as the "diploma disease," the quest for a diploma in order to increase opportunities to work in "the modern economic sector." Schooling is reduced to a competition for securing diplomas, "and the students' efforts from primary school through junior and senior high school become glued to 'prepping' for a succession of entrance examinations."[64] Some work units have tried to remedy this situation by such practices as signing contracts with vocational and ordinary schools that guarantee jobs to their most qualified students. If such practices become common, they undoubtedly will influence the structure of education itself.[65]

Rural Education

Economic reforms implemented since 1978 have also had unintended, but perhaps foreseen, effects on the cultural and educational sectors. In addition to putting a premium on skills and knowledge as the basis for economic success, economic reforms have contributed to the collapse of the *minban* school system in rural areas. When all families were in collectives, which financially supported the locally run schools, student labor after school was used to defer educational costs. But under the household responsibility system, the collective basis for schooling has been destroyed. Wealthy families want their children either to go to the best schools, which are in the often-distant market towns or county seats, or not to go at all, but stay at home and contribute to the family's wealth by working in the fields full-time.

This leaves only the rural poor to support the *minban* schools. But the combined contributions of the rural poor are often insufficient to support a school. And they can ill afford the expenses for room and board in a distant secondary school. *Minban* schools have probably been the lowest quality schools in China. Teachers in these schools rarely have gone beyond the first three years of middle school. Most of those primary school teachers whom China's leaders at the time of the 1979 educational reforms pronounced unqualified to teach were *minban* teachers.[66]

There are statements but no clear evidence that the state itself is willing to finance these rural schools as a necessary supplement to the compulsory school legislation of 1985. Without state funding, "compulsory" schooling will remain a hollow shell. Further, since the best schools in the market towns or county seats tend to have curricula that is academic, not agricultural or vocational in orientation, the rural schooling system will not necessarily contribute in the short run to the advancement of agricultural modernization. It might, in fact, contribute to the migration of the most talented rural youth to the cities.[67]

The tendency for rural residents to see schools as a channel for social mobility and to leave farming is quite common in developing countries. Like them, China's rhetoric is geared toward encouraging the people in rural areas to send their children to schools that present a curriculum relevant to the community's needs; but national policies that reward those who pursue an academic education with social mobility contradict this rhetoric. Thus, it is hardly surprising that China's peasants, no less than peasants and farmers in other countries, resist efforts to transform local schools into agricultural schools.[68] If they are going to attend school at all, then, the children from rural areas are going to do it for the purpose of staying out of farming forever.

Nevertheless, the future of rural education is promising, again because of economic and political reforms that stress the need for expertise and knowledge. With the better jobs, including factory jobs and managerial positions in the countryside, now requiring higher levels of education, families are eager to educate their children. Reforms have created a built-in incentive for becoming educated that used to be missing. This was, without question, a fully intended side effect of the reforms since 1978.

CONSTRAINTS OF SOCIALIST AND DEVELOPMENTAL VARIABLES ON MODERNIZATION OF EDUCATION

It is an unfortunate commentary on the implementation of socialist principles in China that, beginning in the 1960s, those principles did more to interfere with the advancement of the educational level of the Chinese people than did China's underdeveloped and poor conditions or China's traditional culture. Indeed, until 1985, educational *and* political policies, which were founded more on ideological principles than on developmental objectives, made a concerted effort to overcome the traditional Chinese reverence for education and the educated. Only by dint of extreme efforts, such as anti-rightist campaigns, class struggle, and the Cultural Revolution, was the regime able to mute this profound respect for education. That it was largely effective was shown by the extreme reluctance of talented Chinese to enter the teaching profession, or to study the traditionally revered fields in the humanities, notably history, literature, and philosophy. These fields, together with all the social sciences, had become so infused with and controlled by political values, so vulnerable to political attack, that they lost their appeal and their integrity as disciplines. They served primarily as instruments of propaganda at the disposal of the Party, and virtually no talented student from the late 1950s until the mid-1980s would consider entering these fields of study if they could instead be permitted to specialize in mathematics, the sciences, or technology.[69] Yet as is evident from test results, the educated elites taught their children the importance of education, and behind closed doors, they did everything they could to ensure that at least their own children would become educated, regardless of the values the political leadership conveyed.

Similarly, although the Chinese Communists claimed that Marxism was scientific and, therefore, supported values conducive to development, socialist values and policies have actually prohibited the adoption of many values important to successful modernization. This has no doubt reflected an insecure, newly established government, fearful of a challenge to its utopian vision and its fragile claim to moral authority. Given the idealistic foundations of socialism, and the problems that socialism confronted in its effort to become established in China, the regime's concerns were understandable. The unification of the society and the state had to take precedence over independent thinking. Nevertheless, creativity, the exploration of new ideas, free-wheeling discussions and conferences, communication with the international community of scholars, the education of students outside the socialist bloc, open libraries rich with current books and classics in the field—these and other resources that have proven so valuable in advancing the understanding of science, technology, and humanity in the Western world and Japan were virtually nonexistent to the Chinese until 1979.

We have already noted that some of the constraints on modernizing the educational system have been created by developmental factors; but most have been created by *policy choices.* They do not flow directly out of a lack of adequate resources for education. In fact, even according to their own admission, China's *allocation* of funds to the educational sector is "an unusually low proportion of the state budget." Generally speaking, other countries allocate some 15 percent to 20 percent of their total state budget to education, whereas China's allocation has hovered around 10 percent. In 1978, UNESCO ranked China "130th among 149 countries in order of size of allocation for education in proportion to GNP," putting China not only far below countries in the "first" and "second" world, but also at the bottom of the list of most third world countries.[70] One can only conclude from such data that it is the Chinese leaders' choices, based on ideological and political values, not their low level of development, that are primarily responsible for holding back the educational sector.

CONCLUSION

The debate over education is not yet over. The direction taken in the educational sphere will continue to reflect both the debate over policy at the top and the conflict between the goals of rapid growth and egalitarianism. The lineup of political forces is not as clear as might be expected. In fact, well-known intellectuals, not leftist radicals with a more egalitarian set of values, are some of the most vocal supporters for greater resources to basic mass education. The discussion continues about how best to allocate educational resources: whether to train a small high-quality elite, or to broaden egalitarian objectives of eradicating illiteracy and providing "a sound basic education for all."[71]

For the time being, one thing is clear: Economics and experts, not politics and redness, are "in command" in the educational sector as in almost all other sectors. Education toward the objective of increasing China's productivity has now taken precedence over education as a means to achieve political goals.

Finally, as the above analysis indicates, the structuring and restructuring of the educational system and its curriculum have communicated certain values of fundamental importance to the development of socialist political culture in China. The educational system has instilled the following values in its students, in varying combinations over time:

1. Socialist values through political education courses, work-study programs, and the promotion to higher levels of the education ladder of those with correct political attitudes;
2. Chinese traditional values, such as educational elitism, through a system that based promotion to higher levels on academic achievement and respect for

people in positions of authority. This was done through the use of the traditional pedagogical techniques of lecturing and student note-taking, memorization and then regurgitation of what the texts or teachers (authorities) said without analysis, the state determination of texts, curricula, and even research projects, and the teaching of (Chinese) morality in place of political ideology; and

3. Modernization values, through the introduction of a more practical curriculum, geared toward turning out students with academic (and/or technical) skills and a scientific orientation toward problem solving, rather than political skills and an ideological orientation; and through the introduction of foreign educational values, models, and institutional practices.

As the history of China's educational system reveals, the changing balance among these three sets of values in the educational system reflected political struggles within the central leadership. It is unlikely that in the future these values will be any less determined by the central political issues and personalities of the day than they have been thus far.

NOTES

[1]Liu Binyan, "People or Monsters?" translated by James V. Feinerman, with Perry Link, in Perry Link (ed), *People or Monsters? And Other Stories and Reportage From China After Mao* (Bloomington: Indiana University Press, 1983), p. 54.

[2]In China, anyone with a secondary school education is considered an "intellectual."

[3]Nina Halperin, "The Role of Economists in Policy-Making, 1955–1983," paper presented at New England China Seminar, April 16, 1986, Harvard University.

[4]"Notes From the Editor," *BR*, No. 34 (August 24, 1981), p. 3.

[5]"Honesty Is Not All," *China Daily (CD)* (June 16, 1984), p. 4.

[6]"Criteria of Cadres," excerpted from *Jingji Ribao (Economic Daily)*, in *CD* (June 8, 1984), p. 4.

[7]V. I. Lenin, quoted in Paul Cocks, "Bureaucracy and Party Control," in Carmelo Mesa-Lago and Carl Beck, *Comparative Socialist Systems* (Pittsburgh: Center for International Studies, University of Pittsburgh, 1975), p. 223.

[8]Jerome Chen (ed), *Mao Papers* (London: Oxford University Press, 1970), referenced in Susan Shirk, *Competitive Comrades* (Berkeley: University of California Press, 1982), p. 15.

[9]Marianne Bastid, "Chinese Educational Policies in the 1980s and Economic Development," *China Quarterly*, No. 98 (June 1984), p. 215.

[10]Many institutions of higher education were not under the Ministry's authority, and as more and more work units set up their own primary and secondary schools, its control was steadily diluted.

[11]Peter J. Seybolt, "Editor's Introduction," *Chinese Education* (Fall–Winter 1980–81), Vol. XIII, No. 3–4, p. xxviii.

[12]"Members were chosen on the basis of categories descriptive of age, class background, or function in society, not of competence in education . . . ," Suzanne Ogden, "Higher Education in the People's Republic of China: New Directions in the 1980s," *Higher Education*, Vol. 11, No. 1 (January 1982), p. 87.

[13]Ibid., p. 87.

[14]*China: Facts and Figures* (Beijing: Foreign Language Press, 1982), p. 6.

[15]Suzanne Ogden, "The Politics of Higher Education," in *Chinese Law and Government* (Summer 1982), p. 9.

[16]Bastid, "Chinese Educational Policies," pp. 202, 203.

[17]"Education Mainly Belongs to the Production Forces," *GMRB* (March 11, 1981), p. 3, translation in Suzanne Ogden (ed), *Chinese Law and Government*, pp. 99–101.

[18]"Attention to Knowledge Must Go Hand in Hand With Attention to Education," *Red Flag*, No. 8 (April 16, 1983), pp. 2–5, translated in *JPRS* 83808 (July 1, 1983), *China Report*, pp. 2, 4, 6.

[19]Although some scholarships were available for poor children to attend state-run schools, schooling was a major part of most family budgets. Before 1966, the annual costs for a child to attend a junior high school were 14 yuan, 20 yuan for senior high; Shirk, *Competitive Comrades*, p. 24. If they had to live at the school because of distance—and this was usually the case in the countryside—the costs were far greater. By the 1980s the government began to view the alleged inability of parents to pay school tuition as merely an excuse for not sending their children to school. They were, of course, by then advocating compulsory education. See "Attention to Knowledge Must Go Hand in Hand with Attention to Education," p. 3.

[20]Gilbert Rozman (ed), *The Modernization of China* (New York: Free Press, 1981), pp. 410, 411.

[21]Retention of characters, which can only occur if the initial memorization of them is reinforced by repeated usage, is a serious problem for the Chinese. Rote memorization is the only way to learn ideographs, which number in the tens of thousands. The government's standard for measuring literacy is an ability to read 2,000 characters in the cities, but only 800 characters in the countryside. See Rozman, *Modernization of China*, p. 415.

[22]The information for literacy in 1964, estimated at 62%, comes in a Chinese report in 1983. The article implies that China is trying to make up for lost ground in the fight against illiteracy after 1964. "Progress in Literacy Campaigns in Countryside," *CD* (December 24, 1983), p. 3.

[23]Shirk, *Competitive Comrades*, p. 25.

[24]Anita Chan, Stanley Rosen, and Jonathan Unger, "Students and Class Warfare: The Social Roots of the Red Guard Conflict in Guangzhou (Canton)," *The China Quarterly* (September 1980), p. 398. John Cleverly's study disagrees with this conclusion, at least at the national level. His data suggest that the 1958 Great Leap Forward movement of "youth to the countryside," in which 8 million youth left the cities and resettled in the countryside, was in part an effort by China's leaders "to mop up unemployed middle school graduates whose literacy and numeracy skills could be used in the countryside, and to lessen the demand for tertiary (university) places." John Cleverly, *The Schooling of China* (Boston: Allen and Unwin, 1985), p. 147.

[25]Cleverly, *Schooling of China*, pp. 144–146.

[26]Anita Chan, "Images of China's Social Structure: The Changing Perspective of Canton Students," *World Politics*, Vol. XXXIV (April 1982), No. 3, pp. 302, 305, 306, 308.

[27]Chan, Rosen, and Unger, "Students and Class Warfare," p. 406–416, 420.

[28]Mao Tse-tung, "Chairman Mao Discusses Education" (February 13, 1964), in David Milton, Nancy Milton, and Franz Schurmann (eds), *The China Reader: People's China* (New York: Random House, 1974), p. 246.

[29]A student's behavior presumably reflected his or her commitment to socialism. But commitment could be feigned and was, in any event, difficult to measure. The process of selecting candidates to attend universities was arbitrary because of the lack of objective standards. Once again, connections with the appropriate officals and use of the "back door" were the only sure ways to become a candidate for university admission. By 1976 substantial evidence indicates that the vast majority of candidates selected from at least one city were children of high-ranking urban officials. Julia Kwong, "Is Everyone Equal Beofre the System of Grades: Social Background and Opportunities in China," *The British Journal of Sociology*, Vol. 34, No. 1 (March 1983), pp. 94–96.

[30]Soldiers from the ranks only.

[31]Actually a few places were reserved in every class for children from these types of family backgrounds.

[32]Seybolt, "Editor's Introduction," p. xxxiv.

[33]Shirk, *Competitive Comrades*, p. 25.

[34]Stanley Rosen, "Restoring Keypoint Secondary Schools in Post-Mao China: The Politics of Competition and Educational Quality, 1978–1983." Paper prepared for the SSRC Conference on Policy Implementation in Post-Mao China (draft, June 1983; revised in 1984), p. 11. For a more extensive elaboration of some of the ideas and data presented in this paper, see Stanley Rosen, "Recentralization, Decentralization, and Rationalization: Deng Xiaoping's

Bifurcated Educational Policy," *Modern China*, Vol. 11, No. 3 (July 1985), pp. 301–346.

[35]In line with the Soviet model, only China's most talented university graduates would be selected to join these institutes; but graduate training would take place in the institutes themselves. Until the mid-1980s, China had almost no postgraduate schooling. Only in isolated instances, when faculty members at the university also held appointments at these research institutes, was the level of university instruction and research sufficient for its graduating students to move directly into independent research without a long period of training. See Ogden, "Higher Education," p. 92.

[36]This assertion does not take into account the argument that developing countries often suffer from an "internal brain drain" of scientific workers "who tend to work on problems which are irrelevant to their environment." That is, they work on scientific issues of concern to the advanced, industrialized countries, not those of greater relevance to their own country's needs. From the "Sussex Group," *Science and Technology for Development*, United Nations ST/ECA/133 (New York: 1970), p. 18, quoted in Boel Berner, "China's Science Through Visitors' Eyes," (Lund, Sweden: Research Policy Program, University of Lund, June 1975), p. 1.

[37]"Attention to Knowledge," op. cit., p. 3.

[38]Stanley Rosen, "Restoring Keypoint Secondary Schools in Post-Mao China," pp. 5, 6 (draft).

[39]A 1982 Chinese report on education indicated, however, that primary and middle school students were still required to do manual labor and that university students had to spend ten weeks per year working in factories or farms, and an additional twelve weeks "in social investigation and practical work." In short, about five months per year were not for study. See *China: Facts and Figures* (Beijing: Foreign Languages Press, 1982), pp. 2–4.

[40]One estimate of literacy suggests that "illiteracy among rural youth actually increased in the 1970s." Another suggests that as of the late 1970s, China's population had achieved between 60% to 70% literacy (based on school attendance figures). Such figures "place China among the more literate nonmodernized countries, far ahead of India, but behind Sri Lanka." China's own estimate, based on the 1982 national census, indicates a literacy rate of 75% for those above the age of twelve years. Rozman, *Modernization of China*, p. 415; and "Facts and Figures: Education," *BR*, No. 40 (October 3, 1983), p. 26.

[41]The edict required that the most developed areas (especially cities), which encompassed some 25% of China's population, should have nine years of compulsory schooling for youth by about the year 1990. Those areas of "medium-level development," encompassing about 50% of the total population, would be required to fulfill the mandate by about 1995. And economically backward areas (about 25% of the population) would be required to fulfill the mandate with state support, whenever they could manage to do so. "Decision of the [Communist Party's Central Committee] on Reform of the Educational System" (May 27, 1985) *FBIS, Daily Report China*, No. 104 (May 30, 1985), pp. k3, k4.

[42]"Attention to Knowledge," op. cit., p. 3.

[43]Cleverly, *Schooling of China*, p. 233.

[44]"Why Don't Middle School Students Like to Take Politics Classes?," originally published in *Beijing Youth News* (May 22, 1984); and "Political Instructors Should Get Rid of Their Depression," Letter to the Editor of *New Times*, No. 1 (September 1979), p. 42. Both articles are in John P. Burns and Stanley Rosen (eds), *Policy Conflicts in Post-Mao China* (Armonk, N.Y.: M. E. Sharpe, 1986), pp. 63–66.

[45]*Guangming ribao* (January 14, 1983), p. 2, cited in Bastid, "Chinese Educational Policies," p. 207; and "How Is China's Future Shaping Up?" *China Youth News*, in *BR*, No. 38 (September 22, 1986), pp. 28, 29.

[46]For example, Chen Yun, by then one of the five members of the Standing Committee of the Politburo and head of the Party's Disciplinary Inspection Office, displayed his concern in his article warning Party branches at all levels to pay more attention to political education. "Combating Corrosive Ideology," *BR*, No. 41 (October 14, 1985), p. 15. The fact that this was by no means a settled issue is indicated by the simultaneous publication, intentionally or unintentionally, of another article in that same issue of *Beijing Review* stating the opposite point of view. While Chen Yun's article lamented the corrosive effects of capitalist ideology, the other article, translated from the Chinese press, flatly stated that "Capitalism also . . . has some valuable facets, to which we should be attentive." "Open Policy Can Help Moral

Growth," translated from *Workers' Daily,* (October 14, 1985), in *BR,* No. 41 (October 14, 1985), p. 27.

[47]Rosen, "Restoring Keypoint Secondary Schools," p. 8 (draft).

[48]Ibid., pp. 7, 8, 28 (draft).

[49]Stanley Rosen, "Obstacles to Re-education Reform in China," *Modern China,* Vol. 8, No. 1 (January 1982), p. 19.

[50]Wang Zhixin, "Educational Work Needs to Overcome a Harmful Tendency," *People's Daily* (March 12, 1983), p. 3, translated in Burns and Rosen (eds), *Policy Conflicts in Post-Mao China,* pp. 287–289.

[51]For a discussion of some of these ideas, see "Educational Reform and Outdated Ideas," *Red Flag,* in *BR,* No. 36 (September 8, 1986), p. 28.

[52]"Remedial Education for Younger Workers," *BR,* No. 20 (May 17, 1982), p. 7.

[53]One-third of the teachers in primary and secondary schools were enrolled in courses to upgrade their knowledge by 1980. See Bastid, "Chinese Educational Policies," p. 201.

[54]In 1979, there were 72 full-time universities offering correspondence courses. In the city of Shanghai alone, 200 colleges for workers and staff members offered 100 different subjects to 50,000 students. These colleges were full-time, part-time, or spare-time, and enrolled students on the basis of performance on a citywide entrance examination. In 1980, 24 universities ran night universities. Most students in correspondence and night schools have the equivalent of a senior secondary school education. Large enterprises, specialized companies, bureaus, or scientific associations have set up some of the spare-time colleges. *China, Facts and Figures* (Beijing: Foreign Language Press, 1982), pp. 7, 8. Figures for total enrollments in this "nonconventional" sector are projected at 835,000 by 1987. Robert McCormick, "The Radio and Television Universities and the Development of Higher Education in China," *China Quarterly,* No. 105 (March 1986), p. 75.

[55]For a superb analysis of these and other problems facing graduates from the nonconventional sector of education, see McCormick, "The Radio and Television Universities," pp. 76–84.

[56]"Self-Taught Education," *Guangming ribao,* (January 6, 1984), p. 4.

[57]As just one of countless examples of this, see "Notice on Test Score Requirements for Admission to Technician Schools in Jilin Province," *China Youth News* (April 12, 1983), p. 1. Translation in Burns and Rosen (eds), *Policy Conflicts in Post-Mao China,* pp. 303, 304.

[58]"Suitable Jobs for Graduates," *China Daily* (*CD*) (August 9, 1984), p. 4.

[59]"Companies Poach Graduates," *CD,* (September 10, 1985), p. 4.

[60]Privileged treatment refers to the continuation of these students in the "keypoint classrooms" established within the ordinary schools for the best students.

[61]Rosen, "Restoring Keypoint Secondary Schools," pp. 22 and 6 (draft). This drop-out rate has continued, especially in rural areas, where a 40% drop-out rate is not uncommon. See "How Is China's Future Shaping Up?" *China Youth News,* in *BR,* No. 38 (September 22, 1986), pp. 28, 29.

[62]Rosen, "Restoring Keypoint Secondary Schools," p. 29 (draft).

[63]See He Dongchang, Minister of Education, "Plans Are Outlined for Improving Education Further," *CD* (September 10, 1984), p. 4. Nationwide, in 1979 about 9% of the students in senior secondary schools were in technical or vocational schools. Their proportion rose to about 25% by 1983, and was targeted to reach from 40% to 60% by 1987. Bastid, "Chinese Educational Policies," p. 195.

[64]The term "diploma disease" was coined by Ronald P. Dore, in *The Diploma Disease: Education, Qualification and Development* (London: Allen and Unwin, 1976). Referenced in Jonathan Unger, "Bending the School Ladder: The Failure of Chinese Educational Reform in the 1960s," *Comparative Education Review* (1980), Vol. 24, No. 2, part I, p. 221.

[65]Rosen, "Restoring Keypoint Secondary Schools," p. 47 (draft).

[66]Bastid, "Chinese Educational Policies," p. 199.

[67]For an analysis of rural youth's resistance to going into agriculture, see Zhou Zuyou and Ma Li, "Correct Our Guiding Ideology in Running Rural Schools," *People's Daily* (July 3, 1983), p. 3, translation in Burns and Rosen (eds), *Policy Conflicts in Post-Mao China,* pp. 297–300. The authors blame Party and governmental cadres and educational workers, not the peasants, for the resistance.

[68]Brian Holmes, "A Comparatist's View of Chinese Education," in Ruth Hayhoe (ed), *Contemporary Chinese Education* (Armonk, N.Y.: M. E. Sharpe, 1984), pp. 19, 20.

[69]Suzanne Ogden, "China's Social Sciences: Prospects for Teaching and Research in the 1980's," *Asian Survey,* Vol. xxii, No. 7 (July 1982), pp. 582, 583.

[70]"Attention to Knowledge," p. 3.

[71]Rosen, "Restoring Keypoint Secondary Schools," p. 45 (draft).

Chapter Ten
THE MEANING OF SOCIALISM IN CHINA IN THE 1980s

Communism is the ideal. . . . But my property is mine forever.[1]

Drabness is not a tradition, and poverty is not a virtue.[2]

[T]here can be no . . . socialism with pauperism. So to get rich is no sin.[3]

CHINA'S MAJOR SUCCESSES UNDER SOCIALISM

What does "socialism" mean today to the Chinese people and the Chinese Communist Party leadership? Both its achievements and failures help define what socialism means in concrete terms. The people may define socialism in strictly materialistic and developmental terms; but the leadership, as we have seen, has been torn over the meaning of socialism within the context of Chinese culture and underdevelopment.

The theme of this book is that the efforts by China's leaders to pursue policies which simultaneously satisfied the major values associated with each of three major variables, development, culture, and ideology, generated the tensions that inhibited the satisfactory resolution of certain problems China faced after 1949. China's leaders wanted to build socialist institutions (both as means and ends), and to "Sinify" Marxism by "taking the Chinese road to socialism," all for the purpose of developing the material and "spiritual" basis of China without losing a Chinese identity. The results, it was hoped, would demonstrate to the world the superiority of socialism over capitalism, and the superiority of the *Chinese* form of socialism. Their failure to demonstrate either led the Chinese to reexamine their means and ends some thirty years after the socialist experiment began.

Yet China's ongoing problems must not overshadow its extraordinary success under socialism in addressing certain key issues of development. In fact, compared to most less developed countries, China has done remarkably well in *resolving* its developmental problems. Many of China's post-1949 successes have been discussed within the context of the broader unresolved issues addressed in this book. What is striking about the successes is that, with few exceptions, they are in areas in which the objectives of socialism and development are compatible, and where Chinese cultural values are not seriously challenged. China's successes include fulfilling the following policy objectives of the Party leadership:

1. Sustained agricultural and industrial growth rates;
2. A remarkably equitable distribution of goods;
3. Guarantees of minimal food consumption, housing, and medical care for most Chinese;
4. Good preventative health care, resulting in high life expectancy and low infant mortality rates;
5. An ability to mobilize the people effectively for the state's purposes;
6. Stability and unity (except for the self-induced chaos of the "ten bad years";
7. National security;
8. Limited inflation;
9. Industrialization of the countryside (to a degree);
10. Low unemployment;
11. Population control (when the decision was finally made to control it);
12. Limited foreign indebtedness;
13. High level of literacy;
14. The development of science and technology (but not at the middle range);
15. The end of "class exploitation."

The point to be made here is quite simply that the history of post-1949 China is not at all a history of failures, but a mix of some extraordinary successes with some intractable problems. Although this text has focused on the latter, it has done so with the knowledge that, in the context of the conditions the Chinese Communist Party faced in 1949, the successes have been astounding. In addition, any absolute concept of success is virtually impossible to define; and few serious economic, social, or political problems can be resolved with finality. Steps can only be taken along a continuum, so that today's successful resolutions of issues are mere stepping stones to tomorrow's achievements. Finally, in spite of its unresolved issues, China has not been static since 1949. In fact, the interaction of the three major variables shows just how dynamic the situation in China has been, even if this dynamism did not necessarily propel China forward in developmental terms.

SOCIALISM AS CULTURE

There is no agreement among scholars on the role of culture in modernization generally, or in the Chinese case specifically. It may be that culture presents only the possibilities and parameters and does not determine what choices are made. Cultures are composed of a plurality of often contradictory strands, and it is the *leadership* that chooses which cultural elements to build on, which to eliminate, which to ignore. Further, whether traditional Chinese political culture is compatible with modernization or not remains a highly debatable issue.[4]

The leadership repeatedly chose certain quintessentially Chinese cultural elements out of the multitude of possibilities and integrated them into the structuring of its institutions and its "socialist" and "modernization" policies. In the leaders' views, these particular cultural elements served well the needs of an authoritarian Party: hierarchy, elitism, submission to authority, respect for education, and traditions of patriarchy, secrecy, mediation, and centralized control. In this respect, China's leaders have, like the leaders of many developing societies, chosen to build on certain traditions as the best way to modernize and establish socialism. Rarely, however, except when asserting China's nationalism vis-á-vis the outside world, have they admitted, or perhaps even been conscious of, choosing Chinese cultural values or elements.

As the preceding text suggests, China's anxiety over permitting greater contacts with capitalist countries has been as much a concern for protecting traditional cultural values as it has been for protecting socialist values. Their identity as Chinese is reaffirmed by identifying what is not Chinese as "foreign" culture: sex, violence, crime, individualism, materialism, divorce, selfishness. Even within China until the 1980s, policies toward national minorities were conspicuously policies of "great Han chauvinism," that is, policies projecting the superiority of *Chinese* (Han) culture. These policies forced minorities to adopt Chinese practices disguised as socialist practices. Those minorities which refused to do so were criticized for antisocialist, not anti-Chinese, behavior.

The cultural variable is the "Chinese" component of the unresolved problems in the People's Republic of China. In the past, the leadership often ascribed the roots of China's problems to the economic, political, and social chaos inherited from the pre-1949 period, but also to imbedded Chinese cultural factors. Nevertheless, just because China's leaders claim that certain traditional values have negatively influenced people's behavior does not make it true. Within China, for example, people behave differently in different institutional settings, even though they presumably have the same traditional values. A comparative study of structures would enhance our understanding of the effects of similar policies in societies with different cultural traditions.[5]

In any event, the cultural variable reveals much about at least one very significant cluster of values and practices affecting both policy formulation and policy implementation in China. On the one hand, China's cultural characteristics and attitudes in many instances have given it an advantage over other poor and underdeveloped countries. This is one reason why visitors to China often conclude that the Chinese exhibit a kind of cultural strength for modernizing similar to that in war-ravaged Europe after 1945, rather than the general range of attitudes typical for a developing country. The ingenuity, drive, ability to endure sacrifice, obedience to authority, rational intellect, and competitiveness of the Chinese are some of the characteristics reflecting this cultural strength.

On the other hand, certain "feudal" traditions, habits, customs, and ideas have negatively influenced development and the implementation of socialism: the tendency to develop networks of personal relationships, which leads to both corruption and factionalism; fear of authority, to the point of "eating bitterness" rather than speaking out against those who abuse their authority or exploit the people; religion and superstition, which are considered antiscientific, antirational, and hence impediments to modernization; discriminatory treatment of women; the use of the "back door" and personal relationships as the means of distributing scarce resources, goods, and services; bureaucratism; and the cult of the individual. The Chinese Communists have relied on cultural rather than political, developmental, or institutional explanations of such practices, practices that are unacceptable to leaders who have any pretentions of being "socialist" or "modern." And, when they speak of creating a new "socialist political culture," they are referring to their efforts to eradicate those aspects of Chinese culture that threaten both socialism and modernization.

Socialist ethical principles should transform traditional Chinese human relationships and traditions: "The morals advocated in the old society—parents should be kind to their children, children should be filial to their parents, brothers should love and respect each other—can be transformed into socialist ethics of mutual understanding, mutual love and mutual help."[6] Obviously, "good" aspects of Chinese culture find their equivalence in socialism. But the question that some Chinese may raise is, if all those aspects of Chinese culture that are incompatible with socialism and modernization are eradicated, and if even many good aspects of Chinese culture are destroyed as a by-product of modernization, what will be left of Chinese culture?

SOCIALISM AS IDEOLOGY AND INSTITUTIONS

As the foregoing chapters on China's unresolved problems indicate, the socialist system itself has usually been the single greatest obstacle to development while, paradoxically, it is Chinese culture that has been the single greatest obstacle to the implementation of an effective socialism that might well have been a powerful force for development. If we were to boil down the obstacles that the socialist system itself presents to the successful resolution of problems, they would probably fall into three categories:

1. Problems emanating from the rigidity of a highly centralized system.
2. Problems relating to the concentration of power in a highly centralized system.
3. Problems relating to the interaction of socialism with Chinese culture.

There is no doubt that since 1949, the leadership has made some serious errors in the conceptualization and execution of some of its policies. It could be argued that the leadership misinterpreted, or inappropriately applied, the socalist model in the Chinese context. Even in the early years of Communist Party rule, the blind application of the Soviet model of socialism resulted in serious disproportions and imbalances in the Chinese economy. The beauty of Mao "thought," as encapsulated in the Maoist developmental model, was supposed to be its creative application of Marxism-Leninism to Chinese conditions. Obviously it was not creative enough in a number of instances.

The difficulties of adopting socialism for China arise largely from the following:

1. The developmental variable. China lacks the necessary material basis and wealth to sustain a socialist system.
2. The cultural variable. Socialism reinforces those aspects of Chinese culture least supportive of the modernization process; or in apparent (but not actual) contradiction, many aspects of socialism are not quite suitable to the Chinese character, personality, traditions, habits, and customs.

In either case, the leadership was bound to face problems in implementing socialism in the context of Chinese culture. Failing to remold Chinese psychocultural characteristics, the leaders have faced the alternative of either remolding socialist doctrine to mesh better with Chinese culture, or dropping it. The problem in doing either was the leadership's desire to maintain its socialist credentials. Inevitably, this made it far more difficult to be bold and brutal in assessing orthodox socialist policies and values. In short, had the leadership from the beginning been less concerned about appearances, and really interpreted Marxism within the context of Chinese conditions, they might have discovered what was and was not useful in socialism.

Much of this ideological baggage has been jettisoned in the 1980s. Spurred on by the economic results of policies that deviated from their earlier understanding of what socialism had to look like in practice, China's leadership seriously challenged a rigid interpretation of the Marxist-Leninist classics. Party authorities referred to no less an authority than Lenin himself to stress that Marxism was to be interpreted "creatively," and that Marx's theory was in no sense "inviolable." To the contrary, Marxism only laid the basis for socialism, which then had to be developed in whatever direction was necessary to keep pace with the changing times.[7] Further, what counts is *results*, not the blind application of theory. Marxism, as the Chinese have often said, is not a dogma but a guide to action.

> [T]he standard for judging whether an economic policy or a management system is correct does not rest on whether this policy or system has been mentioned in a book, but on whether this policy or system can promote the development of the productive forces.[8]

In fact, a rigidly planned economy could be seen as a "typical example of oversimplification and dogmatization of Marxism." Market forces and encouraging people to "get rich" actually help revitalize communism, and many things in capitalism remain useful to building the foundations of communism.[9]

The *People's Daily* Commentator (the authoritative voice of the Chinese Communist Party), stunned the world by announcing on December 7, 1984, that the works of Marx, Engels, and Lenin, written in some cases over a hundred years ago, could not be expected to provide solutions to China's current problems (or at least not to *all* of its problems, as noted in the following day's correction to this article). By the 1980s, if not long before, Marx's ideas were hopelessly out of date because conditions had changed greatly since he wrote, and many of his ideas had only been tentatively proposed. Further, the classic works of communism did not deal with "the process" of building communism. The only way to solve economic problems was to investigate reality and to see what kinds of policies worked, not simply to espouse a theory.[10] In short, China's reform leaders (though not without considerable opposition from other more "conservative" leaders) have done much in the 1980s to reinterpret the fundamental Communist theories that they had relied on (as dogma) for the first thirty years of Communist Party rule.

Finally, the possibility should not be dismissed that the concern for the integrity of Marxism-Leninism masks an effort to protect Chinese culture. Regardless of how the propaganda apparatus conceptualizes it, the anxiety over "spiritual pollution" and "bourgeois liberalization" may also be an anxiety about protecting Chinese culture.

Yet, as the legitimizing force for the power of the Party and the state, the importance of socialism as ideology has had no equal. Without it, the Party could not lay claim to being a repository of absolute truth, and would therefore lack a legitimate claim to an unchallenged right to rule. Indeed, the leadership's successes in addressing China's problems, although considerable, have not by themselves been adequate to legitimate continued and unchallenged Communist Party rule.

The decade of the 1980s may, in fact, prove to have been a turning point for just this reason: As the leadership could point to more and more successes in resolving some of its most fundamental problems, ideology diminished in its significance as a legitimizing force. Development and modernization brought their own problems, but the solutions to these problems were found outside the realm of orthodox Communist doctrine.

SOCIALISM AS DEVELOPMENT

Underdevelopment and poverty have affected the resolution of almost every problem in China by limiting economic options and forcing the leadership to make unhappy choices as to who will benefit from the allocation of scarce resources. Inadequate economic resources have also affected the realm of power and policy; for without the alternative of an economic solution, political solutions and social engineering became the primary means to address problems in post-1949 China.[11] Political power and the allocation of political power are, in any event, far more important in a society that lacks adequate material wealth. As the preceding chapters suggest, the problems to which poverty contributed went beyond the processes for allocating scarce economic resources, material incentives, and the overall distribution of wealth, to influence such issues as the development of an educational system, leadership recruitment, China's foreign relations, and military development.

All policies since 1949 have tried to merge developmental with socialist values; but when they were in tension, leftists favored socialist values at the expense of developmental ones; and rightists or pragmatists favored developmental values at the expense of promoting socialist values in the short run. In addition, the leftists were more inclined to change policies to conform to a rather rigid interpretation of an ideological ideal, whereas the more pragmatic leaders were willing to redefine the ideology to rationalize policies that would achieve the desired results.

The Maoist view of development, which largely controlled developmental strategies from 1949 to 1979, was not to "modernize" as such, but to move China, including all of its values, institutions, and structures, toward socialism. By implementing socialism, and finally communism, China could *create* the wealth necessary for maintaining communism and for modernizing. Socialist values, institutions, and structures were not, therefore, necessarily modern values and structures. Socialism was the means and the end, modernization only the presumed after-effect of attaining communism. Thus, the debate of the first three decades of Communist rule focused on the question of how to transform socialist values into policies in order to develop toward higher stages of socialism, not how to develop toward becoming a modern society. As such, the primary values of the Maoist strategy were egalitarianism, self-reliance, heavy industrialization, ever-larger state and collectively owned units, and the end of class exploitation.

When the reformers gained control over the leadership in late 1978, the rationale for moving "backward" to capitalism was to create an adequate material basis for socialism. The development of China's "material civilization" had to accompany the development of its "spiritual civilization" (the creation of a higher level of socialist political culture and the new socialist person). Socialism as ideology would not alone be able to fend off the forces that opposed socialism. Regardless of the repeated pauses and even reversals of the economic and political reforms initiated in December 1978, the trend toward further decentralization and liberalization of the economy, and the opening up of China's economy to the outside world have never really been completely halted. In spite of opposition both from the "leftists" outside the leadership, and then from the more "conservative" wing within the leadership itself, the more "radical" reformers who have supported Deng Xiaoping's policies have basically maintained their control over the reins of power.

Of all the reversals and counterreversals since 1978, perhaps the most stunning example of the staying power of the Deng reformers was their ability to respond to the attacks on their policies as both cause and effect of "bourgeois liberalization" (perpetrating ideas of "absolute freedom," individual liberty, a multiparty system, and parliamentarianism) in late 1986 and early 1987, attacks that resulted in the removal of key protagonists of liberalizing policies, such as Hu Yaobang. Their counterattack suggested that the only way to stop "bourgeois liberalization" was to push even harder for political and economic reforms while at least giving lip service to the "four basic principles." Deng Xiaoping and then-Premier Zhao insisted that until socialism could display its superiority over capitalism by producing wealth, which it had thus far failed to do, the people would consider "bourgeois liberalization" and complete Westernization as attractive alternatives.

> To build a socialism which is superior to capitalism, first we must build a socialism which is free from poverty. At present, we are still practising socialism, but only when we have reached the level of medium developed countries in the middle of the next century will we be able to declare that our socialism is superior to capitalism and that we are practising genuine socialism.[12]

Further, the focus of the Maoist model of development on the dialectical relationship between class struggle and building socialism was replaced by the reformers' focus on the dialectic between *political reform* and economic development: Political reforms were the essential underpinnings for economic development.[13] Without them, socialism would again be challenged by "bourgeois liberalization." Although Deng spoke of "democratizing" China through political reforms, he never had in mind a Western-style democracy. His concern was with democratizing social relationships, leadership reform, and economic management, all for the purpose of improving the performance of the economy.

Finally, because neither Marx nor Lenin had addressed the problems of socialism as a model for development and had failed to foresee many of the problems that would challenge socialist systems in the second half of the twentieth century, the reformers came to view socialist dogma as inadequate for development. Most important, Marx and Lenin had not foreseen the possibility that the capitalist states could actually be reined into relationships of equality and, as equals, could aid in the development of socialist states through the transfer of technology, science, know-how, equipment, and capital. Liaisons with the capitalist states are, in the minds of the reformers, a possibility that China ignored to its own detriment in the past. Thus, China's open door policy is a crucial element for China's developmental strategy today.

The new meaning of socialism is, therefore, socialism as development, and this now includes the ideas of decentralization of decision making, decollectivization, private ownership, contractual responsibility, stock ownership, bankruptcy, free markets, democratization of economic management and the political leadership, material incentives, and the opening up of China to the international economy and foreign science and technology. Even more crucial, socialism means competition. Competition is socialist as long as the means of production are publicly owned. By arguing that competition is not an exclusively capitalist feature, the Chinese hope to stimulate greater productivity. This is in spite of the fact that competition can mean losing everything and going bankrupt as well as winning and making profits. Socialism as a developmental strategy has, then, been redefined to mean "whatever works," the ultimate pragmatic strategy.[14]

On the other hand, when the adequate "material civilization" that socialism needs in order to support itself is reached in the mid-twenty-first century, it is not at all evident that socialism will then exist in China: The very industrialization, modernization, and urbanization that reflect and contribute to the development of a wealthier society may also impede the implementation of socialism. Urbanization seems, in fact, to be a fragmenting force, one that tears societies apart instead of contributing to a greater collective consciousness.[15] The differences even within a society between attitudes and relationships in the countryside and those in the cities are suggestive of how alienating urbanization is. Apart from everything else, urban residents tend to rely on services provided by the cities, and they have less need than rural inhabitants to call upon their neighbors for assistance. Thus, although poverty may have made the attainment of socialism difficult, it is not at all certain that wealth will make it any easier.

Finally, the process of development or "modernization" (especially economic development defined as industrialization and technological development) dispels the extremes of ideological and cultural differences in *whatever* society it occurs. Hence, if modernization takes the course it has taken elsewhere, both Chinese culture and socialism will eventually become less important than China's developmental level in determining how China resolves its problems. And the meaning of socialism as a developmental strategy will assume a far greater importance than socialism as ideology.

CONCLUSION: THE MEANING OF SOCIALISM

Since 1949, China has moved along the road toward the "wealth and power" that China sought at the end of the nineteenth century in response to foreign threats. Their search took the course, first of overthrowing foreign (Manchu) rule and ridding China of foreigners, creating the institutions of Western-style republics, building a culture and society more compatible with democracy and a republic, and then redefining democracy to mean socialist democracy. Socialist democracy, in turn, required the implementation of a socialist model of development, one inspired by egalitarian and collectivistic impulses and based on the assumption of a Leninist centralized Party and state structure. The socialist model as implemented after 1949, however, proved incapable of enriching China as quickly as was necessary if socialism was to maintain its legitimacy.

After 1979, then, the Chinese responded to the intractable problems created by socialism's interaction with Chinese traditional culture and the conditions of poverty and underdevelopment by taking a new road to wealth and power. At this point in history, China's more "radical" reform leaders state that China is a poor country that has, since 1956, been in "the preliminary stage of socialism," the first of several stages before communism. During this stage, which will last for at least another thirty years, China must permit a "commodity economy" to flourish, develop the private sector, and encourage the growth of joint ventures and wholly foreign-owned enterprises in China. China must become much wealthier before it can progress to higher stages of socialism and, finally, to communism.[16]

As in the past, individuals within China's central leadership, its intellectuals, and its people wonder about the wisdom of this road. One thing seems clear: Considering that the per capita income of the peasantry has skyrocketed since 1979; that half of peasant income now comes from non-collective sources; that tens of thousands of Chinese have experienced firsthand through study or travel abroad the vibrancy of Western liberal democracy; that Western investment, technology, and science are indispensable if China wishes to advance more rapidly than in the past; and that the Chinese people have been exposed to the phenomenal successes enjoyed by other Chinese people living under non-Communist rule in Taiwan, Singapore, and Hong Kong, the dangers to Communist rule in the PRC of stepping back from economic liberalization and political reforms are at this time at least as great as moving forward with them.

Explaining the issues in the People's Republic of China in terms of development, culture, and ideology provides a far more accurate picture than does a simplistic totalitarian model. The interaction of these three variables permits us to merge historical, cultural, economic, political, and social factors, and to see from this just how rich is the mosaic that today is China.

What, then, is the meaning of socialism in China? As of the late 1980s, its meaning is still changing. The constant pressures to carry out reforms for the purpose of development generate tensions, which in turn force the leadership to reformulate socialist doctrine to address them. Since 1979, not even China's top Party leaders have been able to settle on a meaning for socialism that could last for more than a year. And certainly intellectuals and the ordinary people have different visions of what socialism means. For many of them, socialism is wealth, democracy, legality, and education; and the "four modernizations" that have become the core of today's socialist policies are, in their view, to enrich, to democratize, to legalize, and to raise the educational level.

The steady modification of socialism in the 1980s has centered on three major concerns:

1. Decreasing the "leftist" rigid ideological element in socialism, an interpretation that had put a premium on class struggle, political activism, redness, and egalitarianism;
2. Redistributing power among institutions and individuals in a way that undercuts the most detrimental "feudal" aspect of Chinese culture—the reliance upon networks of personal relationships, a culturally based practice that reinforces inegalitarianism;
3. Emphasizing the developmental purpose of socialism at the expense of socialism as ideology.

In the process of redefining socialism to emphasize development, some strands of traditional Chinese culture are jeopardized. But the more radical wing of the reform leadership thus far seems to believe that the "open door" to foreign investment, trade, science, and technology must be pursued in spite of this challenge to Chinese culture, and that policies to confront spiritual pollution and bourgeois liberalization will counteract the worst of foreign values that (in Deng Xiaoping's words), like so many insects, fly in through the open door. "Socialism with Chinese characteristics" now means anything that helps China modernize.

NOTES

[1]Gu Dehua, a 28-year-old tailor in Shanghai who earns about $70 per month, commenting on his becoming a Communist Party member while he retained his materialistic values. Quoted in article by Pico Iyer, "The Second Revolution," *Time* (September 23, 1985), p. 55.

[2]Editor quoting a Shanghai tailor, *People's Daily* (February 9, 1984).

[3]Deng Xiaoping, "Deng on Issues of World Interest" (Interview on September 2, 1986 with Michael Wallace, CBS), in *BR*, No. 38 (September 22, 1986), p. 6.

[4]For a summary of some of these viewpoints concerning the importance of the cultural variable, including those of Hanna Arendt, Raymond Meyers, Thomas Metzger, and Lucian Pye, see Chalmers Johnson, 'What's Wrong With Chinese Studies?" *Asian Survey*, No. 10 (October 1982), pp. 920–923.

[5]See Susan Shirk, *Competitive Comrades* (Berkeley: University of California Press, 1982), pp. 6–8.

[6]"Socialist Values," *BR*, No. 42 (October 19, 1981), p. 29.

[7]Commentator, "New Lenin Edition Provides Useful Lessons," *Hongqi*, in *CD* (September 28, 1984), p. 4.

[8]"The Way for Fujian," *BR*, No. 32 (August 9, 1982), p. 26.

[9]*People's Daily* (December 1984, and October 1984), as quoted by Christopher S. Wren, "Peking Reshaping Ideology to Fit New Economic Policy," *The New York Times* (December 17, 1984), p. A10.

[10]Commentator, "Theory and Practice," *People's Daily* (December 7, 1984), p. 1, translated in *JPRS* (December 7, 1984), pp. K1, K2.

[11]The frequent use of mass mobilization for economic tasks, reorganization of social and economic units, and class struggle campaigns provide good examples of this kind of alternative.

[12]"Zhao on Reform and Anti-Bourgeois Liberalization," *BR*, No. 29 (July 20, 1987), p. 14.

[13]This analysis is somewhat unfair, however, as the need for class struggle and the ending of class exploitation by redistributing property had already been resolved as issues by the Maoist model. Thus, it was easy for the reformers to move beyond the issue of class exploitation and claim that they were concerned with higher issues.

[14]According to some developmental theorists, Communist and non-Communist strategies for modernization are less and less distinct, since poor and underdeveloped countries, whatever their ideology, face similar conditions that seem to elicit similar policies. See, for example, John H. Kautsky, *Communism and the Politics of Development: Persistent Myths and Changing Behaviors* (New York: John Wiley, 1968), p. 5.

[15]B. Michael Frolic (York University) has done a considerable amount of (unpublished) work on this topic.

[16]Dai Yannian, "Preliminary Stage of Socialism," *BR*, No. 24 (June 15, 1987), p. 4.

BIBLIOGRAPHY

PERIODICALS AND NEWSPAPERS

Asian Survey
Asian Forum
Australian Journal of Chinese Affairs
Beijing Review
China Business Review
China Daily
Chinese Education
Chinese Law and Government
China News Analysis
China Quarterly
Far Eastern Economic Review
Faxue yanjiu (Legal Research)
Foreign Broadcasts Information Service (FBIS)
Guangming Daily (Guangming ribao)
Inside China Mainland (Taipei)
Joint Publications Research Service (JPRS)
Journal of Asian Studies
Minzhu yu fazhi (Democracy and the Legal System)
Modern China

The New York Times
The Washington Post
Pacific Affairs
Renmin ribao (People's Daily)
Social Sciences in China (Beijing)
Zhengfa yanjiu (The Study of Law)

CHINA'S HISTORY

CHANG, K. C., *The Archaeology of China*, 4th edition. New Haven: Conn.: Yale University Press, 1986.

CHANG KWANG-CHIH, *Shang Civilization*. New Haven, Conn.: Yale University Press, 1980.

CHEEK, TIMOTHY, "The Fading of Wild Lillies: Wang Shiwei and Mao Zedong's *Yen'an Talks* in the First CPC Rectification Movement," *The Australian Journal of Chinese Affairs*, No. 11 (1984), pp. 25–58.

CREEL, HERRLEE G., *The Birth of China: A Study of the Formative Period of Chinese Civilization*. New York: Frederick Ungar Publishing Co., 1937.

CHOW TSE-TSUNG, *The May Fourth Movement*. Stanford, Calif.: Stanford University Press, 1967.

EASTMAN, LLOYD E., *The Abortive Revolution: China Under Nationalist Rule, 1927–1937*. Cambridge, Mass.: Harvard University Press, 1974.

FAIRBANK, JOHN K. (ed.), *The Chinese World Order: Traditional China's Foreign Relations*. Cambridge, Mass.: Harvard University Press, 1968.

FRIEDMAN, EDWARD, *Backward Toward Revolution: The Chinese Revolutionary Party*. Published for the Center for Chinese Studies of the University of Michigan by Stanford University Press, 1974.

GRIEDER, JEROME B., *Hu Shih and the Chinese Renaissance*. Cambridge, Mass.: Harvard University Press, 1970.

HO PING-TI, *The Ladder of Success in Imperial China*. New York: John Wiley and Sons, 1964.

HUANG SUNG-K'ANG, *Lu Hsun and the New Culture Movement of Modern China*. Amsterdam: Djambatan, 1957.

LANG, OLGA, *Pa Chin and His Writings*. Cambridge, Mass.: Harvard University Press, 1967.

LEVENSON, JOSEPH R., *Liang Ch'i-ch'ao and the Mind of Modern China*. Berkeley: University of California Press, 1967.

MAO TSE-TUNG, *Selected Works*, Vols I–IV. Peking: Foreign Languages Press, 1965–1969.

MEISNER, MAURICE, *Li Ta-chao and the Origins of Chinese Marxism*. Cambridge, Mass.: Harvard University Press, 1968.

MUNRO, DONALD J., *The Concept of Man in Early China*. Stanford, Calif.: Stanford University Press, 1969.

NATHAN, ANDREW J., *Chinese Democracy*. New York: Alfred A. Knopf, 1985.

DEBARY, THEODORE (ed.), *Sources of Chinese Tradition*, Vols I and II. New York: Columbia University Press, 1964.

SCHURMANN, FRANZ, AND SCHELL, ORVILLE (eds.), *The China Reader: Imperial China*. New York: Vintage Books, 1967.

SCHWARTZ, BENJAMIN I., *Chinese Communism and the Rise of Mao*. Cambridge, Mass.: Harvard University Press, 1964.

SCHWARTZ, BENJAMIN I., *In Search of Wealth and Power: Yen Fu and the West*. New York: Harper & Row, 1968.

SHARMAN, LYON, *Sun Yat-sen: His Life and Its Meaning*. Stanford, Calif.: Stanford University Press, 1968.

SNOW, EDGAR, *Red Star Over China*. New York: Grove Press, 1973.

THAXTON, RALPH, *China Turned Rightside Up: Revolutionary Legitimacy in the Peasant World*. New Haven, Conn.: Yale University Press, 1983.

WHEATLEY, PAUL, *The Pivot of the Four Corners*. Chicago: Aldine Publishing Co., 1971.

WRIGHT, MARY CLABAUGH (ed.), *China in Revolution: The First Phase, 1900–1913*. New Haven, Conn.: Yale University Press, 1968.

THE CHINESE COMMUNISTS IN SEARCH OF THEIR GOALS, 1949 TO THE PRESENT

AHN, BYUNG-JOON, *Chinese Politics and the Cultural Revolution.* Seattle: University of Washington Press, 1976.

BAUM, RICHARD, *Prelude to Revolution: Mao, the Party and the Peasant Question 1962–1966.* New York: Columbia University Press, 1975.

BERNSTEIN, THOMAS P., *Up to the Mountains and Down to the Villages: The Transfer of Youth from Urban to Rural China.* New Haven, Conn.: Yale University Press, 1977.

BURNS, JOHN P., AND ROSEN, STANLEY (eds.), *Policy Conflicts in Post-Mao China: A Documentary Survey With Analysis.* Armonk, N.Y.: M. E. Sharpe, 1986.

BUSH, RICHARD C. (ed.), *China Briefing, 1982.* Boulder, Colo.: Westview Press, 1982.

CHENG NIEN, *Life and Death in Shanghai.* New York: Grove Press, 1986.

CROOK, ISABEL, AND CROOK, DAVID, *Revolution in a Chinese Village: Ten Mile Inn.* London: Routledge, 1959.

FROLIC, B. MICHAEL, *Mao's People.* Cambridge, Mass.: Harvard University Press, 1980.

GAO YUAN, WITH A FOREWORD BY WILLIAM A. JOSEPH, *Born Red: A Chronicle of the Cultural Revolution.* Stanford, Calif.: Stanford University Press, 1987.

GARDNER, JOHN, *Chinese Politics and the Succession to Mao.* New York: Holmes and Meier, 1982.

GARSIDE, ROGER, *Coming Alive: China After Mao.* New York: McGraw-Hill Book Co., 1981.

HINTON, WILLIAM, *Fanshen: A Documentary of Revolution in a Chinese Village.* New York: Vintage, 1966.

HINTON, WILLIAM, *Shenfan.* New York: Random House, 1983.

HOUN, FRANKLIN W., *A Short History of Chinese Communism.* Englewood Cliffs, N.J.: Prentice-Hall, 1967.

ISRAEL, JOHN, "The Red Guards in Historical Perspective: Continuity and Change in China's Youth Movement," in Lenard J. Cohen and Jane P. Shapiro (eds.), *Communist Systems in Comparative Perspective.* New York: Anchor Press, 1974, pp. 400–426.

LIU, ALAN P. L., *How China Is Ruled.* Englewood Cliffs, N.J.: Prentice-Hall, 1986.

MACFARQUHAR, RODERICK, *The Origins of the Cultural Revolution,* Vols. I and II. New York: Columbia University Press, 1974 and 1983, respectively.

MILTON, DAVID, MILTON, NANCY AND SCHURMANN, FRANZ (eds.), *The China Reader: People's China.* New York: Random House, 1974.

NEE, VICTOR, AND MOZINGO, DAVID (eds.), *State and Society in Contemporary China.* Ithaca, N.Y.: Cornell University Press, 1983.

SHUE, VIVIENNE, *Peasant China in Transition.* Berkeley: University of California Press, 1980.

THOMAS, HUGH (translator), *Comrade Editor: Letters to the People's Daily.* Hong Kong: Joint Publishing Company, 1980.

TOWNSEND, JAMES, *Politics in China,* 2nd edition. Boston: Little, Brown, 1980.

VOGEL, EZRA F., *Canton Under Communism.* New York: Harper & Row, 1969.

WANG, JAMES C. F., *Contemporary Chinese Politics: An Introduction,* 2nd edition. Englewood Cliffs, N.J.: Prentice-Hall, 1985.

YOUNG, GRAHAM, "Control and Style: Discipline Inspection Commissions Since the Eleventh Congress," *China Quarterly,* No. 97 (March 1984), pp. 24–52.

YUE DAIYUN, AND WAKEMAN, CAROLYN, *To the Storm.* Berkeley: University of California Press, 1986.

CLASS AND CLASS CONFLICT

DAHRENDORF, RALF, *Class and Class Conflict in Industrial Society.* Stanford, Calif.: Stanford University Press, 1959.

DJILAS, MILOVAN, *The New Class: An Analysis of the Communist System.* San Diego: Harcourt Brace Javanovich, 1982.

HINTON, WILLIAM, *Fanshen: A Documentary of Revolution in a Chinese Village.* New York: Vintage, 1966.

KRAUS, RICHARD C., *Class Conflict in Chinese Socialism.* New York: Columbia University Press, 1981.

LOEWI, MICHAEL, "The Order of Aristocratic Rank of Han China," *T'oung Pao*, Vol. 48, Nos. 1–3 (1960), pp. 97–174.

LOH, ROBERT (as told to Humphrey Evans), *Escape from Red China.* New York: Coward, McCann, 1962.

SCHRAM, STUART R., "Classes, Old and New, in Mao Zedong Thought, 1949–1976," in James L. Watson (ed.), *Class and Social Stratification in Post-Revolution China.* Cambridge, U.K.: Cambridge University Press, 1984.

WATSON, JAMES L. (ed.), *Class and Social Stratification in Post-Revolution China.* Cambridge, U.K.: Cambridge University Press, 1984.

DEMOCRACY AND POLITICAL PARTICIPATION

BLECHER, MARC, "Consensual Politics in Rural Chinese Communities: The Mass Line in Theory and Practice," *Modern China*, Vol. 5, No. 1 (January 1979), pp. 105–126.

BURNS, JOHN P., *Political Participation in Rural China.* Berkeley: University of California Press, forthcoming.

CHAN, ANITA, ROSEN, STANLEY, AND UNGER, JONATHAN (eds.), *On Socialist Democracy and the Chinese Legal System: The Li Yizhe Debates.* Armonk, N.Y.: M. E. Sharpe, 1985.

CHEN ERJIN, *China: Crossroad Socialism. An Unofficial Manifesto for Proletarian Democracy.* London: Verson Editions, 1984.

COOPER, JOHN F., MICHAEL, FRANZ, AND WU YUANLI, *Human Rights in Post-Mao China.* Boulder, Colo.: Westview, 1985.

CROIZIER, RALPH, "The Thorny Flowers of 1979: Political Cartoons and Liberalization in China," *Bulletin of Concerned Asian Scholars*, China Special, Part 2, Vol. 13, No. 3 (1981), pp. 50–59.

DEBARY, WILLIAM THEODORE, *The Liberal Tradition in China.* New York: Columbia University Press, 1983.

DITTMER, LOWELL, "China in 1980: Modernization and Its Discontents," *Asian Survey*, Vol. XXI, No. 1 (January 1981), pp. 31–50.

EDWARDS, RANDALL R., HENKIN, LOUIS, AND NATHAN, ANDREW J., *Human Rights in Contemporary China.* New York: Columbia University Press, 1986.

FALKENHEIM, VICTOR C. (ed.), *Citizens and Groups in Contemporary China.* Ann Arbor: Center for Chinese Studies, University of Michigan Press, 1987.

FALKENHEIM, VICTOR C., "Political Participation in China," *Problems of Communism*, Vol. XXVII (May–June 1978), pp. 18–32.

GOODMAN, DAVID S. G., *Beijing Street Voices: The Poetry and Politics of China's Democracy Movement.* London: Marion Boyars, 1981.

HUNTINGTON, SAMUEL, AND NELSON, JOAN M., *No Easy Choice: Political Participation in Developing Countries.* Cambridge, Mass.: Harvard University Press, 1976.

JIE JI, "Whoever Enjoys Democracy Must Obey Law," *Minzu yu fazhi (Democracy and the Legal System)*, No. 10 (October 1983).

McCORMICK, BARRETT L., "Leninist Implementation: The Election Campaign," in David M. Lampton (ed.), *Policy Implementation in Post-Mao China.* Berkeley: University of California Press, 1987, pp. 383–413.

MOODY, PETER R., *Opposition and Dissent in Contemporary China.* Stanford, Calif.: Hoover Institute, Stanford University Press, 1977.

NATHAN, ANDREW J., *Chinese Democracy.* New York: Alfred A. Knopf, 1985.

OKSENBERG, MICHEL, "Occupational Groups in Chinese Society and the Cultural Revolution," in Lenard J. Cohen and Jane P. Shapiro (eds.), *Communist Systems in Comparative Perspective.* New York: Anchor Press, 1974.

PYE, LUCIAN W., *The Spirit of Chinese Politics.* Cambridge, Mass.: The MIT Press, 1967.

QI XIN (ed.), *China's New Democracy.* Hong Kong: Cosmos Books Ltd., 1979.

ROSEN, STANLEY, "Guangzhou's Democracy Movement in Cultural Revolution Perspective," *China Quarterly*, No. 101 (March 1985), pp. 1–31.

SCHRAM, STUART (ed.), *Chairman Mao Talks to the People. Talks and Letters: 1945–1971*. New York: Pantheon Books, 1974.

SEYMOUR, JAMES D., *China's Satellite Parties*. Armonk, N.Y.: M.E. Sharpe, 1987.

SEYMOUR, JAMES D. (ed.), *The Fifth Modernization: China's Human Rights Movement, 1978–1979*. Stanfordville, N.Y.: Human Rights Publishing Group, 1981.

TOWNSEND, JAMES R., *Political Participation in Communist China*. Berkeley: University of California Press, 1969.

VERBA, SIDNEY, NIE, NORMAN H., AND KIM, JAE-ON, *Participation and Political Equality: A Seven Nation Comparison*. Cambridge, U.K.: Cambridge University Press, 1978.

WALDER, ANDREW, *Communist Neotraditionalism: Work and Authority in Chinese Industry*. Berkeley: University of California, 1986.

WHYTE, MARTIN KING, *Small Groups and Political Rituals in China*. Berkeley: University of California Press, 1974.

WOMACK, BRANTLY, "The 1980 County-Level Elections in China: Experiment in Democratic Modernization," *Asian Survey*, Vol. XXII, No. 3 (March 1982), pp. 261–277.

THE ECONOMY

CHAN, ANITA, AND UNGER, JONATHAN, "Grey and Black: The Hidden Economy of Rural China," *Pacific Affairs*, Vol. 55, No. 3 (Fall 1982), pp. 452–471.

CHANG, KING-YUH (ed.), *Perspectives on Development in Mainland China*. Boulder, Colo.: Westview Press, 1985.

China's Economy Looks Toward the Year 2000: Selected Papers. Selected Papers Submitted to the Joint Economic Committee, Congress of the United States. Washington D.C.: Government Printing Office, 1986.

CHOSSUDOVSKY, MICHAEL, *Toward Capitalist Restoration? Chinese Socialism After Mao*. New York: St. Martin's Press, 1986.

CHOW, GREGORY C., *The Chinese Economy*. New York: Harper & Row, 1985.

ECKSTEIN, ALEXANDER, *China's Economic Revolution*. Cambridge, U.K.: Cambridge University Press, 1977.

FROLIC, B. MICHAEL, "Reflections on the Chinese Model of Development," *Social Forces*, Vol. 57, No. 2 (December 1978), pp. 384–417.

HAGEN, EVERETT E., *On the Theory of Social Change: How Economic Growth Begins*. Cambridge, Mass.: The MIT Press, 1962.

IMAI HIROYUKI, "China's New Banking System: Changes in Monetary Management," *Pacific Affairs*, Vol. 58, No. 3 (Fall 1985), pp. 451–472;

JIANG YIWEI, "The Theory of An Enterprise-Based Economy," *Social Sciences in China*, No. 1 (March 1980), pp. 48–70.

JOHNSON, CHRISTOPHER, "Economic Reform in China," *The World Today* (March 1985).

JOHNSON, GRAHAM E., "The Production Responsibility System in Chinese Agriculture: Some Examples from Guangdong," *Pacific Affairs*, Vol. 55, No. 3 (Fall 1982), pp. 430–451.

KAUTSKY, JOHN H., *Communism and the Politics of Development: Persistent Myths and Changing Behaviors*. New York: John Wiley, 1968.

LARDY, NICHOLAS R., *Agriculture in China's Modern Economic Development*. Cambridge, U.K.: Cambridge University Press, 1983.

LARDY, NICHOLAS R., "Consumption and Living Standards in China, 1978–83," in *China Quarterly*, No. 100 (December 1984), pp. 849–865.

LIN, CYRIL CHIHREN, "The Reinstatement of Economics in China Today," *China Quarterly*, No. 85 (March 1981), pp. 1–48.

LYONS, THOMAS P., *Economic Integration and Planning in Maoist China*. New York: Columbia University Press, 1987.

O'LEARY, GREGORY, AND WATSON, ANDREW, "The Production Responsibility System and the Future of Collective Farming," *Australian Journal of Chinese Affairs*, No. 8 (1982), pp. 1–34.

MARUYAMA NOBUO, "The Mechanism of China's Industrial Development—Background to the Shift in Development Strategy," *The Development Economies* (Tokyo), Vol. XX, No. 4 (December 1982), pp. 437–471.

NAUGHTON, BARRY, "The Decline of Central Control Over Investment in Post-Mao China," in David M. Lampton (ed.), *Policy Implementation in Post-Mao China*, Berkeley: University of California Press, 1987, pp. 51–80.

OI, JEAN C., "Commercializing China's Rural Cadres," *Problems of Communism* (September–October 1986), pp. 1–15.

OI, JEAN C., "Peasant Households Between Plan and Market," *Modern China*, Vol. 12, No. 2 (April 1986), pp. 230–251.

OI, JEAN C., "Peasant Grain Marketing and State Procurement: China's Grain Contracting System," *China Quarterly*, No. 106 (June 1986), pp. 272–290.

ROZMAN, GILBERT (ed.), *The Modernization of China*. New York: Free Press, 1981.

SKINNER, G. WILLIAM, "Rural Marketing in China: Repression and Revival," *China Quarterly*, No. 103 (September 1985), pp. 393–413.

SOLINGER, DOROTHY J., *Chinese Business Under Socialism: The Politics of Domestic Commerce, 1949–1980*. Berkeley: University of California Press, 1984.

STAVIS, BENEDICT, AND MEISNER, MAURICE (Guest Editors), "China's Cropping System Debate," *Chinese Economic Studies* (Winter 1981–1982), pp. 7–24.

WALTER, CARL E., "Dual Leadership and the 1956 Credit Reforms of the Bank of China," *China Quarterly*, No. 102 (June 1985), pp. 277–290.

WEIL, MARTIN, "Tightening Up," *The China Business Review* (May–June 1982), pp. 32–35.

WONG, CHRISTINE, "The Second Phase of Economic Reform in China," *Current History* (September 1985), pp. 260–263, 278.

XUE MUQIAO (ed.), *Almanac of China's Economy, 1981*. Hong Kong: Modern Cultural Company, Ltd., 1982.

ZWEIG, DAVID, AND BUTLER, STEVEN, *China's Agricultural Reform: Background and Prospects.* (Booklet.) New York: China Council of the Asia Society, 1985.

ZWEIG, DAVID, "Context and Content in Policy Implementation: Household Contracts and Decollectivization, 1977–1983," in David M. Lampton (ed.), *Policy Implementation in Post-Mao China* Berkeley: University of California Press, 1987, pp. 255–283.

ZWEIG, DAVID, "Prosperity and Conflict in Post-Mao Rural China," *China Quarterly*, No. 105 (March 1986), pp. 1–18.

EDUCATION, INTELLECTUALS, AND SOCIALIST POLITICAL CULTURE

BARME, GEREMIE, AND MINFORD, JOHN (eds), *Seeds of Fire: Chinese Voices of Conscience*. Hong Kong: Far Eastern Economic Review, Ltd., 1986.

BASTID, MARIANNE, "Chinese Educational Policies in the 1980's and Economic Development," *China Quarterly*, No. 98 (June 1984).

CHAN, ANITA, "Images of China's Social Structure: The Changing Perspective of Canton Students," *World Politics*, Vol. XXXIV, No. 3 (April 1982).

CHAN, ANITA, *Children of Mao: Personality Development and Political Activism in the Red Guard Generation*. Seattle: University of Washington, 1985.

CHANG, ARNOLD, *Painting in the People's Republic of China: The Politics of Style*. Boulder, Colo.: Westview Press, 1980.

CLARKE, DONALD C., "Political Power and Authority in Recent Chinese Literature," *China Quarterly*, No. 102 (June 1985), pp. 234–252.

CLEVERLY, JOHN, *The Schooling of China*. Boston: George Allen and Unwin, 1985.

DUKE, MICHAEL S., *Blooming and Contending: Chinese Literature in the Post-Mao Era*. Bloomington: Indiana University Press, 1985.

DUKE, MICHAEL S. (ed.), *Contemporary Chinese Literature: An Anthology of Post-Mao Fiction and Poetry*. Published for the Bulletin of Concerned Asian Scholars. Armonk, N.Y.: M. E. Sharpe, 1985.

EBON, MARTIN (ed.), *Five Chinese Communist Plays*. New York: John Day Co., 1975.

GOLD, THOMAS, "Back to the City: The Return of Shanghai's Educated Youth," *China Quarterly*, No. 84 (December 1980), pp. 755–770.

GOLDBLATT, HOWARD (ed.), *Chinese Literature for the 1980s: The Fourth Congress of Writers and Artists.* Armonk, N.Y.: M. E. Sharpe, 1982.

GOLDMAN, MERLE, *China's Intellectuals: Advise and Dissent.* Cambridge, Mass.: Harvard University Press, 1981.

HAMRIN, CAROL, AND CHEEK, TIMOTHY (eds.), *China's Establishment Intellectuals.* Armonk, N.Y.: M. E. Sharpe, 1986.

HAYHOE, RUTH (ed.), *Contemporary Chinese Education.* Armonk, N.Y.: M. E. Sharpe, 1984.

HOLMES, BRIAN, "A Comparativist's View of Chinese Education," in Ruth Hayhoe (ed.), *Contemporary Chinese Education.* Armonk, N.Y.: M. E. Sharpe, 1984, pp. 7–25.

JIANG YIWEI, "The Theory of an Enterprise-Based Economy," *Social Sciences in China* (Beijing), No. 1 (March 1980).

KWONG, JULIA, "Is Everyone Equal Before the System of Grades: Social Background and Opportunities in China," *The British Journal of Sociology*, Vol. 34, No. 1 (March 1983), pp. 93–108.

LIANG HENG, AND SHAPIRO, JUDITH, *Intellectual Freedom in China: An Update.* A Report of Asia Watch Committee. New York: The Fund for Free Expression, July 1985.

LINK, PERRY (ed.), *People or Monsters? Liu Binyan.* Bloomington: Indiana University Press, 1983.

McCORMICK, ROBERT, "The Radio and Television Universities and the Development of Higher Education in China," *China Quarterly*, No. 105 (March 1986), pp. 72–94.

OGDEN, SUZANNE, "China's Social Sciences: Prospects for Teaching and Research in the 1980's," *Asian Survey*, Vol. XXII, No. 7 (July 1982), pp. 581–608.

OGDEN, SUZANNE, "Higher Education in the People's Republic of China: New Directions in the 1980's," *Higher Education*, Vol. II (January 1982), pp. 85–109.

OGDEN, SUZANNE, "The Politics of Higher Education in the PRC," *Chinese Law and Governemnt* (Summer 1982), pp. 4–23.

McDOUGALL, BONNIE S. (ed.), *Popular Chinese Literature and Performing Arts in the People's Republic of China, 1949–1979.* Berkeley: University of California Press, 1984.

McDOUGALL, BONNIE S., "Preface," *Mao Zedong's "Talks at the Yen'an Conference on Literature and Art".* Center for Chinese Studies, Ann Arbor: University of Michigan Press, 1980.

PEPPER, SUZANNE, "China's Universities," *Modern China*, Vol. 8, No. 2, (April 1982), pp. 147–204.

ROSEN, STANLEY, "Obstacles to Re-education Reform in China," *Modern China*, Vol. 8, No. 1 (January 1982), pp. 3–40.

ROSEN, STANLEY, "Recentralization, Decentralization, and Rationalization: Deng Xiaoping's Bifurcated Educational Policy," *Modern China*, Vol. 11, No. 3 (July 1985), pp. 301–346.

ROSEN, STANLEY, "Restoring Key Secondary Schools in Post-Mao China: The Politics of Competition and Educational Quality," in David M. Lampton (ed.), *Policy Implementation in Post-Mao China.* Berkeley: University of California Press, 1987, pp. 321–353.

Seven Contemporary Chinese Women Writers. Beijing: Panda Books, Chinese Literature, 1982.

SHIRK, SUSAN L. *Competitive Comrades: Career Incentives and Student Strategies in China.* Berkeley: University of California Press, 1982.

SOLOMON, RICHARD H., *Mao's Revolution and the Chinese Political Culture.* Berkeley: University of California Press, 1971.

THURSTON, ANN F., "Victims of China's Cultural Revolution: The Invisible Wounds," Parts I and II, in *Pacific Affairs*, Vol. 57, No. 4 (Winter 1984–1985), pp. 599–620; and Vol. 58, No. 1 (Spring 1985), pp. 5–27.

UNGER, JONATHAN, "Bending the School Ladder: The Failure of Chinese Educational Reform in the 1960's," *Comparative Education Review*, Vol. 24, No. 2, Part I (1980), pp. 221–237.

UNGER, JONATHAN, *Education under Mao: Class and Competition in Canton Schools, 1960–1980.* New York: Comumbia University Press, 1982.

WHITE, GORDON, *Party and Professionals: The Political Role of Teachers in Contemporary China.* Armonk, N.Y.: M. E. Sharpe, 1981.

YU SHIAO-LING, "Voice of Protest: Political Poetry in the Post-Mao Era," *China Quarterly*, No. 96 (December 1983), pp. 703–719.

ZHANG JIE, *Love Must Not Be Forgotten.* Beijing: Panda Books, and San Francisco: China Books and Periodicals, 1986.

IDEOLOGY AND POLITICAL THOUGHT

CHEN, JEROME (ed.), *Mao Papers*. London: Oxford University Press, 1970.
CHI HSIN, *The Case of the Gang of Four*. Hong Kong: Cosmos Books, 1978.
DENG XIAOPING, *The Selected Works of Deng Xiaoping, 1975–1982*. Beijing: Foreign Languages Press, 1983.
FREMANTLE, ANNE (ed.), *Mao Tse-tung: An Anthology of His Writings*. New York: Mentor Books, 1962.
GINSBURGS, GEORGE, "Soviet Critique of the Maoist Political Model," in James C. Hsiung (ed.), *The Logic of "Maoism."* New York: Praeger Publishers, 1974, pp. 137–162.
KAU, MICHAEL YING-MAO, AND LEUNG, JOHN (eds.), *The Writings of Mao Zedong, 1949–1976*, Vol. I. Armonk, N.Y.: M. E. Sharpe, 1986.
JOSEPH, WILLIAM, *The Critique of Ultraleftism in China, 1958–1981*. Stanford, Calif.: Stanford University Press, 1984.
LENIN, V. I., *Selected Works*, Vol. II. Moscow: Foreign Languages Publishing House, 1952.
MAO TSE-TUNG, *Selected Works*, Vols I–IV. Beijing: Foreign Languages Press, 1965–1969.
MEISNER, MAURICE (ed.), *Marxism, Maoism, and Utopianism*. Madison: University of Wisconsin Press, 1982.
Quotations from Chairman Mao Tse-tung, 2nd edition (With a Foreword by Lin Biao). Peking: Foreign Languages Press, 1967.
SCHRAM, STUART, *Chairman Mao Talks to the People. Talks and Letters: 1956–1971*. New York: Pantheon Books, 1974.
SCHRAM, STUART, *The Political Thought of Mao Tse-tung*. New York: Praeger Publishers, 1969.
SCHURMANN, FRANZ, *Ideology and Organization in Communist China*. Berkeley: University of California Press, 1966.
SU SHAOZHI, WU DAKUN, RU XIN, AND CHENG RENQIAN, *Marxism in China*. Nottingham, U.K.: Spokesman, 1983.

LEGALITY, DEVIANCE, AND SOCIAL CONTROL

ALLEN, PAUL A., AND PALAY, MARC S., "China Law: Economic Courts," *The China Business Review* (November–December 1981), pp. 44–48.
BENNETT, GORDON A., "China's Mass Campaign and Social Control," in Wilson, Amy, Greenblatt, Sidney L., and Wilson, Richard (eds.), *Deviance and Social Control in Chinese Society*. New York: Praeger Special Studies, 1977.
BENNETT, GORDON, *Yundong: Mass Campaigns in Chinese Communist Leadership*. Berkeley: University of California Press, 1976.
BONAVIA, DAVID, *Verdict in Peking: The Trial of the Gang of Four*. London: Burnett Books, 1984.
CELL, CHARLES P., *Revolution at Work: Mobilization Campaigns in China*. New York: Academic Press, 1977.
CHIU HUNGDAH, "China's Legal Reforms," *Current History* (September 1985), pp. 268–271, 275–276.
CLARKE, DONALD C., "Concepts of Law in the Chinese Anti-Crime Campaign," *Harvard Law Review*, Vol. 98, No. 8 (June 1985), pp. 1890–1908.
COHEN, JEROME ALAN, "China's Changing Constitution," *China Quarterly* (December 1978), pp. 794–841.
COHEN, JEROME ALAN, "Chinese Mediation on the Eve of Modernization," *California Law Review*, Vol. 54 (1966).
COHEN, JEROME ALAN, *The Criminal Process in the People's Republic of China 1949–1963*. Cambridge, Mass.: Harvard University Press, 1968.
COHEN, JEROME ALAN, GELATT, TIMOTHY A., LI, FLORENCE (translators) "Chinese Criminal Code Symposium" (which includes a "Foreword" by Cohen, and translations of China's Criminal Law and Criminal Procedure Law), *Journal of Criminal Law and Criminology*, Vol. 73, No. 1 (1982), pp. 135–203.

COHEN, JEROME ALAN, "Will China Have a Formal Legal System?" *American Bar Association Journal*, Vol. 64, (October 1978), pp. 1510–1515.

FALKENHEIM, VICTOR, "Autonomy and Control in Chinese Organization: Dilemmas of Rural Administrative Reform," in Sidney Greenblatt, Richard Wilson, and Amy Wilson (eds.), *Organizational Behavior in Chinese Society*. New York: Praeger Special Studies, 1981, pp. 190–208.

FELKENES, GEORGE T., "Criminal Justice in the People's Republic of China: A System of Contradictions," *Judicature*, Vol. 69 (April–May 1986).

FOREIGN LANGUAGES PRESS, *China: Facts and Figures, the Legal System*. (Pamphlet.) Beijing: Foreign Languages Press, 1982.

FYFIELD, T. A., *Re-educating Chinese Anti-Communists*. New York: St. Martin's Press, 1982.

GELATT, TIMOTHY A., AND SYNDER, FREDERICK E., "Legal Education in China: Training for a New Era," *China Law Reporter*, Vol. 1, No. 2 (Fall 1980), pp. 41–60.

GREENBLATT, SIDNEY L., "Campaigns and the Manufacture of Deviance," in Amy A. Wilson, Sidney L. Greenblatt, and Richard W. Wilson (eds.), *Deviance and Social Control in Chinese Society*. New York: Praeger Special Studies, 1977, pp. 82–120.

LENG SHAO-CHUAN, "The Chinese Judicial System: A New Direction," in Sidney L. Greenblatt, Richard W. Wilson, and Amy A. Wilson (eds.), *Organizational Behavior in Chinese Society* New York: Praeger Special Studies, 1981, pp. 112–133.

LENG SHAO-CHUAN, *Justice in Communist China*. Dobbs Ferry, N.Y.: Oceana, 1967.

LUBMAN, STANLEY, "Mao and Mediation," *California Law Review*, Vol. 55 (1967), pp. 1284–1300.

LUBMAN, STANLEY, AND WAJNOWSKI, GREGORY C., "Criminal Justice and the Foreigner," *The China Business Review* (November–December 1985), pp. 27–30.

NEE, OWEN D., CHU, FRANKLIN D., AND MOSER, MICHAEL J. (eds.), *Commercial, Business and Trade Laws, The People's Republic of China*. Dobbs Ferry, N.Y.: Oceana 1982.

OGDEN, SUZANNE, "China and International Law: Implications for Foreign Policy," *Pacific Affairs*, Vol. 49, No. 1 (Spring 1976), pp. 24–48.

SKINNER, G. WILLIAM, AND WINCKLER, EDWARD A., "Compliance Succession in Rural Communist China: A Cyclical Theory," in Amitai Etzioni (ed.), *A Sociological Reader on Complex Organizations*, 2nd edition. New York: Holt, Rinehart & Winston, 1969, pp. 410–438.

WHITE, LYNN T., III, "Deviance, Modernization, Rations, and Household Registers in Urban China," in Amy A. Wilson, Sidney L. Greenblatt, and Richard W. Wilson (eds.), *Deviance and Social Control in Chinese Society*. New York: Praeger Special Studies, 1977, pp. 151–172.

WILSON, AMY A., GREENBLATT, SIDNEY L., AND WILSON, RICHARD W. (eds), *Deviance and Social Control in Chinese Society*. New York: Praeger Special Studies, 1977.

THE PARTY AND STATE STRUCTURE AND LEADERSHIP

BARNETT, A. DOAK, *Cadres, Bureaucracy and Political Power in Communist China*, with a contribution by Ezra Vogel. New York: Columbia University Press, 1967.

BURNS, JOHN P., "Local Cadre Accommodation to the 'Responsibility System,' in Rural China," *Pacific Affairs*, Vol. 58, No. 4, pp. 607–625.

BURNS, JOHN P., AND ROSEN, STANLEY (eds.), *Policy Conflicts in Post-Mao China*. Armonk, N.Y.: M. E. Sharpe, 1986.

CHANG, PARRIS H., "The Last Stand of Deng's Revolution," *Journal of Northeast Asian Studies*, Vol. I, No. 2 (June 1982), pp. 3–20.

DENG XIAOPING, *The Selected Works of Deng Xiaoping, 1975–1982*. Beijing: Foreign Language Press, 1983.

DITTMER, LOWELL, *Liu Shao-ch'i and the Chinese Cultural Revolution*. Berkeley: University of California Press, 1974.

FONTANA, DOROTHY, "Background to the Fall of Hua Guofeng," *Asian Survey*, Vol. XXII, No. 3 (March 1982), pp. 237–260.

GOODMAN, DAVID S. G., "The National CCP Conference of September 1985 and China's Leadership Changes," *China Quarterly*, No. 105 (March 1986), pp. 123–130.

HARDING, HARRY, *Organizing China: The Problem of Bureaucracy, 1949–1976*. Stanford, Calif.: Stanford University Press, 1981.

JOSEPH, WILLIAM A., "The Dilemma of Political Reform in China," *Current History* (September 1985).

KAU, MICHAEL YINGMAO (ed.), *The Lin Biao Affair: Power, Politics and Military Coup*. White Plains, New York: International Arts and Sciences Press, 1975.

KAU, MICHAEL YINGMAO (ed.), "The Case Against Lin Biao," *Chinese Law and Government*, Vol. V, Nos. 3, 4 (Fall/Winter 1972–73).

LIEBERTHAL, KENNETH, "The Future of Reform in China," *AEI Foreign Policy and Defense Review*, Vol. 6, No. 3 (1986), pp. 3–10.

MADSEN, RICHARD, *Morality and Power in a Chinese Village*. Berkeley: University of California Press, 1984.

MAO TSE-TUNG, *Selected Works*, Vols. I–IV. Beijing: Foreign Languages Press, 1965–1969.

MARTIN, ROBERTA, *Party Recruitment in China: Patterns and Prospects. A Study of the Recruitment Campaign of 1954–1956 and Its Impact on Party Expansion Through 1980*. Occasional Papers of the East Asian Institute, Columbia University, N.Y., 1981.

MANION, MELANIE, "The Cadre Management System, Post-Mao: The Appointment, Promotion, Transfer, and Removal of Party and State Leaders," *China Quarterly*, No. 102 (June 1985), pp. 203–233.

MILLER, LYMAN H., "China's Administrative Revolution," *Current History* (September 1983), pp. 270–274.

MOODY, PETER R., JR., "Political Liberalization in China: A Struggle Between Two Lines," *Pacific Affairs*, Vol. 57, No. 1 (Spring 1984), pp. 26–44.

NG-QUINN, MICHAEL, "Deng Xiaoping's Political Reform and Political Order," *Asian Survey*, Vol. XXII, No. 12 (December 1982), pp. 1187–1205.

PERROLLE, PIERRE M. (ed.), *Fundamentals of the Chinese Communist Party*. White Plains, N.Y.: International Arts and Sciences Press, 1976.

PYE, LUCIAN, *The Dynamics of Chinese Politics*. Cambridge, U.K.: Oelgeschlager, Gunn & Hain, Publishers, 1981.

ROSEN, STANLEY, "Prosperity, Privatization and China's Youth," *Problems of Communism* (March–April 1985), pp. 1–28.

SCHURMANN, FRANZ, *Ideology and Organization in Communist China*, 2nd edition. Berkeley: University of California Press, 1968.

TERRILL, ROSS, *Mao: A Biography*. New York: Harper & Row, 1980.

TEIWES, FREDERICK C., *Leadership, Legitimacy, and Conflict in China*. Armonk, N.Y.: M. E. Sharpe, 1984.

WILSON, DICK, *The People's Emperor: Mao*. New York: Doubleday, 1980.

WITKE, ROXANE, *Comrade Chiang Ch'ing*. Boston: Little, Brown, 1977.

YAO MING-LE, *The Conspiracy and Death of Lin Biao*. New York: Alfred A. Knopf, 1983.

YOUNG, GRAHAM, "Control and Style: Discipline Inspection Commissions Since the 11th Congress," *China Quarterly*, No. 97 (March 1984), pp. 24–32.

SOCIAL STRUCTURE AND SOCIAL ISSUES

BLOCH, MARC L. B., *Feudal Society*, Vol. I (translated by L. A. Manyon). Chicago: University of Chicago Press, 1961.

CHAN, ANITA, MADSEN, RICHARD, AND UNGER, JONATHAN, *Chen Village*. Berkeley: University of California Press, 1984.

CHANCE, NORMAN A., *China's Urban Villages: Life in a Beijing Commune*. New York: Holt, Rinehart & Winston, 1984.

CROLL, ELISABETH, *The Family Rice Bowl: Food and the Domestic Economy in China*. Geneva: United Nations Research Institute for Social Development, 1982.

CROLL, ELISABETH, *Feminism and Socialism in China*. London: Routledge & Kegan Paul, 1978.

CROLL, ELISABETH, *Food Supply and the Nutritional Status of Children*. Geneva: United Nations Research Institute for Social Development, 1986.

CROLL, ELISABETH, *Chinese Women Since Mao*. London: Zed Books, Ltd., 1983.

CROLL, ELISABETH, *The Politics of Marriage in Contemporary China.* Cambridge, U.K.: Cambridge University Press, 1981.
CROLL, ELISABETH, DAVIN, DELIA, AND KANE, PENNY (eds.), *China's One-Child Family Policy.* London: The MacMillan Press, 1985.
DAVIS-FRIEDMANN, DEBORAH, *Long Lives: Chinese Elderly and the Communist Revolution.* Cambridge, Mass.: Harvard University Press, 1983.
DIXON, JOHN, *The Chinese Welfare System, 1949–1979.* New York: Praeger Special Studies, 1981.
GU HUA, *A Small Town Named Hibiscus* (translated by Gladys Yang). Beijing: Chinese Literature, Panda Books, 1983.
LEVY, MARION, *Modernization and the Structure of Societies.* Princeton, N.J.: Princeton University Press, 1966.
PARISH, WILLIAM L., AND WHYTE, MARTIN KING, *Village and Family in Contemporary China.* Chicago: University of Chicago Press, 1978.
PERRY, ELIZABETH J., "Rural Violence in Socialist China," *China Quarterly,* No. 103 (September 1985), pp. 414–440.
POPULATION CENSUS OFFICE AND DEPARTMENT OF POPULAR STATISTICS, STATE STATISTICAL BUREAU, PRC, *A Census of One Billion People: Papers for International Seminar on China's 1982 Population Census.* Boulder, Colo.: Westview Press, 1986.
ROSENTHAL, MARILYN M., *Health Care in the People's Republic of China.* Boulder, Colo.: Westview Press, 1987.
WHYTE, MARTIN KING, AND PARISH, WILLIAM L., *Urban Life in Contemporary China.* Chicago: University of Chicago Press, 1984.
WILSON, RICHARD, WILSON, AMY, AND GREENBLATT, SIDNEY (eds.), *Value Change in Chinese Society.* New York: Praeger Special Studies, 1979.
WOLF, MARGERY, *Revolution Postponed: Women in Contemporary China.* Stanford, Calif.: Stanford University Press, 1985.

SCIENCE AND TECHNOLOGY

LUBMAN, STANLEY B., "Technology Transfer in China: Policies, Practice and Law," *China's Economy Looks toward the Year 2000: Selected Papers Submitted to the Joint Economic Committee of the United States.* Washington, D.C.: U.S. Government Printing Office, 1986.
ORLEANS, LEO A. (ed.), *Science in Contemporary China.* Stanford, Calif.: Stanford University Press, 1980.
SIMON, DENIS FRED, "The Evolving Role of Technology Transfer in China's Modernization," *China's Economy Looks toward the Year 2000: Selected Papers Submitted to the Joint Economic Committee of the United States.* Washington, D.C.: U.S. Government Printing Office, 1986.
SIMON, DENIS FRED, "Implementing China's S & T Modernization Program," in David M. Lampton (ed.), *Policy Implementation in Post-Mao China.* Berkeley: University of California Press, 1987, pp. 354–379.
TANG, TONG B., *Science and Technology in China.* London: Longman Group, Ltd., 1984.
VOLTI, RUDI, *Technology, Politics, and Society in China.* Boulder, Colo.: Westview Press, 1982.
XU LIANGYING AND FAN DAINIAN, *Science and Socialist Construction in China.* Translated by John C. S. Hsu. Armonk, N.Y.: M. E. Sharpe, 1982.

MISCELLANEOUS

FRIEDMAN, EDWARD, "In Defense of China Studies: Review Article," *Pacific Affairs,* Vol. 55, No. 2 (Summer 1982), pp. 252–266.
HARDING, HARRY, "From China, with Disdain: New Trends in the Study of China," *Asian Survey,* No. 10 (October 1982), pp. 934–958.
JOHNSON, CHALMERS, "What's Wrong with Chinese Studies?" *Asian Survey,* No. 10 (October 1982), pp. 919–933.

INDEX